I0753232

HISTORIC PHOTOS OF ANAHEIM

TEXT AND CAPTIONS BY STEPHEN J. FAESSEL

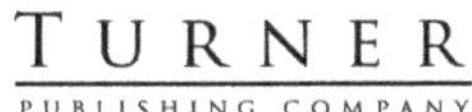

This aerial view of Anaheim was snapped on July 14, 1953, and begins to show the growth of the community outward from its downtown core. By now many of the area's orange groves were being paved over for housing—the city's population had surpassed 22,000, an increase of more than 7,000 in just two years. By 1955, Anaheim would embark on a journey that would make it the entertainment and tourism destination for Southern California.

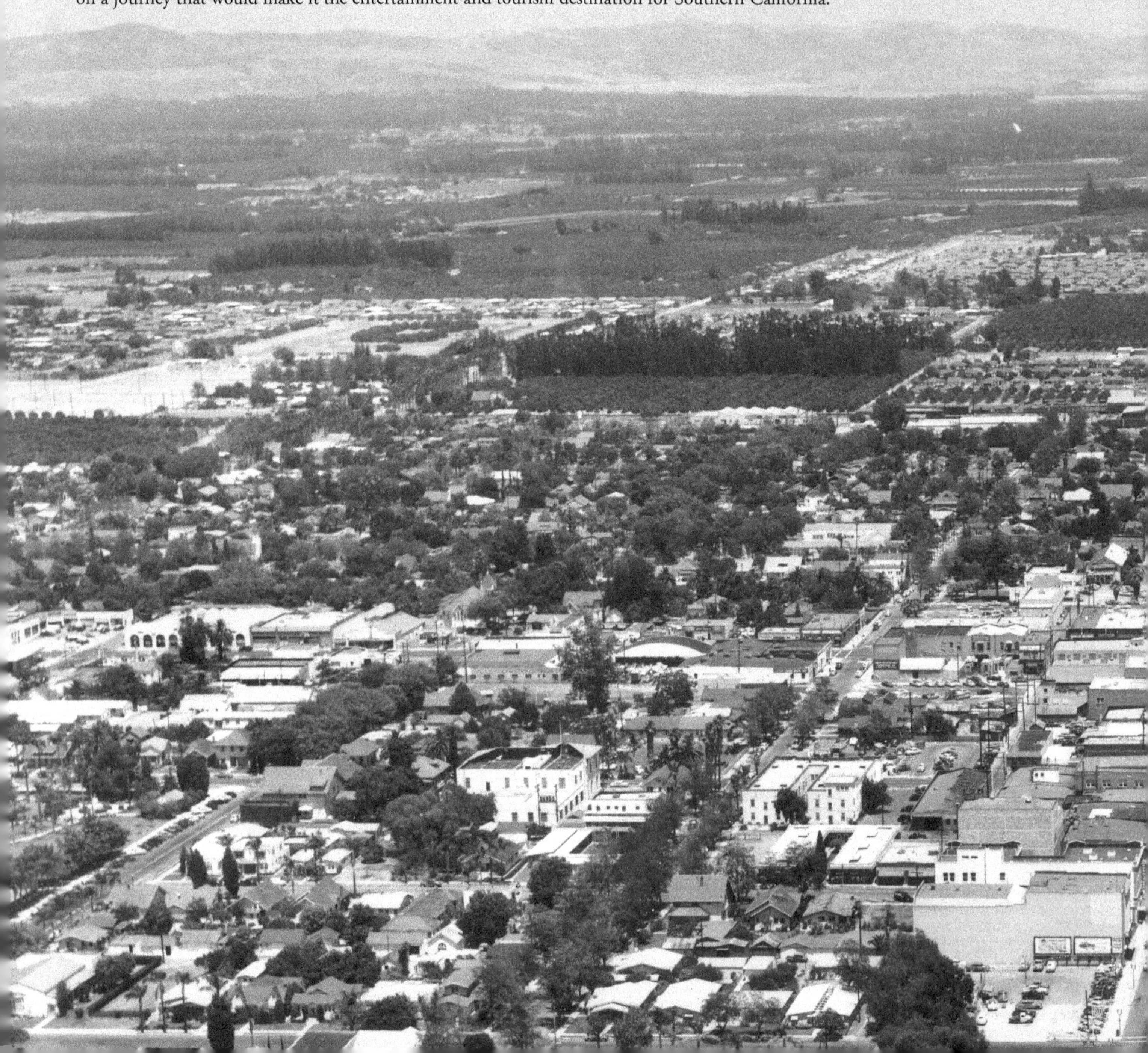

HISTORIC PHOTOS OF
ANAHEIM

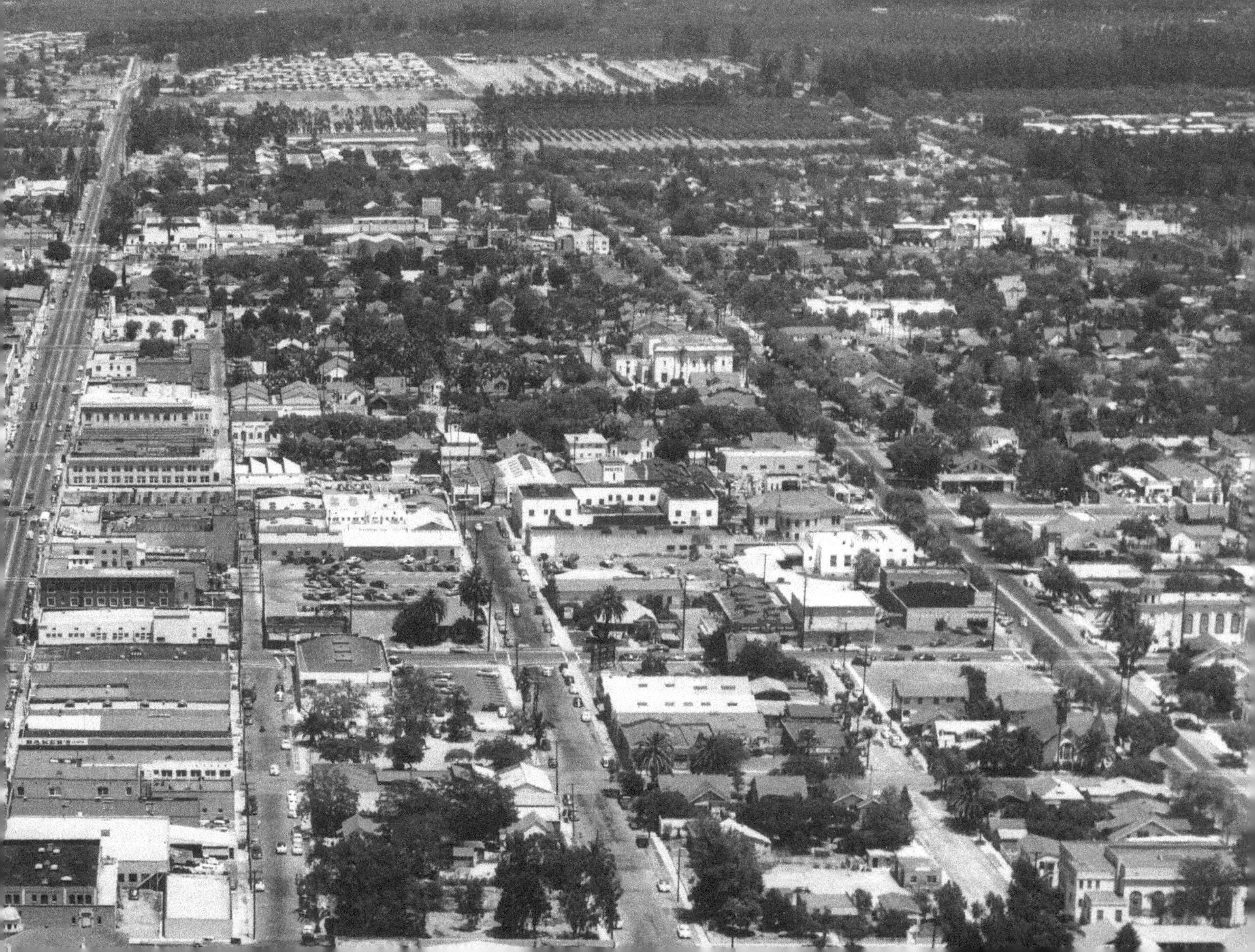

Turner Publishing Company
www.turnerpublishing.com

Historic Photos of Anaheim

Library of Congress Control Number: 2007923452

ISBN-13: 978-1-59652-333-3
ISBN: 1-59652-333-6

Printed in the United States of America

ISBN 978-1-68336-947-9 (hc)

Contents

Reinforcing Anaheim's position as an international destination, on December 21, 1976, Anaheim signed its first "Sister City" agreement with Mito, Japan. We see Anaheim Mayor Bill Thom and Mayor Pro Tem John Seymour join Yunosuke Wada the Mayor and Kan Kimura, Chairman of the City Council of Mito, Japan, in ratifying the official declaration. The Sister City program gives communities of different nations a forum to share ideas and information. In 1998, Anaheim's second Sister City became Victoria-Gasteiz, of Spain.

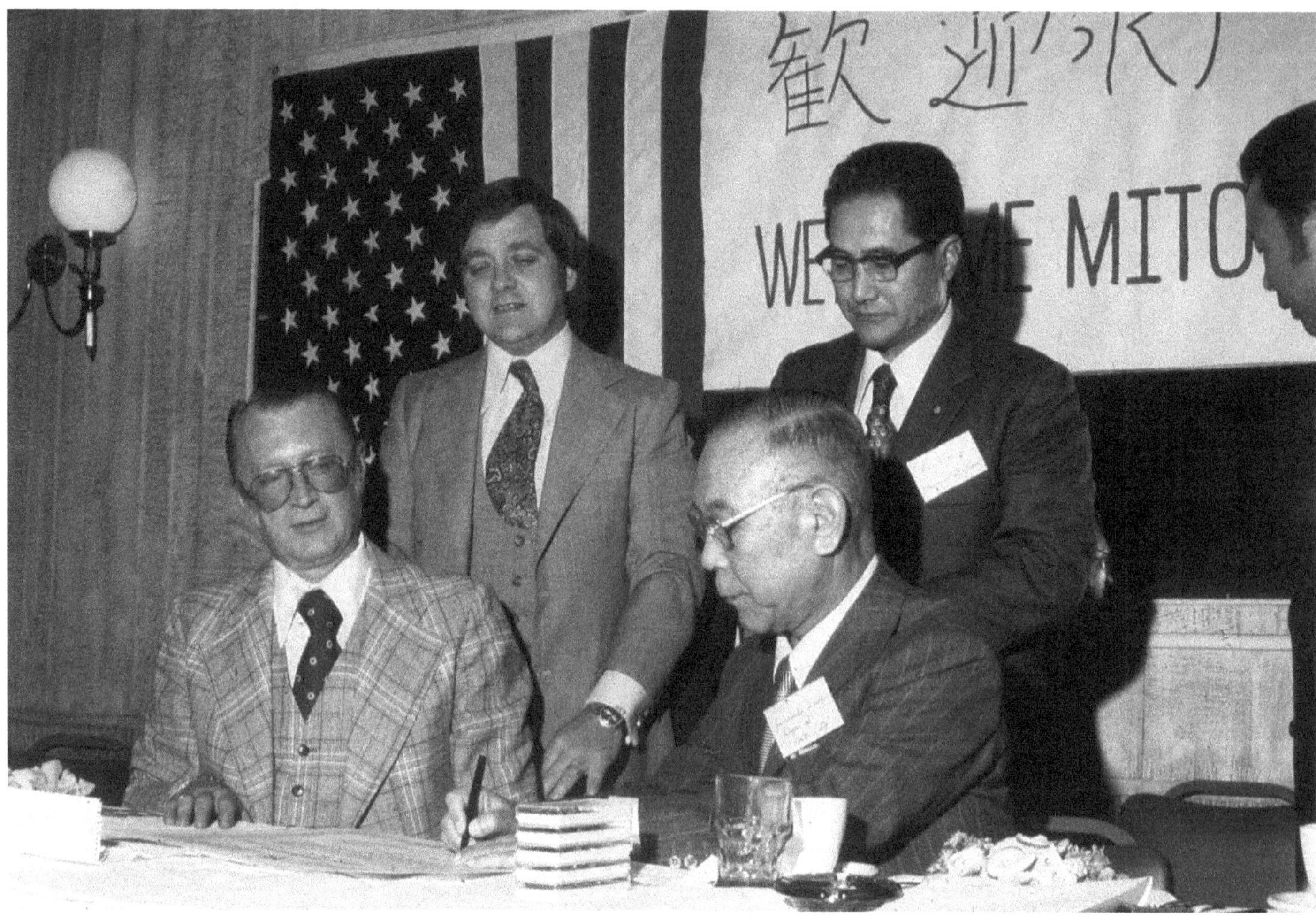

Acknowledgments

This volume, *Historic Photos of Anaheim,* is the result of the cooperation and efforts of many individuals, organizations, and corporations. It is with great thanks that we acknowledge, in particular, the valuable contribution of the Anaheim Public Library for their generous support.

We would also like to thank Stephen J. Faessel, our writer, for valuable contributions and assistance in making this work possible.

As the author, I would like to thank Ms. Jane Newell, Local History Curator of the Elizabeth J. Schultz History Room, Anaheim Public Library, for her very generous assistance and support in the creation of this book. Mrs. Ymelda Ventura and Mr. Sal Addotta, History Room staff, have also contributed their time and encouragement to this project. Thanks to a special friend, Marcie, for enlightened guidance.

Finally, I must acknowledge the loving assistance of my wife, Susan, for her unwavering support of this undertaking. Without her it would not have been completed.

PREFACE

Anaheim has thousands of historic photographs that reside in archives, both locally and nationally. This book began with the observation that, while those photographs are of great interest to many, they are not easily accessible. During a time when Anaheim is looking ahead and evaluating its future course, many people are asking, How do we treat the past? These decisions affect every aspect of the city—architecture, public spaces, commerce, infrastructure—and these, in turn, affect the way that people live their lives. This book seeks to provide easy access to a valuable, objective look into the history of Anaheim.

The power of photographs is that they are less subjective than words in their treatment of history. Although the photographer can make decisions regarding subject matter and how to capture and present it, photographs do not provide the breadth of interpretation that text does. For this reason, they offer an original, untainted perspective that allows the viewer to interpret and observe.

This project represents countless hours of review and research. The researchers and writer have reviewed thousands of photographs in numerous archives. We greatly appreciate the generous assistance of the individuals and organizations listed in the acknowledgments of this work, without whom this project could not have been completed.

The goal in publishing this work is to provide broader access to this set of extraordinary photographs that seek to inspire, provide perspective, and evoke insight that might assist people who are responsible for determining Anaheim's future. In addition, the book seeks to preserve the past with adequate respect and reverence.

With the exception of touching up imperfections caused by the vicissitudes of time and cropping where necessary, no other changes have been made. The focus and clarity of many images is limited to the technology and the ability of the photographer at the time they were taken.

The work is divided into eras. Beginning with some of the earliest known photographs of Anaheim, the first section features images from the earliest period, 1865 through 1899, with a focus on Anaheim's vineyards. The second section spans the years 1900 to 1939, taking a look at the city's citrus industry. Section Three moves from 1940 and the World War II era to 1953. The last section covers the years 1954, with the advent of Disneyland, forward to recent times.

In each of these sections we have made an effort to capture various aspects of life through our selection of photographs. People, commerce, transportation, infrastructure, religious institutions, and educational institutions have been included to provide a broad perspective.

We encourage readers to reflect as they go walking in Anaheim, strolling through the city, or wandering its parks and neighborhoods. It is the publisher's hope that in utilizing this work, longtime residents will learn something new and that new residents will gain a perspective on where Anaheim has been, so that each can contribute to its future.

Todd Bottorff, Publisher

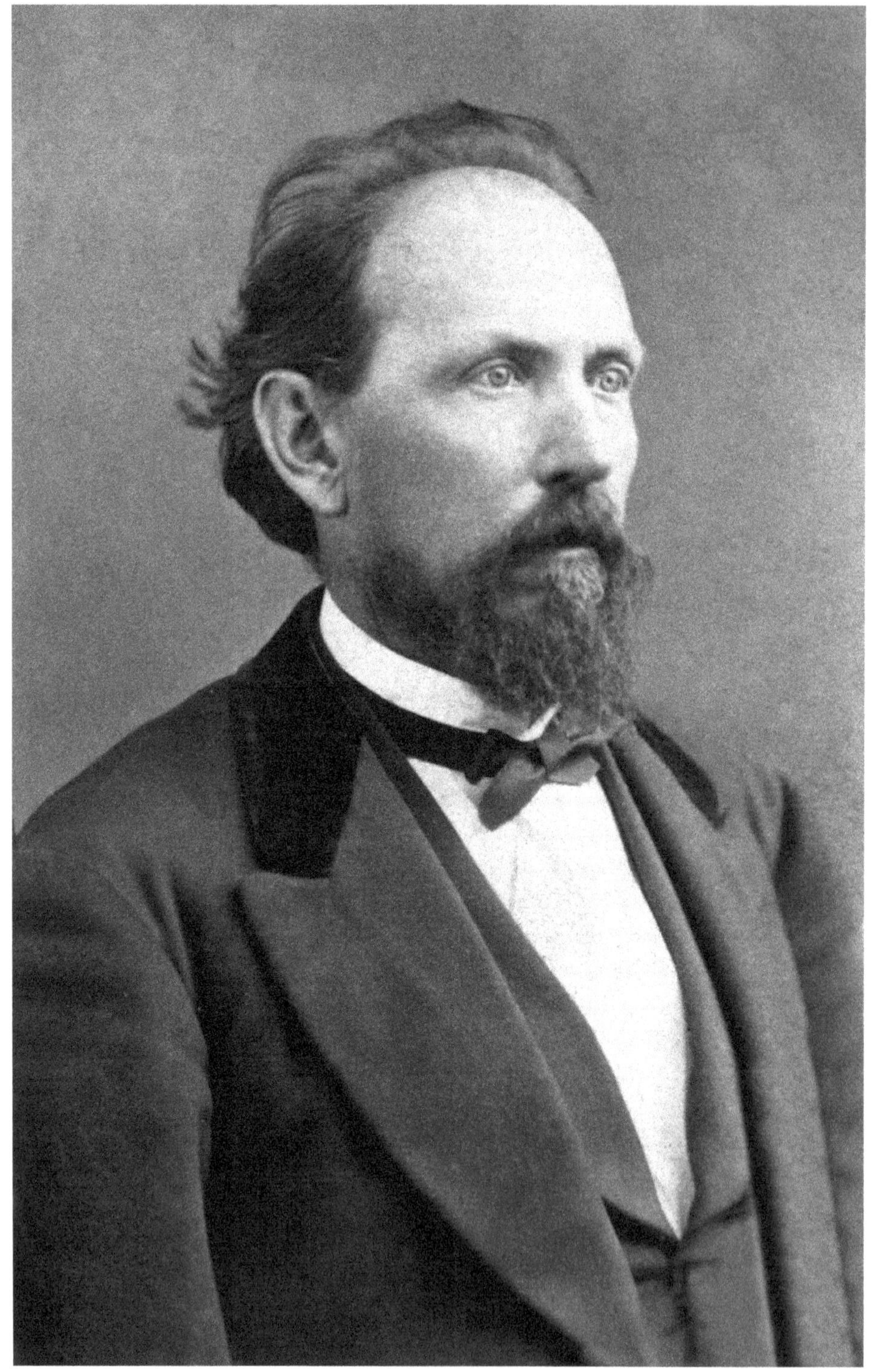

German born, George Hansen was hired by the Los Angeles Vineyard Society as their superintendent. A deputy surveyor and civil engineer, he was able to locate suitable land and water rights in the Southern California area on which the society could build their model community of Anaheim. For his efforts in both locating and laying out the town, he became known as the "Father of Anaheim."

The Mother Colony

(1865–1899)

The name *Anaheim,* a combination of Spanish and German, meaning "home on the Santa Ana River," was founded in 1857 by a group of 50 German immigrants living in San Francisco. John Froehling and Charles Kohler, both Germans by birth, needed greater vineyard capacity for their rapidly growing Los Angeles wine business. The two partners, along with other San Francisco investors, organized themselves as the Los Angeles Vineyard Society with the goal of establishing a colony of vineyardists in Southern California.

One of their first orders of business was to hire a superintendent to find a suitable location and secure the necessary land and water rights. The society had the good fortune of hiring a fellow German, George Hansen, a deputy Los Angeles County surveyor who was already familiar with the Southern California area through his surveys undertaken in 1855.Unable to finalize a land purchase with a number of landowners, Hansen made contact with Juan Pacifico Ontiveros, whose Rancho San Juan Cajon de Santa Ana he had earlier surveyed. The Ontiveros Rancho, a 35,970-acre Spanish Land Grant, adjoined the Santa Ana River, which was not wholly dependable as a water source. Regardless, a deal was struck on September 12, 1857, to buy 1,165 acres at $2 an acre on behalf of the impatient San Francisco investors. An easement for a water canal connecting the town site to the Santa Ana River was arranged with neighboring landowner Bernardo Yorba.

With land in hand and assured of a water source, Hansen began to lay out the town's 20-acre vineyard lots, employing American Indian and Mexican laborers, who called the settlement Campo Aleman, or "German Country." By 1859, an irrigation system had been installed and the Mission grapes planted by Hansen were beginning to take root. By 1864, more than 300,000 gallons of wine a year were being produced from Anaheim's 400,000 vines.

The colonists were a group of talented, well-educated gentlemen and ladies with only one having any wine-making experience. Nevertheless, the community thrived and a small downtown was built. Churches and schools soon followed, as did the requisite social and fraternal clubs and lodge halls. The region's first newspaper, the *Anaheim Gazette,* was started in 1870, the Southern Pacific Railroad arrived in 1875, and the thrifty Germans installed their own municipal water system in 1879. By 1880, Anaheim had become the second-largest town in Los Angeles County.

This 1858 view shows August Langenberger's two-story adobe store and residence. In 1857, Langenberger, the son-in-law of Juan Pacifico Ontiveros, partnered with another Anaheim pioneer, Benjamin Dreyfus, to start the town's first general store. The Langenberger's home was on the second floor and an adjoining large room was used for dances and other social functions. Ruggedly built, the adobe survived the historic flood of 1862 and was finally razed in 1915 to make way for a business block of modern buildings.

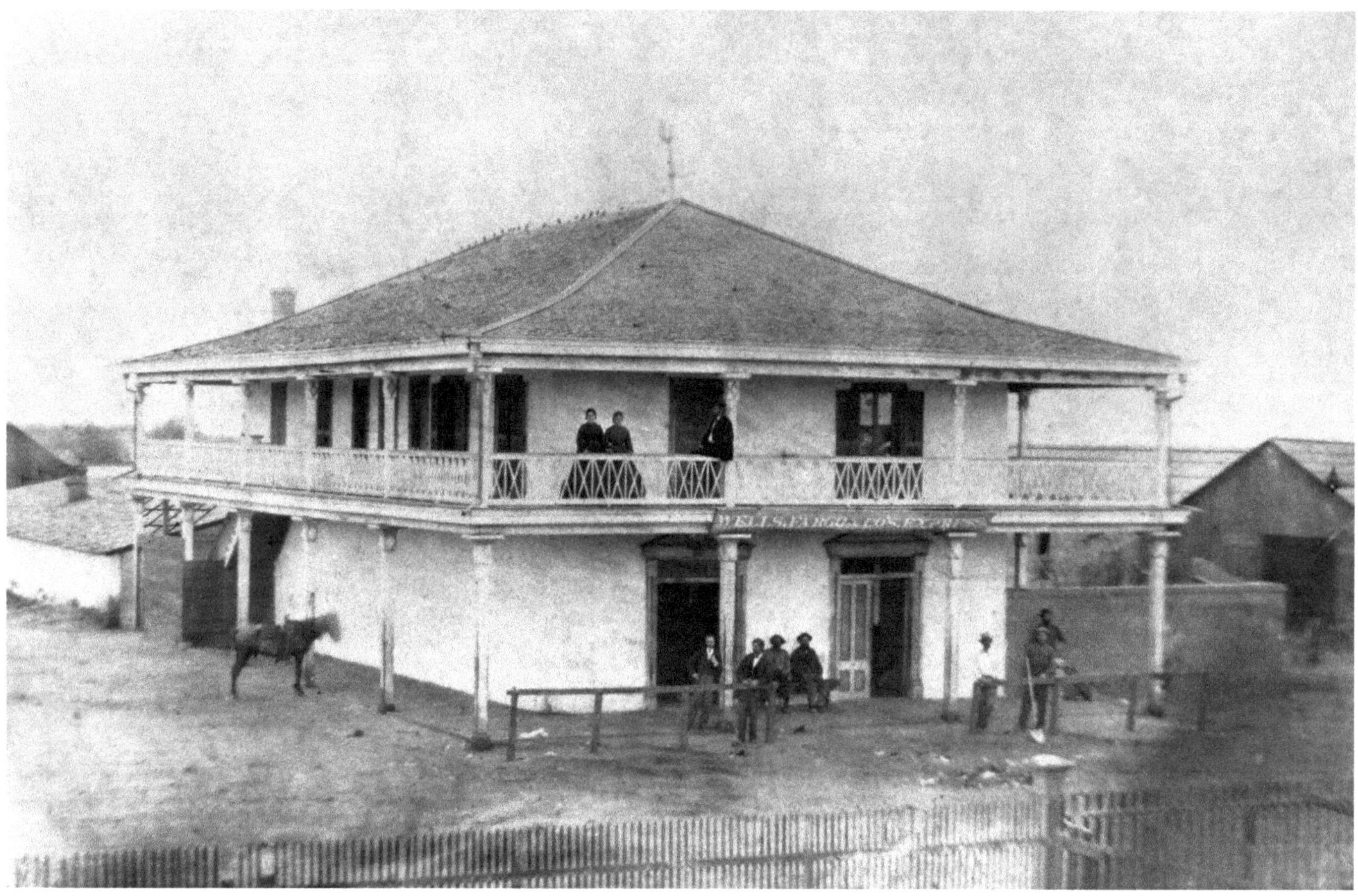

This double portrait shows Juan Pacifico Ontiveros and his wife, Maria Martina Osuna, who in 1857 sold for $2 an acre 1,165 acres of their Rancho San Juan Cajon de Santa Ana to the Los Angeles Vineyard Society's pioneers. Ontiveros later described the land as too poor to support a single goat.

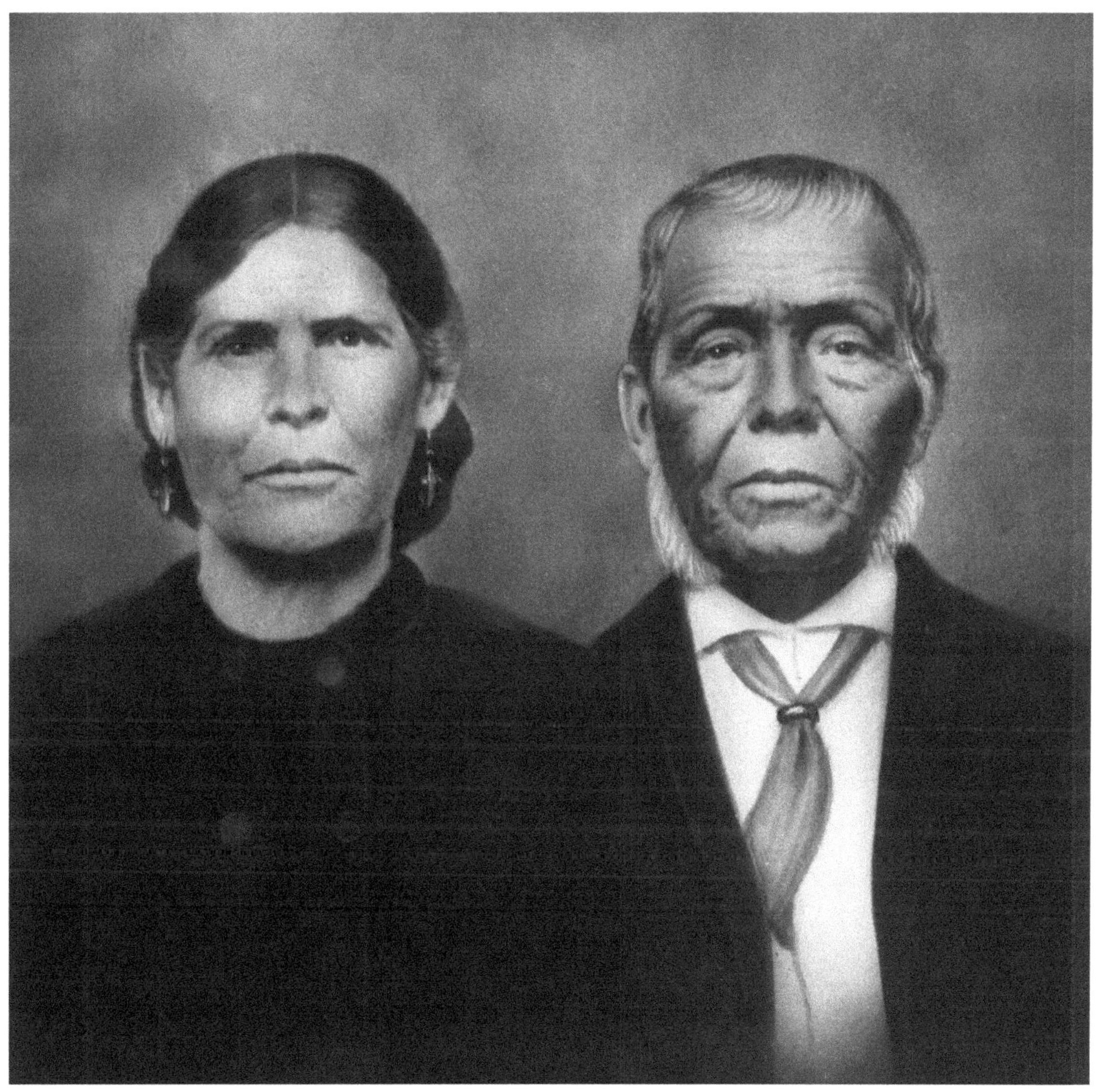

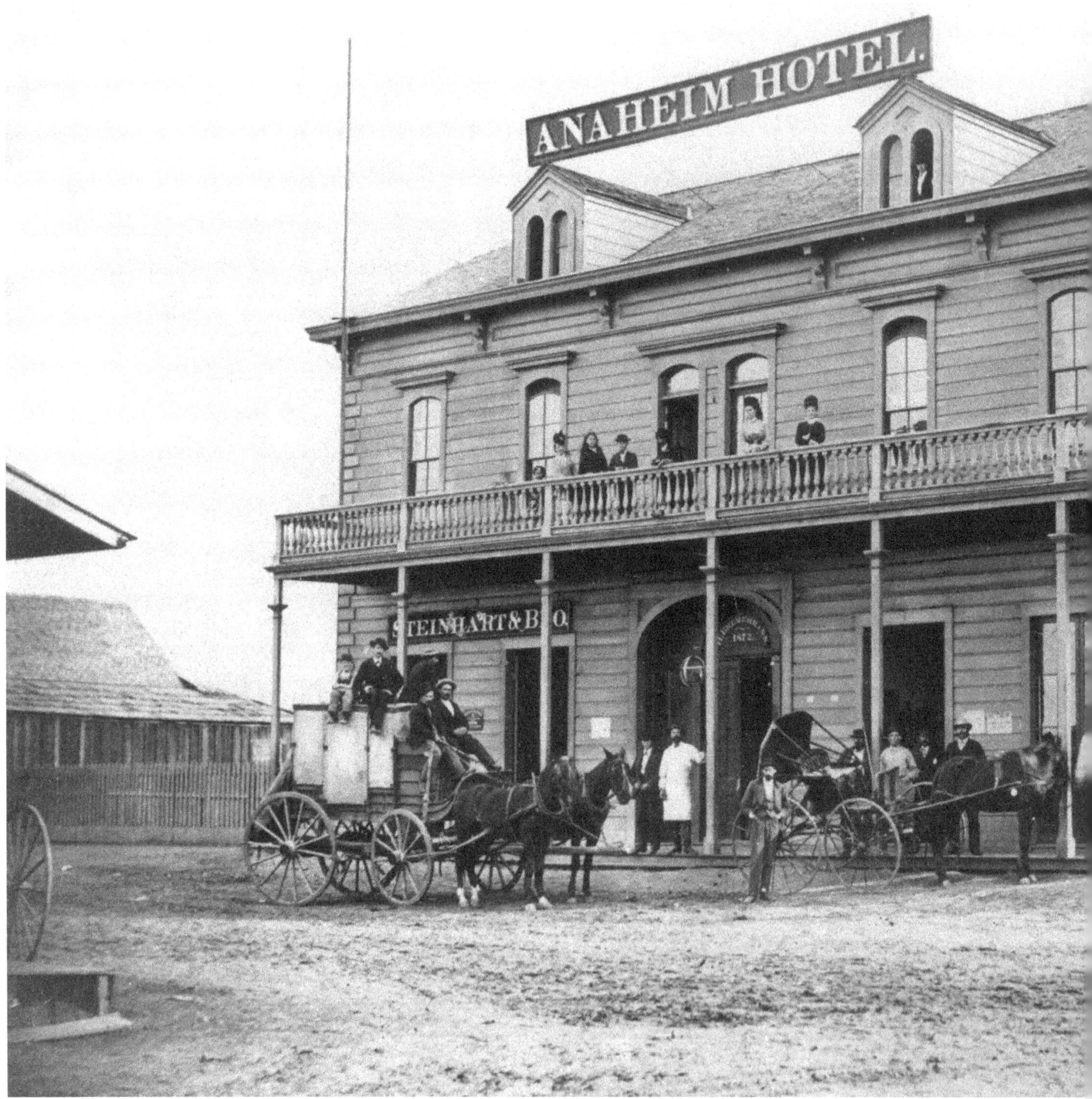
ANAHEIM HOTEL.
STEINHART & BRO.

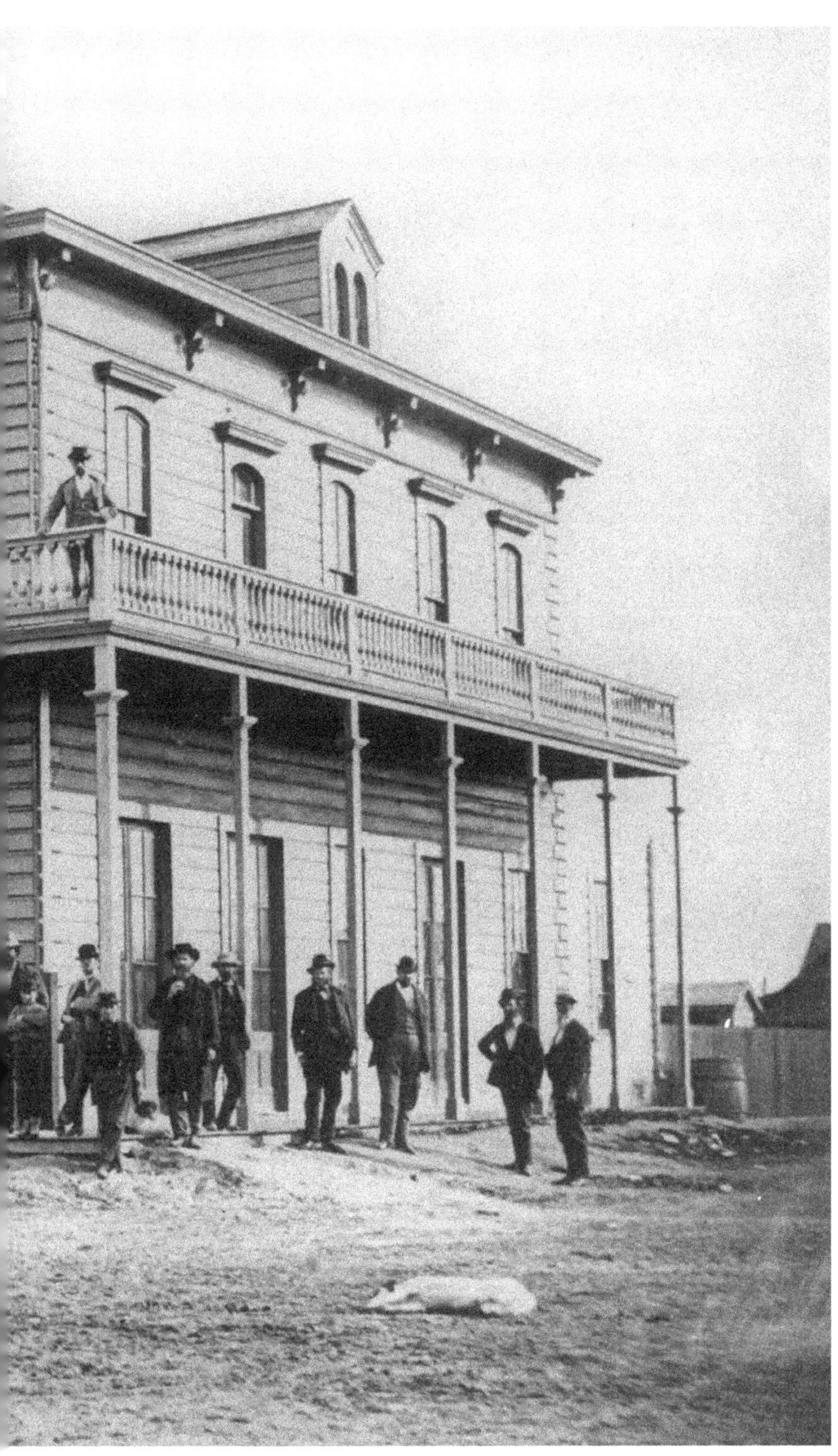

Anaheim's second mayor, Henry Kroeger, built the Anaheim Hotel at the southwest corner of Lemon and Center (now Lincoln Ave.) streets in 1871. Advertised with "well lighted and heated" rooms the interior furnishings were of high quality. Max Nebelung was the proprietor for many years. Renamed the Commercial Hotel in 1890, it passed through a number of hands before being sold to John B. Ziegler in 1905, who operated it until 1915 when it was razed and replaced with the Hotel Valencia.

This view of Center Street (now Lincoln Ave.) from ca. 1873 faces west past Los Angeles Street (now Anaheim Blvd.). Paving would not come for more than 40 years. The rural character of the town can be clearly seen. Anaheim's impressive, although financially fragile, two-story Planters Hotel is visible at center. This structure replaced the original Planters Hotel that burned in 1871, but it too burned on the morning of July 5, 1890. The hostelry was never rebuilt, the vacant lot taking the name Planters Park.

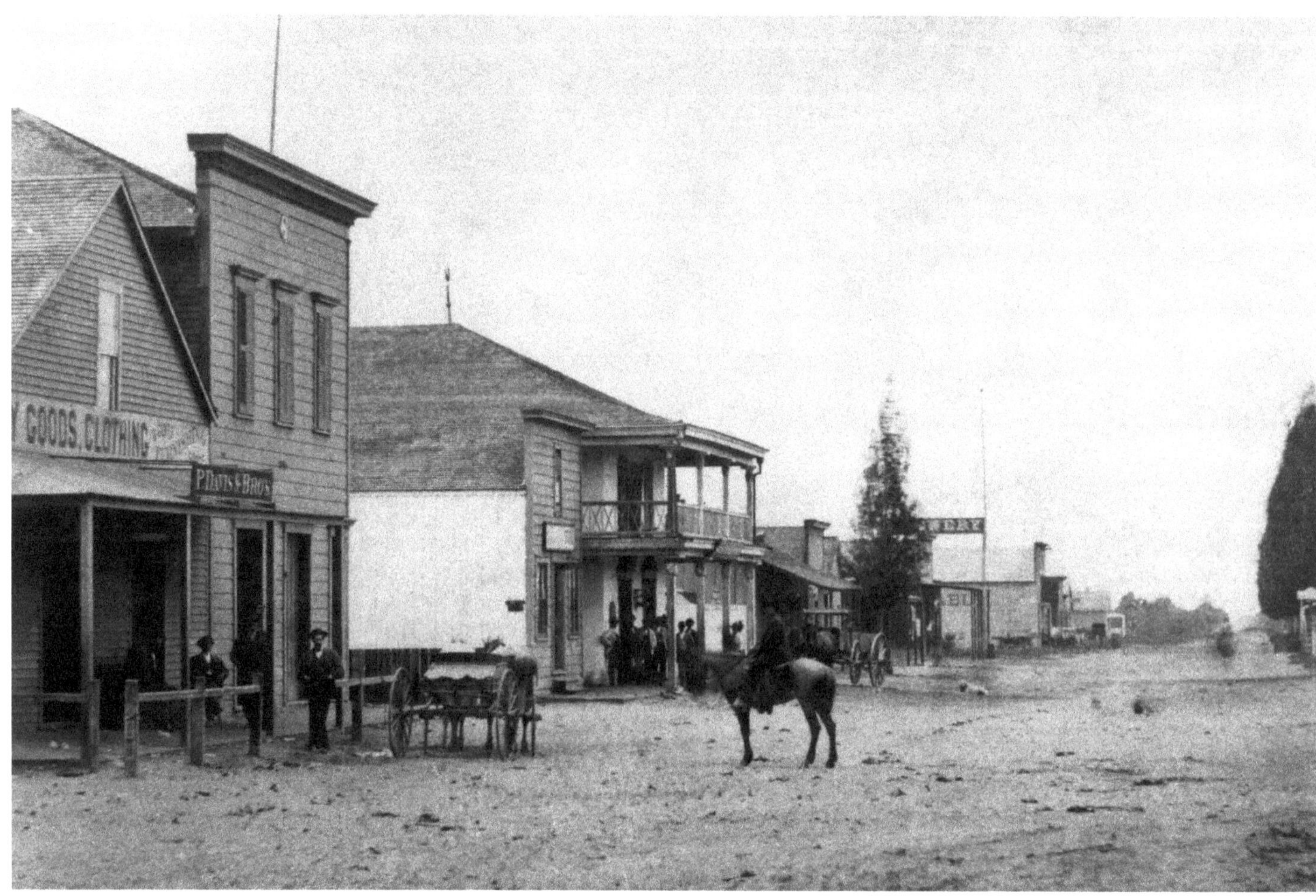

A local dog relaxes in the afternoon sun in this view facing east on Center Street (now Lincoln Ave.) from Lemon Street. The Anaheim Hotel, later named the Commercial Hotel, is visible at right. Center Street remained the main commercial thoroughfare in Anaheim well into the late twentieth century.

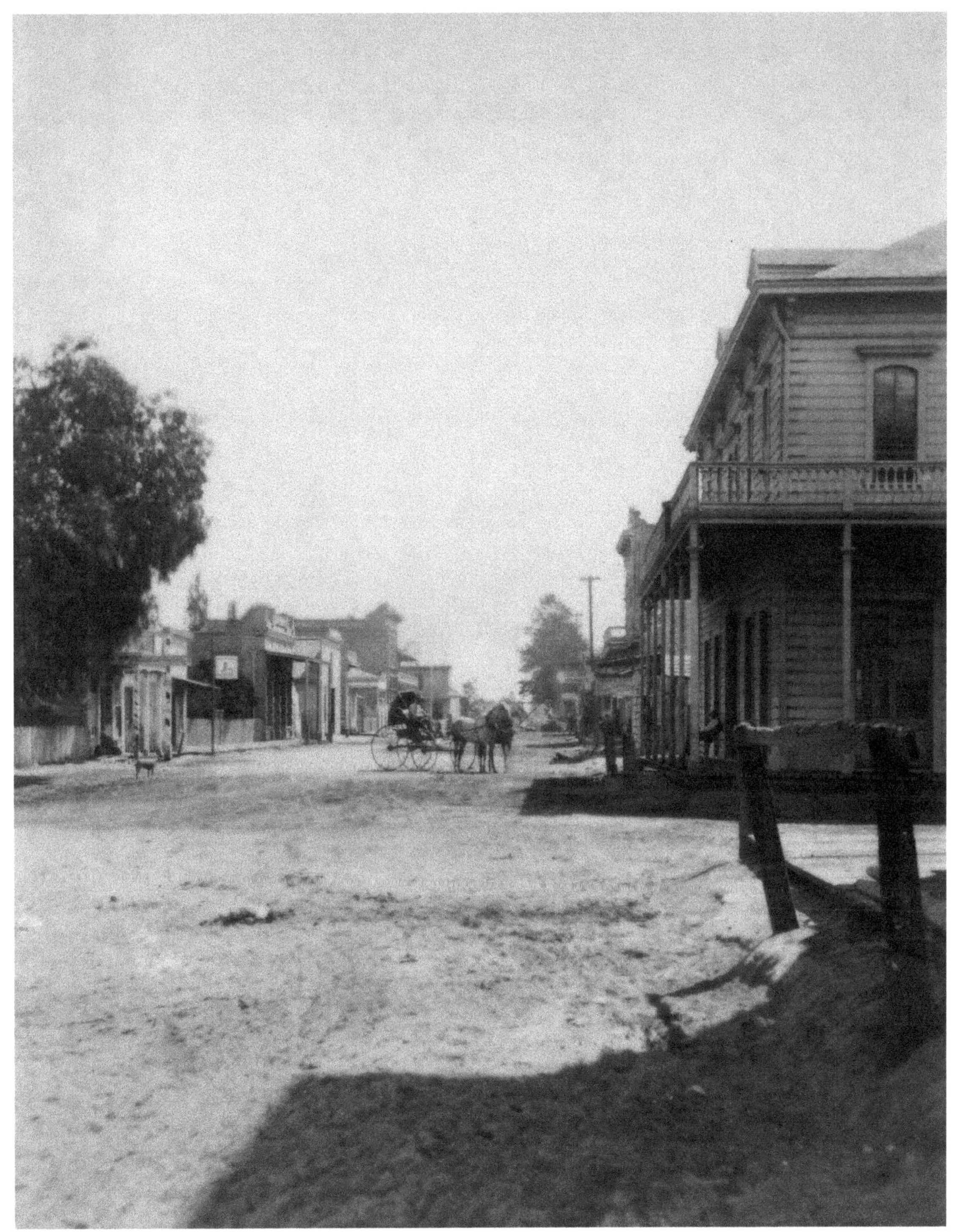

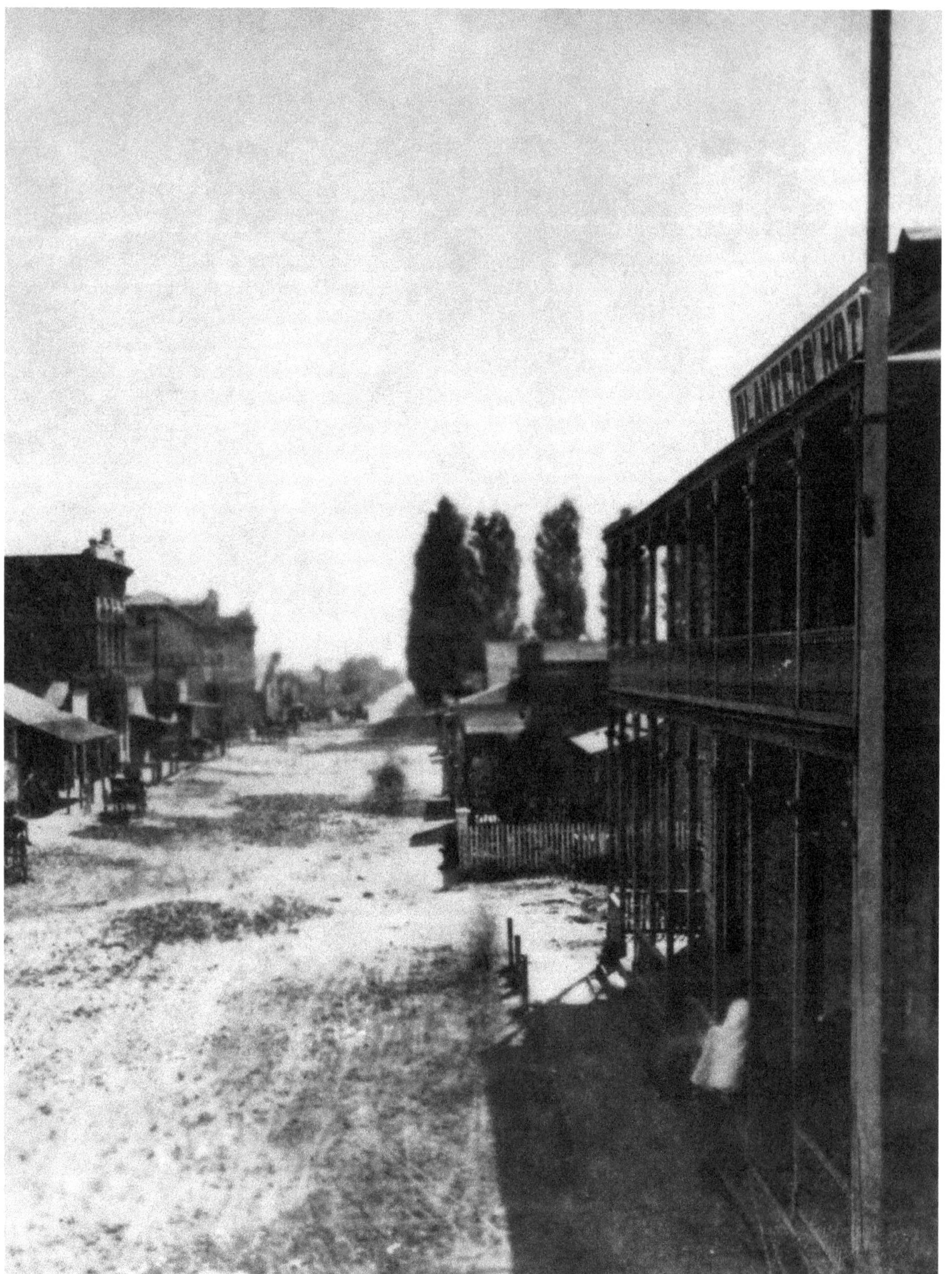

In 1872, Center Street facing west from Los Angeles Street was the geographical center of town. The two-story adobe Langenberger store, built in 1858, is visible to the left. Anaheim's Planters Hotel stands to the right.

Anaheim's 1884 Fourth of July parade makes its way down Center Street. The horse-drawn wagon is driven by Nick A. Bittner, foreman of Anaheim's Volunteer Confidence Fire Company #1. The volunteers were organized in October 1883 and took every opportunity to participate in local events. Their bunting-draped wagon also sports a pump organ.

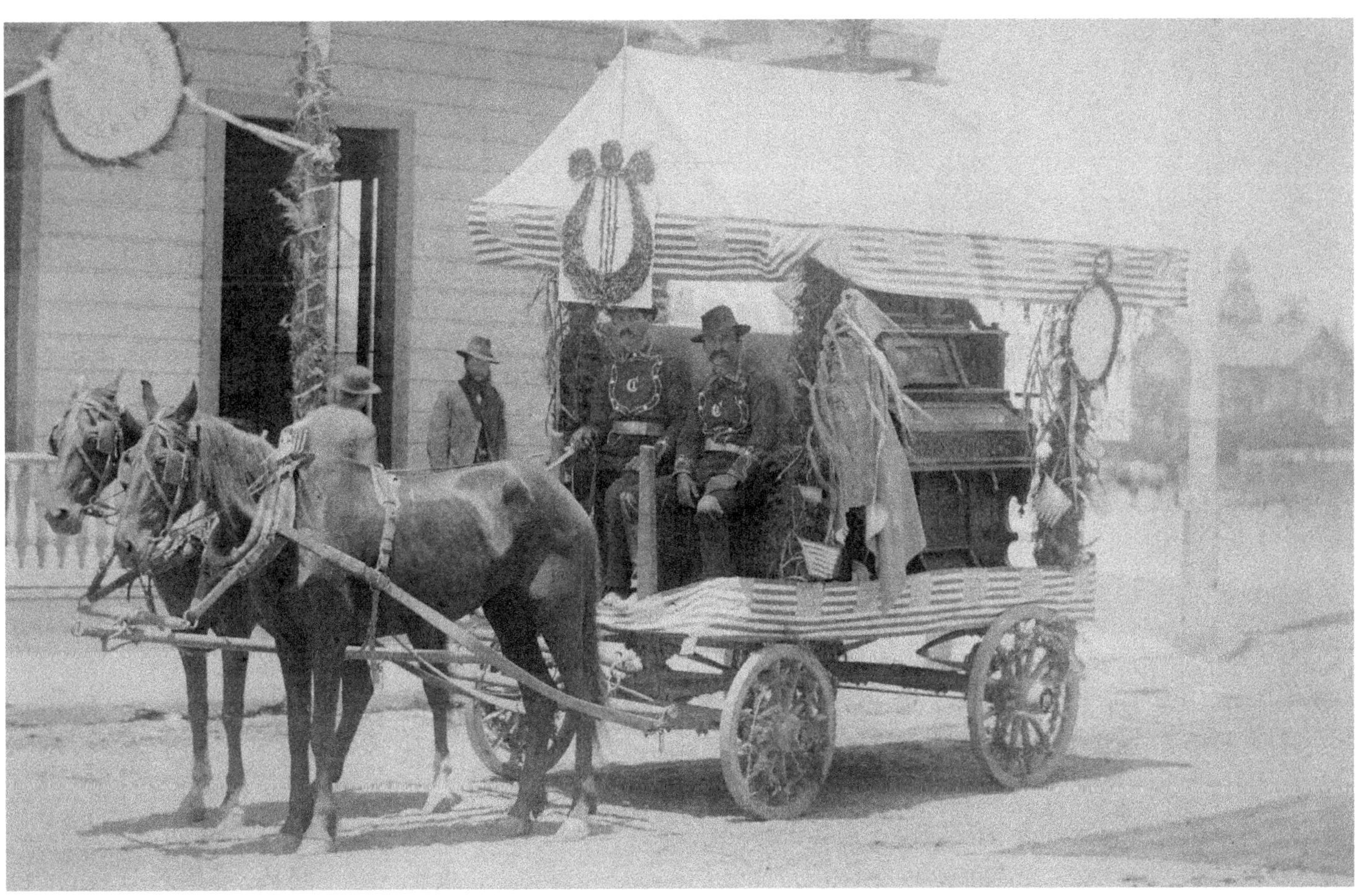

From the tower of Central School, Anaheim's two-story Planters Hotel is visible at the corner of Center Street and Los Angeles Street. The Planters Hotel, built by Anaheim pioneer and first postmaster John Fischer in 1865, burned to the ground in 1871; the second also was lost to fire, in 1890.

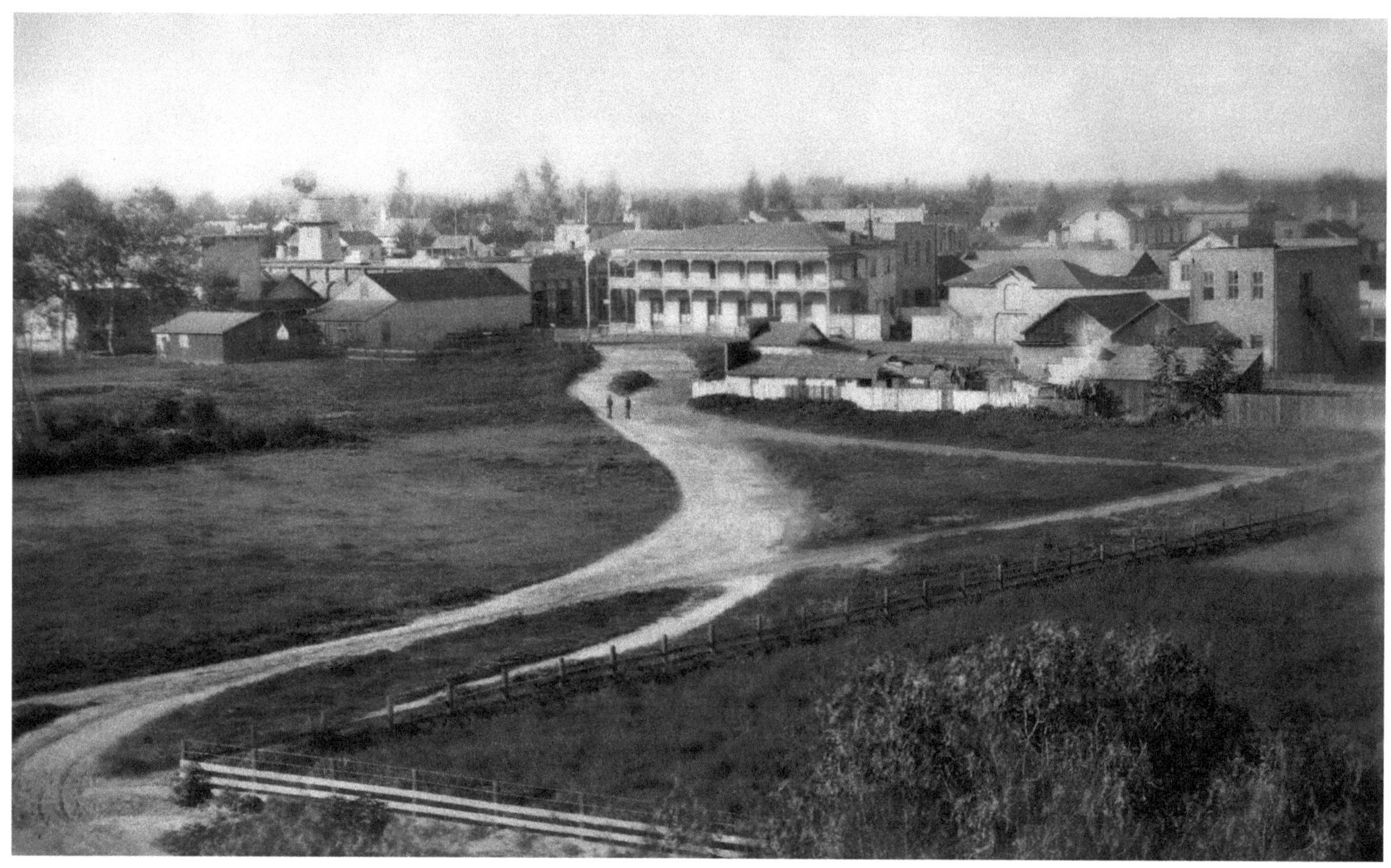

The second St. Boniface Catholic Church building was built in 1879 and replaced a much smaller edifice built in 1870 as Anaheim's first permanent church building. The Anaheim Union Water Company, the successor to the Los Angeles Vineyard Society, donated the lot for the church, located on Cypress Street next to the city jail. Here a group of parishioners is dressed for their first Holy Communion.

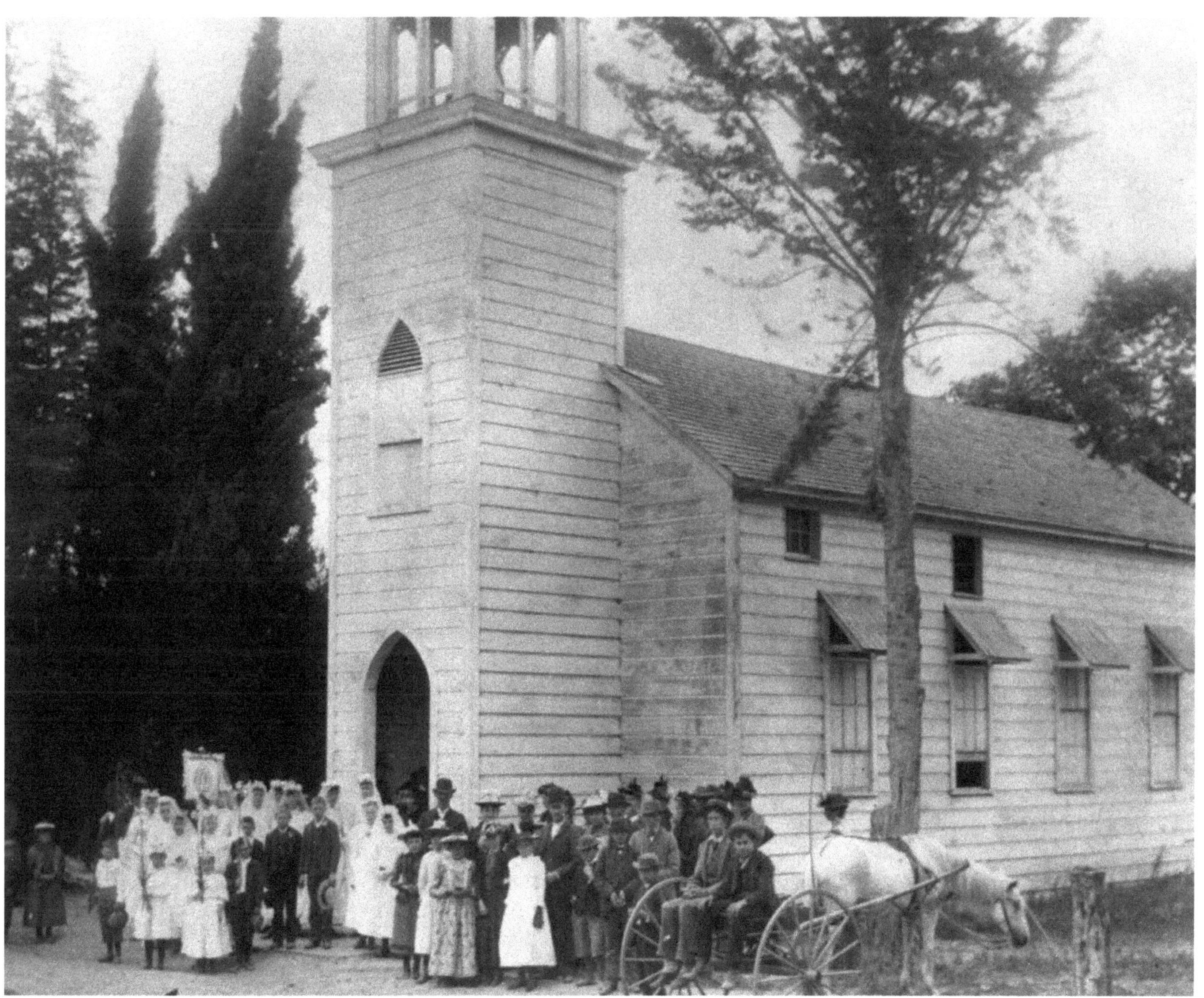

The Los Angeles stage has just arrived at Anaheim's Planters Hotel here in 1882. When rebuilt after the first structure burned in 1871, local advertisements noted that it was "Lighted With Gas" and that "no pains or expense has been spared to make this in every respect a FIRST CLASS HOUSE!" Despite the hyperbole, the Planters never lived up to the financial expectations of its various owners.

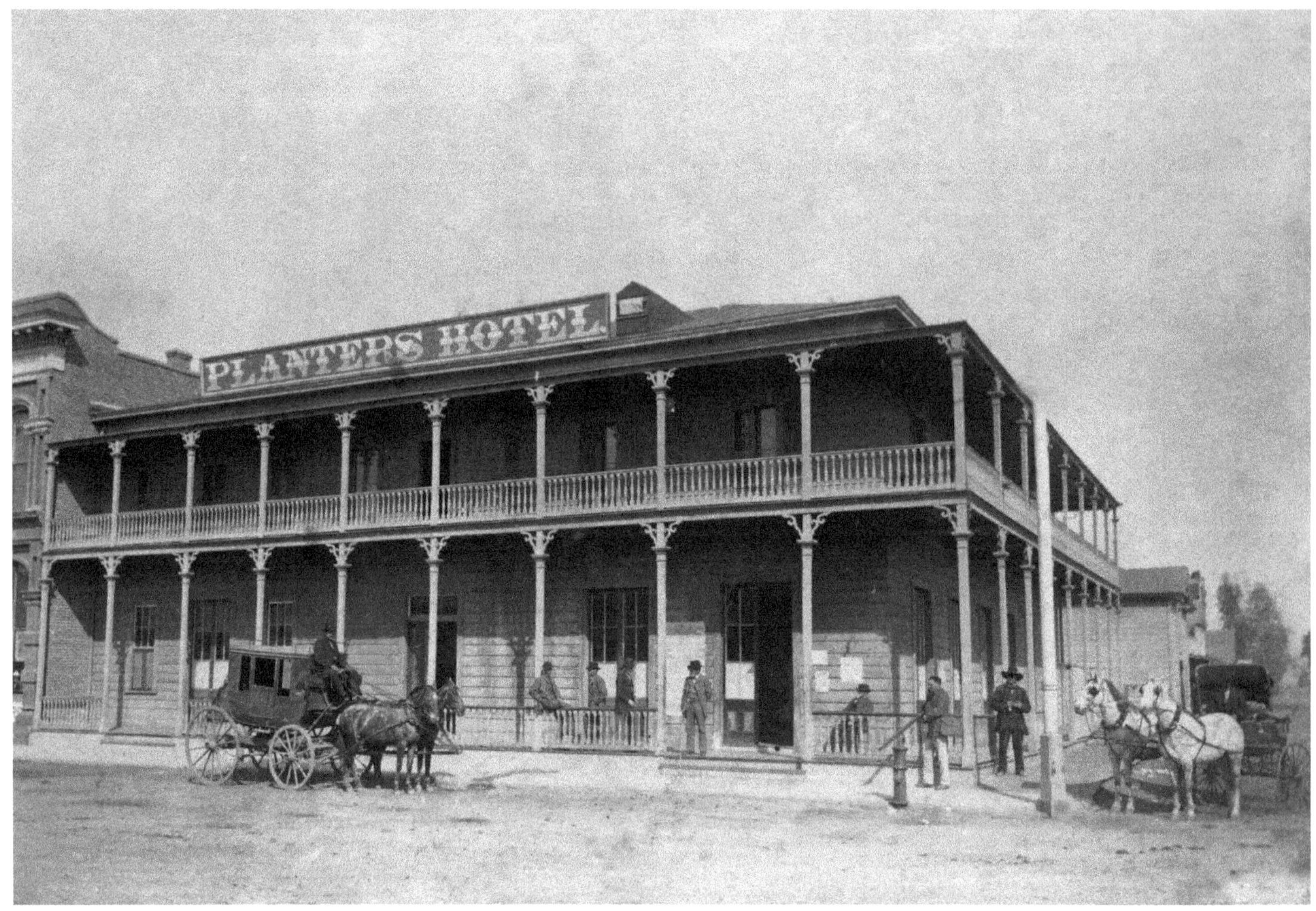

Bavarian-born Benjamin Dreyfus's first winery on Center Street is shown here in 1884. In 1857, Dreyfus formed a partnership with August Langenberger to run a mercantile store in the new town. Standing third from the right of the wine barrel, Dreyfus organized the Anaheim Wine Growers Association, which acted as a marketing agency for member vintners. His firm, B. Dreyfus and Company, had become California's largest wine distributor by the late 1870s.

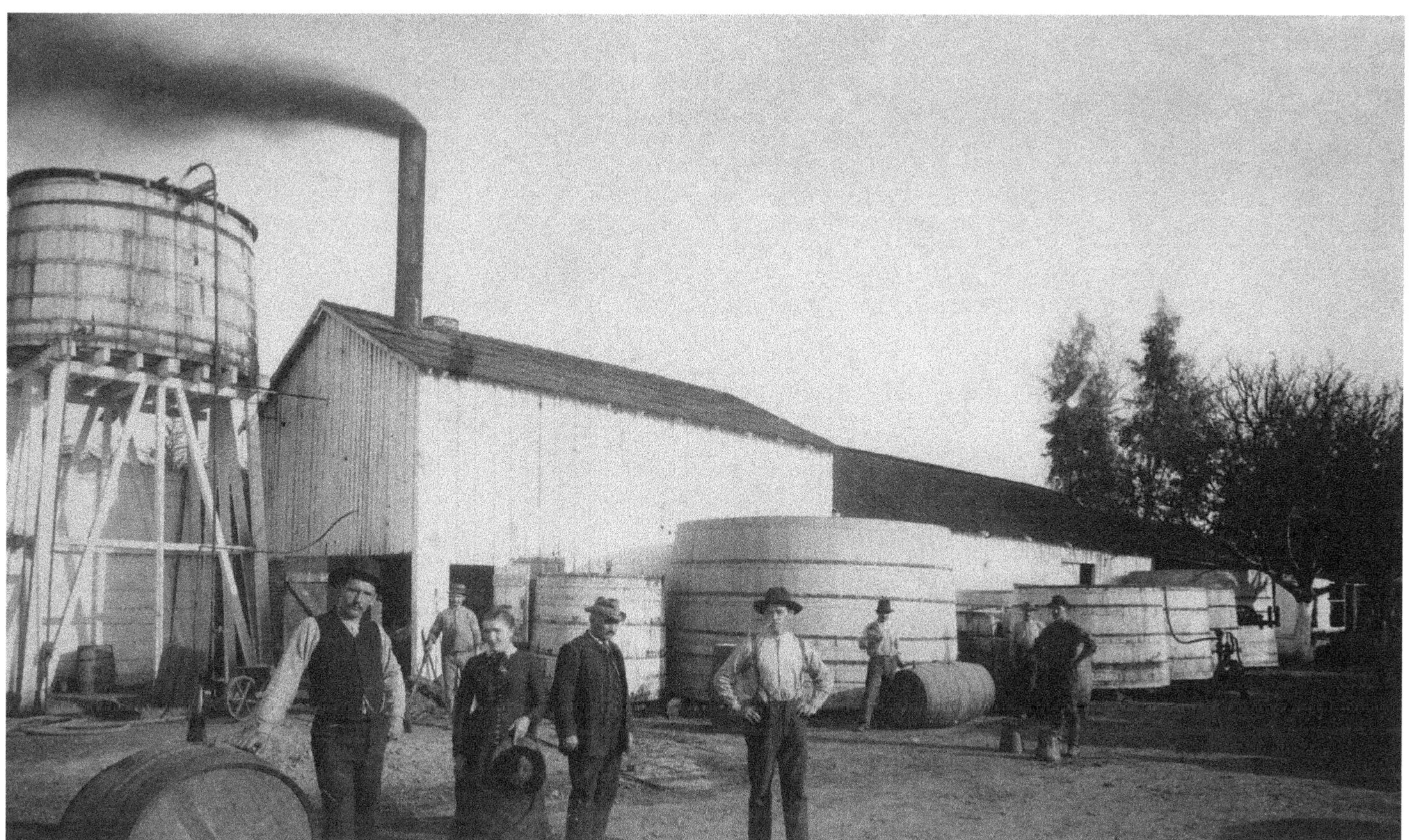

Around 1885, Henry Oelkers plows the William Koenig vineyard on South Los Angeles Street (now Anaheim Blvd.). Oelkers came to Anaheim in 1884 from his native Hamburg in order to assist his uncle, William Koenig, in his winery.

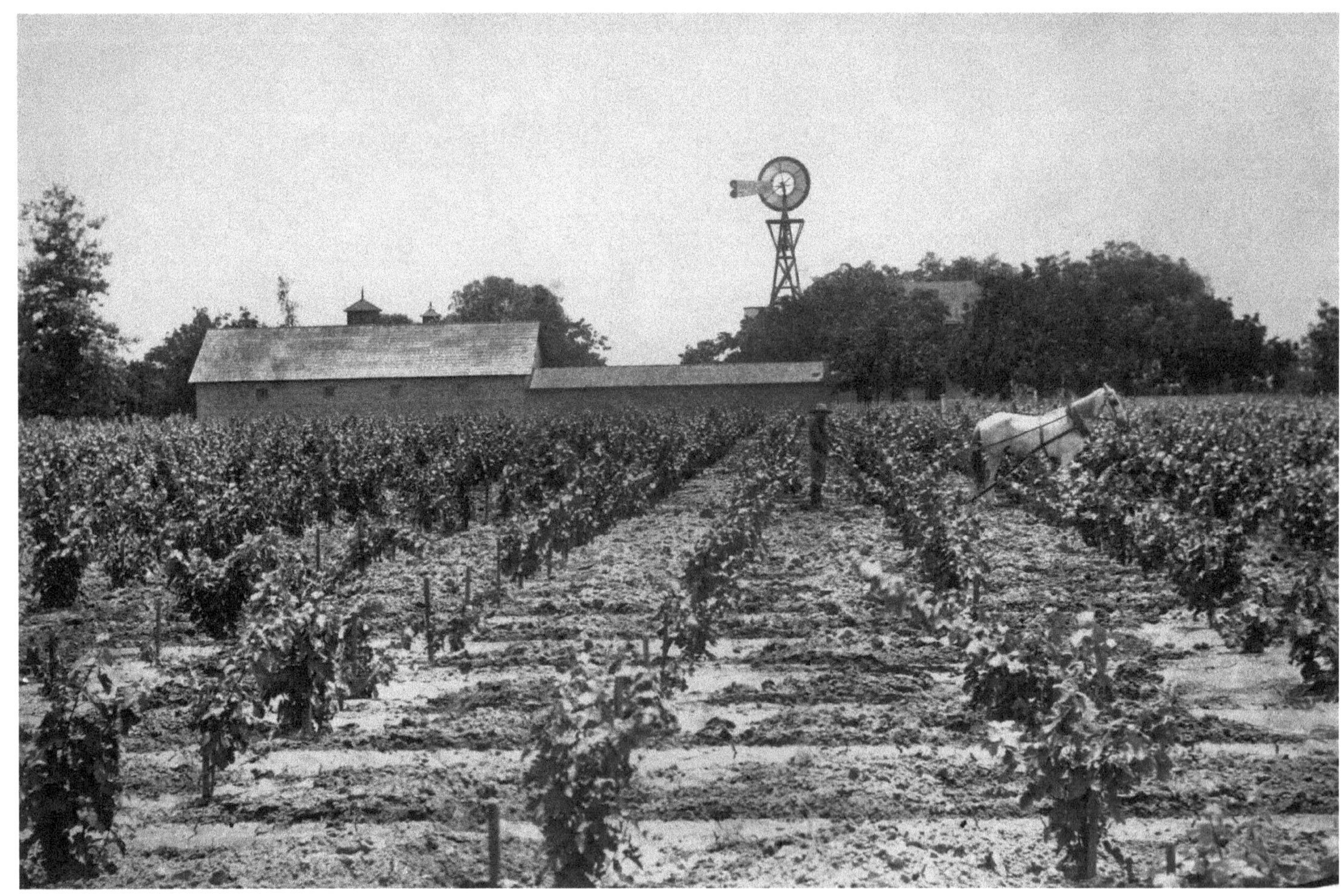

Doctor James Hovey Bullard and two friends stand in front of his office on Los Angeles Street (now Anaheim Blvd.) in 1885. In addition to being one of Anaheim's pioneer physicians, Bullard also ran a modest winery.

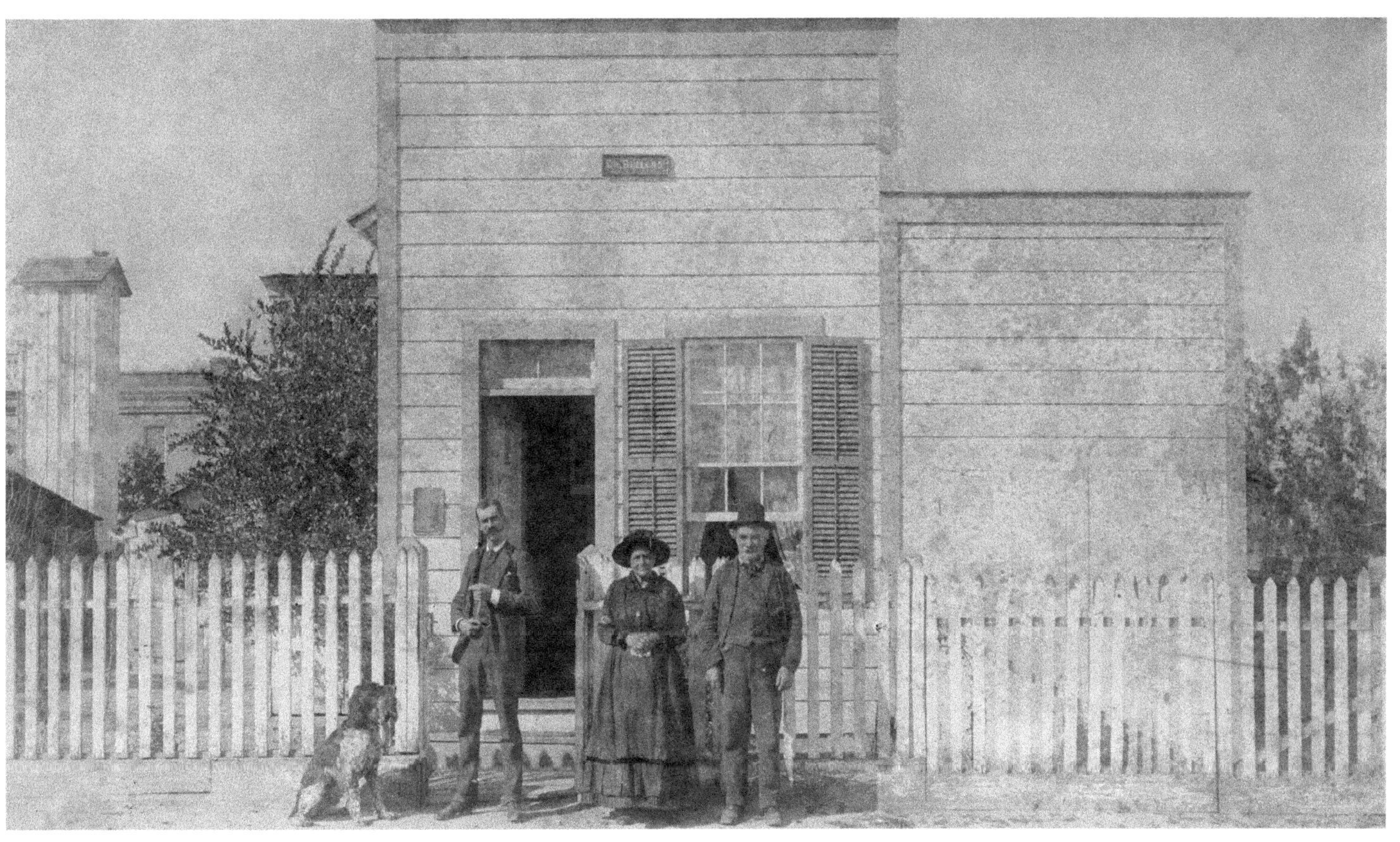

Following Spread: In 1885 Dr. James H. Bullard bottles a recent pressing of local grapes. Winemaking was often a small affair with the vintner doing a great deal of the work. Bullard also purchased a stock interest in the Anaheim Improvement Company, which planned to build the much-anticipated Del Campo Hotel.

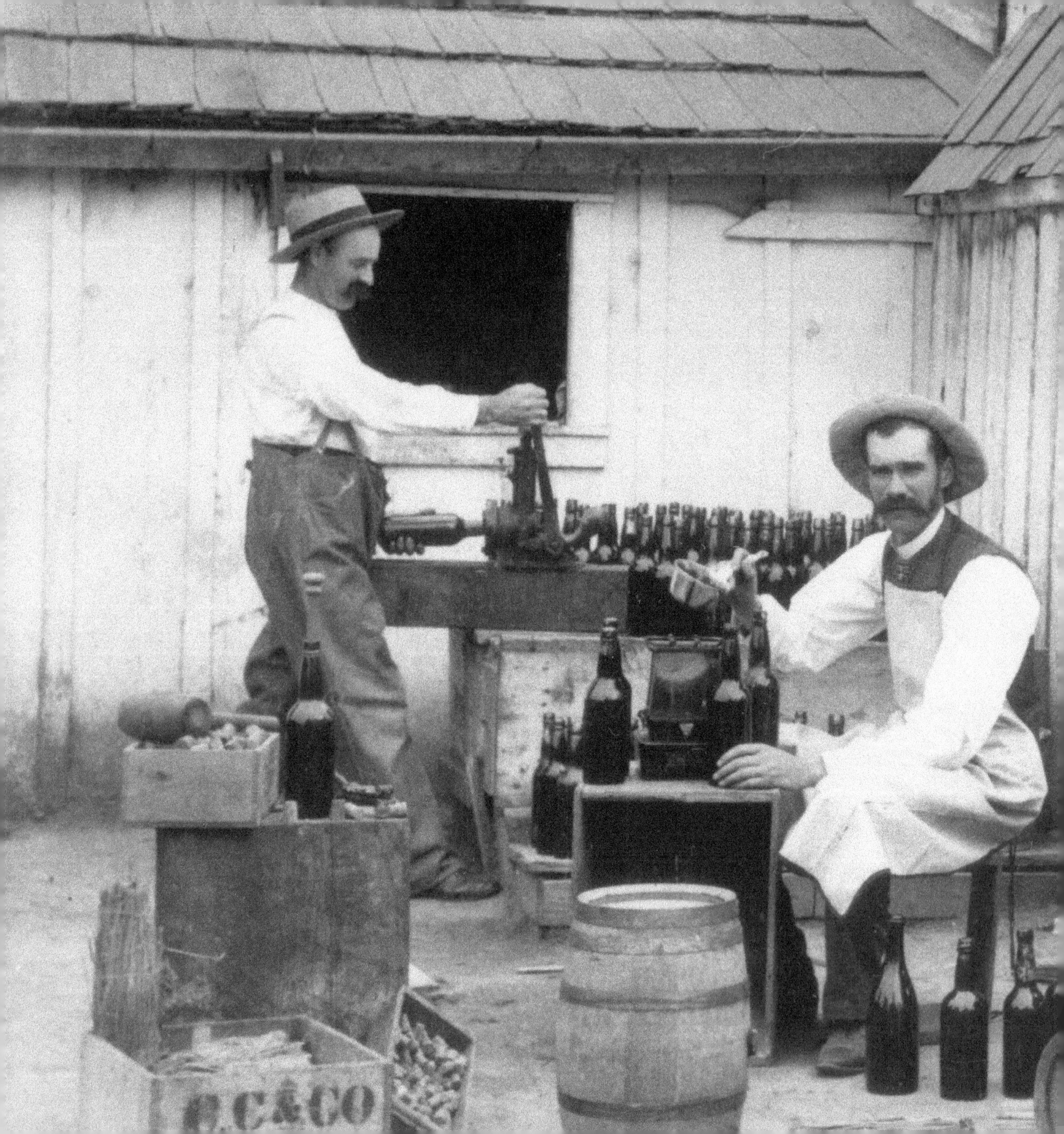
C&CO

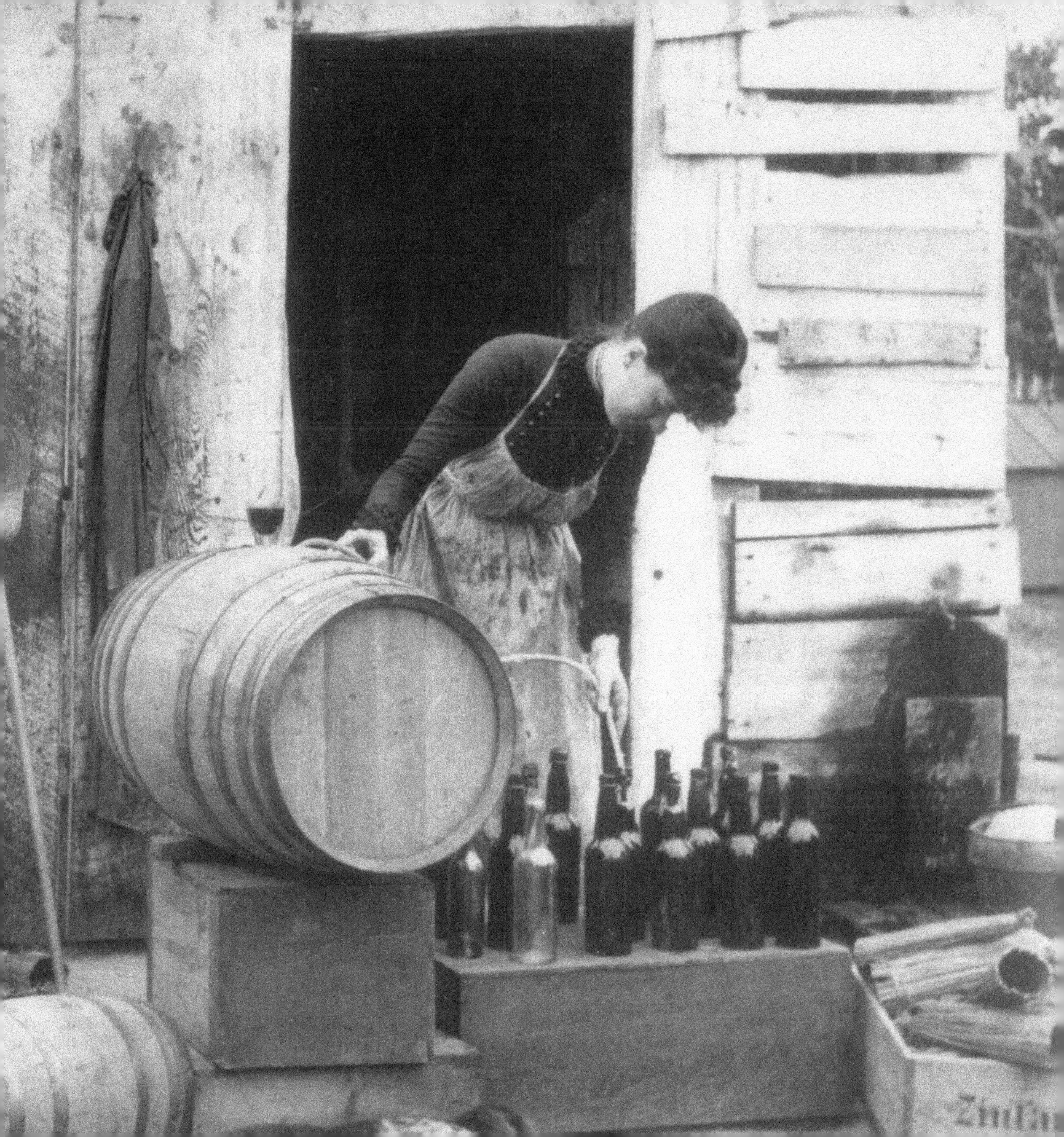

These substantial, brick business buildings indicate the success that the original colonists had in creating a growing community from the dry scrub of the Santa Ana plains. This view faces west on Center Street (now Lincoln Ave.) from the corner of Los Angeles Street (now Anaheim Blvd.). Within the next few years, the crop on which this economy depended would be lost and the colonists would eventually find a profitable substitute.

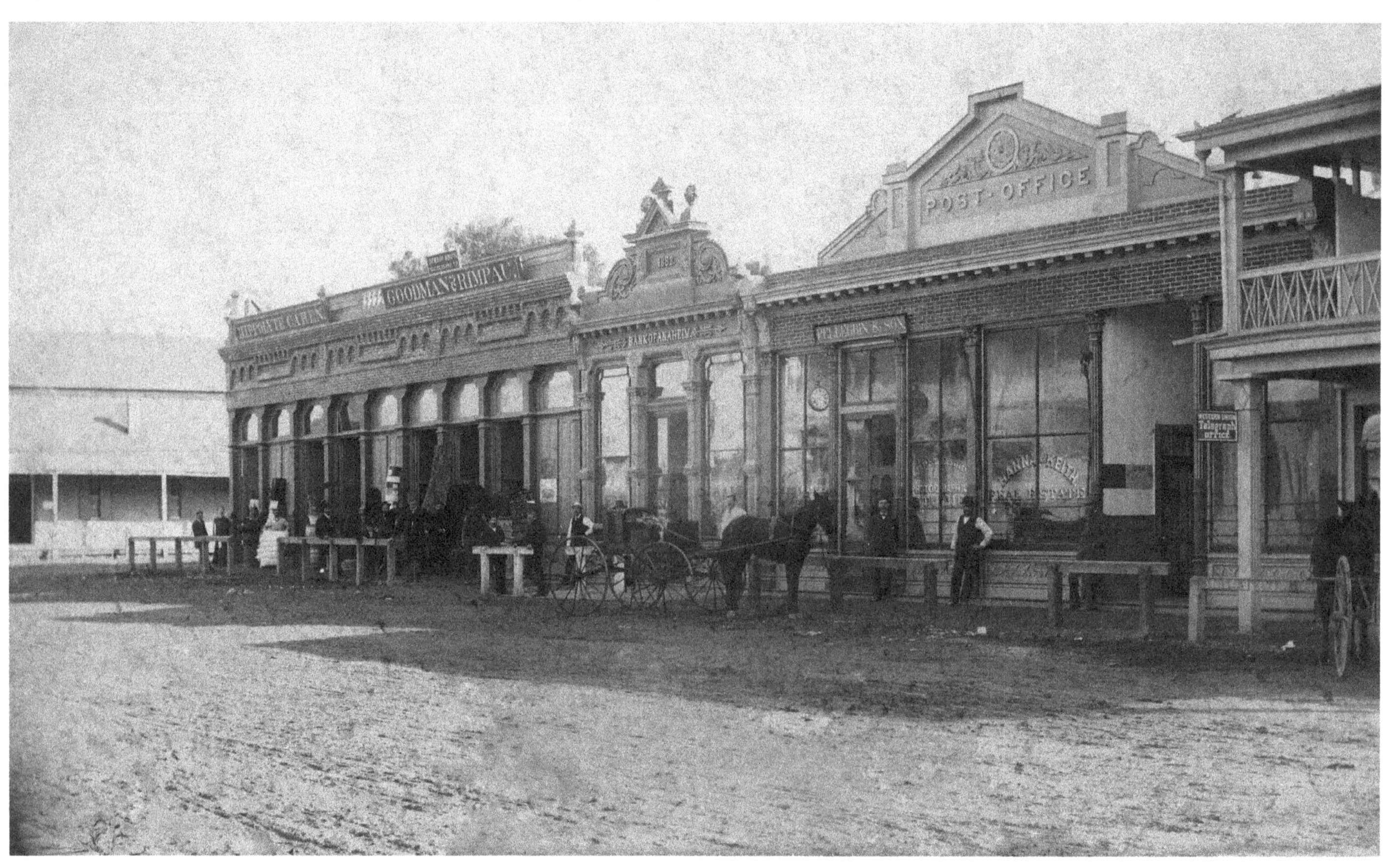

Benjamin Dreyfus built this impressive 80-foot by 200-foot brick winery in Anaheim in 1885. Dreyfus was co-founder of Anaheim's first general store and later served as a town trustee and its mayor in 1881 and 1882. The construction of this ambitious structure unfortunately coincided with the outbreak of the "Anaheim Disease" that killed almost every vine in the region. By the end of the decade, the local industry that Dreyfus had contributed so much to had literally dried up.

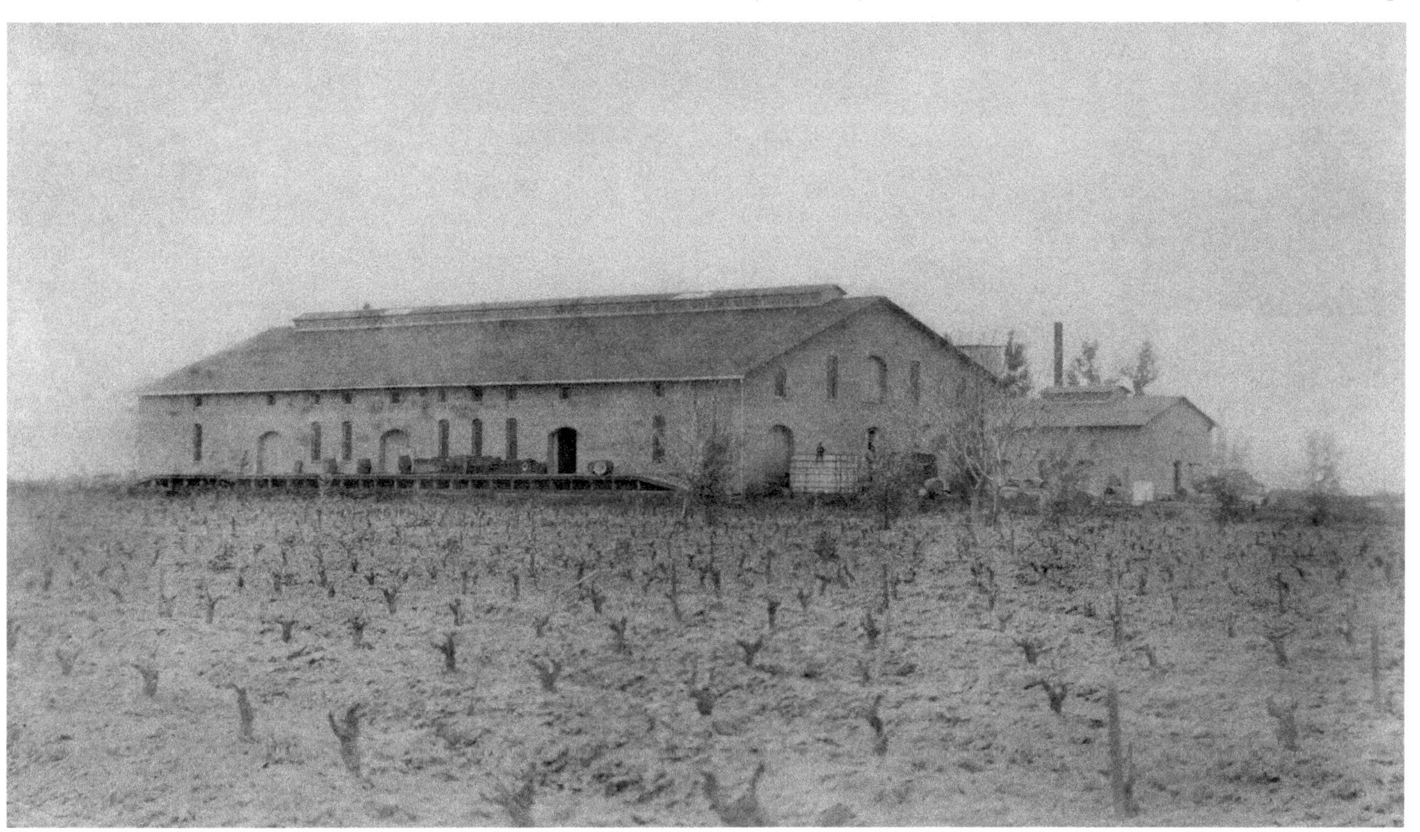

The Fritz Ruhmann building at 217 North Los Angeles Street in 1886. Ruhmann, a native of Schleswig-Holstein, arrived in California after being shanghaied at Hoboken, New Jersey, in 1875. When his sailing vessel dropped anchor at Anaheim Landing several months later, Fritz was given his freedom and met Max Nebelung, who introduced him to a number of his fellow countrymen living in Anaheim.

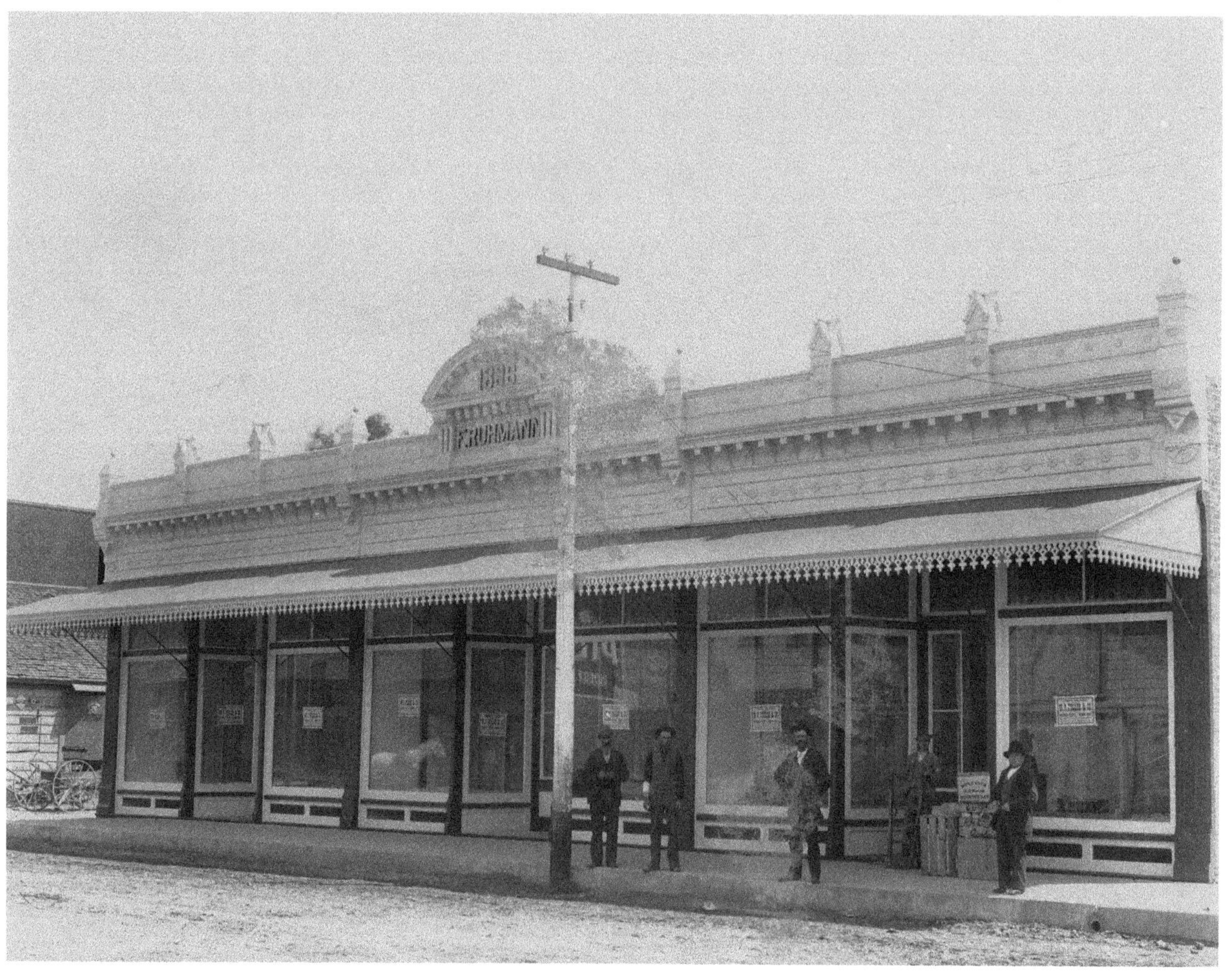

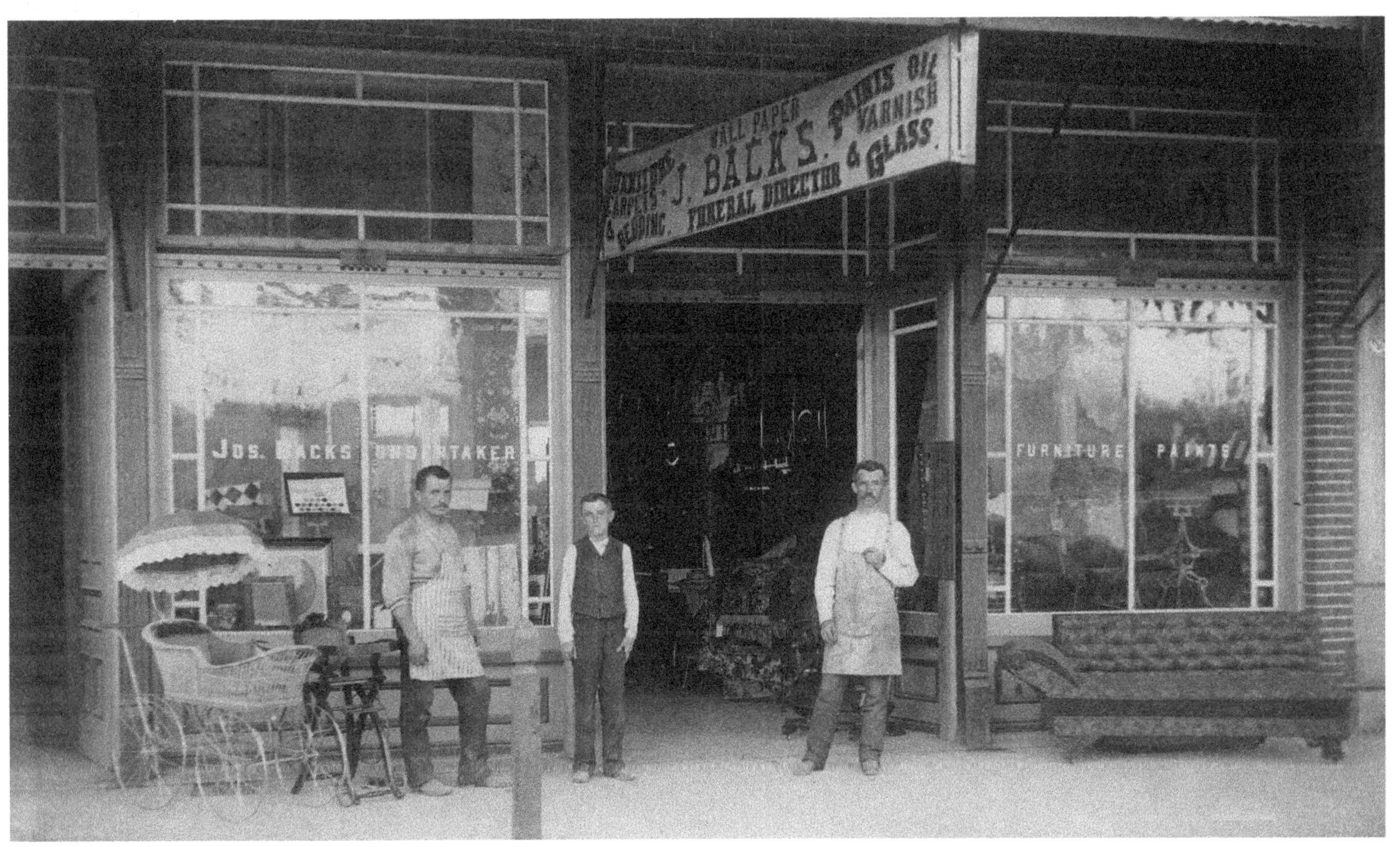

From ca. 1886, this view of the Joseph Backs store at 125 North Los Angeles Street shows Joseph Backs at far right and Joseph Backs, Jr., at center. In addition to maintaining a thriving mercantile store, Backs also served as the town's undertaker.

Asher T. Wallop's Grocery Store in 1886 was located at the northeast corner of Center and Los Angeles streets. A. T. Wallop stands in the doorway, his children Bill, Adelia, and Rudolph, respectively, to his left.

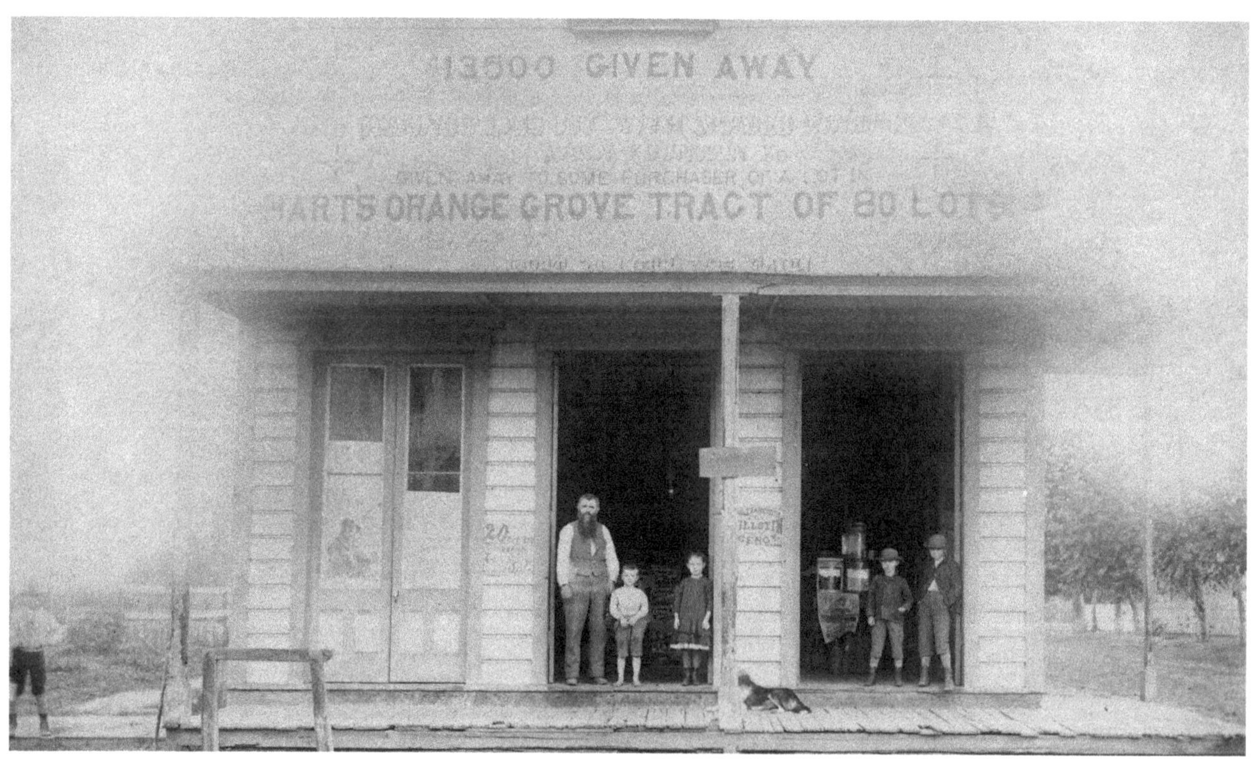

West Center Street in 1887. Lafayette Lewis started the Fashion Stables, on the south side of the street, in 1872. The Commercial Hotel with its signature balcony is visible on the corner of Lemon and Center streets.

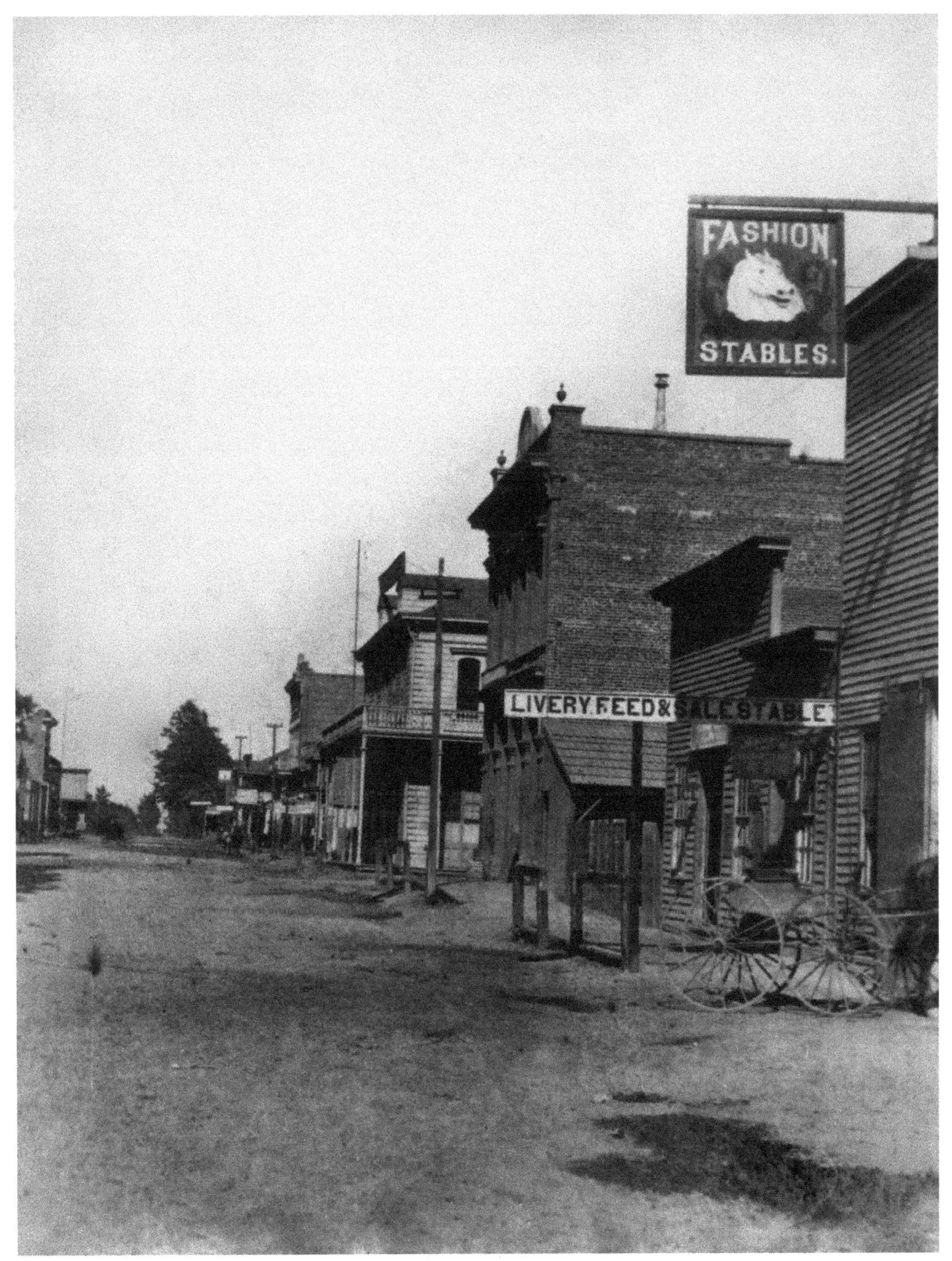

This 1887 view of August Langenberger's vineyard shows his home in the background. Langenberger was the son-in-law of Juan Pacifico Ontiveros, from whom the early vineyardists purchased the land that would become Anaheim. His residence, located on Sycamore Street, was named "Villa Mon Plaisir" (Home of My Pleasure). One of his original 20-acre vineyard lots was sold to the city of Anaheim in 1920 for the future development of City Park (now Pearson Park).

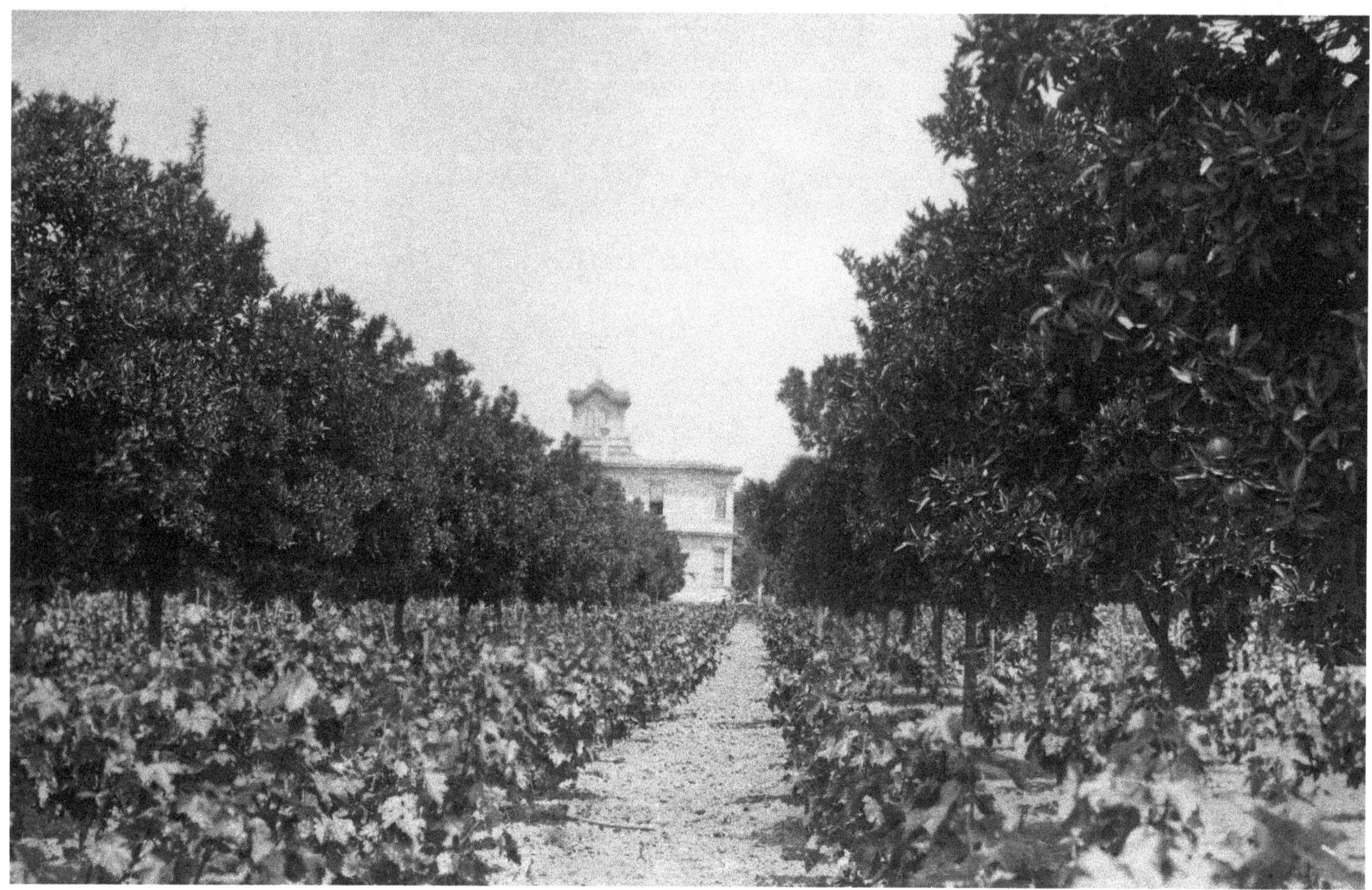

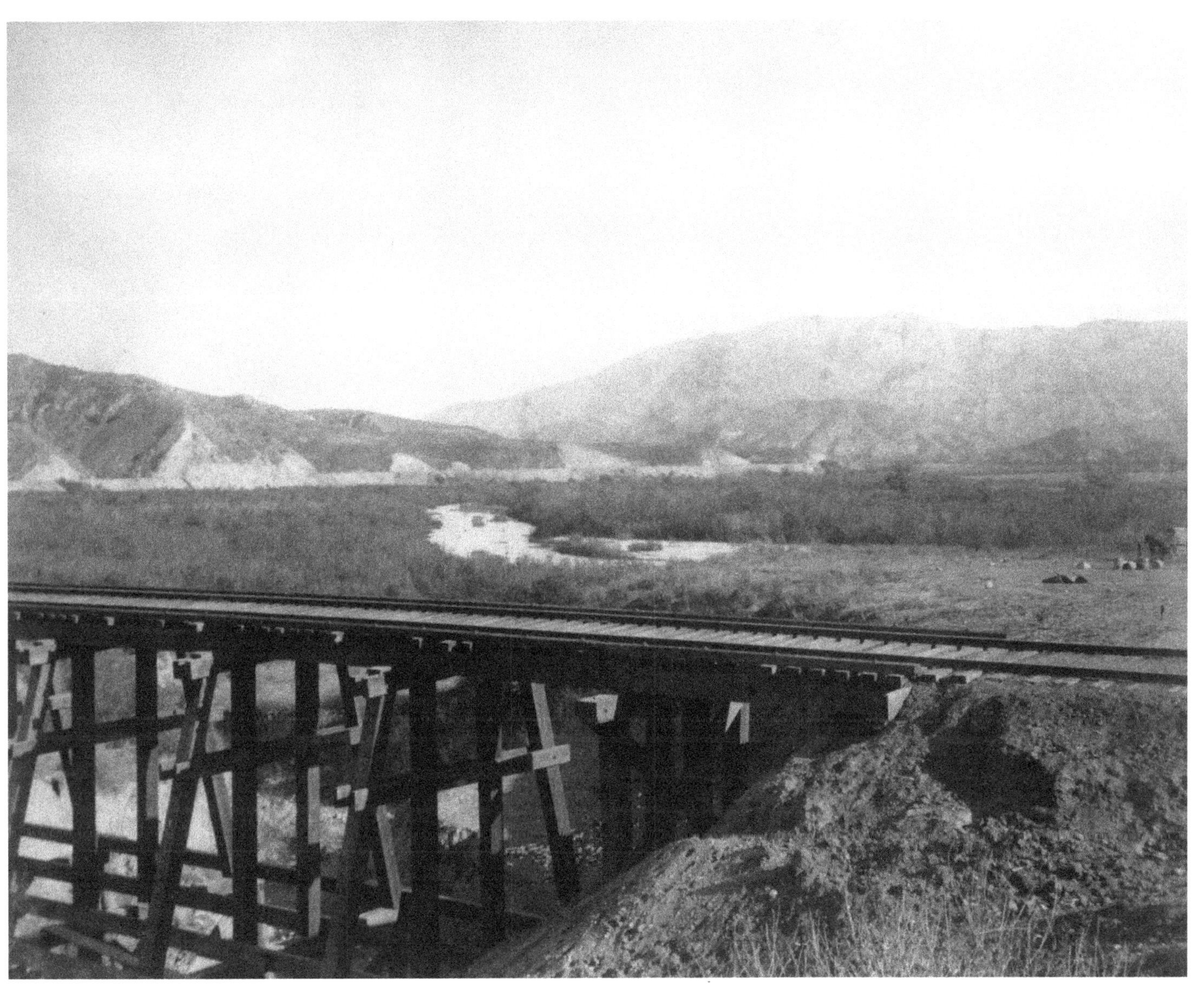

The Atchison, Topeka, and Santa Fe Railway built a line through the Santa Ana Canyon toward Anaheim in 1887. This trestle, one of several required to cross the meandering Santa Ana River, is located in an area that came to be known as Prado. The river provided the Anaheim colonists irrigation water needed by their thirsty vineyards.

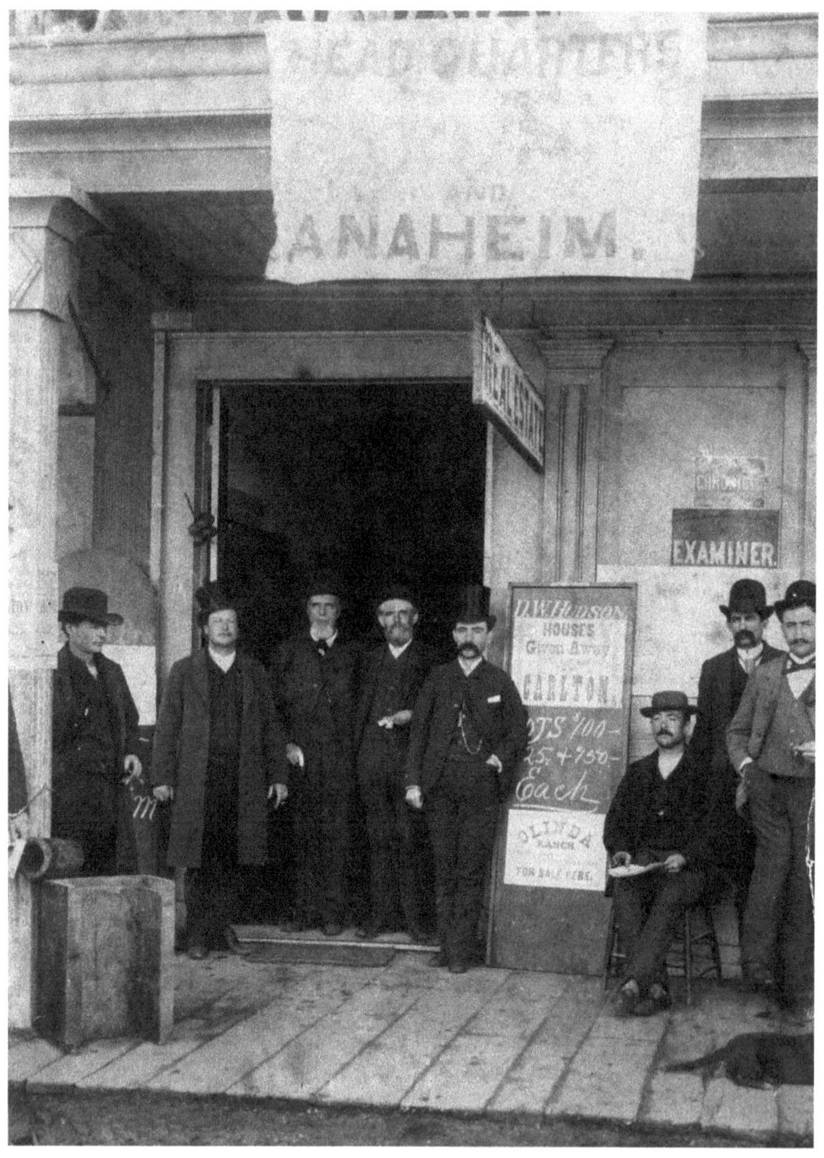

The region experienced a land boom in the 1880s and both real and paper communities were platted. Seen here is the Hudson Real Estate office advertising building lots for a modest $100. Among those pictured are Dr. A. V. Fox (3rd from left), Dr. V. C. Hardin (4th from right), Adolph and Frederick Rimpau, D. W. Hudson, Fred Smithe, Joseph Helmsen, and William Harker.

Lafayette Lewis arrived from his native New York in 1872 and opened the Fashion Stables on Center Street. Anaheim's streetcar line was incorporated by Anaheim's first mayor, Max Von Strobel, but his death in 1873 stalled construction until 1887. The one-mile line connected the Southern Pacific Depot on the west side of town to the Santa Fe Depot on the east side. It never generated the income foreseen by its owners and quietly closed in 1899.

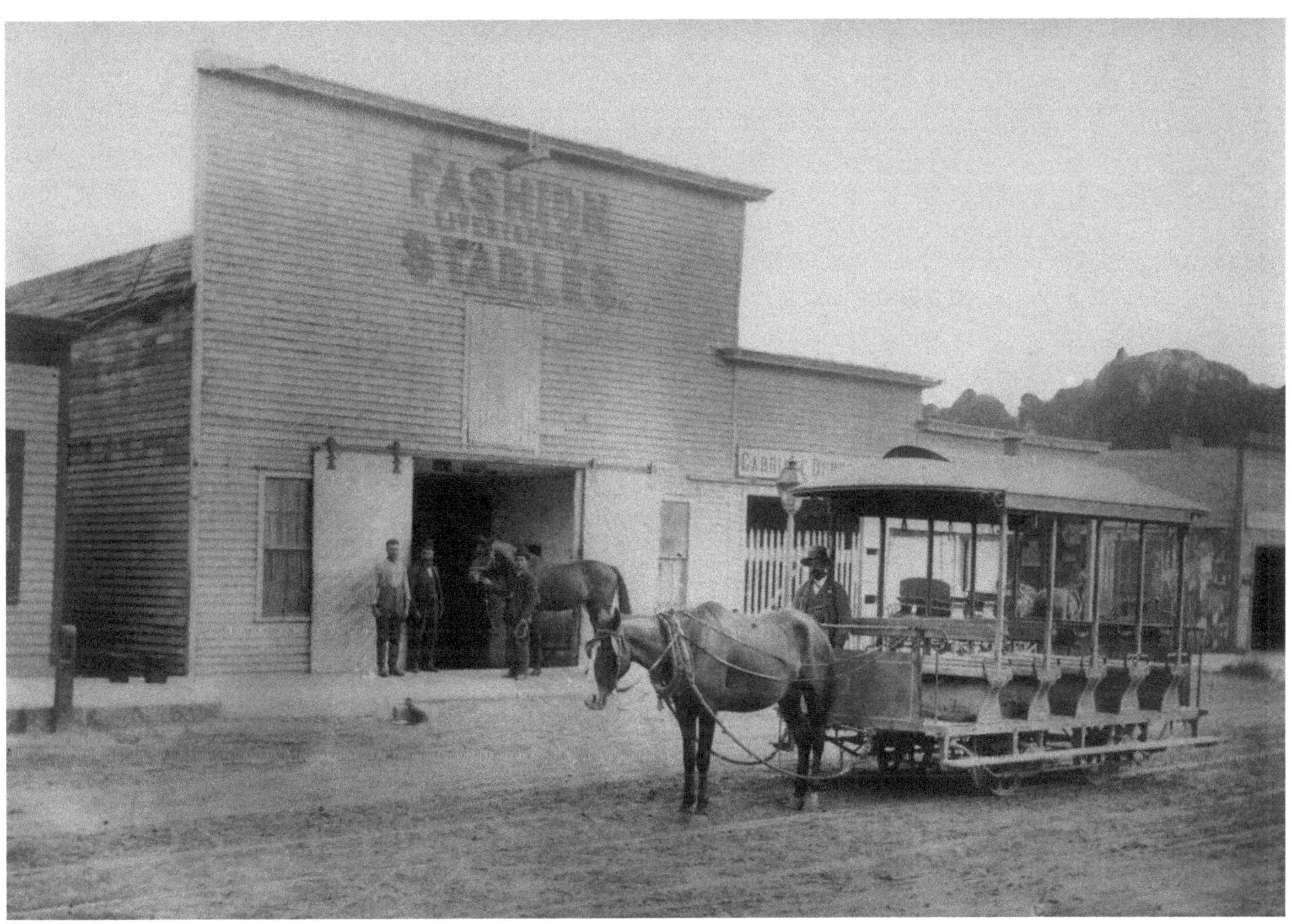

This 1888 view of North Los Angeles Street (now Anaheim Blvd.) shows the Palace Market owned by Mr. D. A. Brunswicker, and F. & J. Backs Furniture and Undertakers. Anaheim's downtown streets sported coal oil streetlamps, permitting some evening shopping.

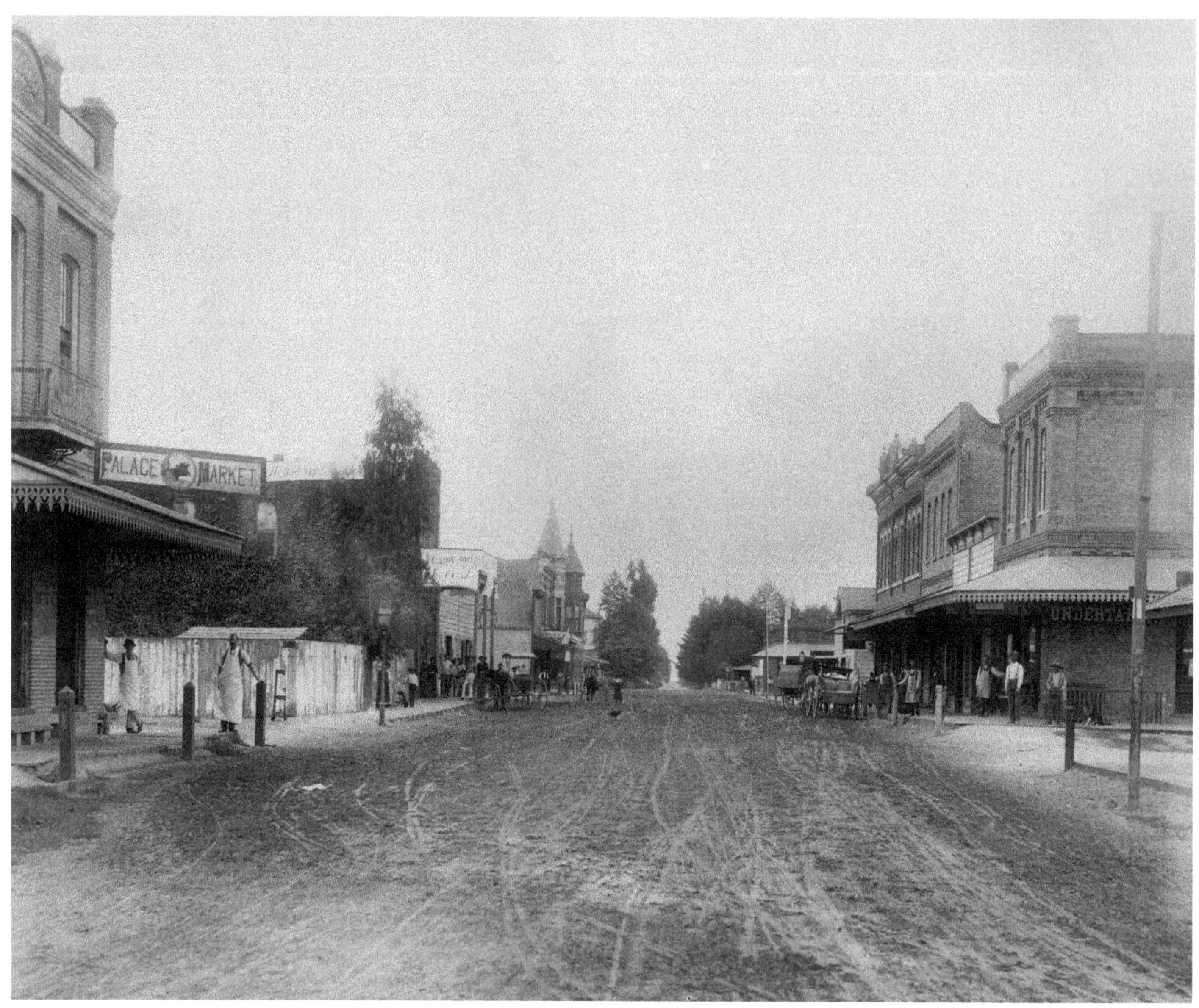

The Goodman and Rimpau Building, the Langenberger Building, and Anaheim's Planters Hotel can be seen in this 1888 photo of Center Street facing west from the corner of Los Angeles Street. Many of the wooden buildings of earlier years were beginning to be replaced with substantial brick structures, indicating the financial success of the original pioneers.

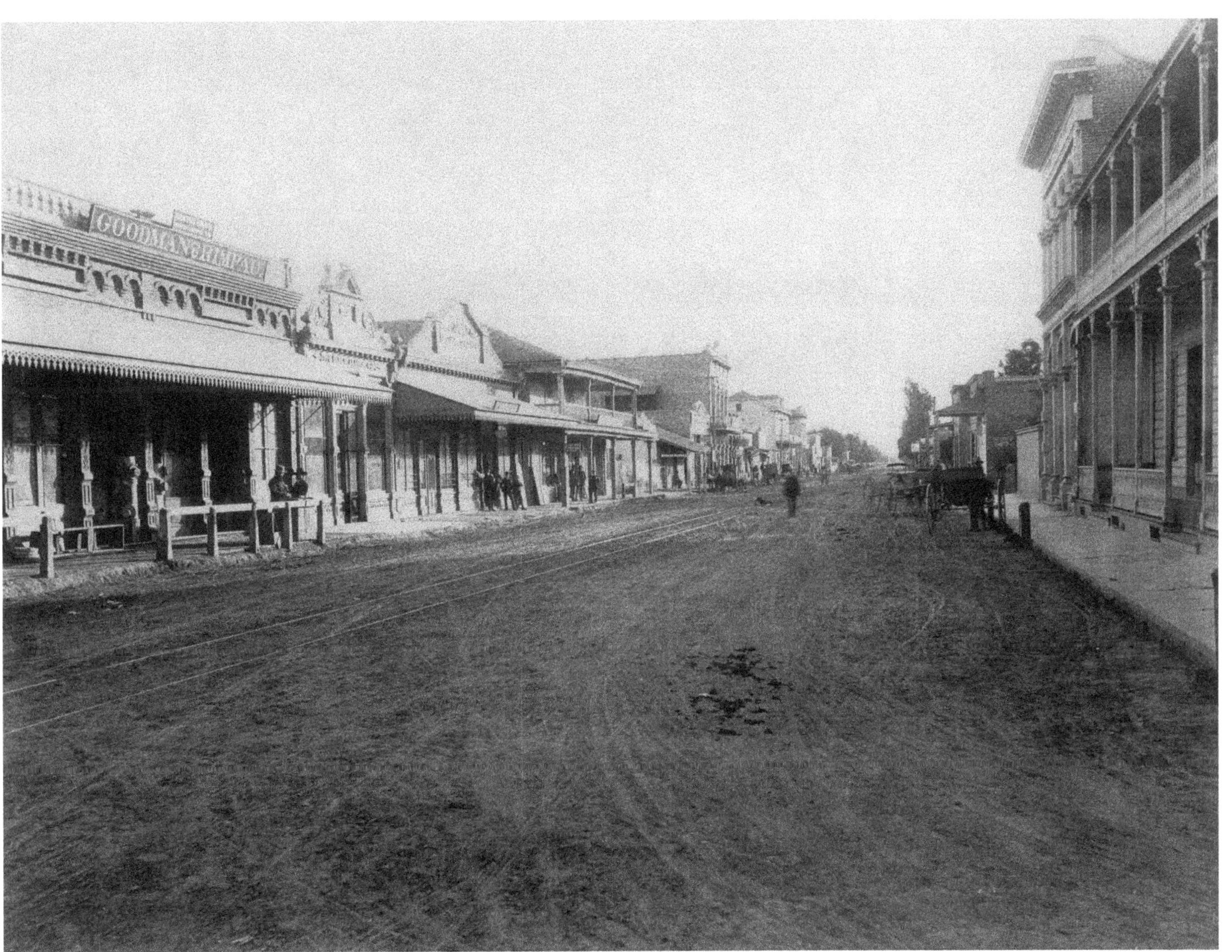

The Anaheim vintners established a port south of Alamitos Bay originally called Bolsa Chiquita. In 1857, just after Anaheim's founding, Frederick Schneider established the Anaheim Lighter Company to ferry goods from the anchored ships to the shore. This area became known as Anaheim Landing and was popular as a seaside vacation destination in the last years of the nineteenth century.

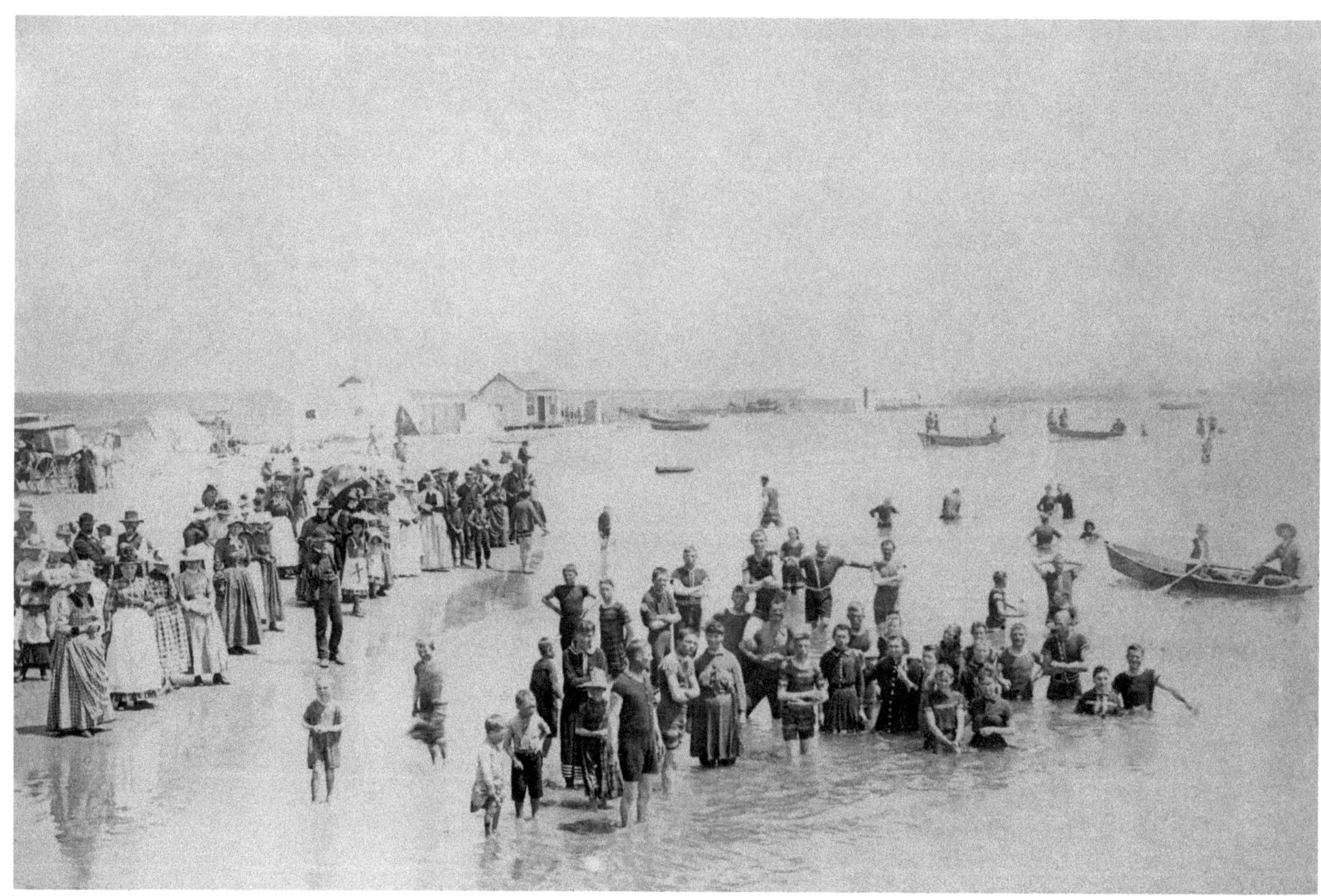

Anaheim Landing, despite its treacherous ocean outlet, enjoyed popularity as a vacation spot for the whole of the Santa Ana Valley. A number of semi-permanent tents were erected for the convenience of visitors.

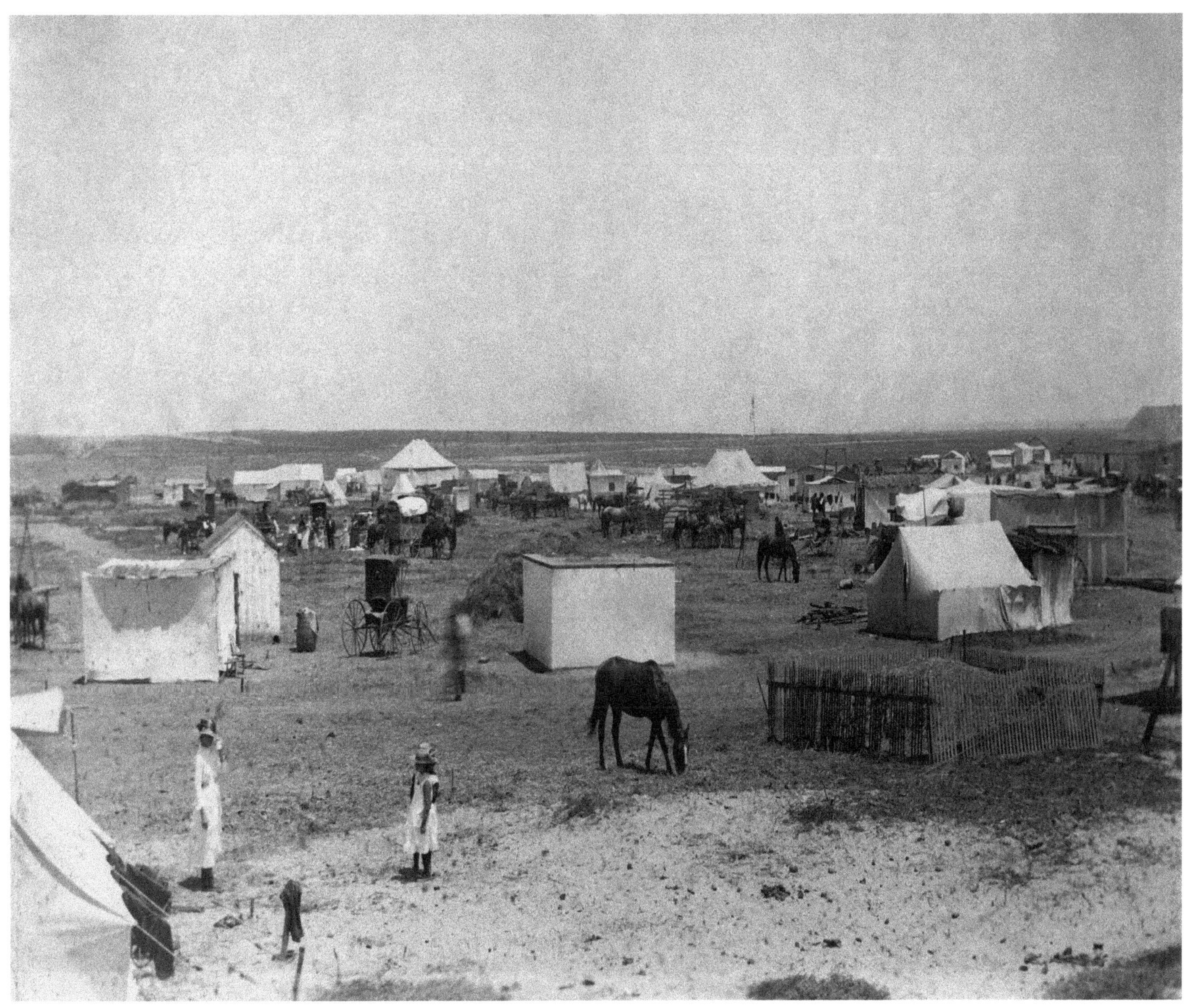

Once regular railroad transportation became available in Anaheim after 1875, Anaheim Landing became more of a seaside attraction than an active port. This 1891 portrait features a vacationing family enjoying one of the vacation cottages that were available. Today, as part of Seal Beach, this area is known as Anaheim Bay and rests inside the U.S. Navy Naval Weapons Station.

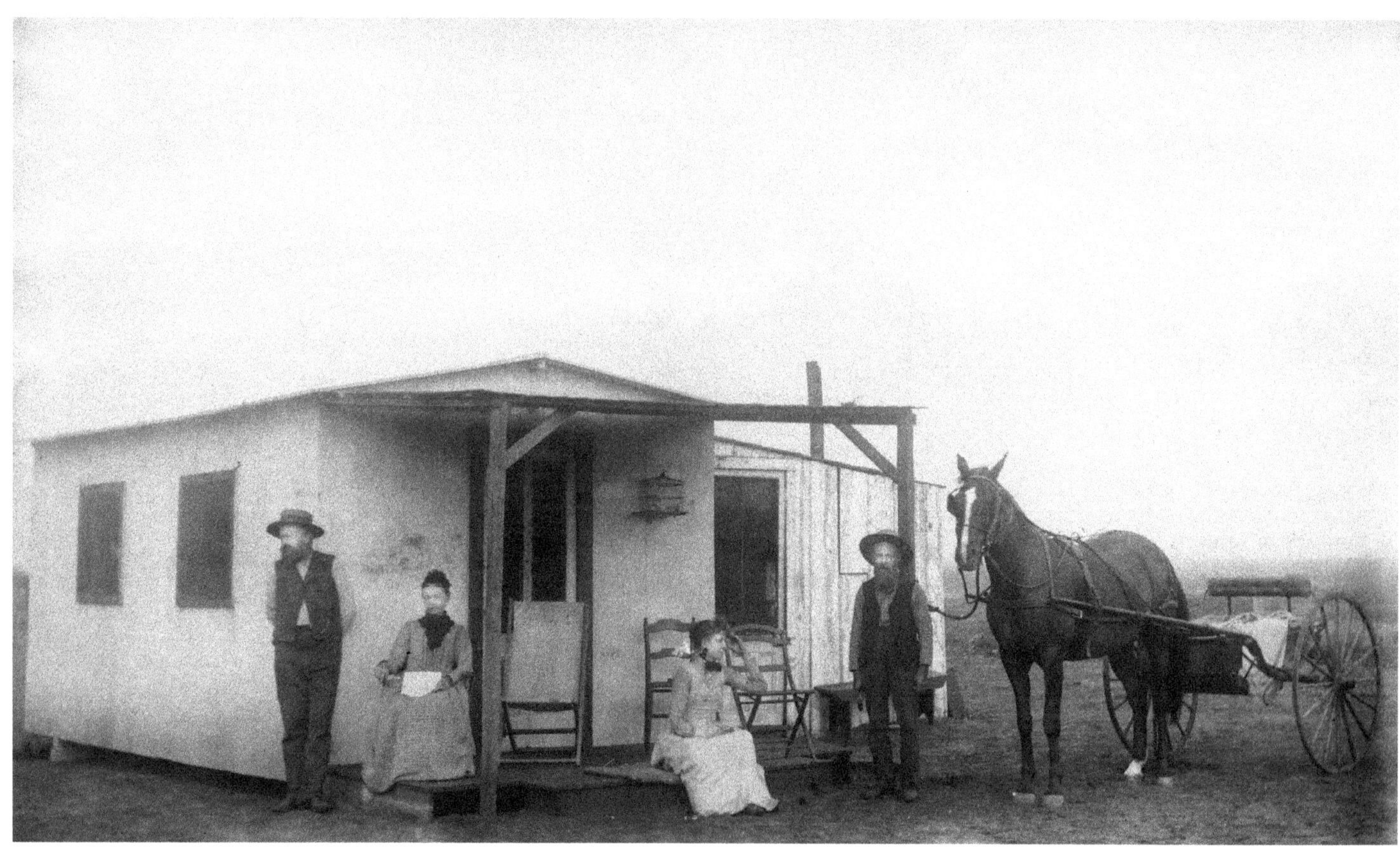

After the area's viticulture succumbed to "Anaheim Disease," later renamed Pierce's Disease in recognition of the USDA agent who studied the problem, several crops were cultivated in the region. From ca. 1890, this view of Walnut Street in West Anaheim shows a row of walnut trees, a significant replacement crop for the hardy German farmers. A grove of young orange trees can be seen at left, beyond the walnuts. Citriculture by the early years of the twentieth century turned the tide financially for the region with Anaheim later becoming known as the "Capital of the Valencia Orange Empire."

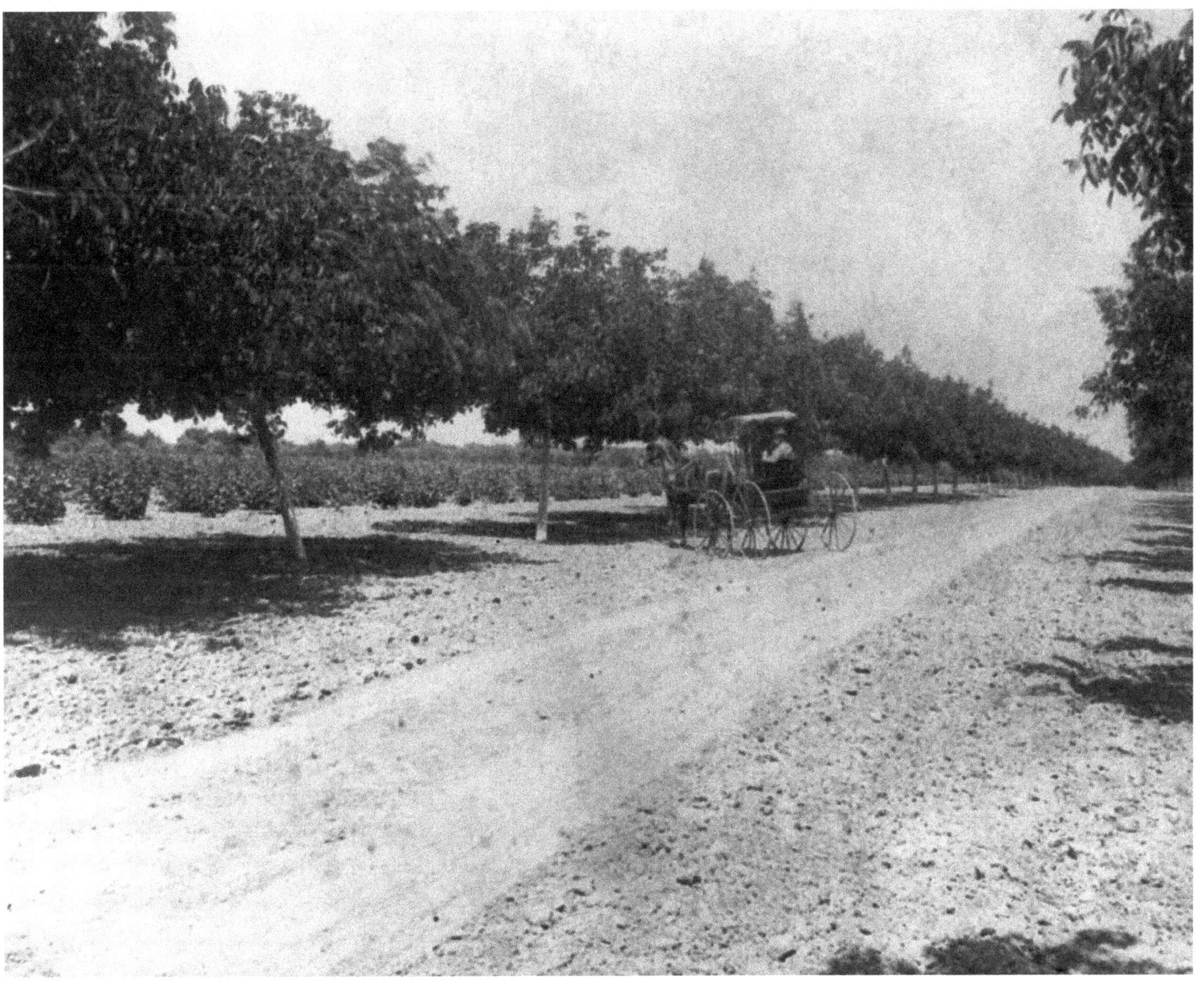

When George Hansen decided on the town site for Anaheim in 1857, a dependable water source was of greatest concern. The Santa Ana River supplied the entire Santa Ana Valley including Anaheim with irrigation water. The irregular flow of the river was claimed by a number of local irrigation companies, and arguments, lawsuits, and even armed conflict were not uncommon. In 1884, most of the competing parties were consolidated into two firms, the Santa Ana Valley Irrigation Company (SAVI) and the Anaheim Union Water Company. The division headgates for the Cajon Canal, part of the Anaheim Union Water Company, are shown here ca. 1890.

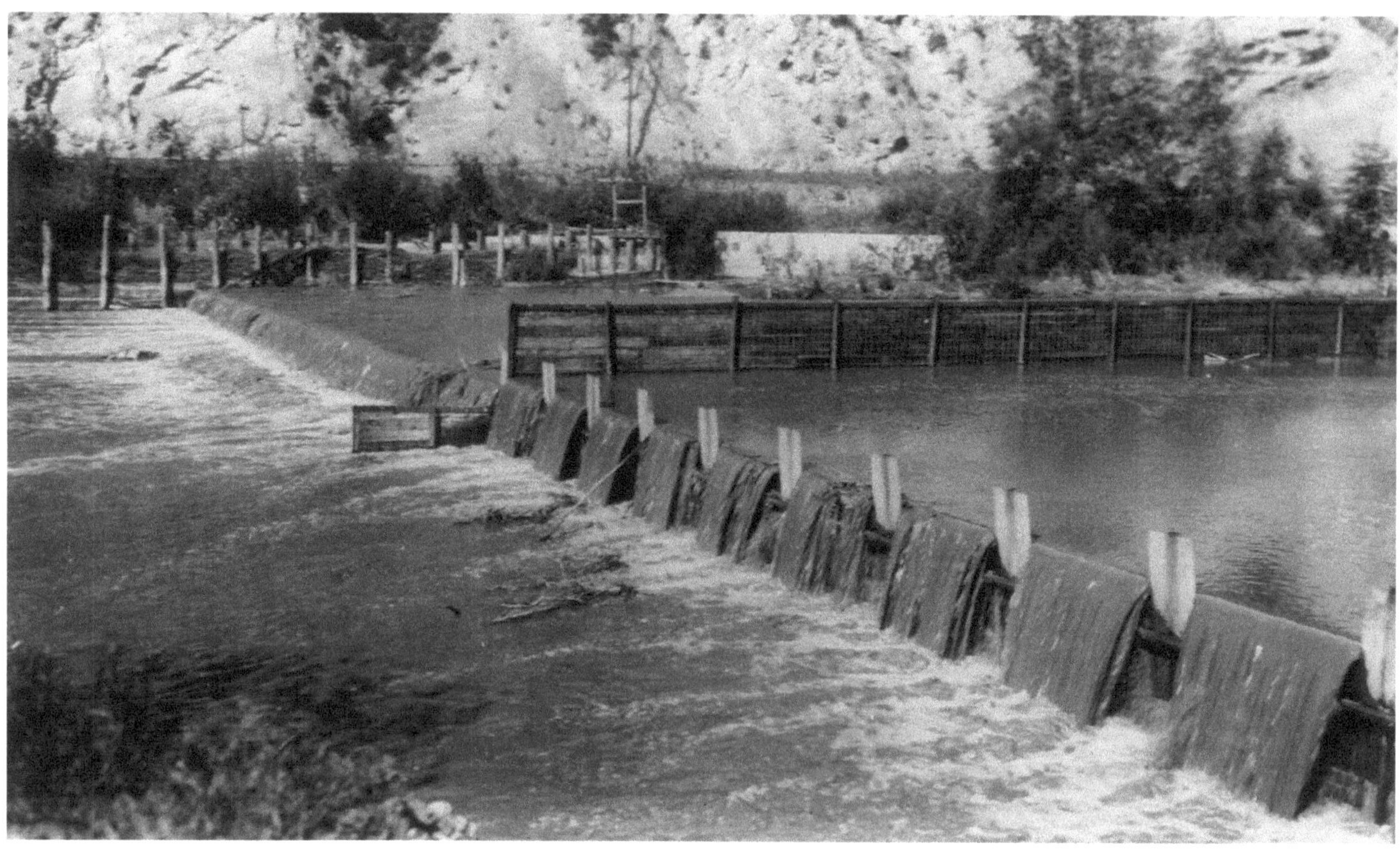

Here in October 1891, the firm of Wille and Albrecht installs a new 60,000-gallon water tank at the town's municipal water works plant at 119 West Cypress Street. Anaheim's frugal German trustees started their city-owned water department in 1879 to generate a small income for the community. The original facility had one shallow steam-driven pump and a 20,000-gallon redwood tank, which served most of the domestic water needs of the town's 883 residents.

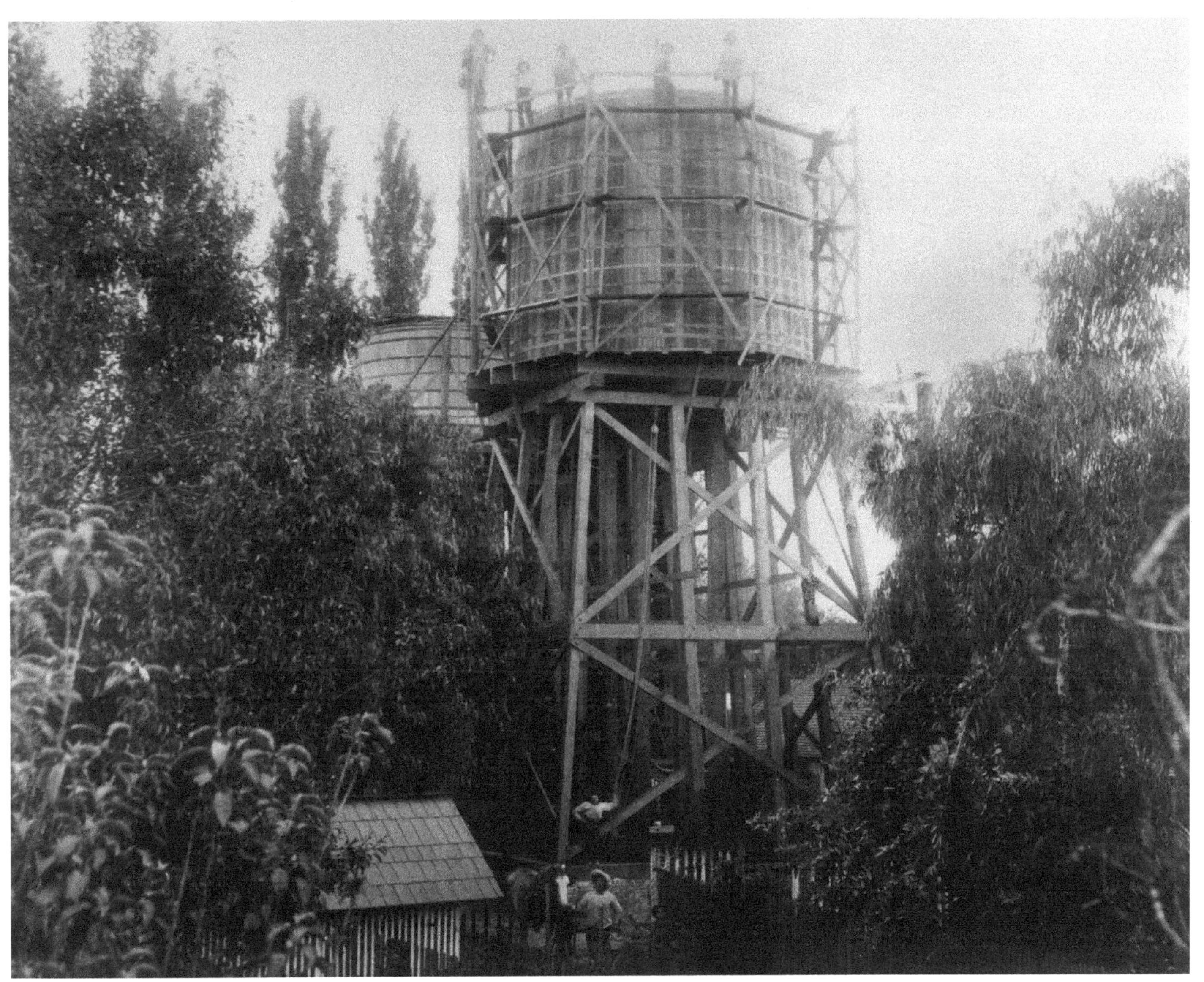

This 1891 elevated view of Anaheim faces west down Center Street from Los Angeles Street. The two-story brick Backs building stands to the right of center. At this time, Anaheim had not moved far beyond its original boundaries of North, South, East, and West streets.

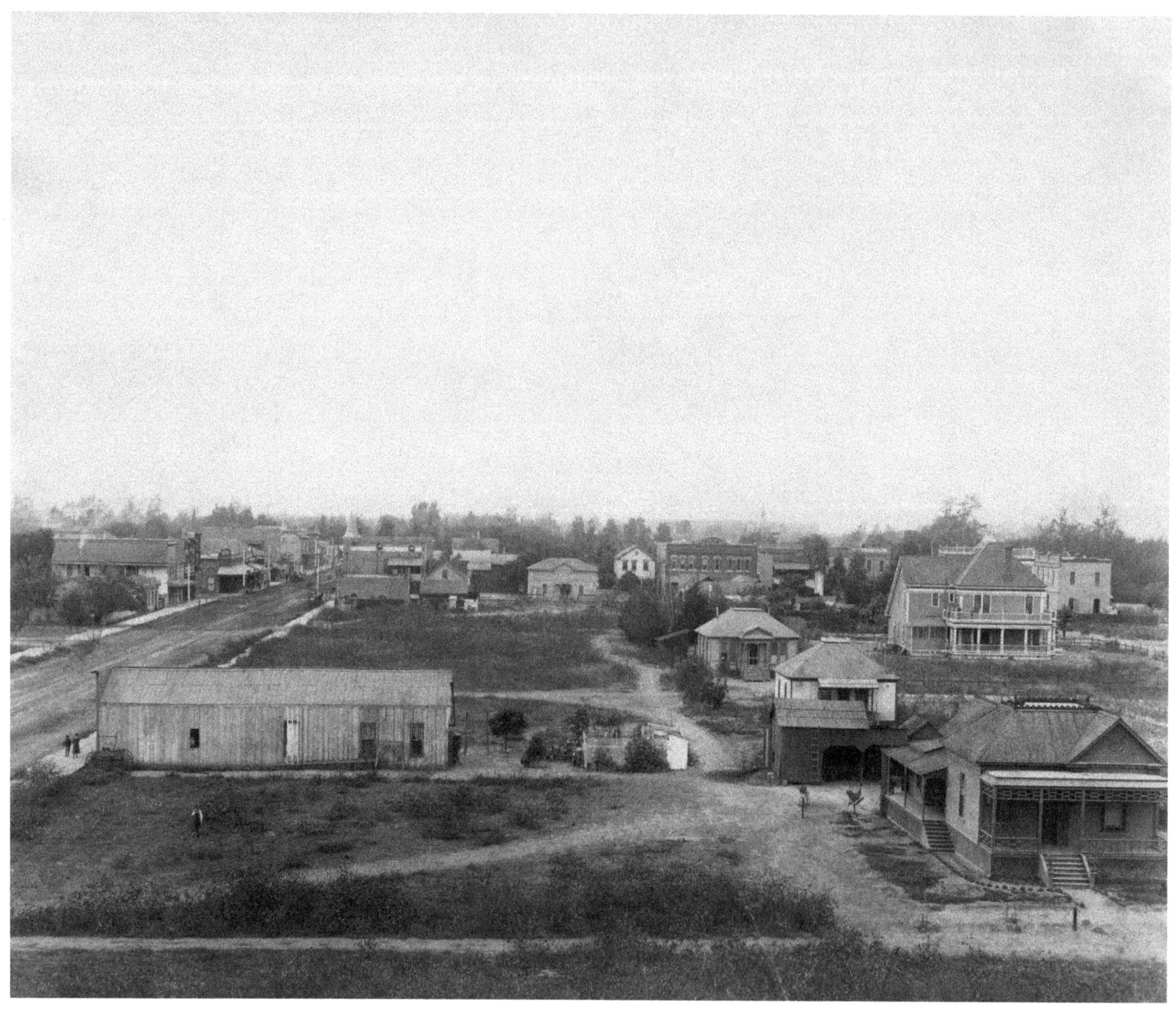

The stagecoach was still an important mode of transportation prior to the twentieth century. Anaheim was a popular stop on the stage route between Los Angeles and San Diego, as much for its saloons as for its bustling business district; the German settlers maintained a "wet" town for the convenience of citizens and visitors.

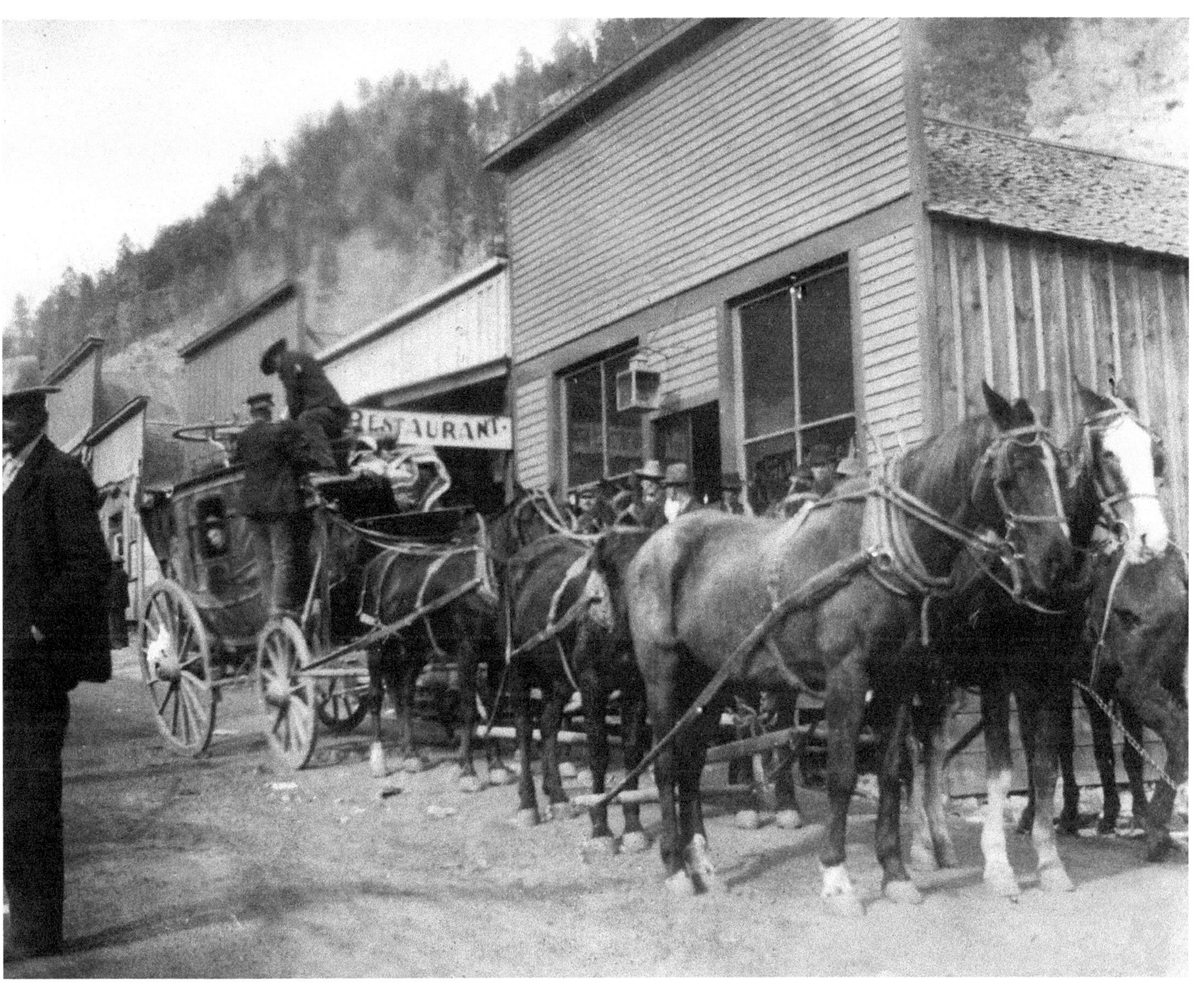

For the Fourth of July, 1892, celebration, Anaheim erected a double triumphal arch. The city built a number of arches in the early years to recognize the nation's independence. Although usually substantial edifices, they remained standing only through the celebration and parade.

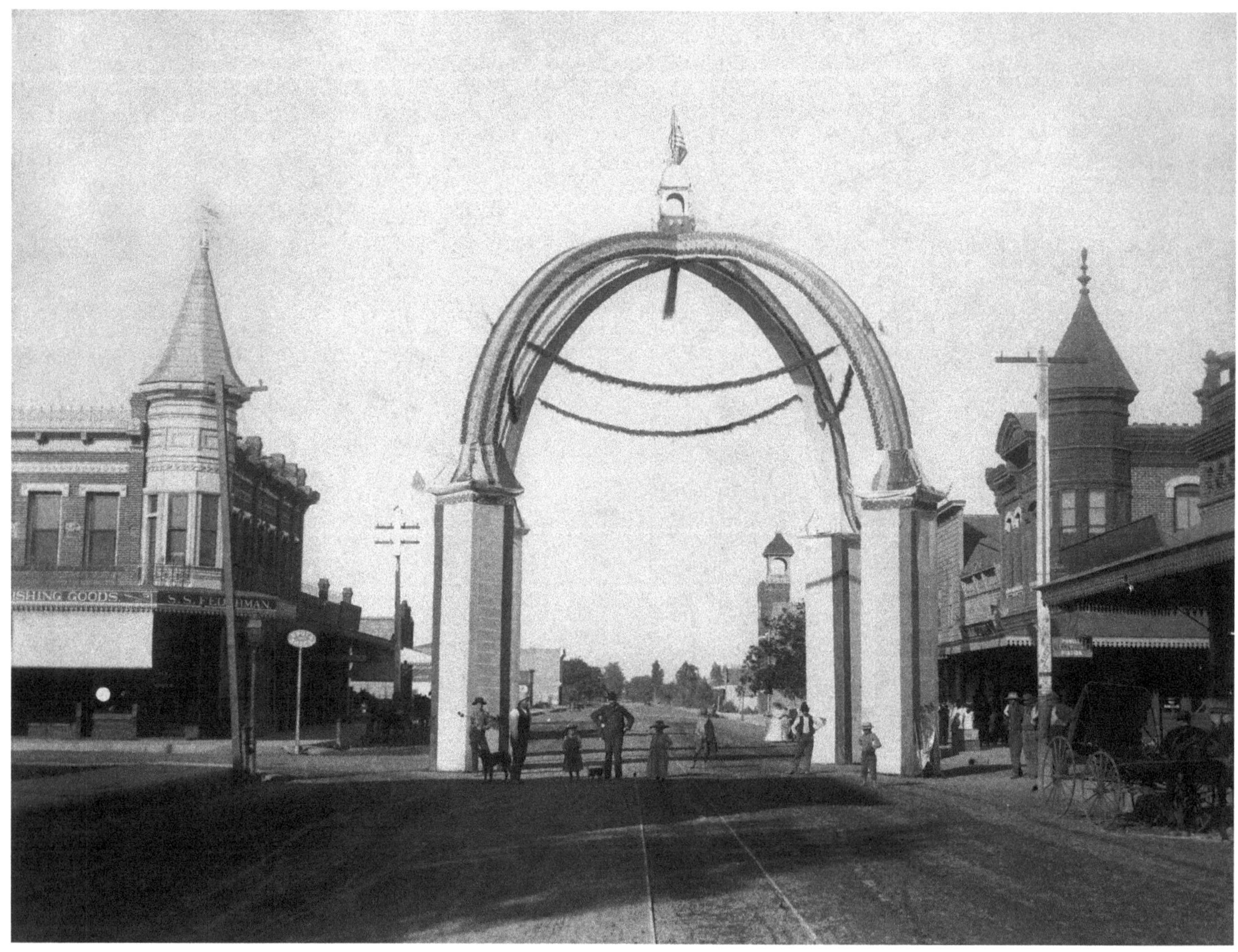

A rabbit hunting party stands in front of Frank Ey's barbershop in 1893. The men and boys proudly display their catch and possible dinner. The "country" was just outside town and hunting was an activity widely pursued.

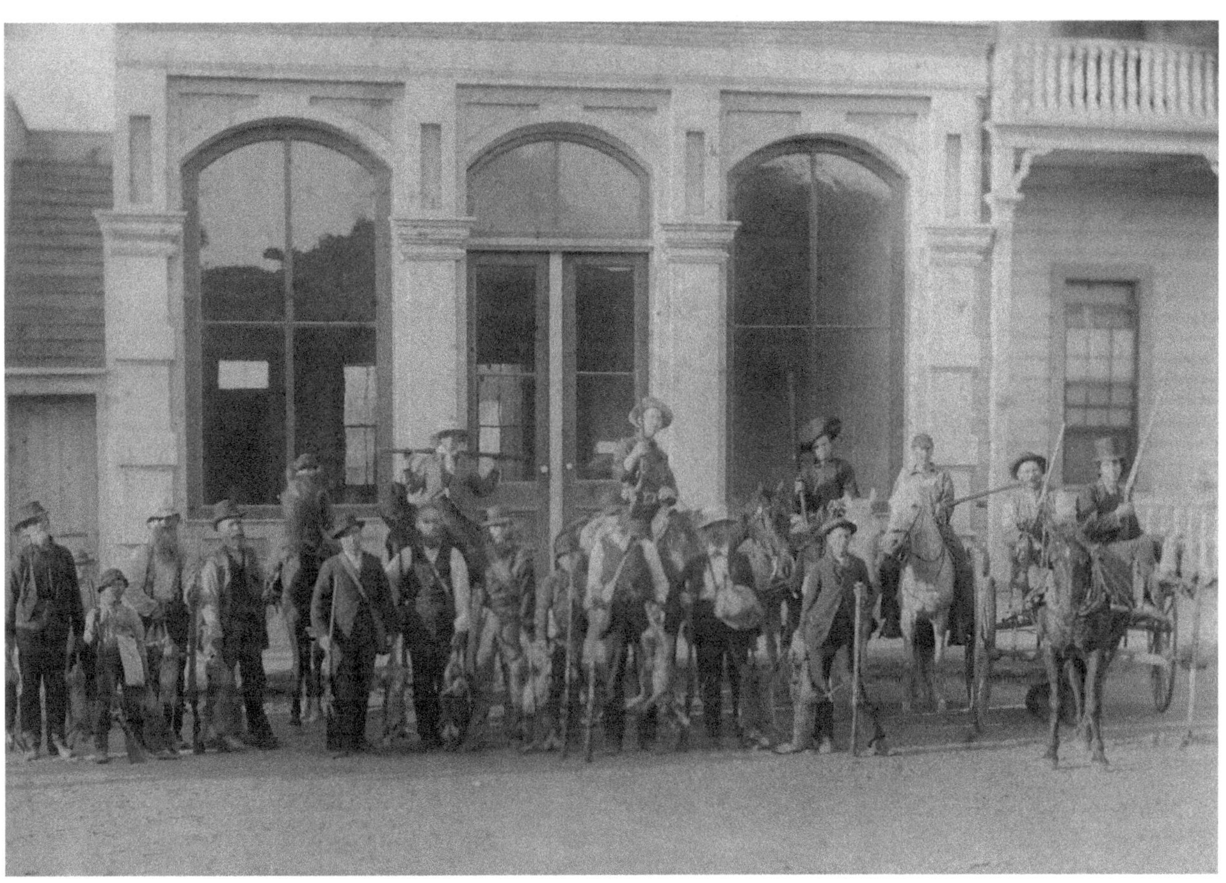

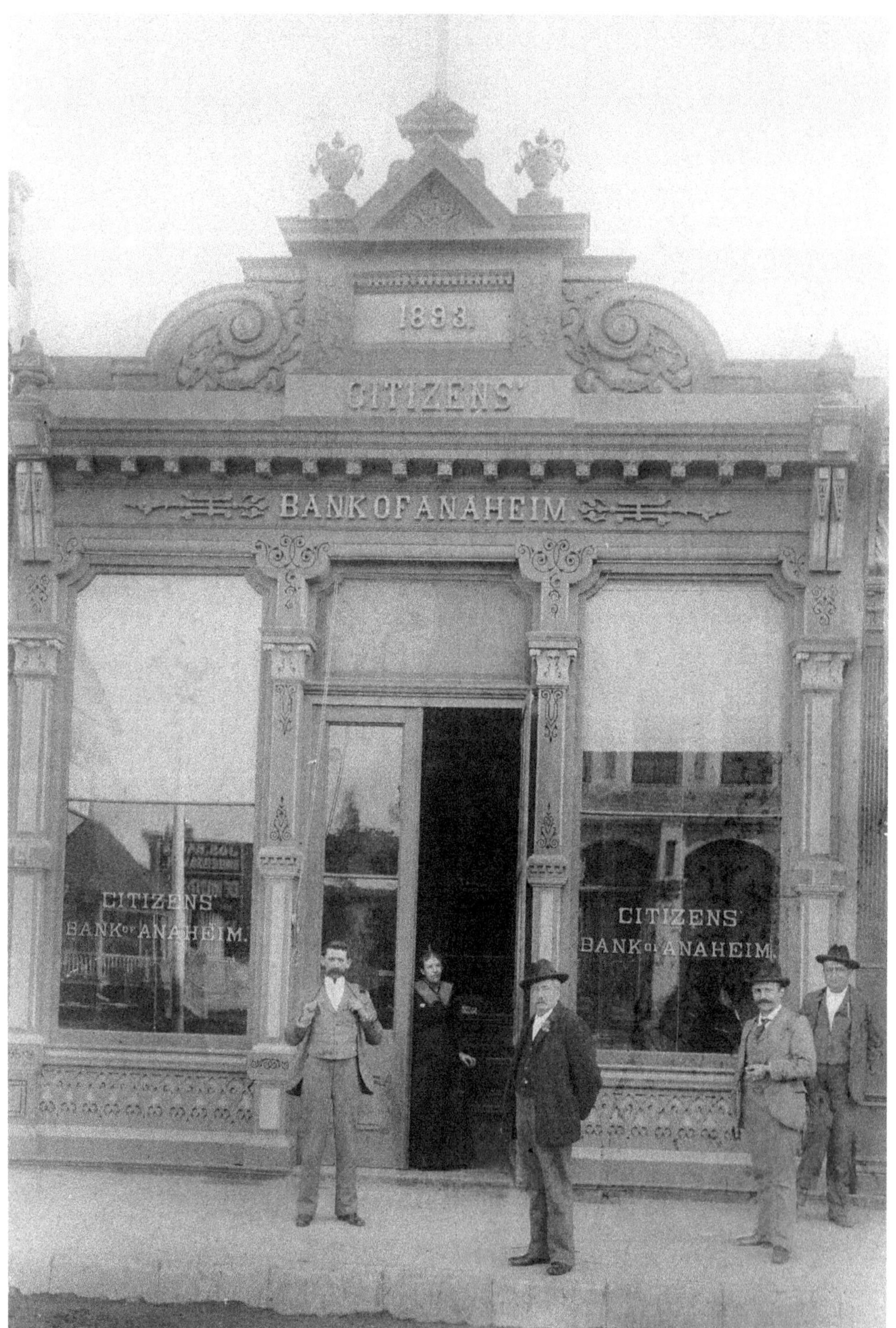

Pictured here is the ornate building of the Citizens Bank of Anaheim.

Kistler's Boston Bakery stood at the corner of Los Angeles Street and Cypress Street from 1891 to 1896. Identified from left to right are Stephen Kistler, Miss Mary Kaiser (Stephen's sister-in-law), and Caroline Kaiser Kistler (Kistler's wife). In addition to baked goods, the Kistlers maintained an ice cream parlor, much to the delight of the local youngsters.

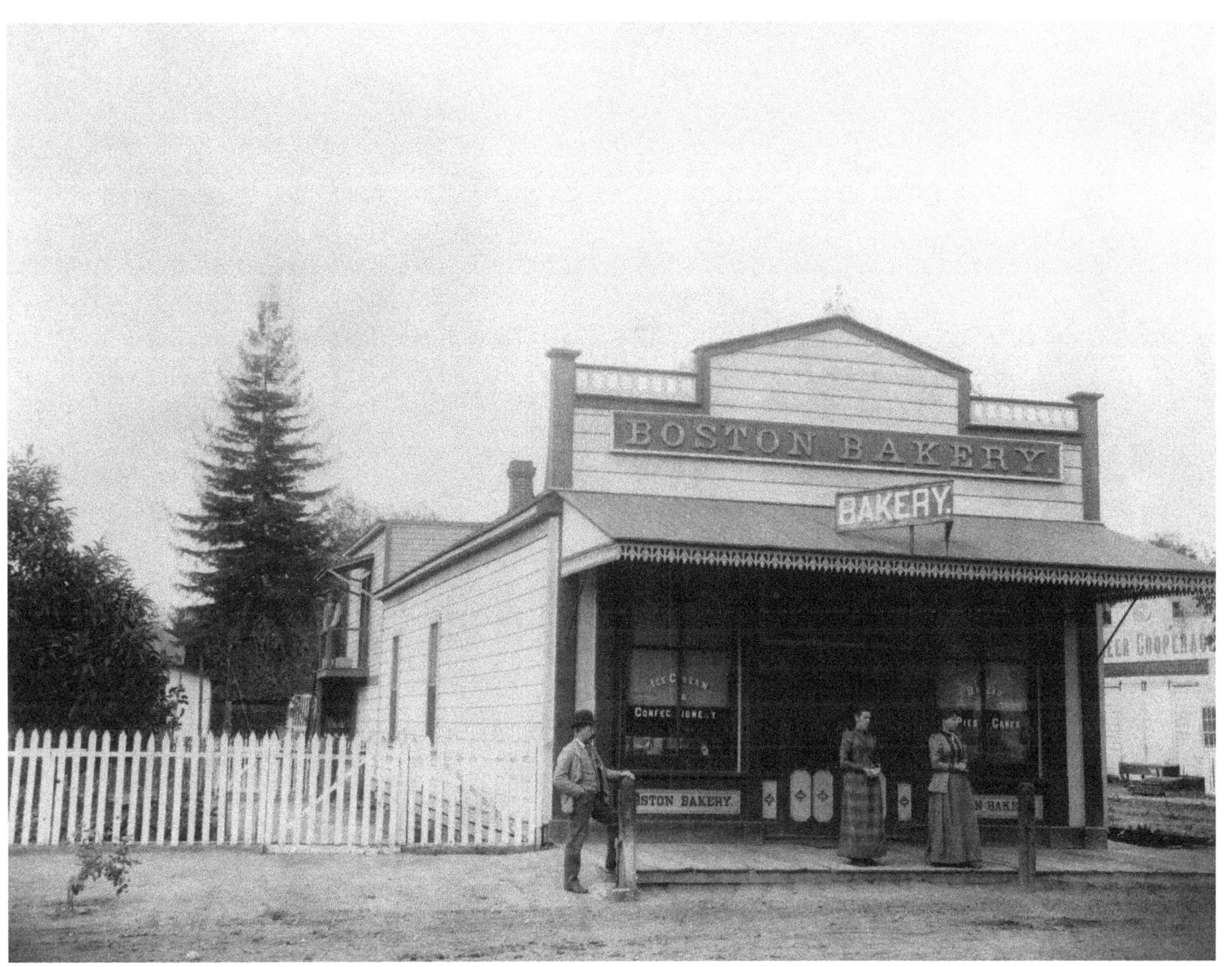

Mable Street in West Anaheim was home to the Evergreen Nursery, owned by Timothy Carroll, an Irishman who arrived in Anaheim in 1863. His well-respected nursery supplied most of Anaheim's early agricultural rootstock. West Anaheim School (later renamed Loara School) and the Hund residence are just visible in the background.

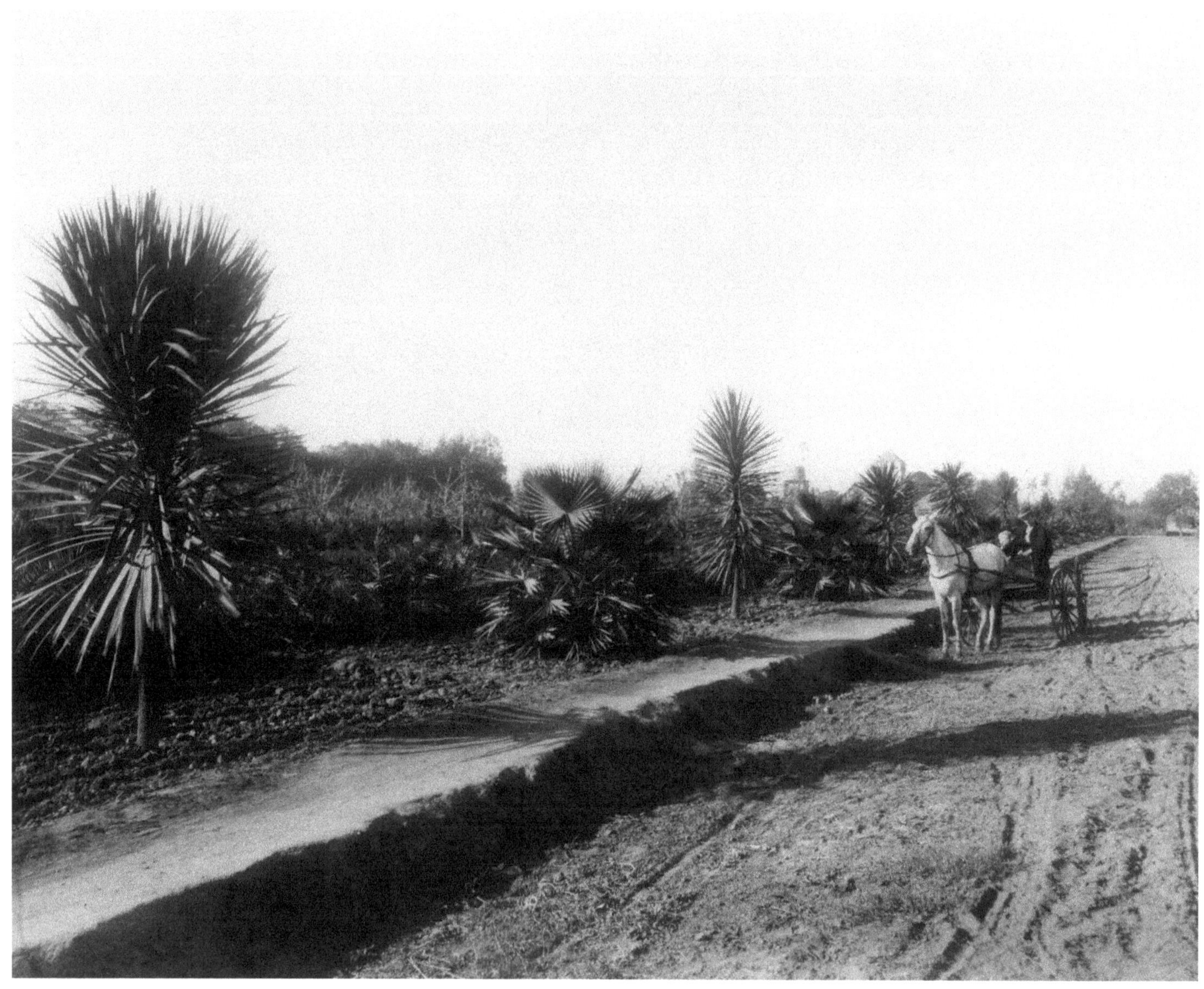

Around 1894, the newly constructed Metz Block building occupies the southeast corner of Center Street and Los Angeles Street. Built by Margaretha Metz in memory of her late husband, John, who died in 1869, this impressive structure dominated downtown Anaheim for many decades. Isaac Lyon's hardware store occupied most of the first floor.

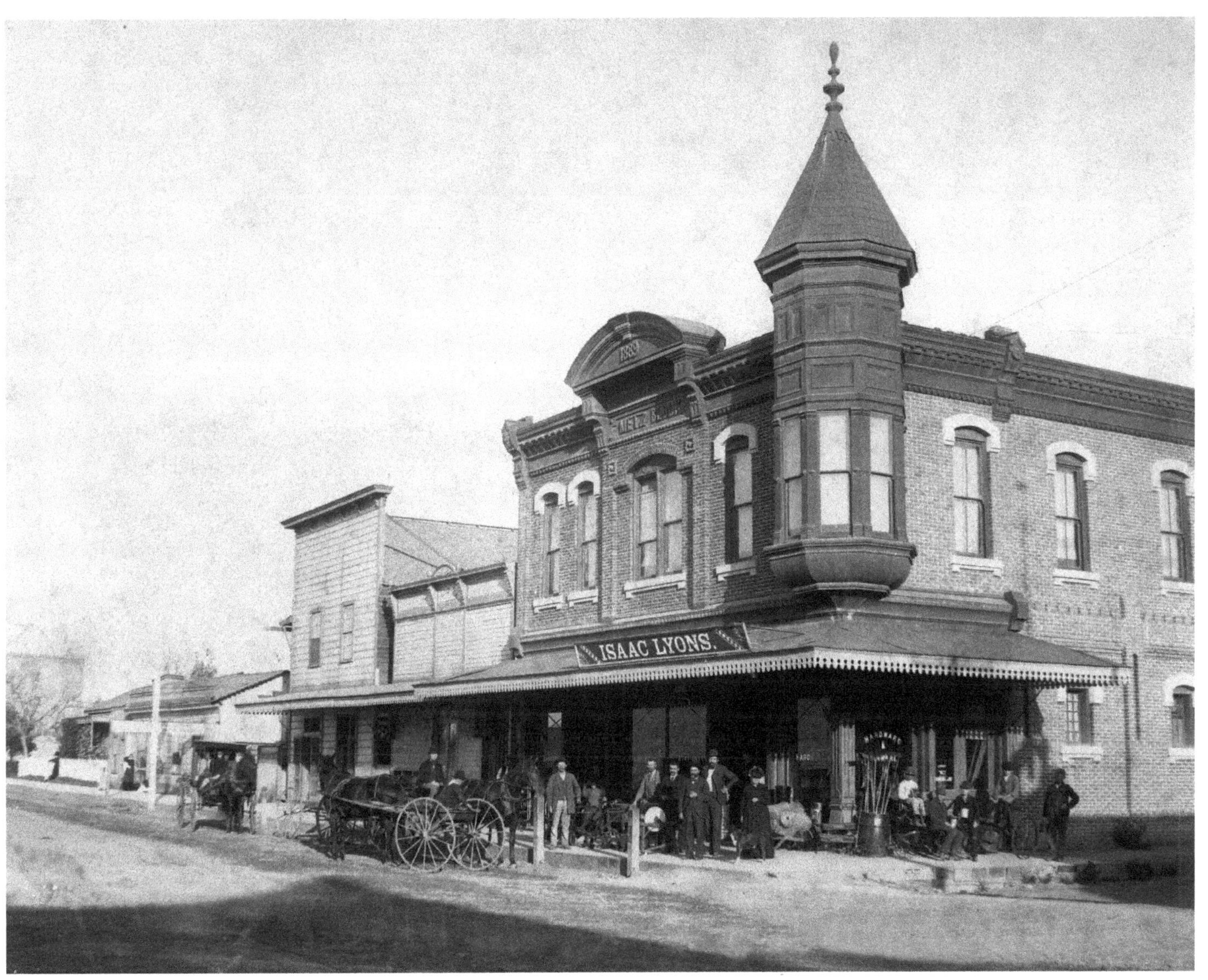

By 1895, William Boyd had taken over the hardware business located in the Metz Block. Boyd supplied the growing community with housekeeping necessities including "Quick Meal Gasoline Stoves." The Cowan dentist office and the Pacific Boarding House occupied the upper floors.

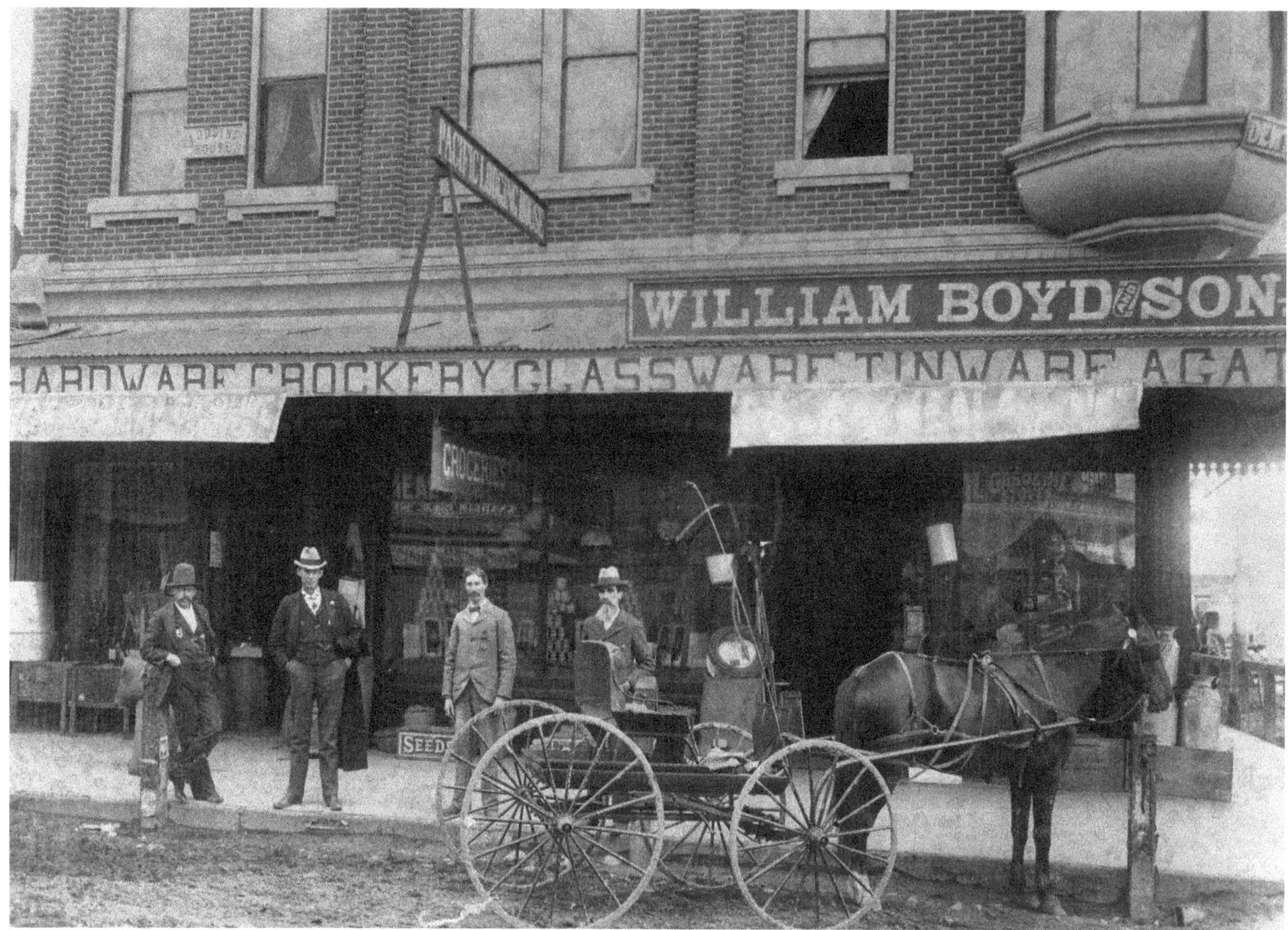

A late 1890s view of Center Street facing west features various buildings on both sides of the street flanking the Anaheim Streetcar tracks. Identified left to right are the Palace Restaurant, the landmark Metz Block building, Bentz & Steadman Meats, S. S. Federman clothing store, the telegraph office, post office, and Pellegrins Music Store.

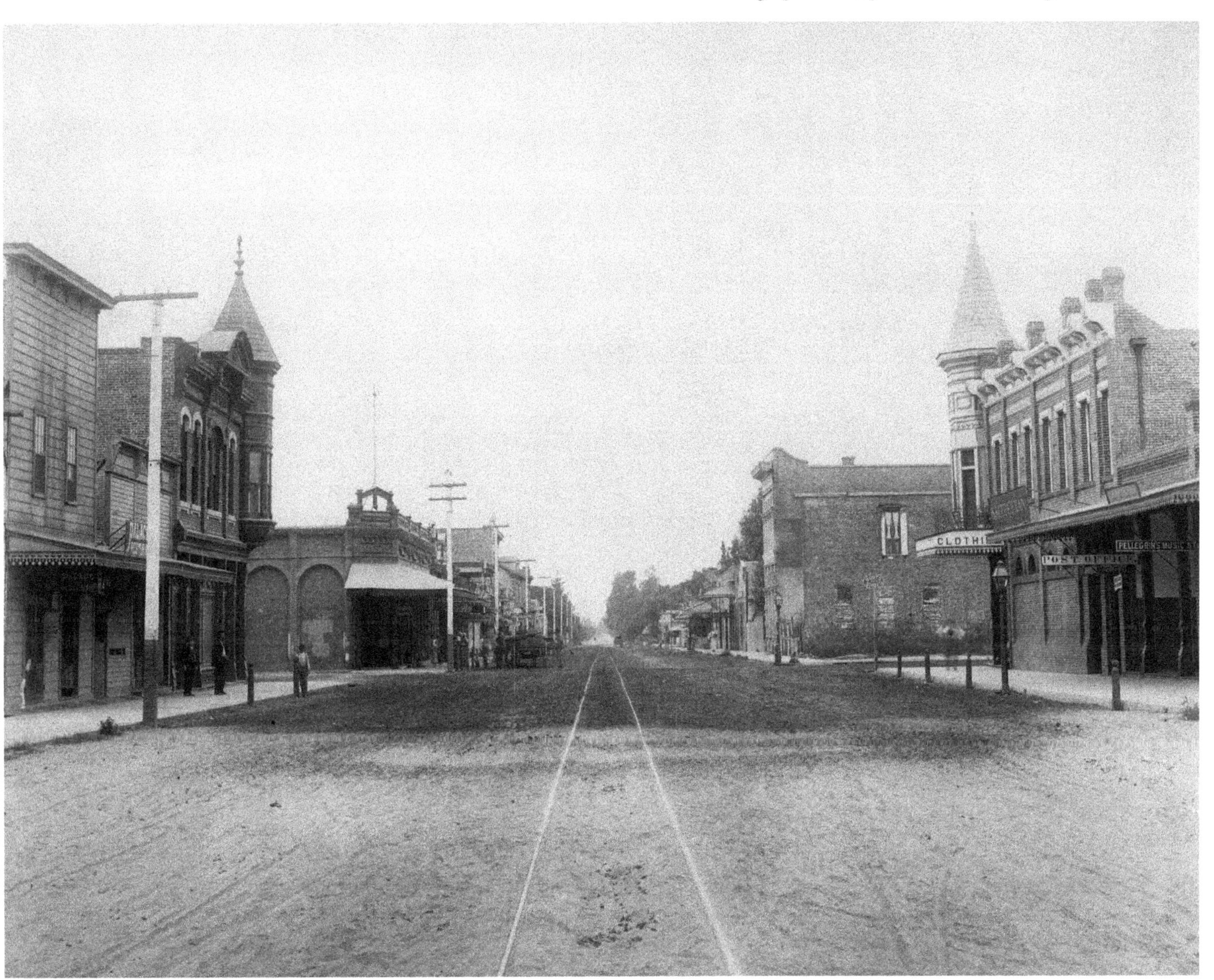

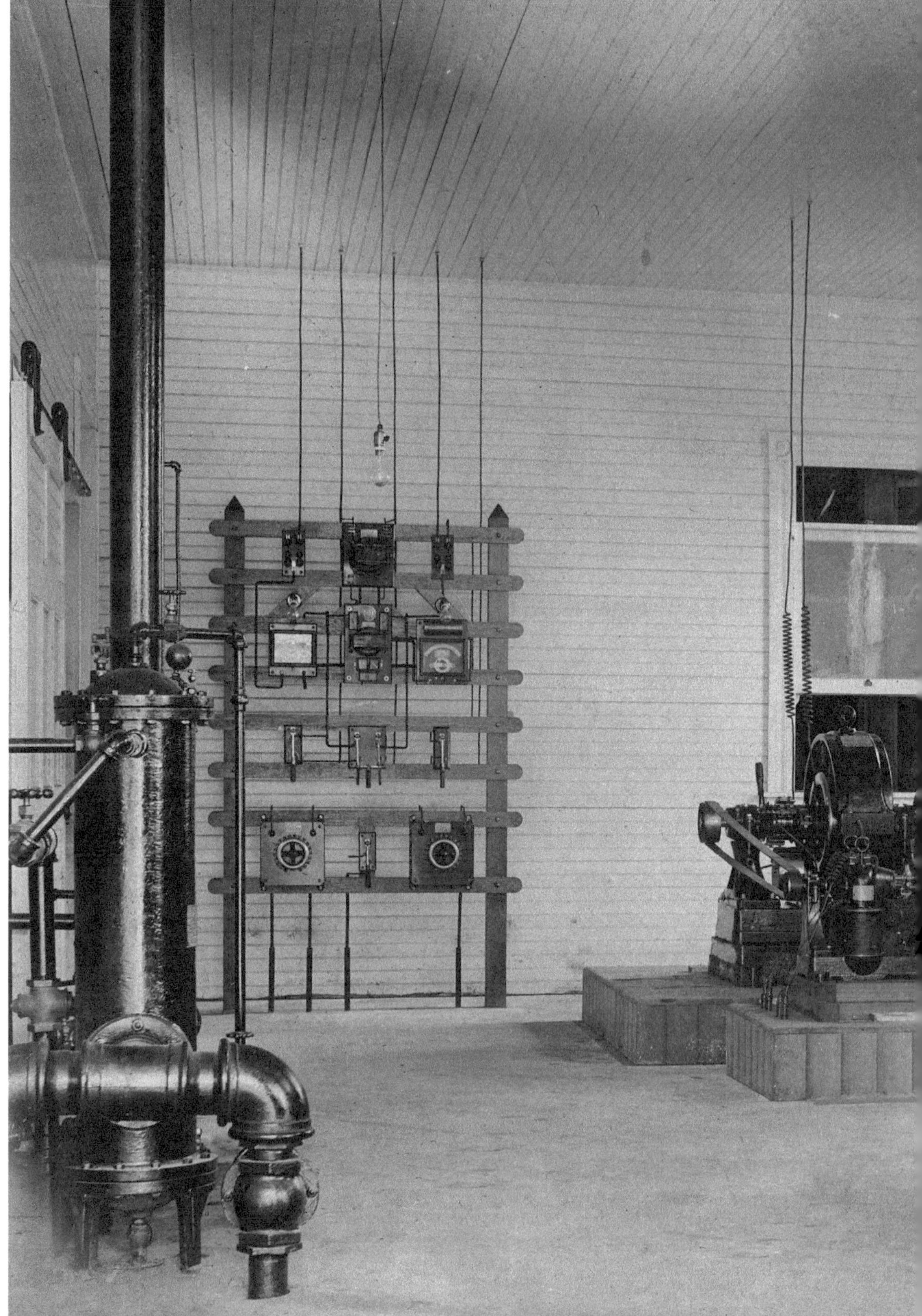

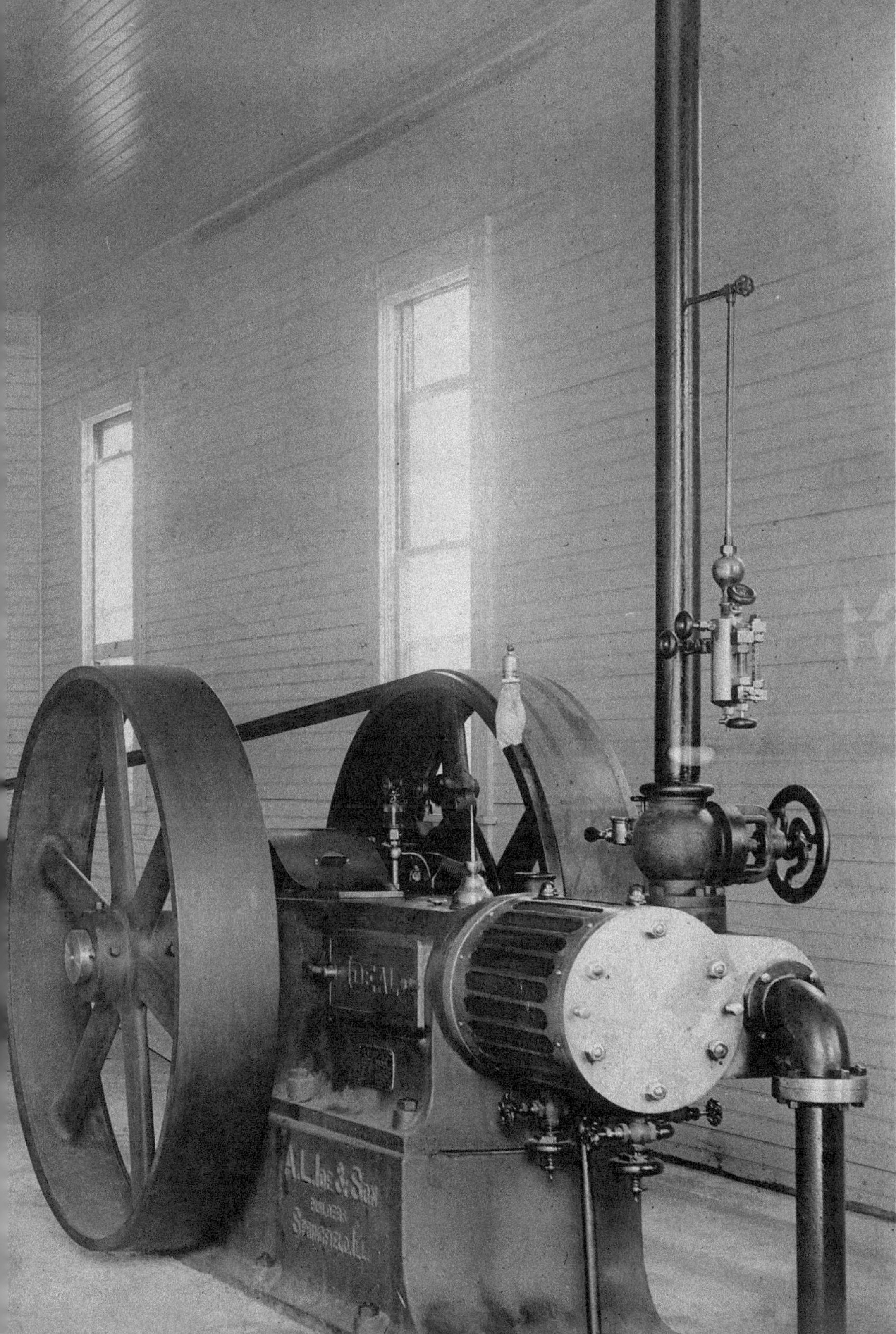

In 1894, the entrepreneurial city trustees entertained the idea of electrifying the community. When a Los Angeles firm offered to install and operate streetlights in the downtown area for $125 a month, Trustee Joseph Helmsen claimed that the city "could easily maintain the plant on their own account." A $7,000 bond issue followed for construction of the "500-light" plant located on West Cypress Street. On April 11, 1895, Charles Lorenz, the town's oldest living resident, "pushed the button" inaugurating Southern California's first municipally owned electric utility.

Electric streetlights have arrived in downtown Anaheim in this late-nineteenth-century view east on Center Street (now Lincoln Ave.). Fred Pressel's Blacksmith Shop at 218 West Center stands at right. The tracks of Orange County's second oldest horsecar would be removed in 1901.

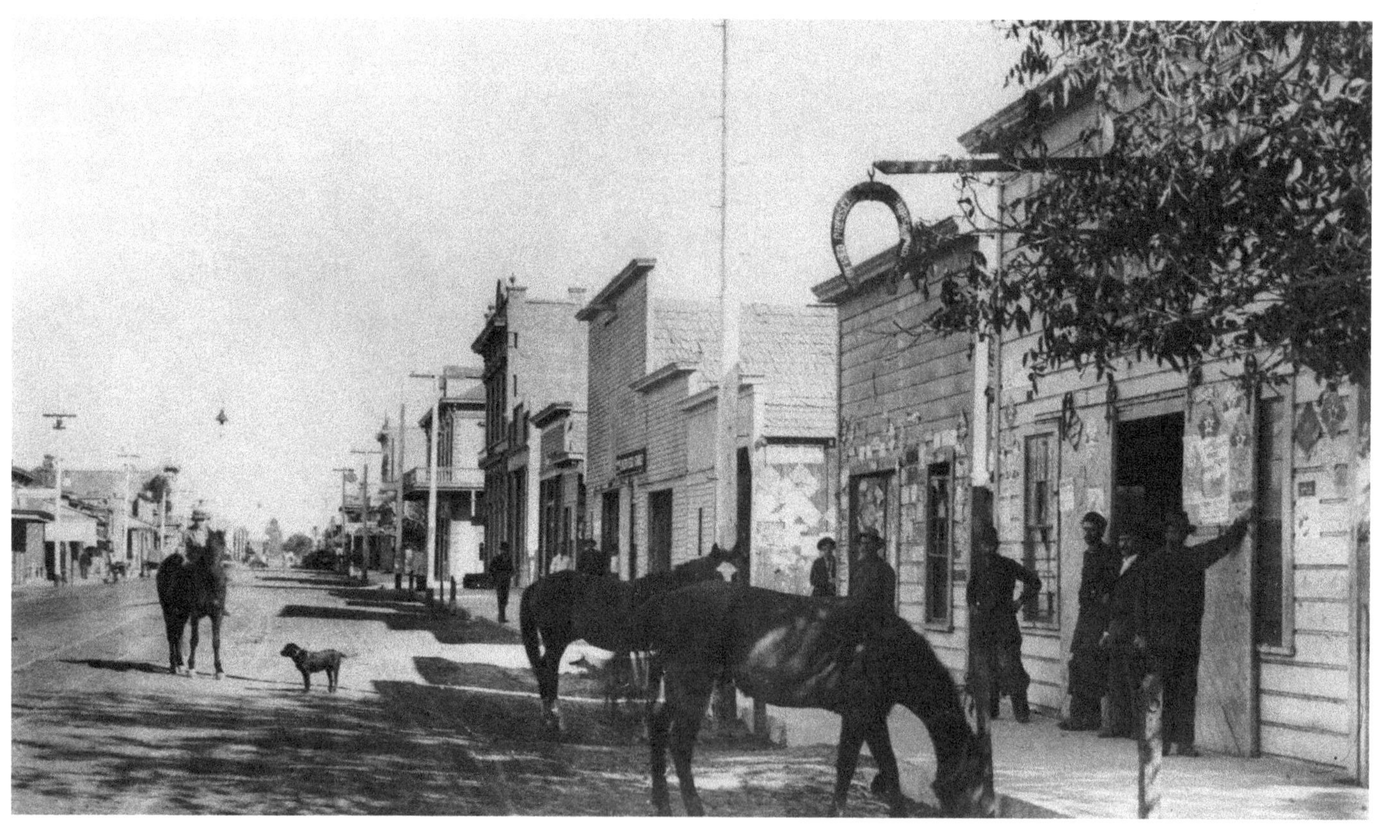

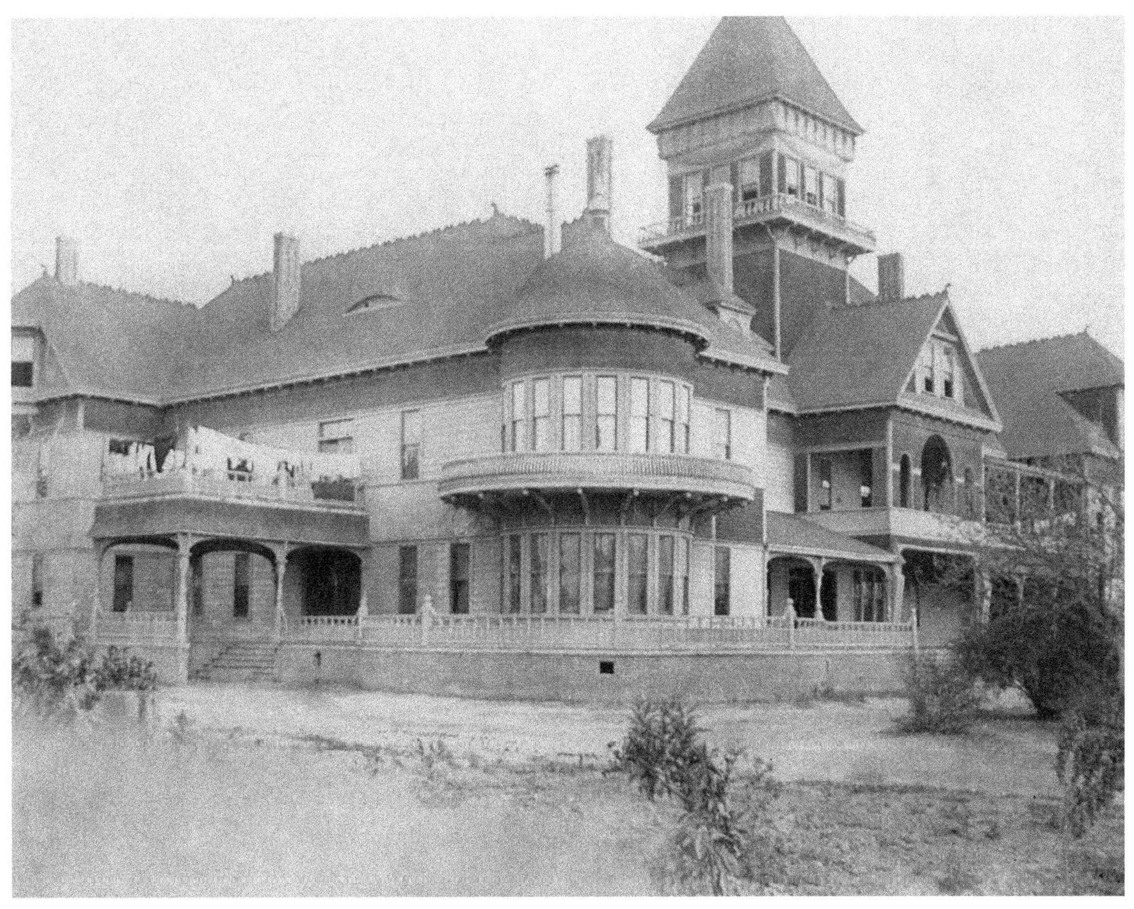

The stately Del Campo Hotel was located at the northeast corner of Broadway and South Olive streets. Erected over a period of two years (1888–1890), it was built and furnished with quality materials. Despite its impressive reputation, financial setbacks forced its closure and conversion into the Pacific Sanitarium and School of Osteopathy in 1896. In 1905 the hotel was sold and razed, the resulting serviceable lumber sold for $6,000, and the lumber used to build a number of houses.

The Knights of Pythias, Anaheim Lodge No. 105, parade down Center Street in the late 1890s. The Knights of Pythias was founded in 1864 as an international, social brotherhood that promotes the principles of friendship, charity, and benevolence.

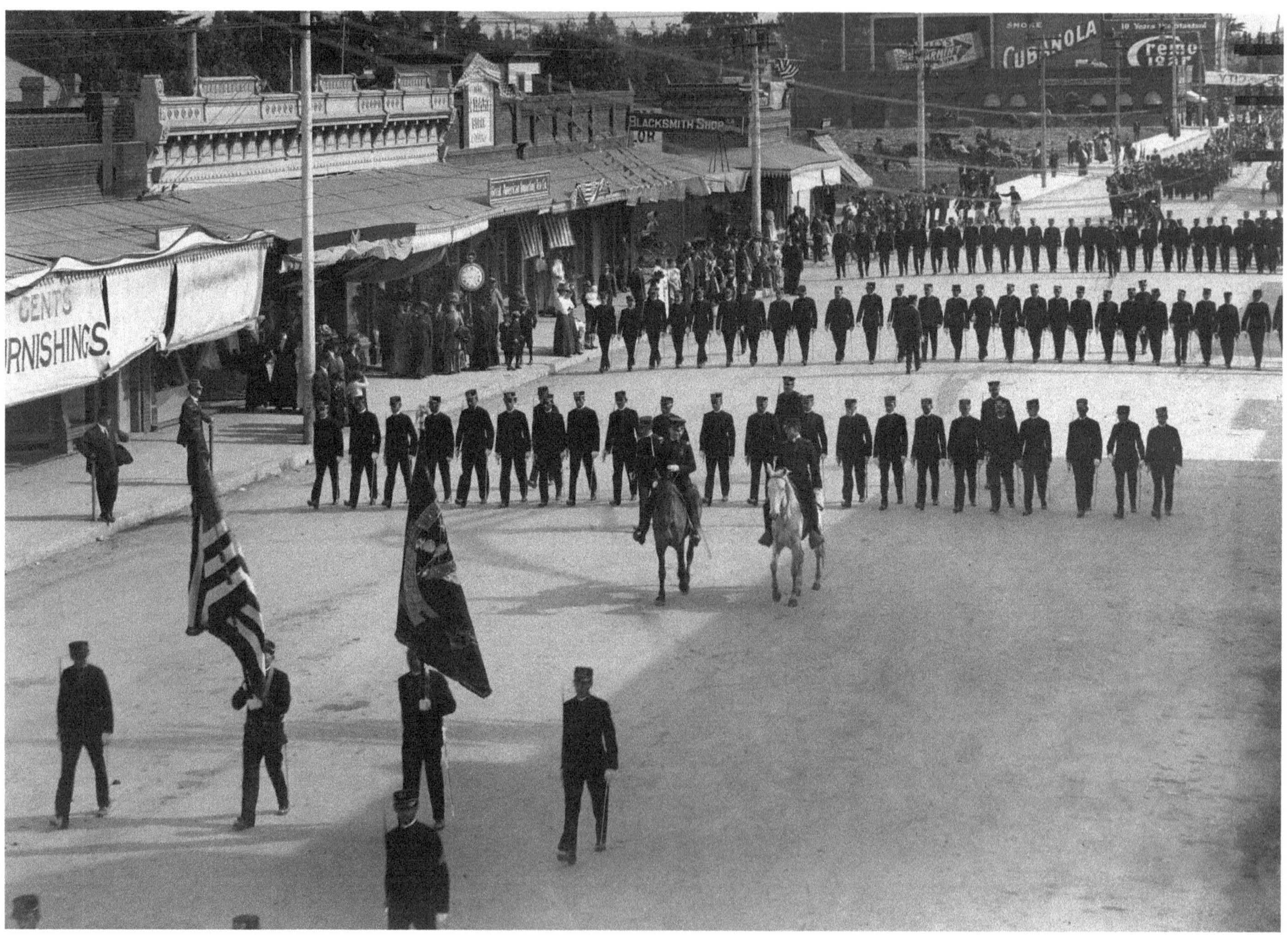

Anaheim's original First Presbyterian Church was built in 1873 at the corner of Los Angeles Street and Sycamore Street, at a cost of $3,000. Lemuel L. Webber, who later founded the neighboring community of Westminster, was its first pastor. The building was later moved to 125 East Cypress and Claudina streets, where it stands today owned by the Salvation Army.

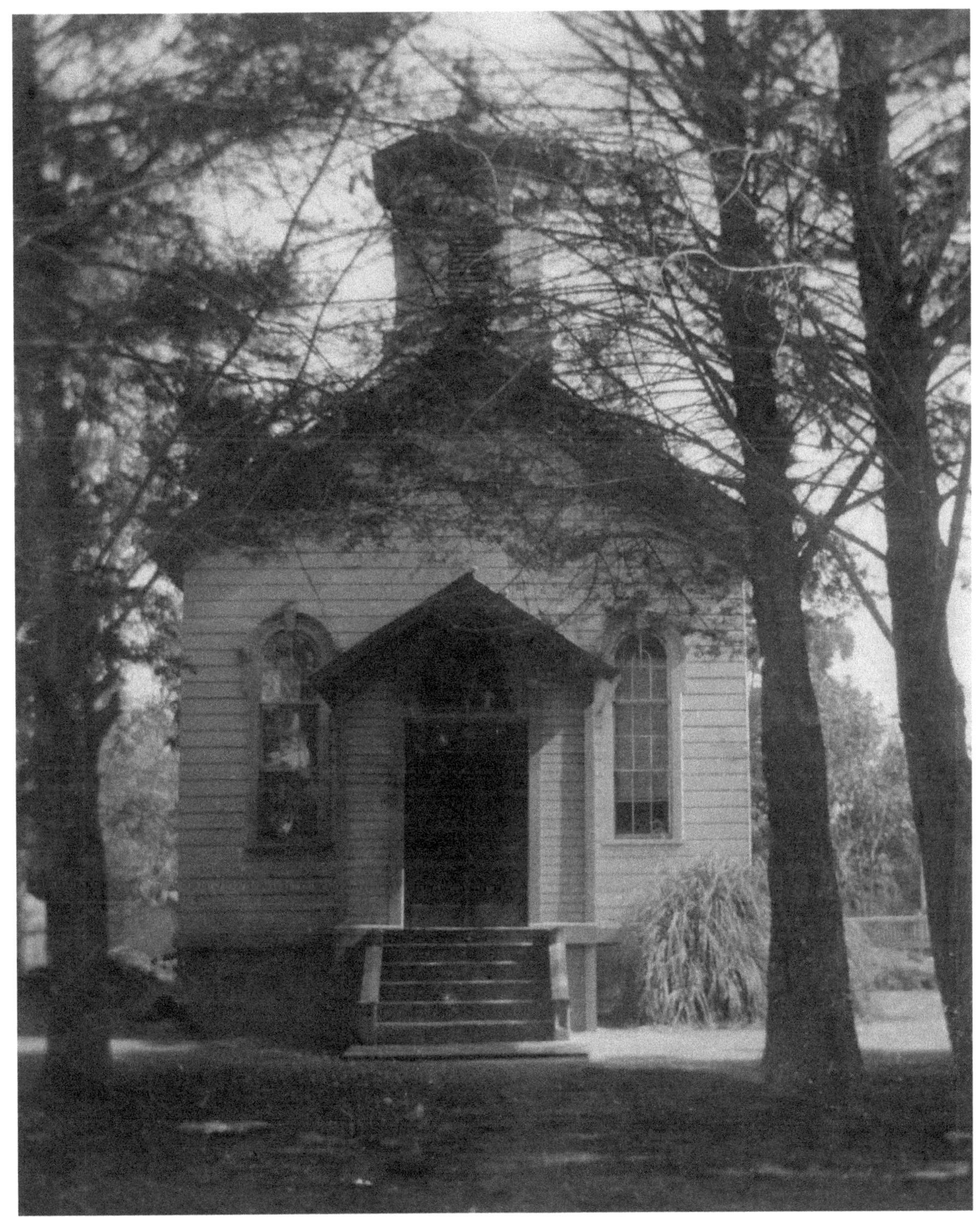

Anaheim's second city hall, located at 202 East Center Street, is shown here around 1895. Built in 1892, it also housed the fire and police departments. This proud structure replaced the town's original three-room city hall and jail built on West Cypress Street in 1870.

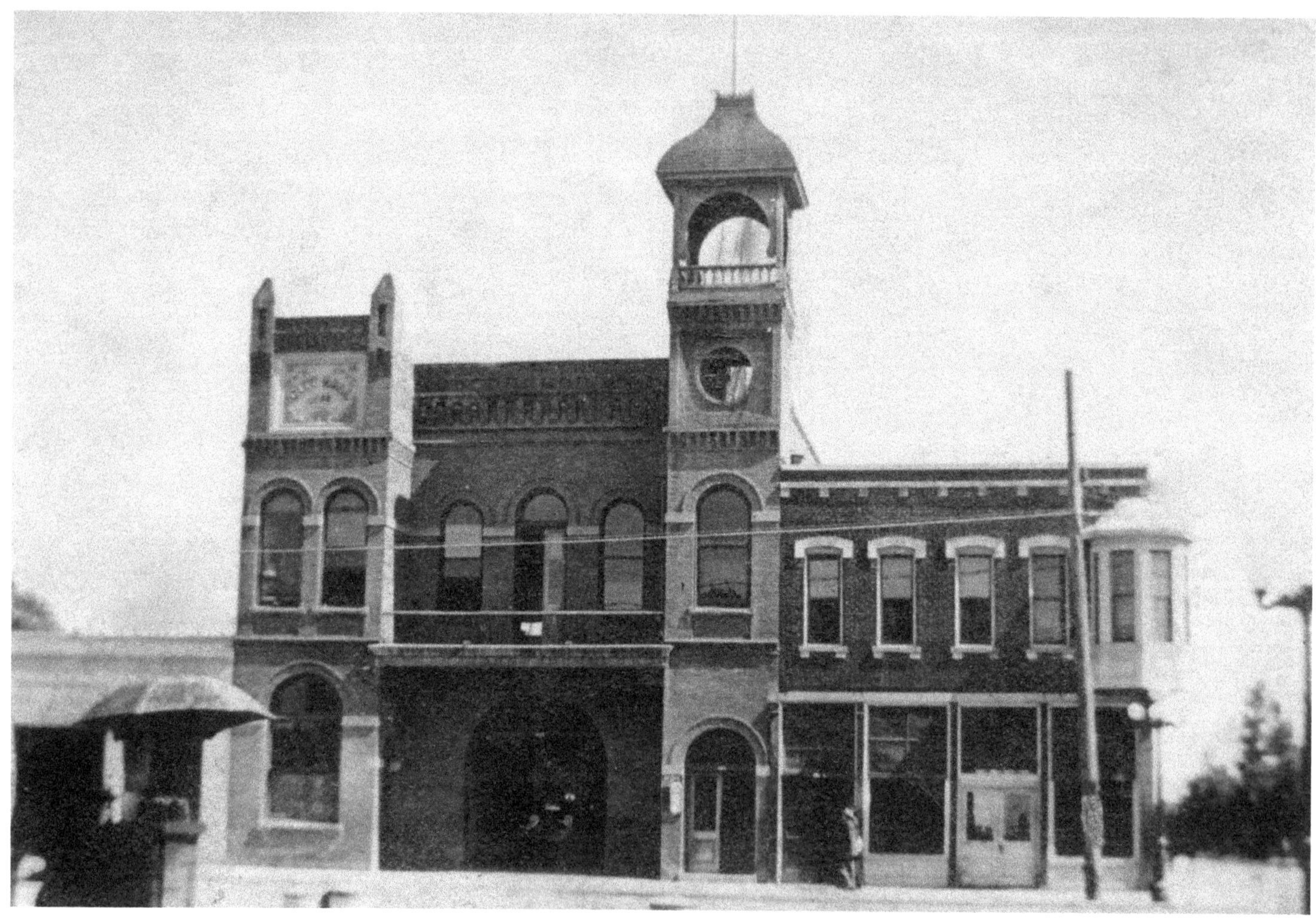

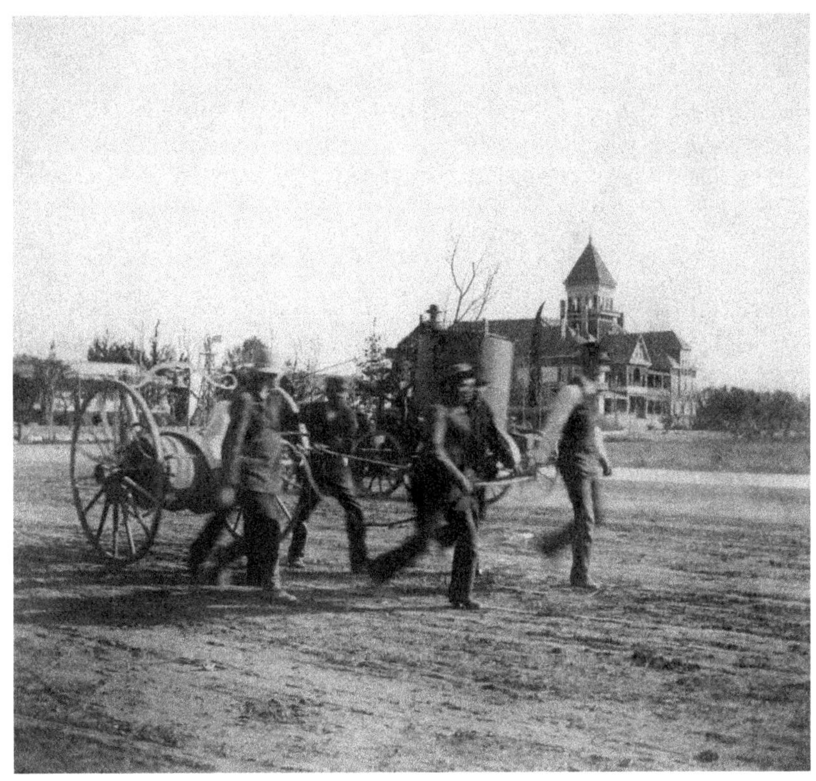

Anaheim's volunteer "Fire Laddies" are seen pulling the town's four-wheel hose cart in this late-nineteenth-century image. Behind the hose cart can be seen Rudolph Fossek's street sprinkler wagon, which was also used as a water supply for fire fighting. Anaheim's stately Del Campo Hotel rises in the background.

E. H. Susmil stands in the doorway of his harness shop in the 100 block of Center Street (now Lincoln Ave.). Susmil occupied the ground floor of the two-story Kroeger building, built by Anaheim's second mayor, Henry Kroeger.

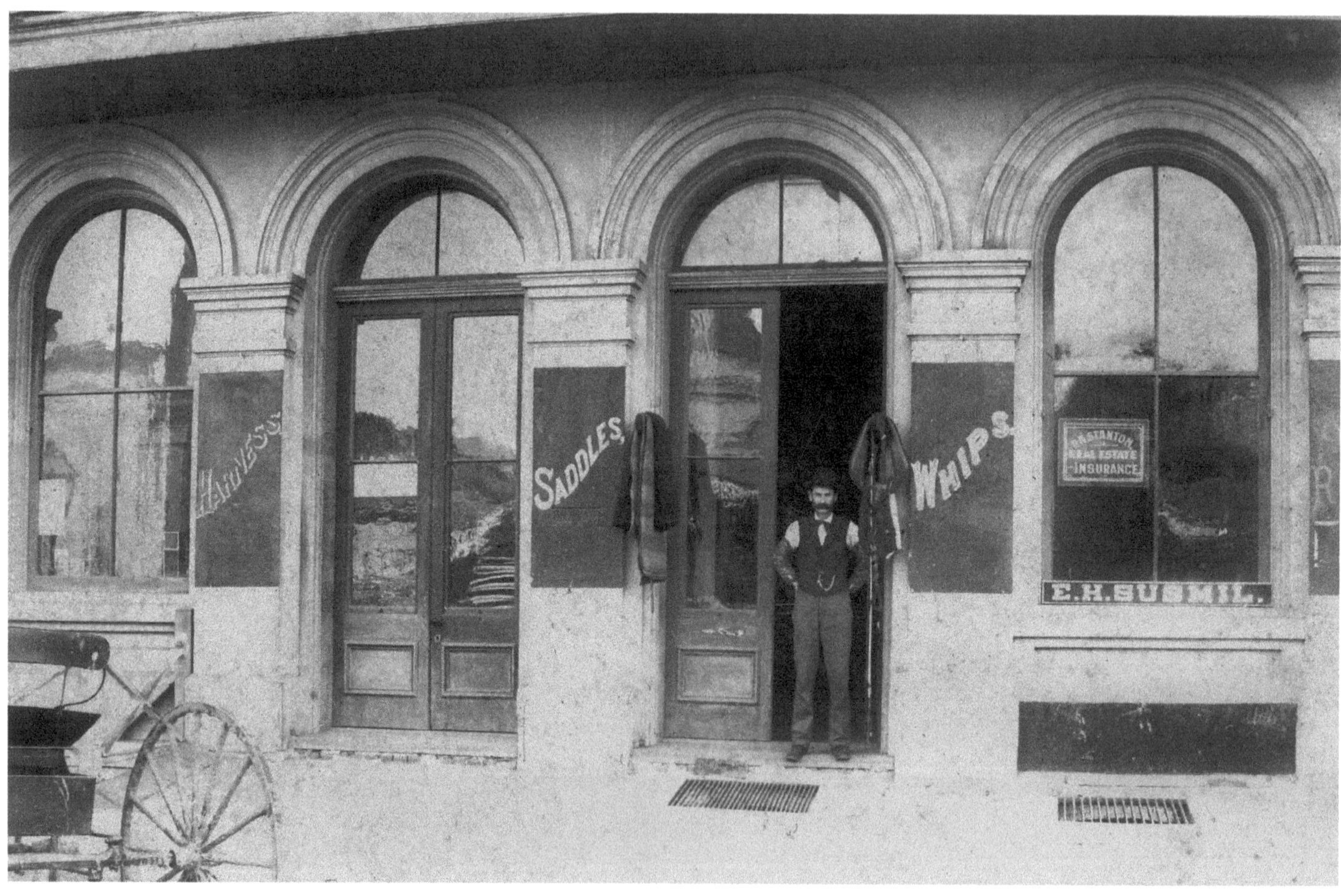

This late-nineteenth-century view shows Anaheim's second Southern Pacific Railroad depot at the corner of South Los Angeles Street (now Anaheim Blvd.) and Santa Ana Street. This "Standard #23" depot was built in 1895 when the railroad built a cut-off through the town to serve the new packinghouses opening there. Here wagonloads of cabbage are being prepared to be shipped to market.

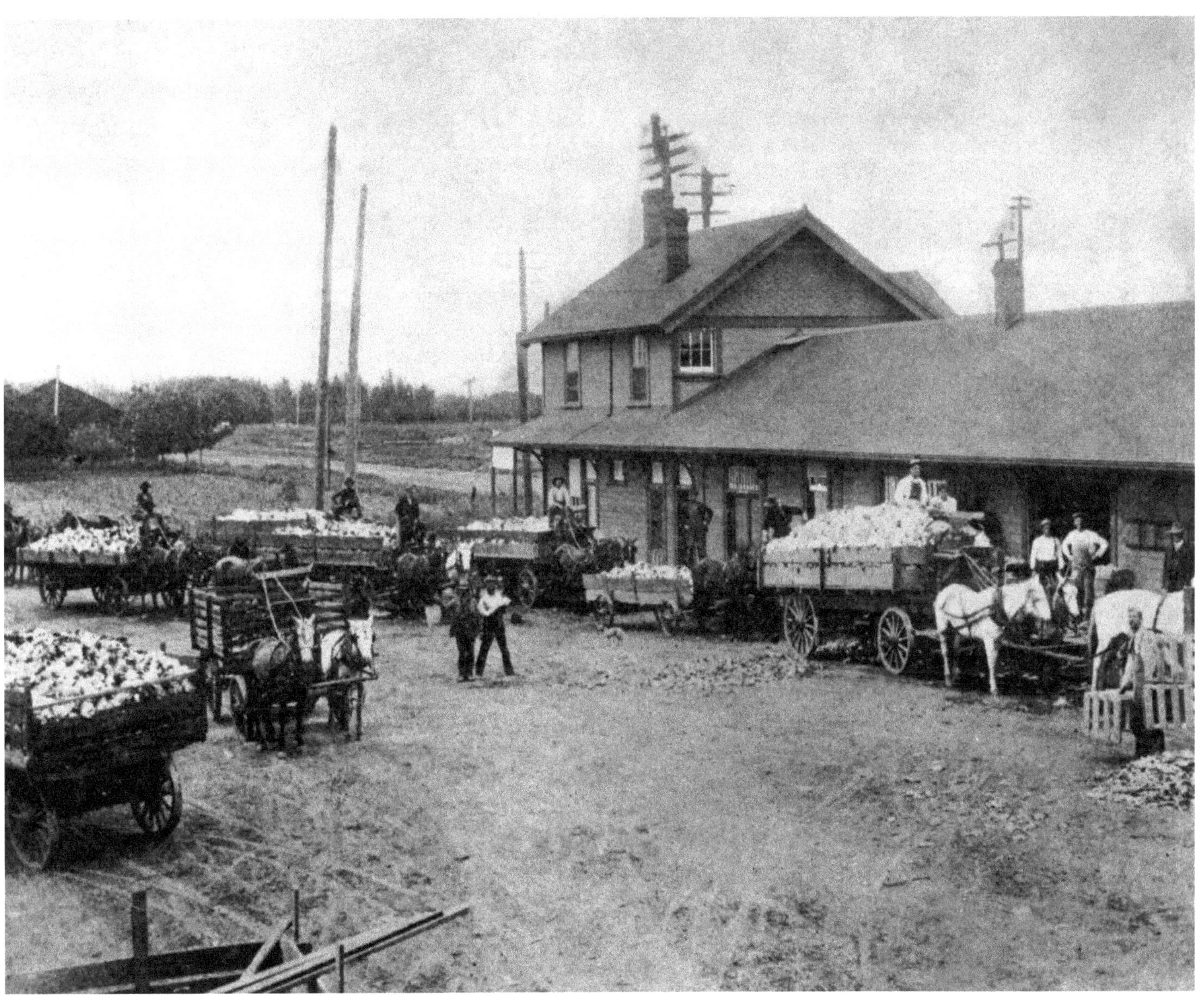

Anaheim barber Willard A. Frantz and postman Frank Eastman, advertised as having "the first trained Ostrich in the United States," trained ostriches in the early years. Their two running stars were named Napoleon and Josephine. The two men and one of their stars pose for the camera at the Coronado Beach racetrack in 1896.

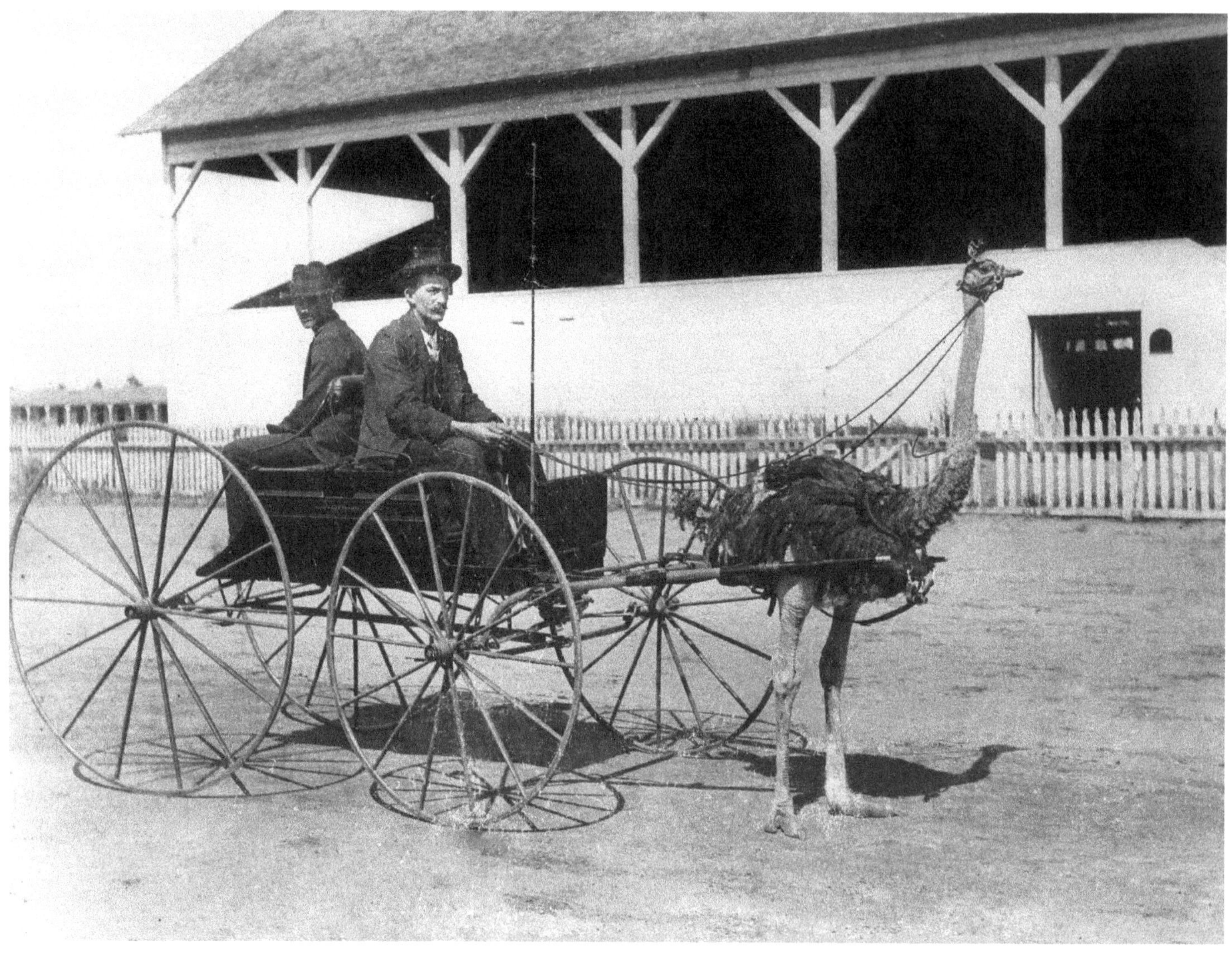

Frank Eastman, Anaheim's earliest mail carrier, appears here in his R.F.D. (Rural Free Delivery) horse-drawn mail carriage. Anaheim's R.F.D. Route 1 covered most of the town of Anaheim in 1896, when this photograph was made. Eastman covered the route on foot before building his homemade carriage.

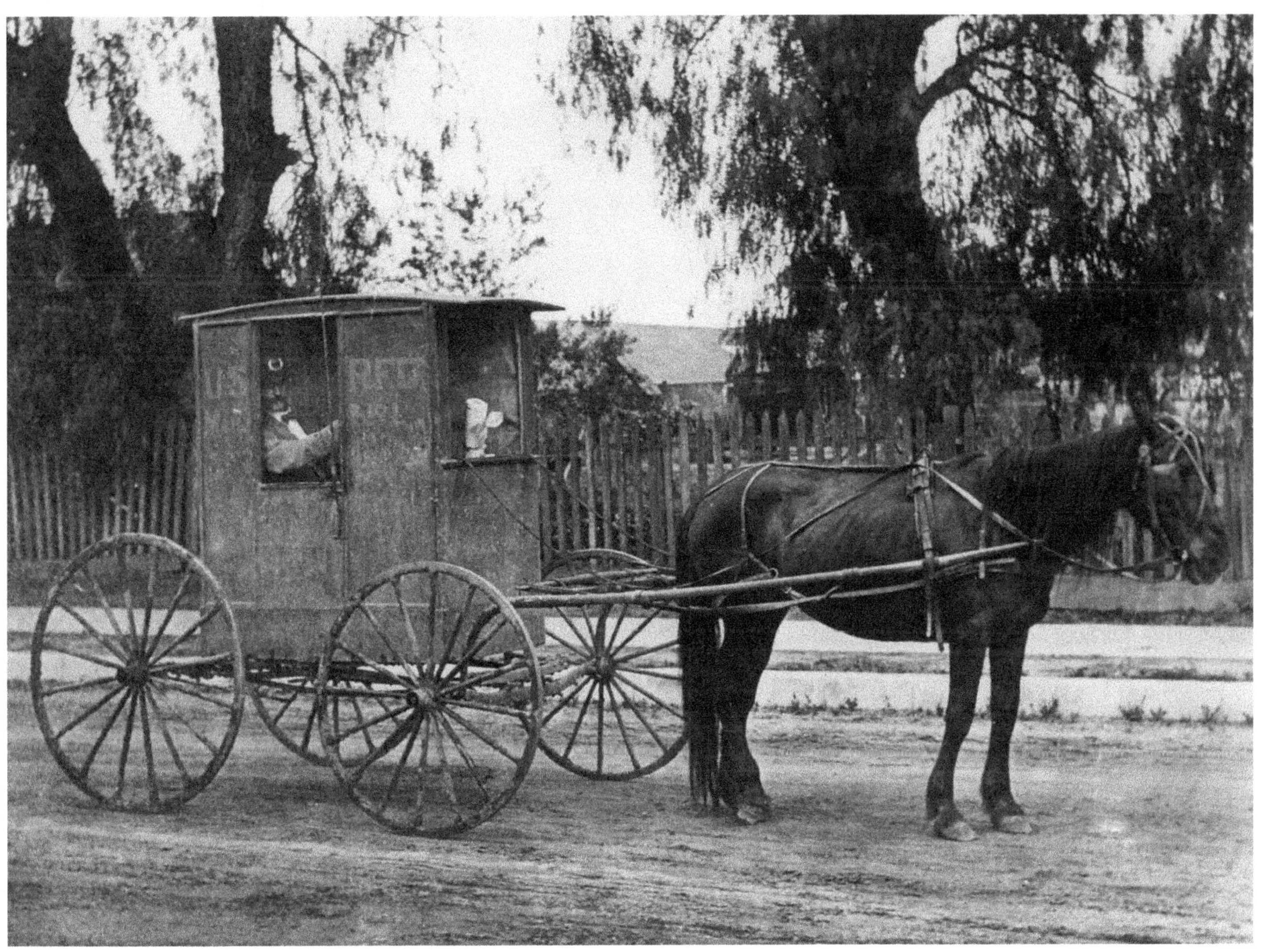

Following Spread: In view here is the front of Anaheim's Del Campo Hotel. A group of Anaheim locals enjoys the hotel's expansive porch. Although an impressive building and lavishly furnished, the hotel was not a financial success and was converted into the Pacific Sanitarium and School of Osteopathy in 1896. Its brief career ended in 1905 when the property was sold and the building razed.

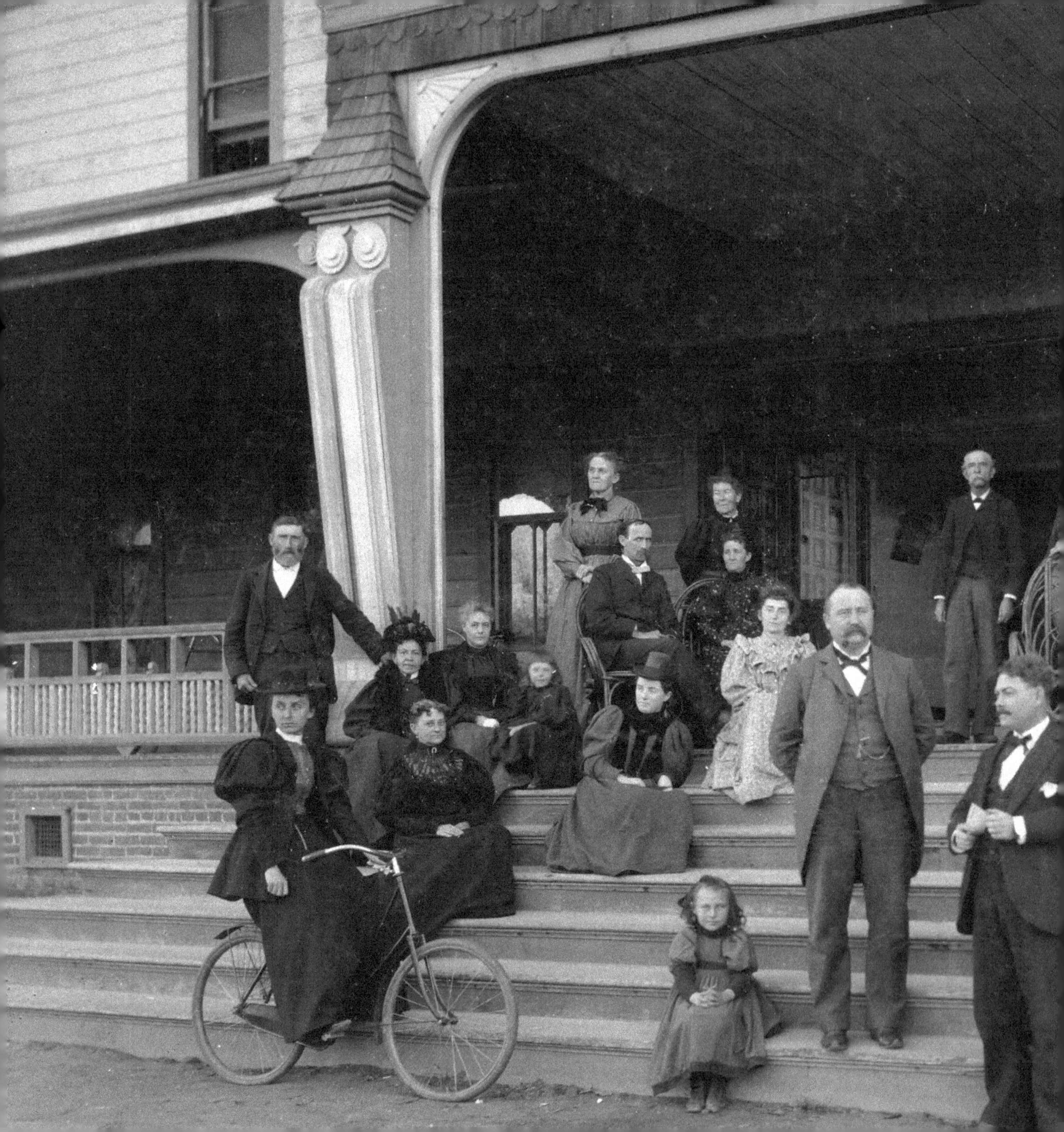

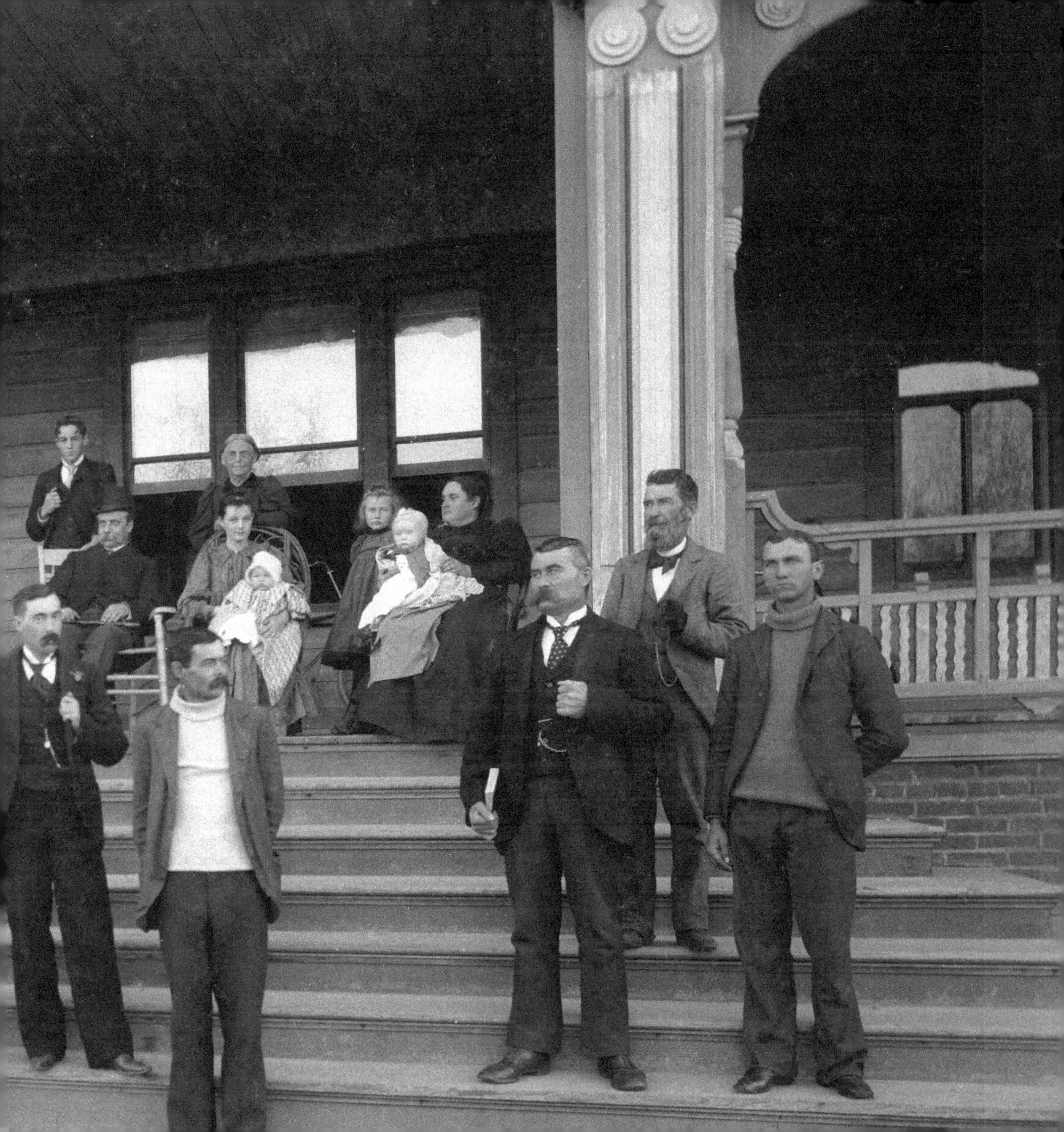

A late-nineteenth-century interior view of Richard Henry Seale's neatly arranged grocery store. Bert F. Fulwider stands in front of the left side counter; Seale stands at right. By this time, many of Anaheim's business houses were sporting electric lights, which arrived in 1895. This improvement, long awaited by the local businessmen, permitted evening shopping.

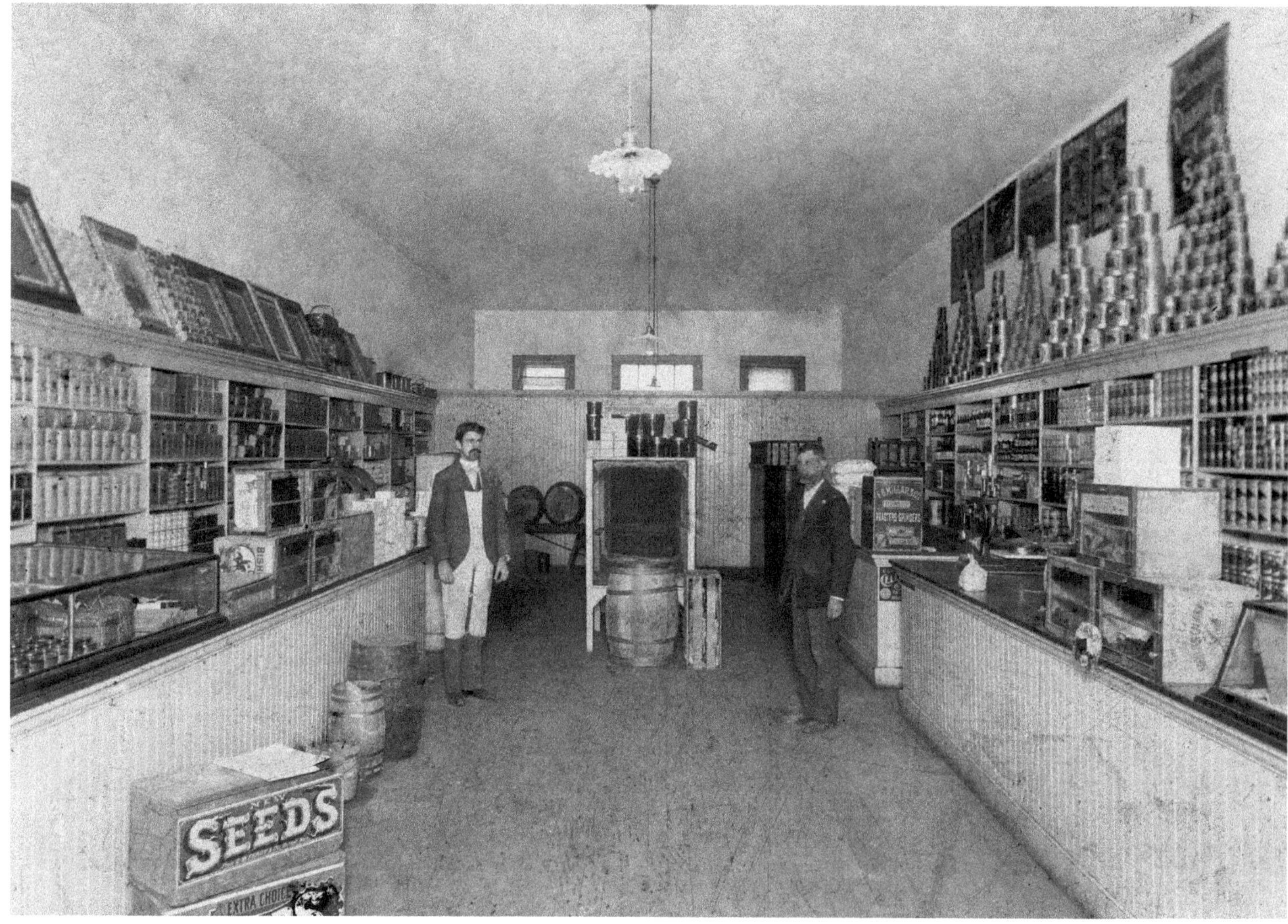

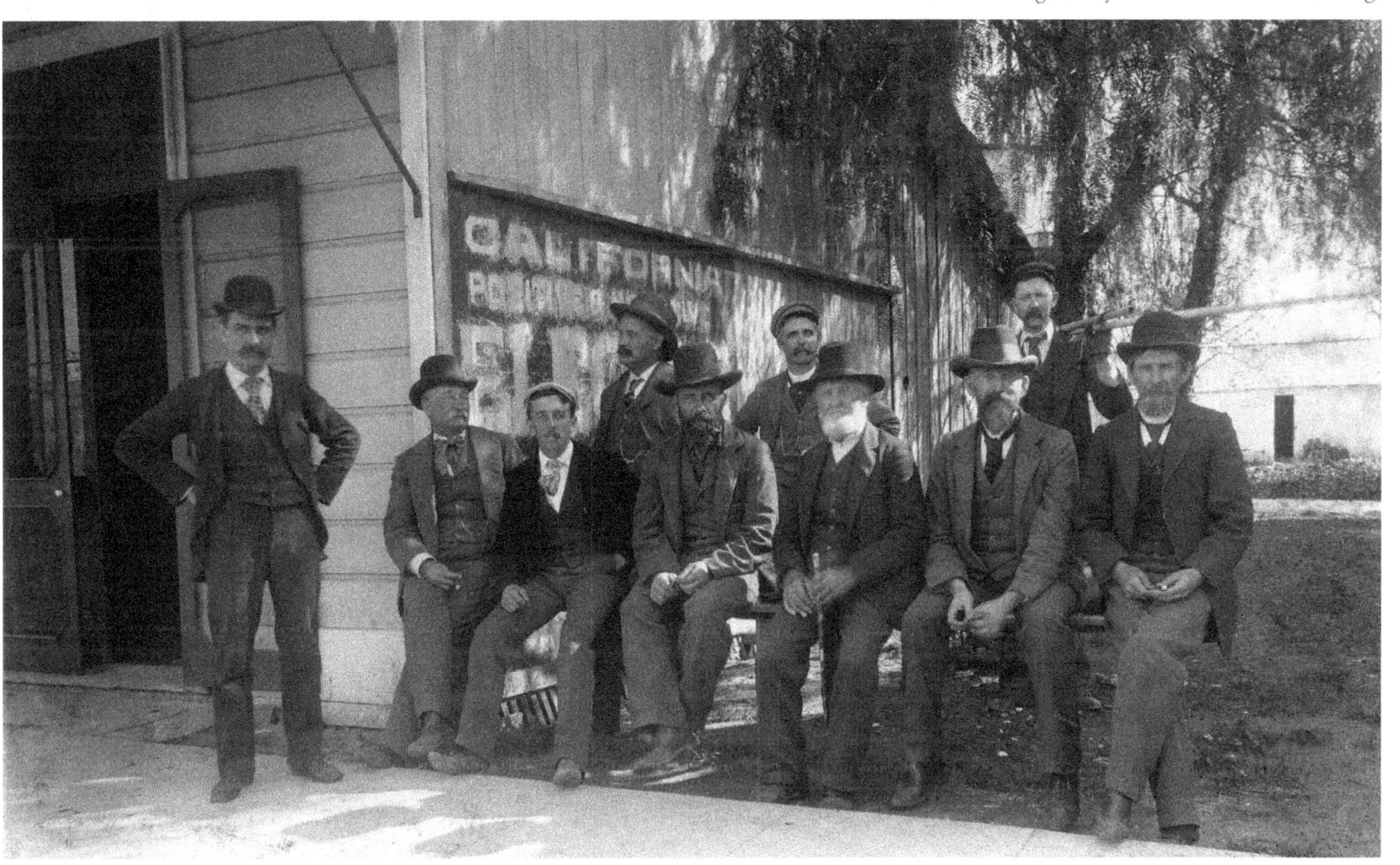

Ten local business leaders of the Anaheim Ways and Means Committee pose outside Cornelius Bruce's Candy Kitchen at 106 East Center Street (now Lincoln Ave.) ca. 1898. Identified left to right are Louis E. Miller, E. P. Fowler, W. J. Newberry, Capt. Irwin Barr, John B. Rae, E. B. Merritt, Henry Kroeger, Cornelius Bruce, August Nagel, and J. P. Zeyn. Bruce, in addition to his candy store, maintained the town's lending library in the rear of his building.

Federman & Co. was one of Anaheim's premier clothing merchants in the last days of the nineteenth century. Their store, housed in the Federman Block building, was located at 102-104 North Los Angeles Street (now Anaheim Blvd.). This substantial brick turreted building was an Anaheim landmark for many years.

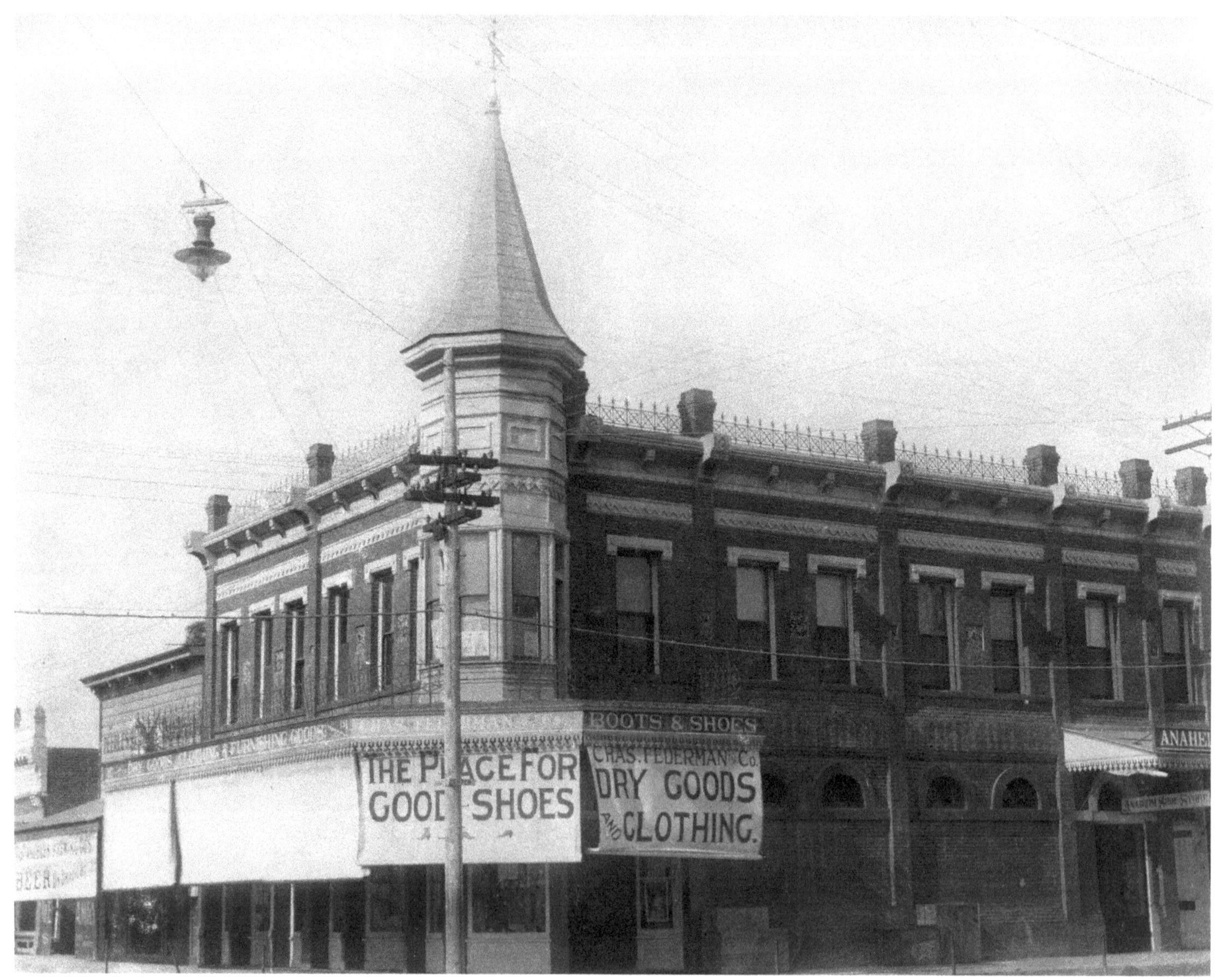

A group portrait of the children from Anaheim's Central School, recorded in the waning years of the nineteenth century. The school, at 231 East Chartres Street, was built in 1877 and housed elementary through high school grades. This edifice held the distinction of being the first school in California built through the sale of bonds.

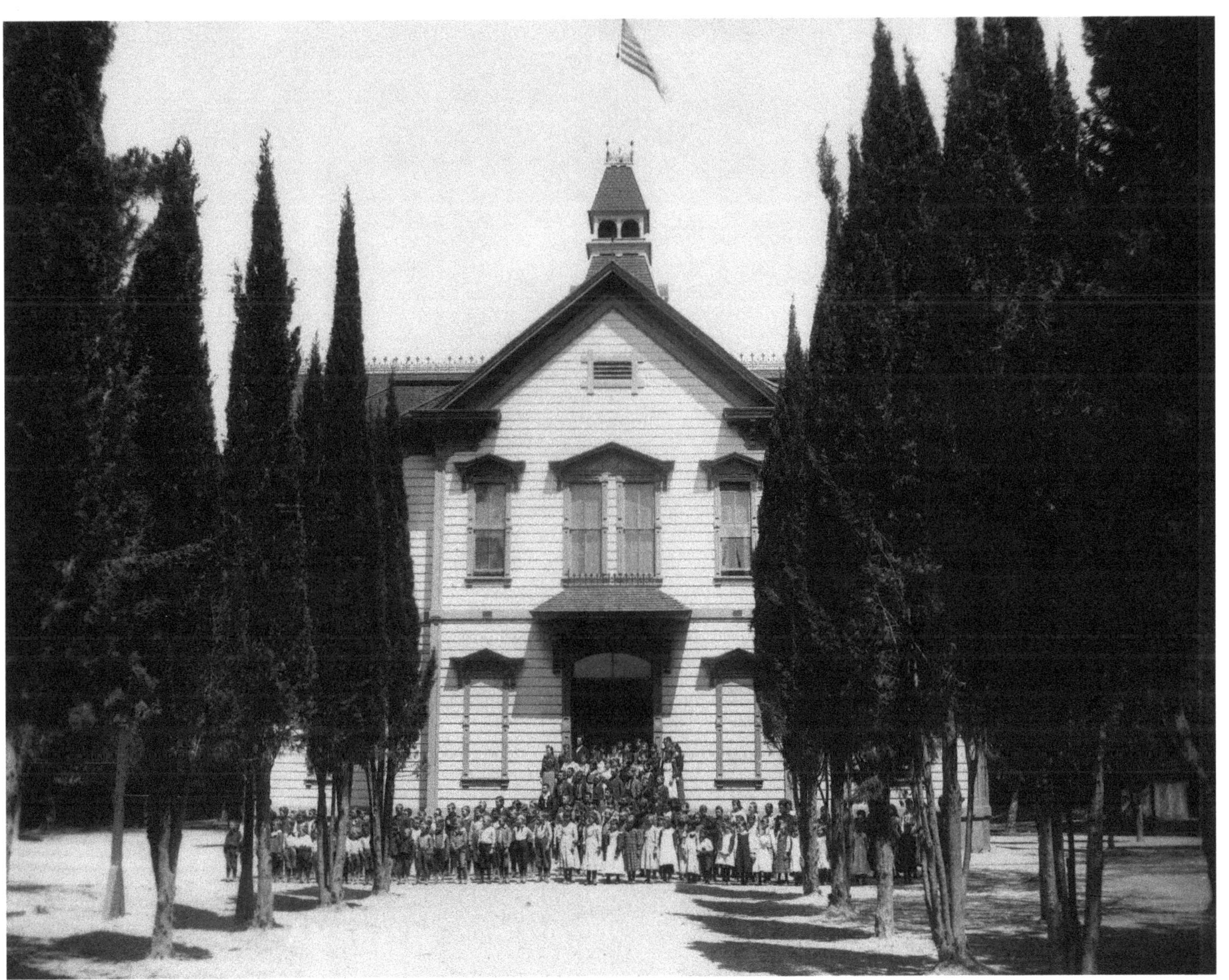

Charles E. Bauer maintained a blacksmith shop in Anaheim at the turn of the century. The blacksmith, in addition to his regular duties as farrier, was also the town's general repairman and mechanic. Activity in Anaheim was enough to keep Bauer and his competitor Fred Pressel quite busy.

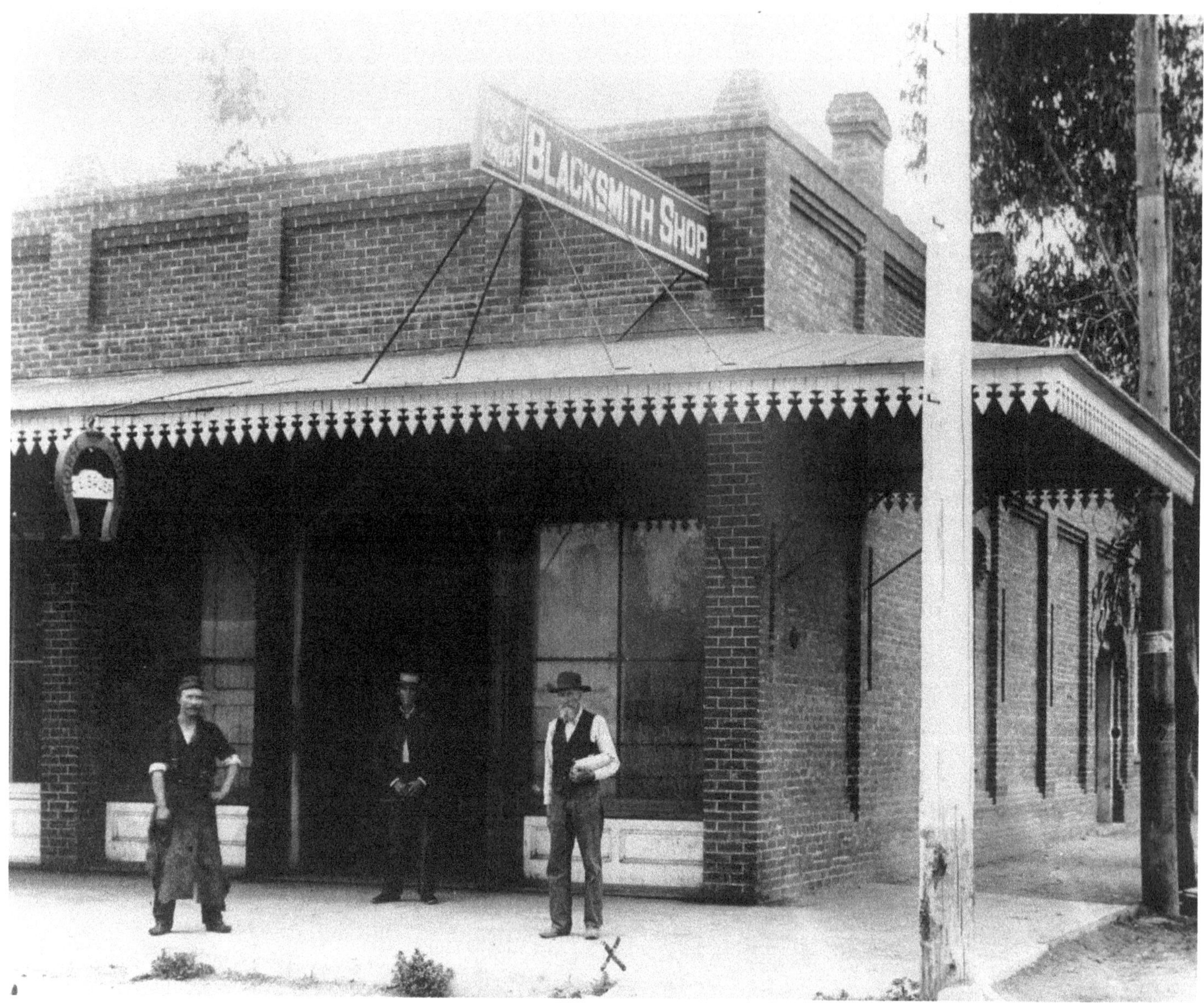

August Langenberger's Wells Fargo and Co. Express building was built in 1875 at the corner of Center Street (now Lincoln Ave.) and Lemon Street. For many years it housed the Dickel Grocery and Hardware Store, with the local telephone office upstairs. This landmark structure survived until August 1925, when it was razed for the construction of the new S.Q.R. department store. The horse-drawn vehicles on the street demonstrate the continuing importance of horsepower in turn-of-the-century Anaheim.

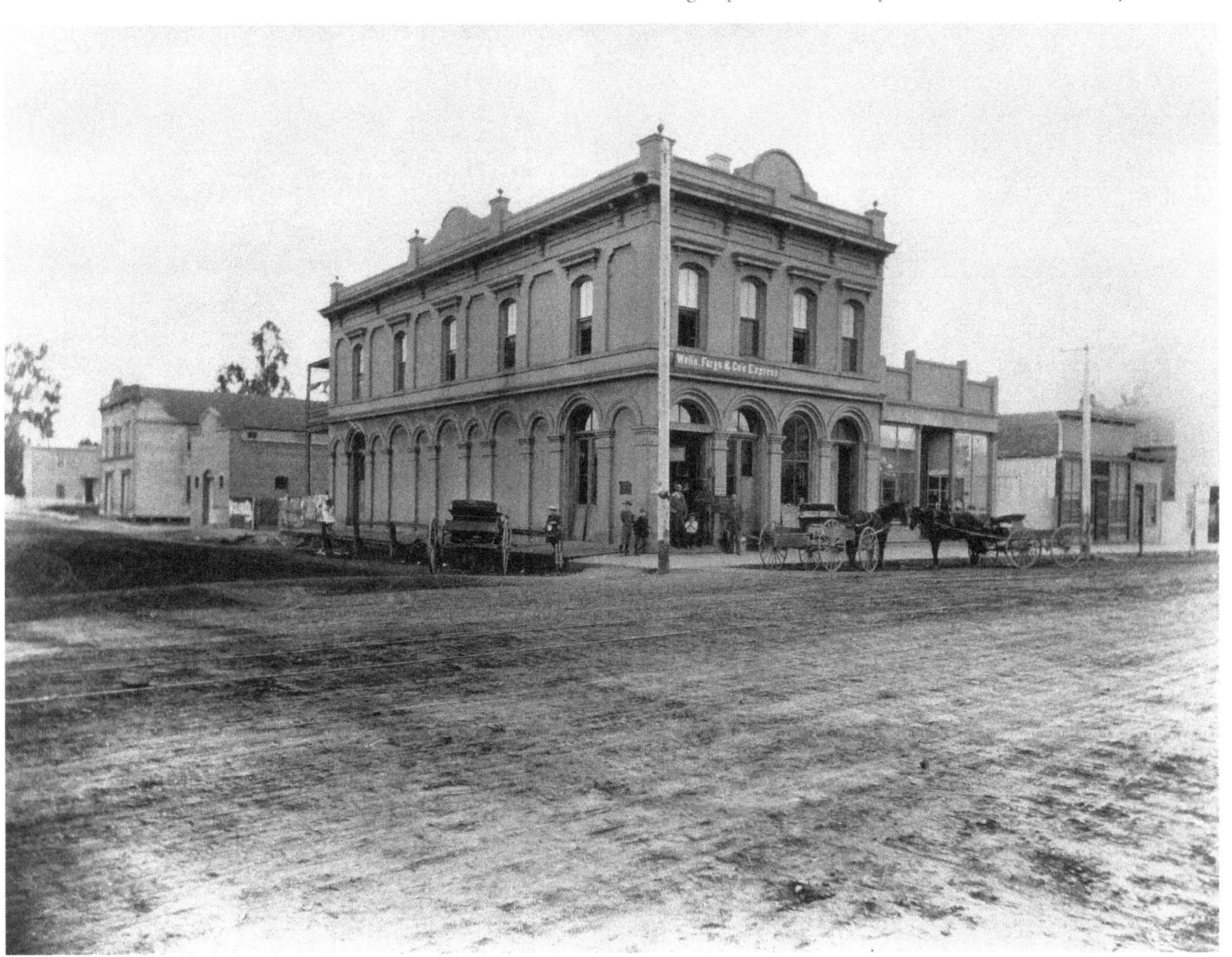

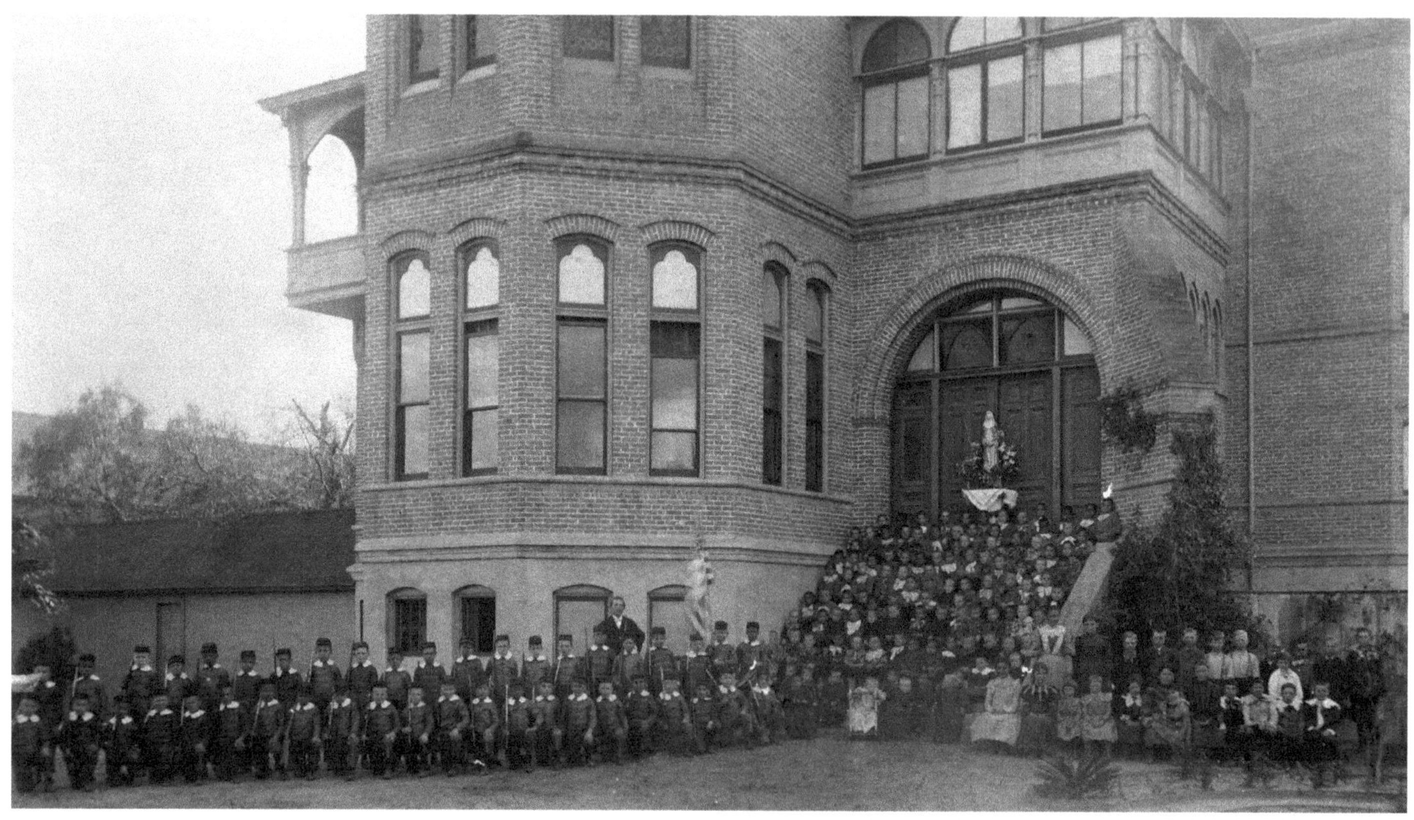

The residents of St. Catherine's Orphanage have their portrait taken on March 21, 1899. In 1887, the Dominican Sisters arrived at the urging of the pastor of Anaheim's St. Boniface Church, Peter Stoetters, to start a new Catholic school. Unable financially to survive with the twenty students who attended, the sisters turned the school into an orphanage. Later, with a fall in the number of orphans, the sisters converted the facility into a military school for boys, where it continues today as St. Catherine's Military Academy.

The photographer opened his lens from the top of the Del Campo Hotel to expose this view of turn-of-the century Anaheim. To the south is the residence of Mr. and Mrs. C. E. Ramella, at lower left, and the home of George E. Boyd, co-owner of the Orange County Preserving Company, at lower right. Anaheim's rural character is conspicuous, with houses still having the required "outbuildings" as well as the windmills that pumped water.

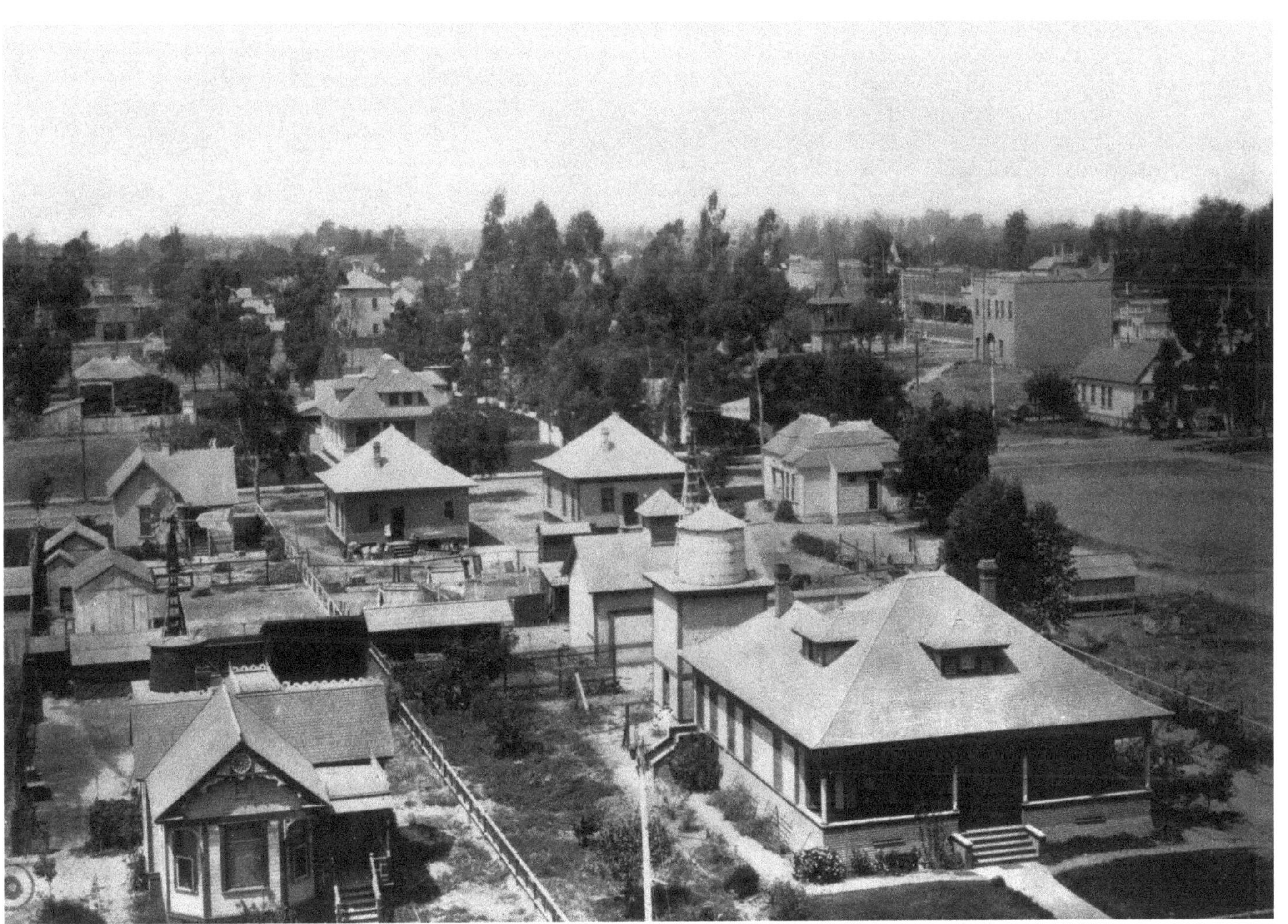

The new century had just dawned when this photograph of Fred Pressel's blacksmith shop was made. Located at 218 West Center Street (now Lincoln Ave.), this was the first of two that he built at this address. The Pressel family continued their business presence in Anaheim well into the late twentieth century.

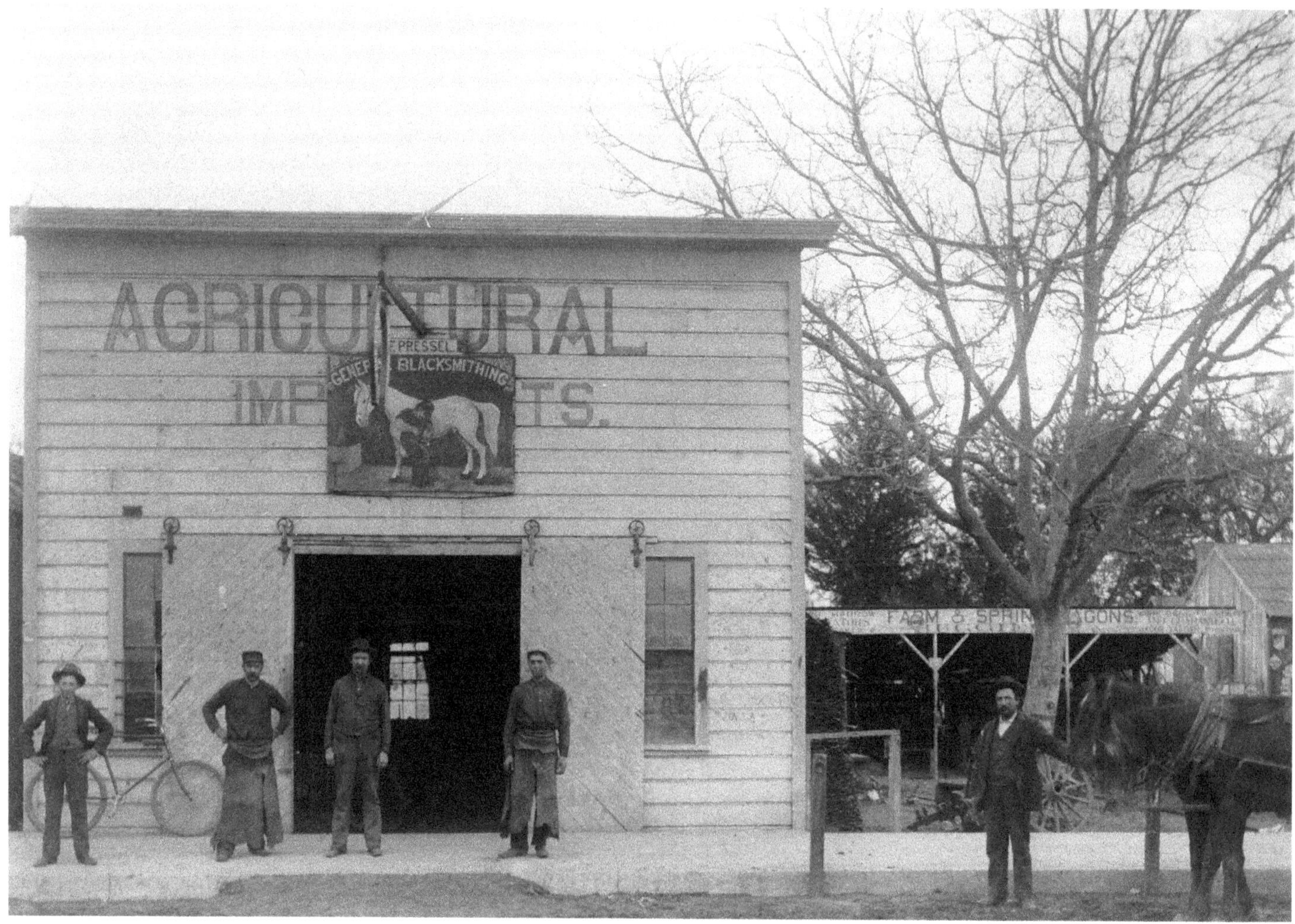

Citriculture Brings Growth (1900–1939)

By 1884, Anaheim's 50 wineries were producing more than one million gallons of wine a year, but tragedy was close at hand. In the mid 1880s, the vines began to wither and by 1890 almost every grapevine in the Orange County area had died. After the loss of Anaheim's grape and wine industry to this disease, the stalwart Germans, who had by now established themselves as competent agriculturists, pursued alternative crops for their livelihood.

Walnuts were found to be a profitable crop for several of the local growers and a large green chili, later named for Anaheim, also flourished. Sugar beets, lemon trees, and apricot trees also grew well in some areas of the Santa Ana Valley. The crop that would change Anaheim's fortunes however was the Valencia orange. In 1886, the Southern California Citrus Fair was held in Chicago, and Anaheim sponsored an impressive booth showing examples of the fruits and vegetables the area was now producing. Perfectly suited to the region's Mediterranean-like microclimate, this thin-skinned sweet orange became the dominant source of income for much of Orange County by the beginning of the twentieth century.

By 1889, Orange County had been created with neighboring Santa Ana as the County Seat. Citriculture, driven by the Valencia orange, enabled the town of Anaheim to continue to grow into a significant business center for early Orange County. Center Street drew visitors and shoppers from far and wide. The local chamber of commerce continued to promote the area as a desirable place to live, and Anaheim's population continued to grow from 1,456 in 1900 to more than 11,000 by 1940. The significance of the citrus industry to Anaheim prompted the chamber of commerce to begin the California Valencia Orange Show in 1921. This annual spring event held through 1931 would showcase not only the area's most important crop but also boost the local communities as desirable places to live and work. In 1924, Anaheim leaders inaugurated the annual Halloween Parade as a way of building civic pride; this well-loved event continues to march Anaheim streets yet today.

Civic improvements including paved streets, improved water and electric services, ornamental streetlights, the building of a beautiful city park, a new city hall, and connection to a regional sanitary sewer system all overseen by the town's frugal trustees came about in the pre–World War II era. Many early vineyard lots gave way to neighborhoods, and combined with the construction of sturdy downtown business buildings, the small town took on an aura of wealth and permanence.

The community would again suffer at the hands of mother nature when both earthquake and flood visited the area in the 1930s.

Anaheim's civic leaders realized early on that dependence on agriculture would hinder the city's growth, so the search for industry prompted a number of businessmen to create the Anaheim Industrial Land Development Company in 1924. This privately funded organization would offer potential manufacturing firms land at far-below-market rates as an inducement to settle in Anaheim. The creation of this company, combined with the creation of Orange County's first Planning Commission in 1927, ensured that Anaheim would be a local leader in commercial and residential growth as it approached midcentury.

The Peerless Bar, owned by Andrew Fuhrberg, was one of several drinking establishments in the town. Anaheim at one time boasted more saloons than churches, a fact that the residents of many "dry towns" in Orange County appreciated. In this 1903 view, Oscar Renner, one of the three owners of Anaheim's S.Q.R. mercantile store, stands at far right.

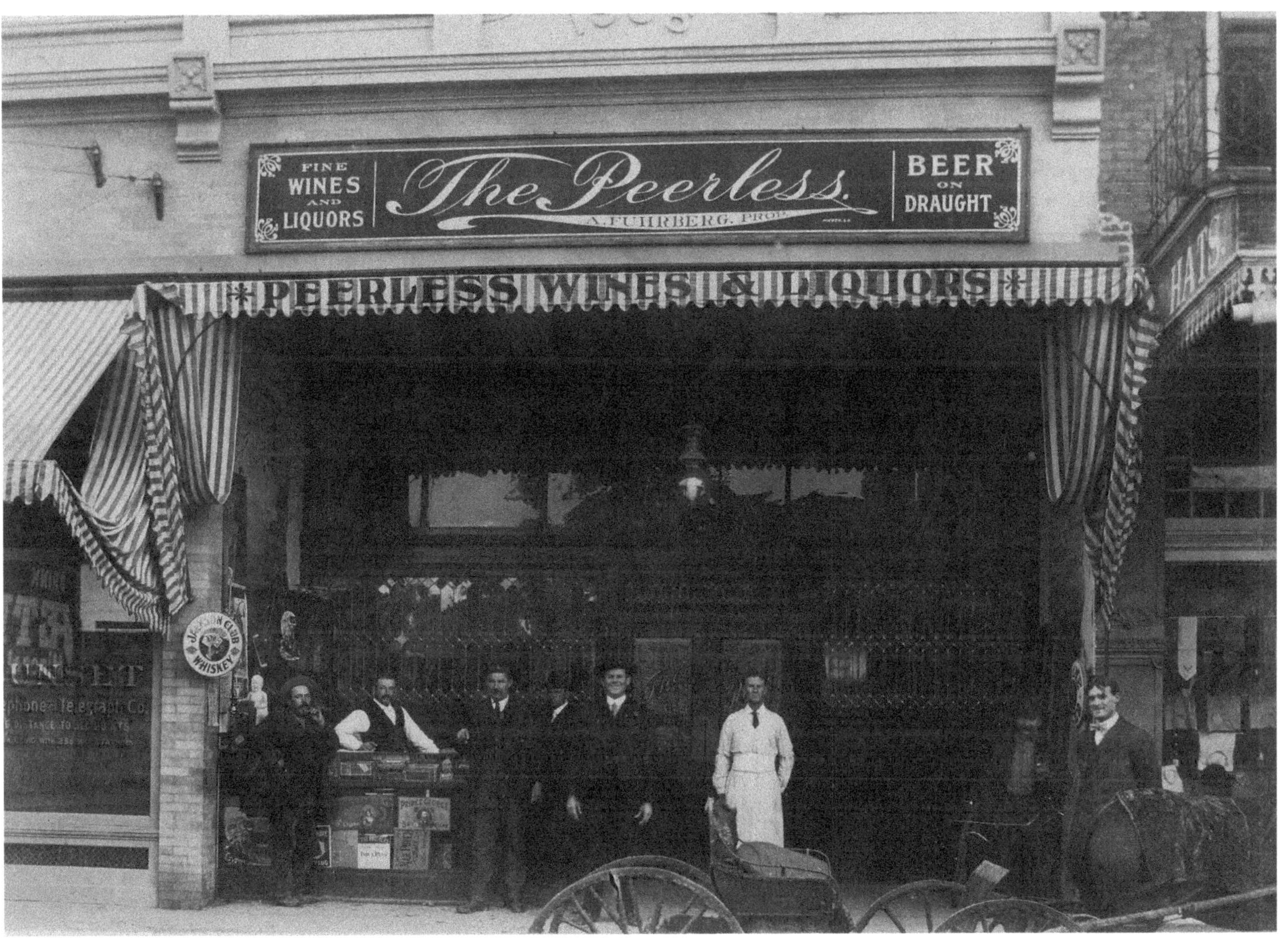

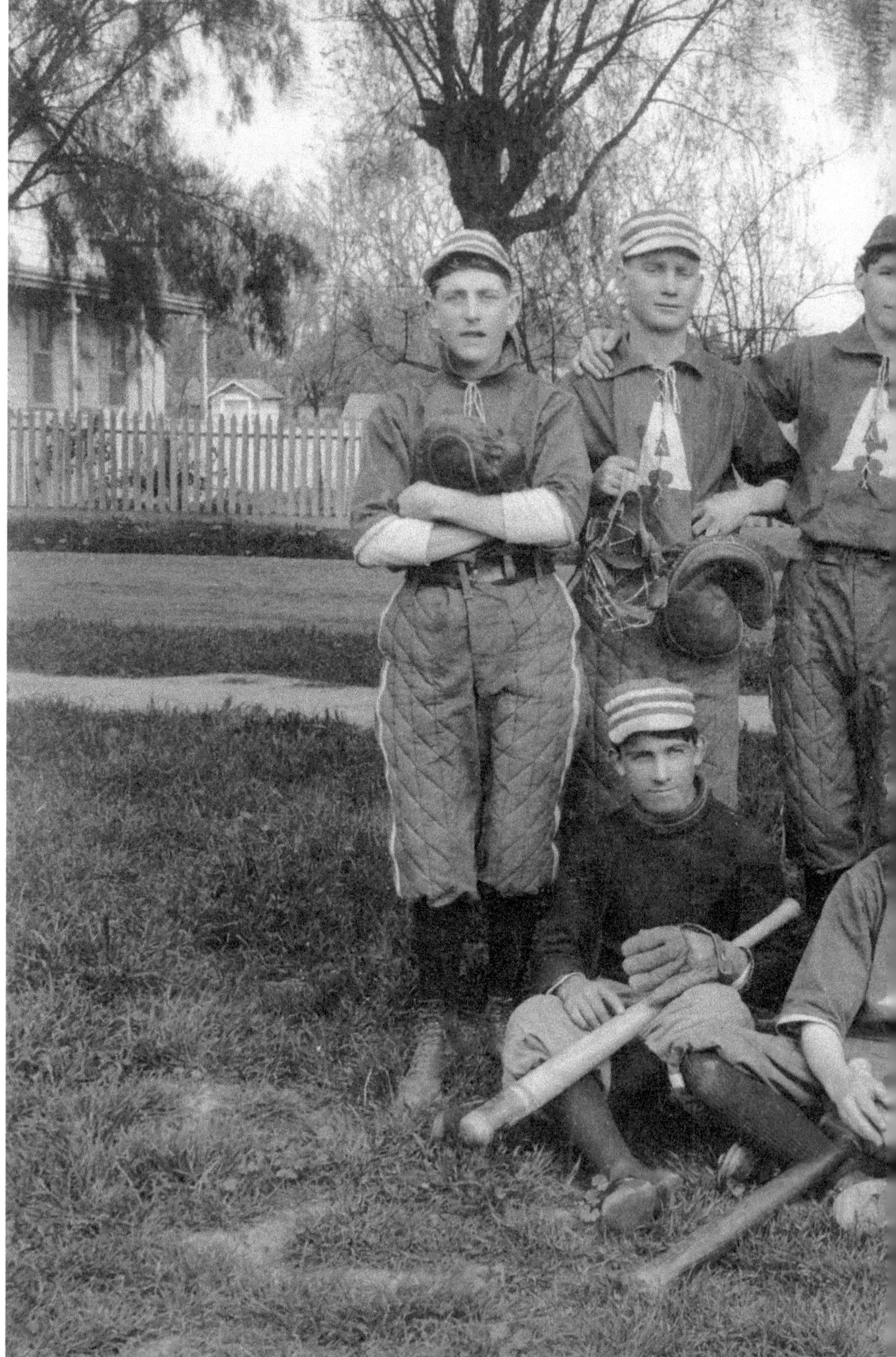

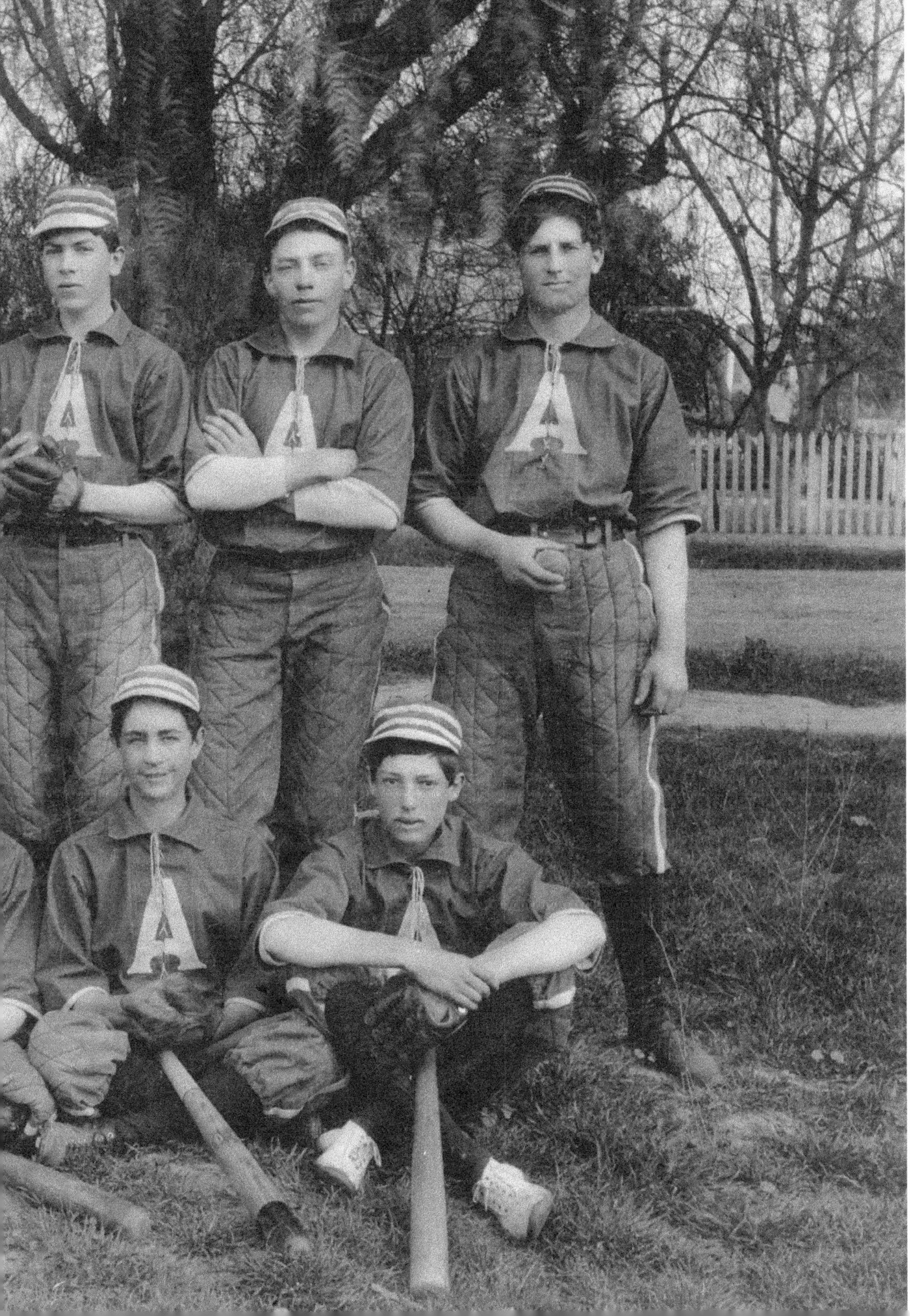

Anaheim had long been a baseball town with a number of fraternal and business organizations fielding teams. Shown here is the Anaheim Baseball Team in 1900, with the young players identified left to right: (back row) Edgar J. Hartung, Bill Fischer, Theodore Dickel, Elmer Stone, H. Westerman, and Fred Conrad; (front row) Ned Merritt, Charles H. Fischer, Lafayette A. Lewis, and Dwight Stone.

Rudolph "Rudy" Fossek was employed by the city to sprinkle the town's dusty streets from 1902 until 1913. Here in 1902 Rudy and his new 700-gallon horse-drawn wagon work the streets of early Anaheim. Fossek also joined the town's volunteer firemen at local fires to provide an additional water supply. In 1913, business interests finally persuaded the frugal trustees to begin paving the important streets of town, rendering Rudy's task obsolete.

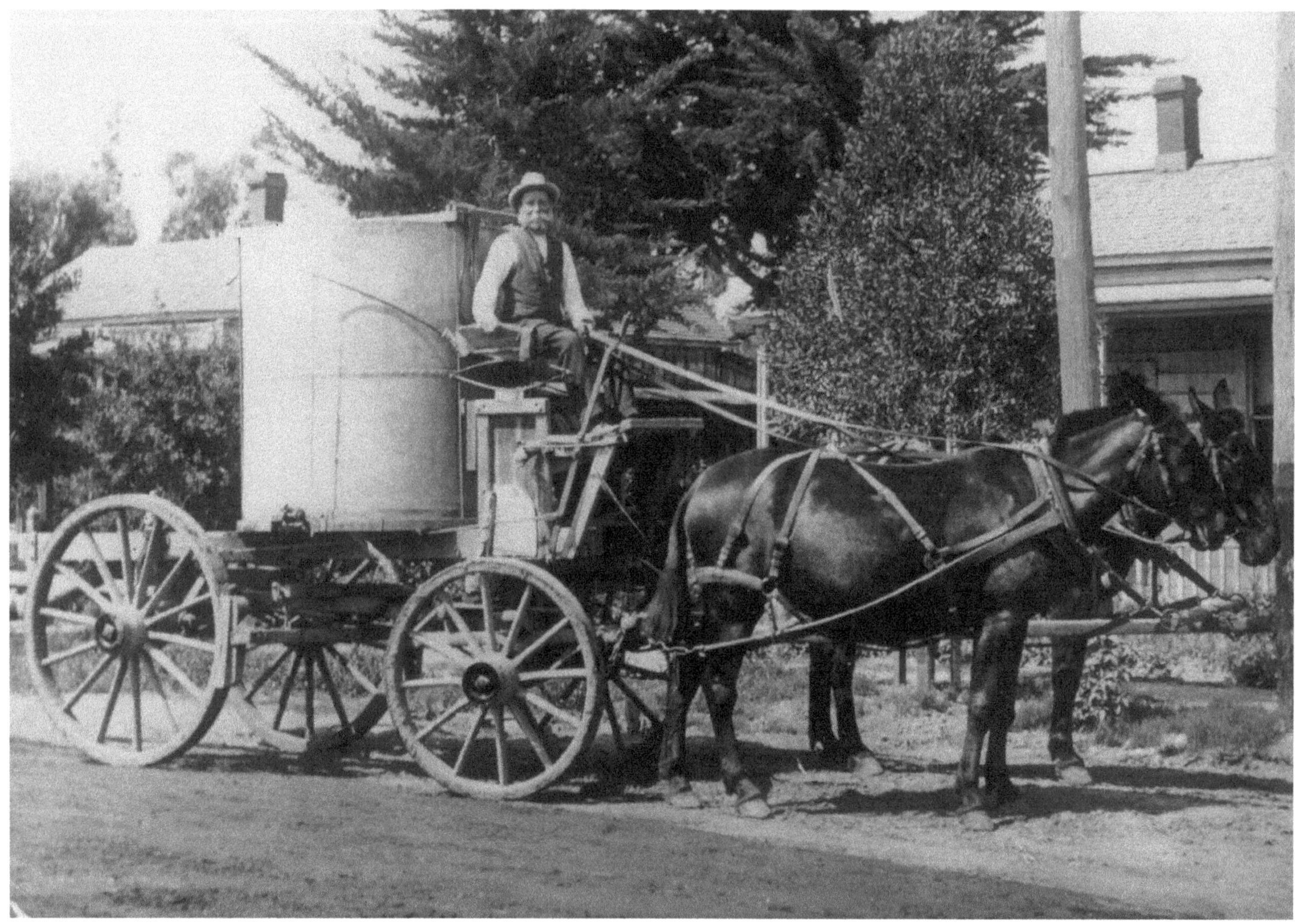

Anaheim's Judge James H. Howard captured this view of four wagons of palm trees leaving Timothy Carroll's Evergreen Nursery. Carroll, who had settled in Anaheim in 1863, owned 500 acres of land in what was known as West Anaheim. His nursery supplied all manner of trees and vegetable rootstock to early Anaheim. In addition to this business interest, he was an accomplished inventor with a number of patented machines to his credit.

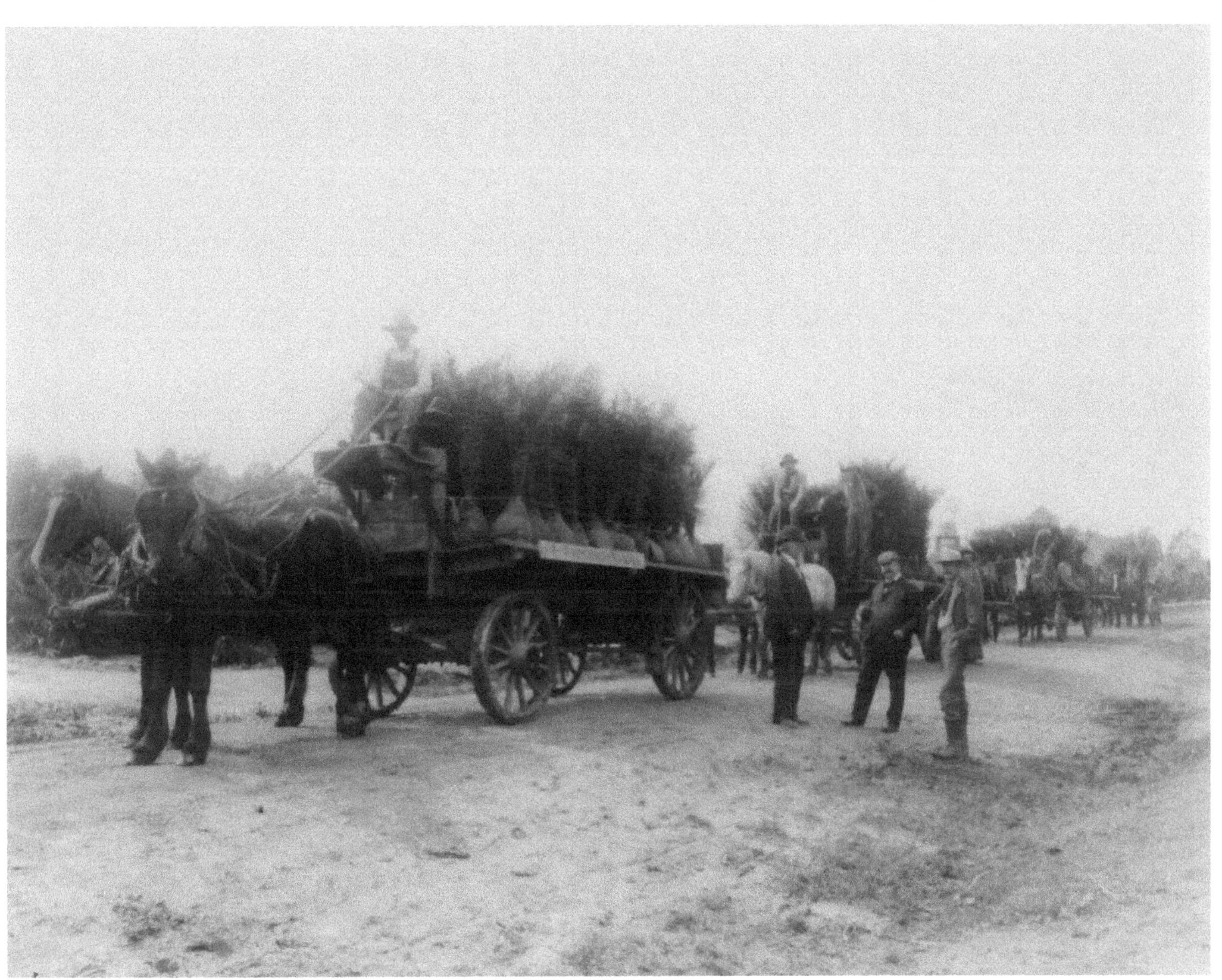

The Commercial Hotel is draped in patriotic bunting on July 4, 1903. Built by Anaheim's second mayor, Henry Kroeger, the Commercial Hotel was located on West Center Street at Lemon Street, and was one of Anaheim's popular hotels until replaced by the Hotel Valencia in 1916.

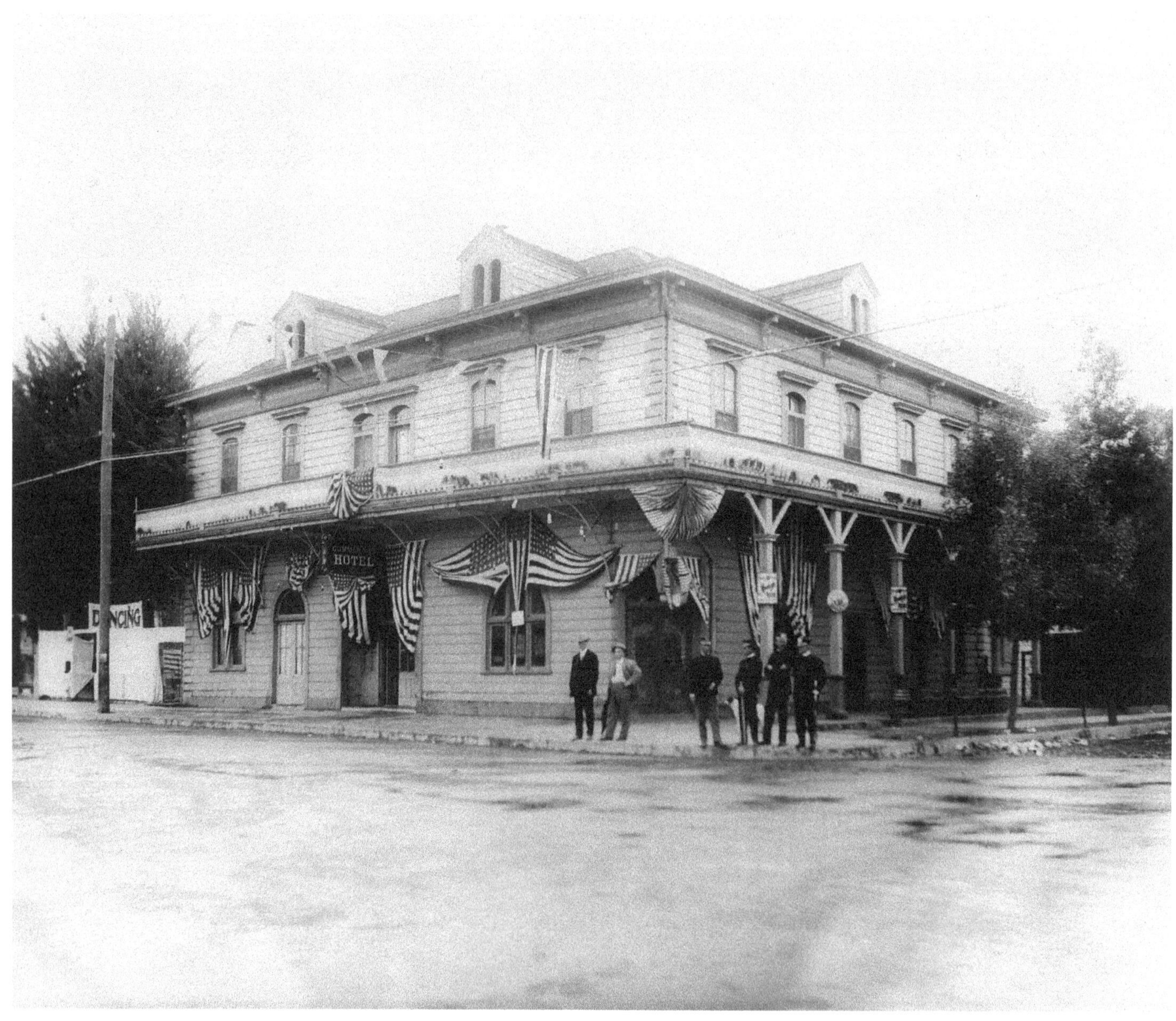

This 1904 image shows Anaheim's own Company E of the State Militia, posed at attention on the steps of the Del Campo Hotel. Most towns maintained militias, which were more often called for parade duty than to protect the residents.

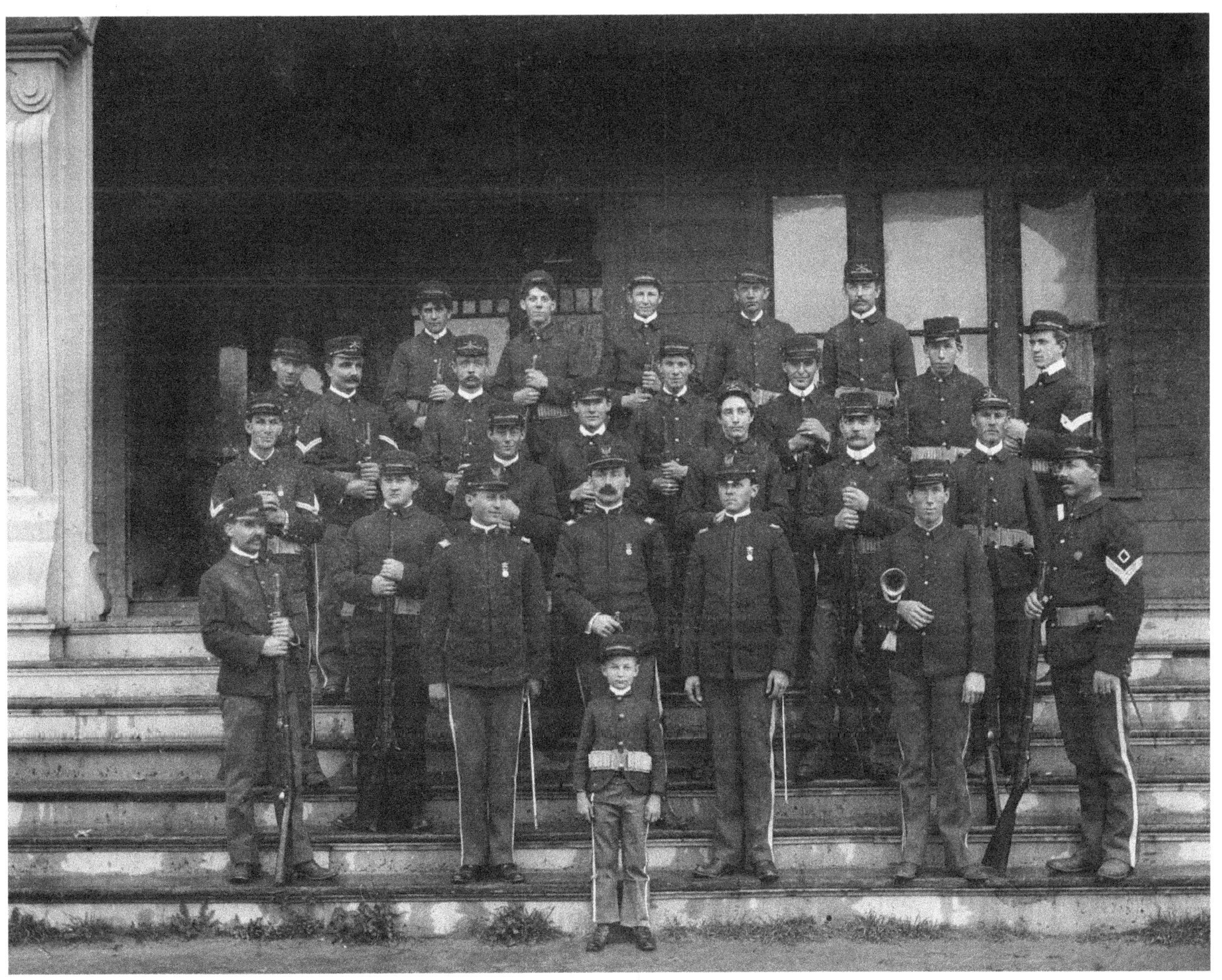

C. G. McKinley ran his feed yard and ice depot at 111-113 North Los Angeles Street. In addition to wood, coal, hay, and feed, he was the town's exclusive supplier of Aetna Mineral Water.

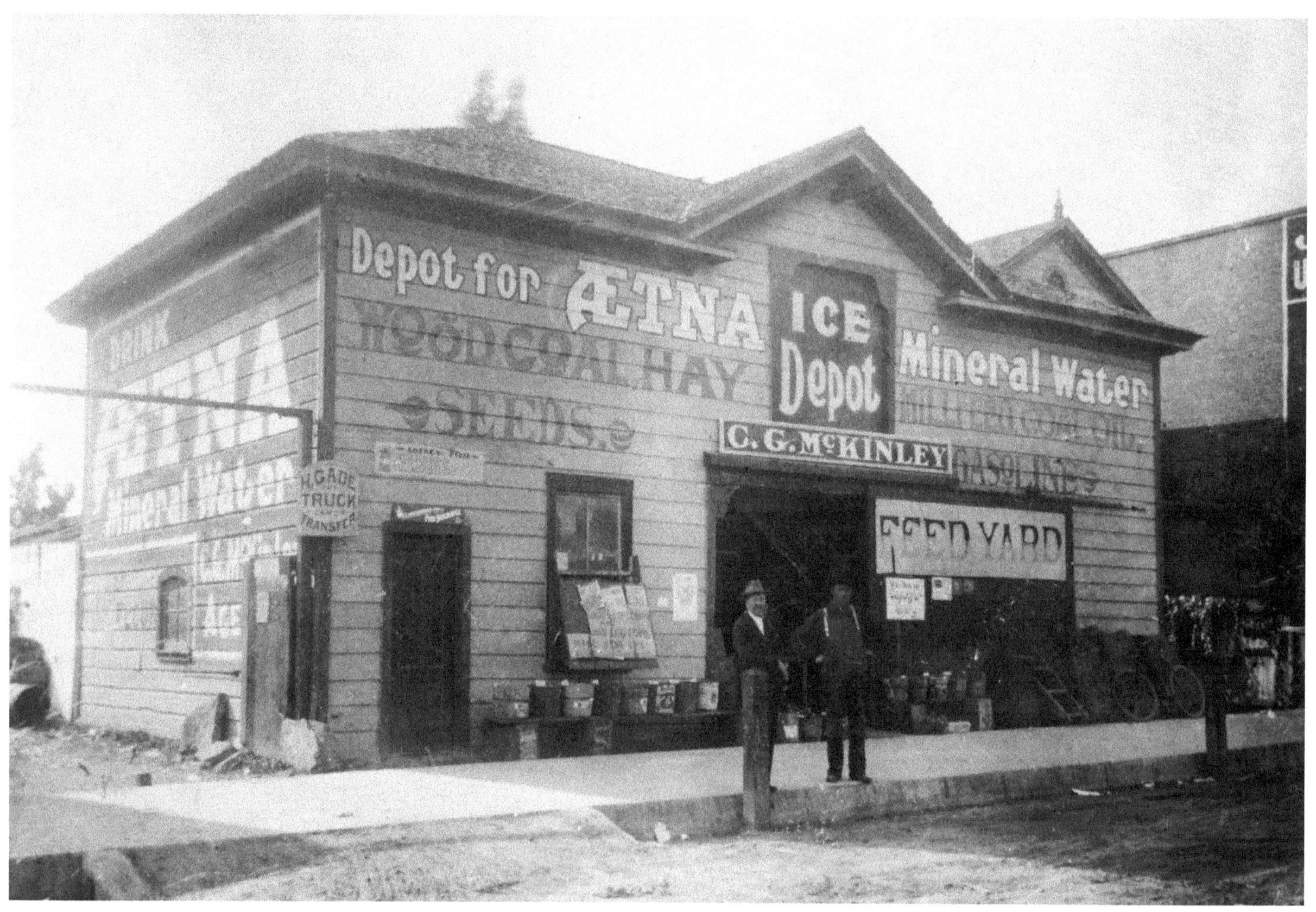

The second railroad to reach Anaheim was the Santa Fe, which entered Anaheim in 1888, building this wood frame depot at 708 East Center Street. The arrival of the Santa Fe provided competition to the Southern Pacific, which had reached Anaheim in 1875. A rate war ensued that ignited a regional real estate boom complete with speculators, brass bands, paper cities, and free lunches for potential landowners. A group of travelers poses for the photographer at the depot in 1905.

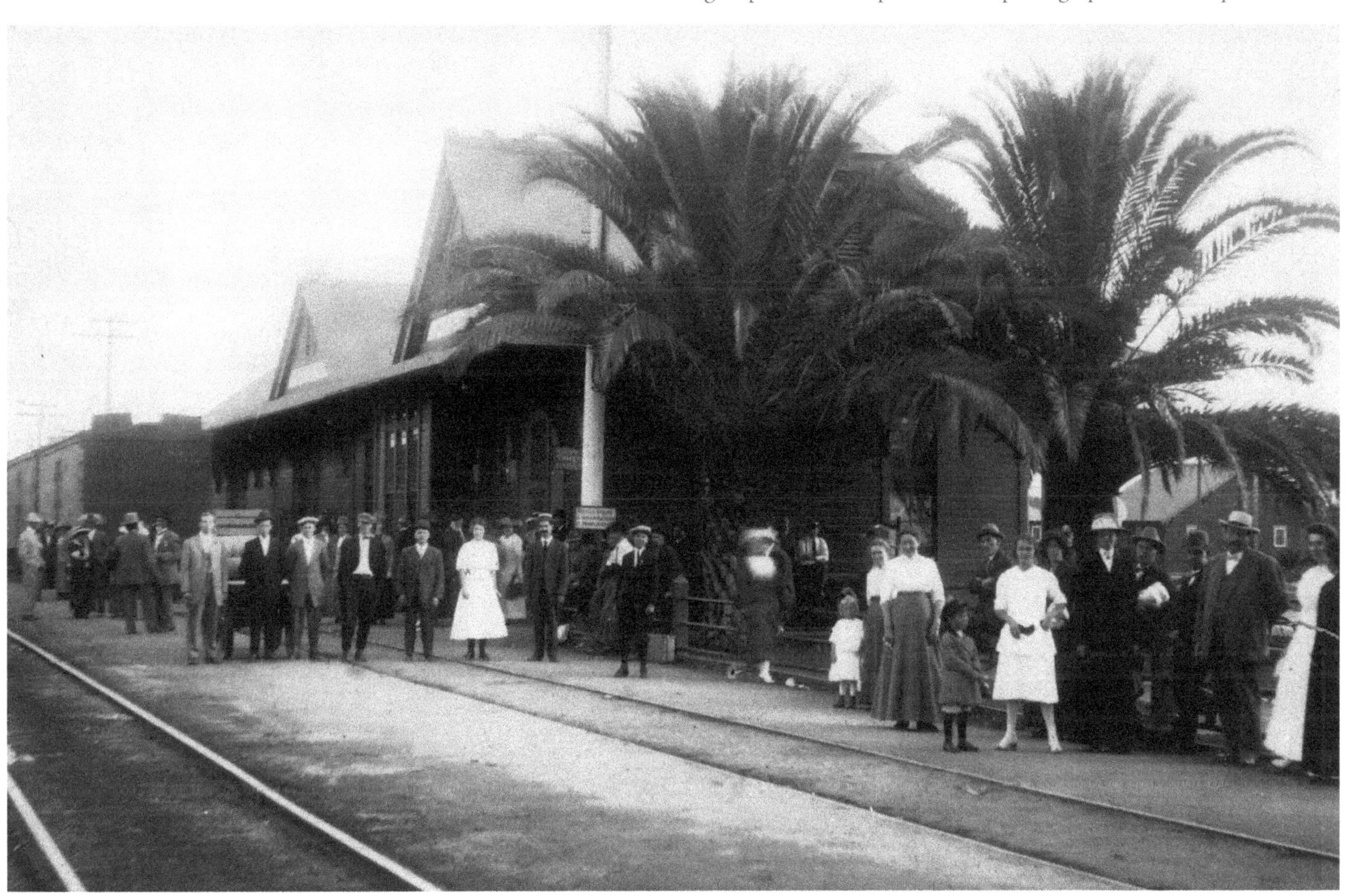

This interior view of the Orange County Preserving Company at 801 East Center Street shows graders packing an early crop of Valencia oranges. In addition to citrus, George Boyd's firm packed and shipped deciduous fruit, walnuts, and vegetables of all kinds.

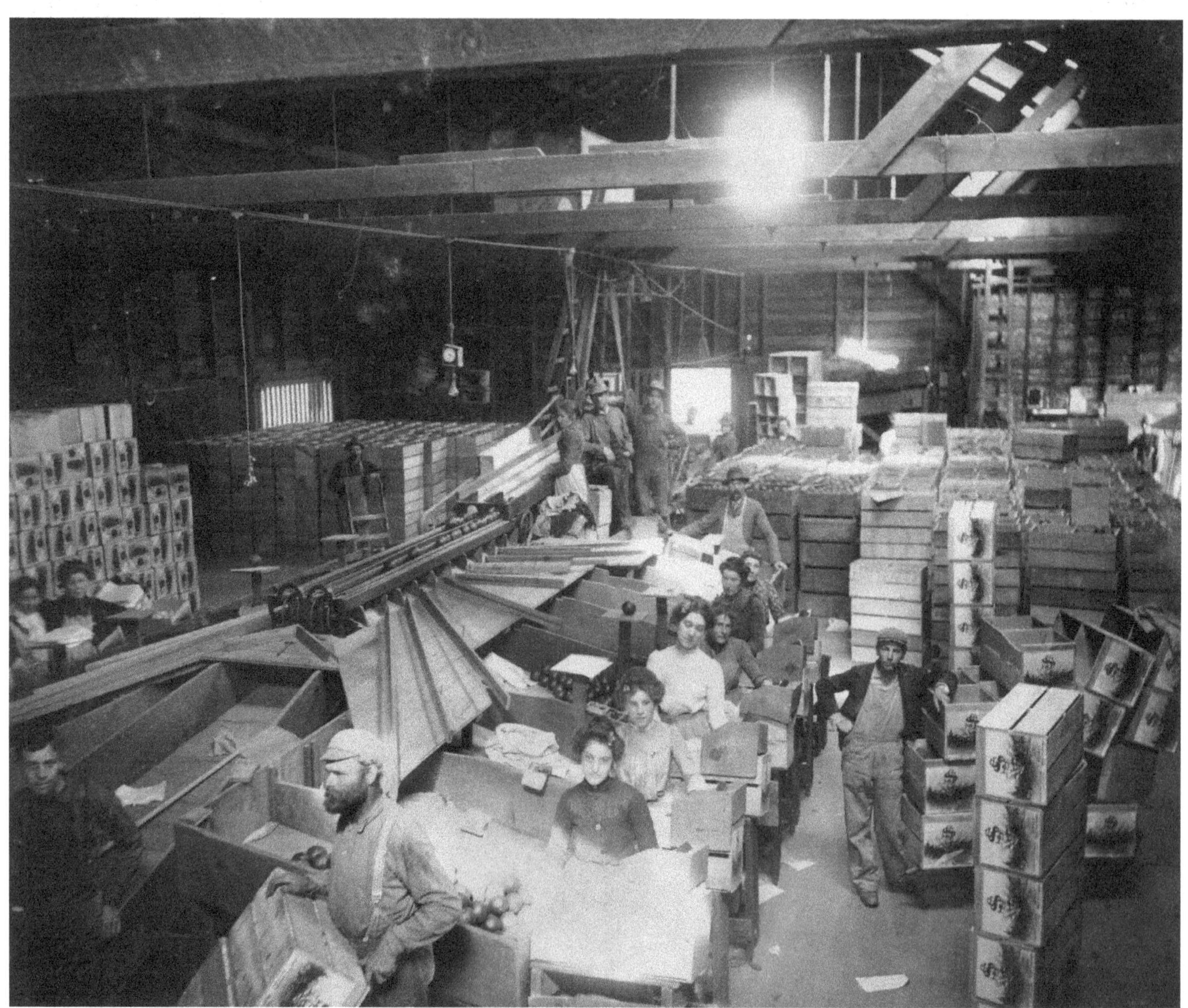

Anaheim's Philadelphia Street is lined with neatly maintained homes in this 1907 view. Right to left are the residences of Sidney and Emma Holman, Cornelius and Zilphia Bruce, Ira and Hilda Chandler, George and Ina May Dietrich, and Thomas and Ellen Hollingworth.

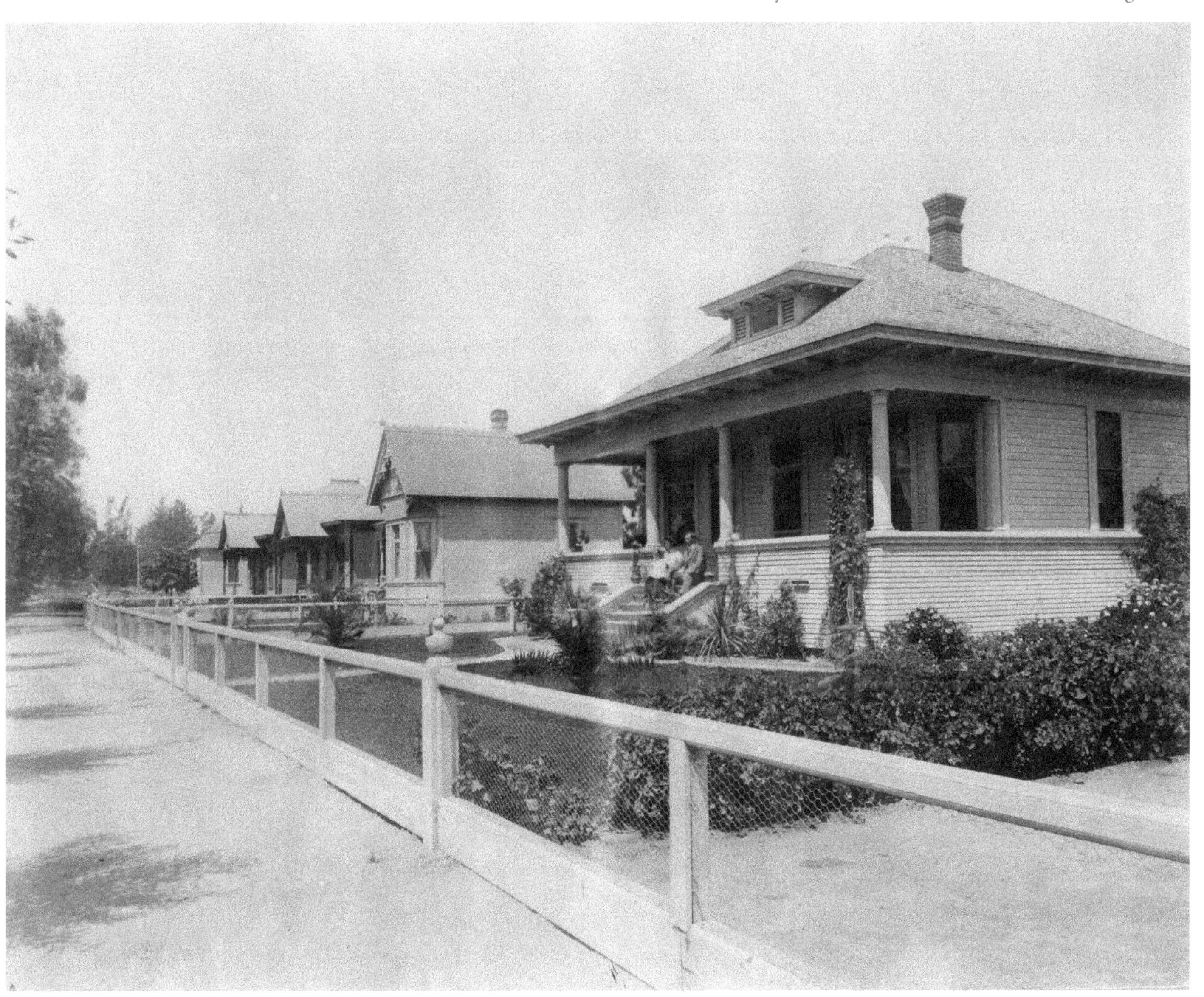

John Wirsching sits in his mule-drawn wagon in front of the Anaheim Union Water Company building at 123 North Los Angeles Street here around 1905. Wirsching's wagon was a rolling billboard for his "Advertising Agency."

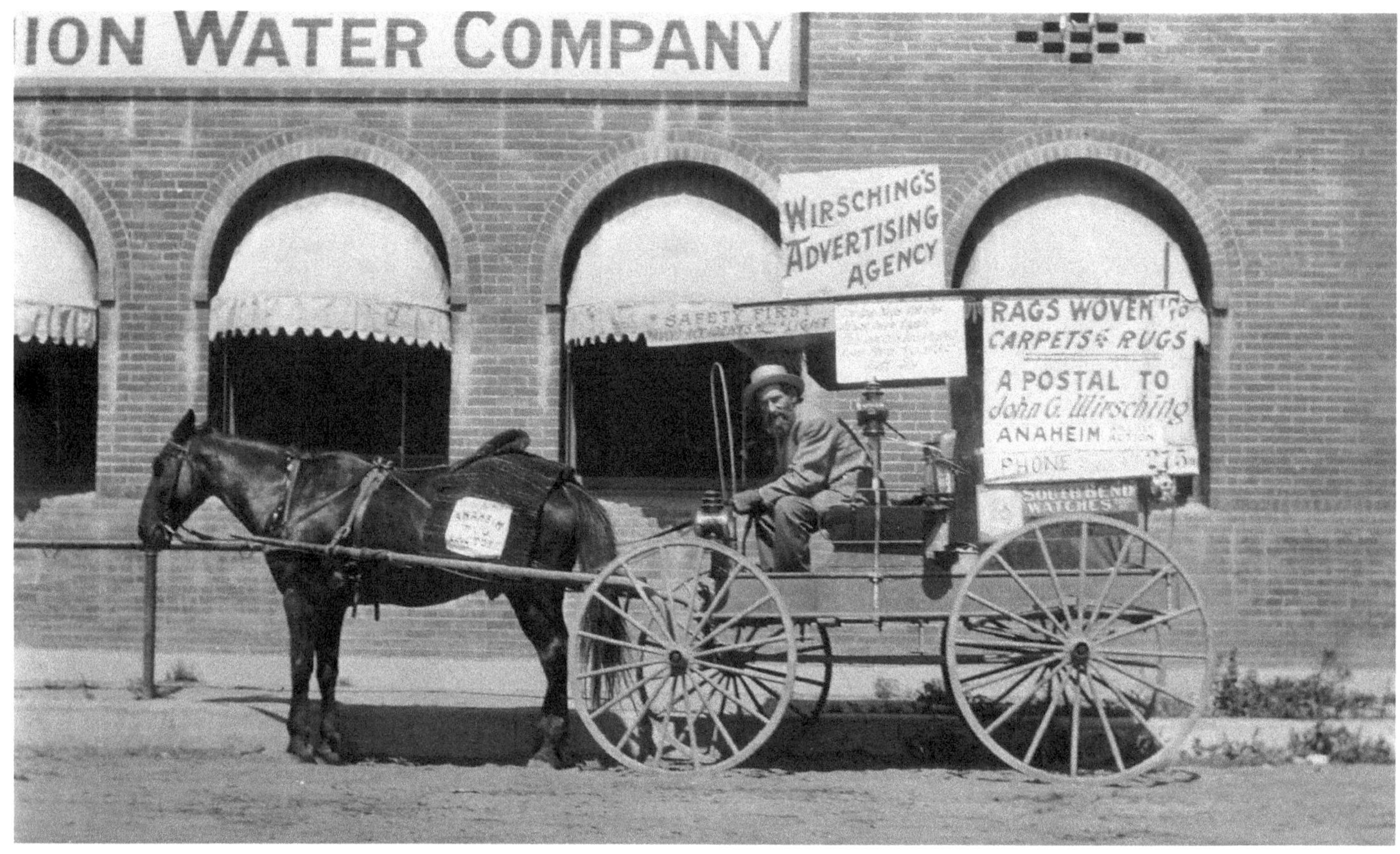

Charles Fischer ran Chilie's Place, a pool and billiards hall, located at 112 North Los Angeles Street. A place for men to relax, these establishments, filled with tobacco smoke and spittoons, were shunned by the town's proper ladies.

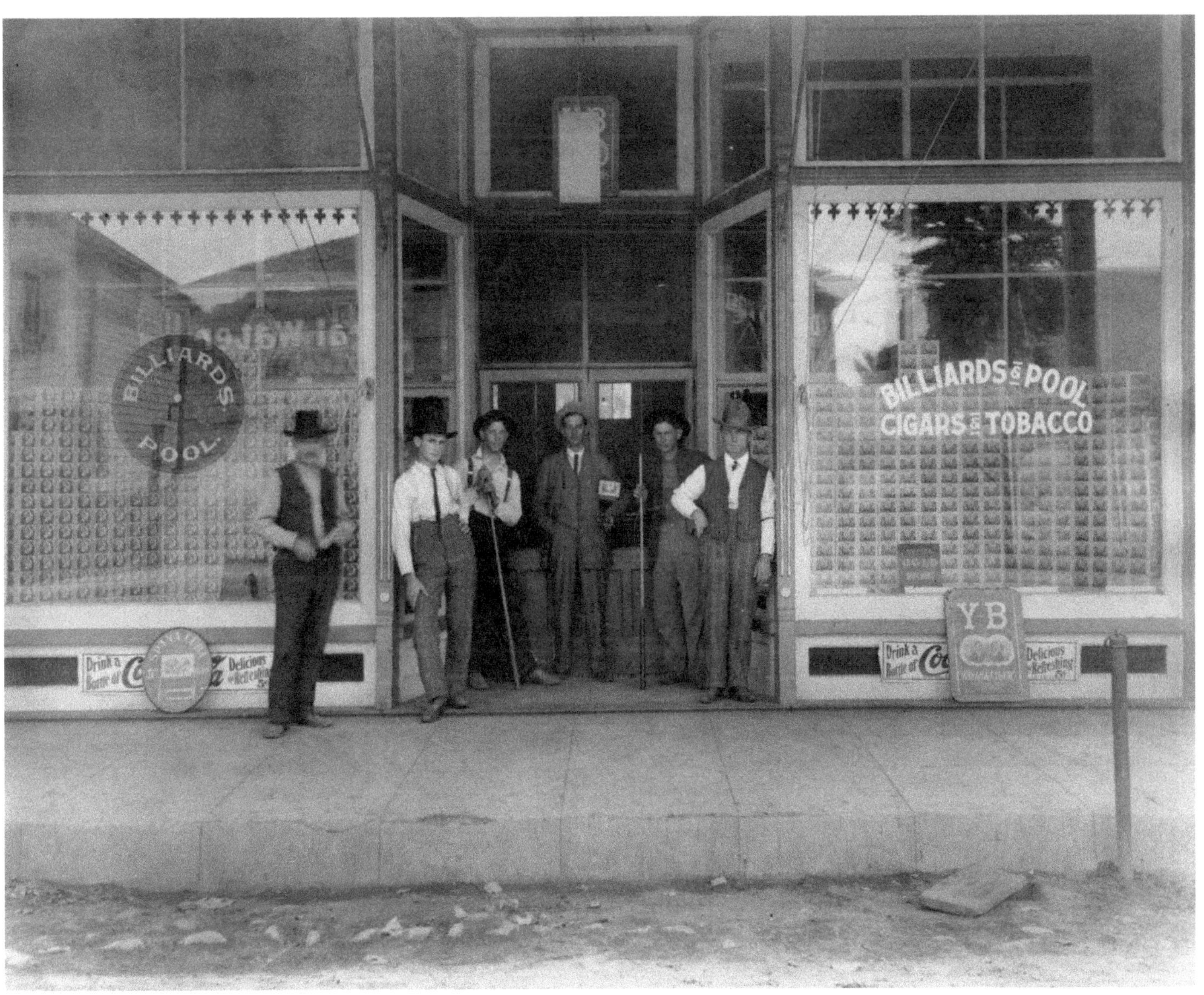

Anaheim's growth exceeded the capacity of its original electric and water works on West Cypress Street at the turn of the century. On April 14, 1906, Anaheim voters agreed to indebt themselves in the amount of $46,000 for a new utility facility. A lot was purchased on South Los Angeles Street and after many debates, the new facility was finally erected. Anaheim's new very-modern powerhouse went "on-line" December 20, 1907.

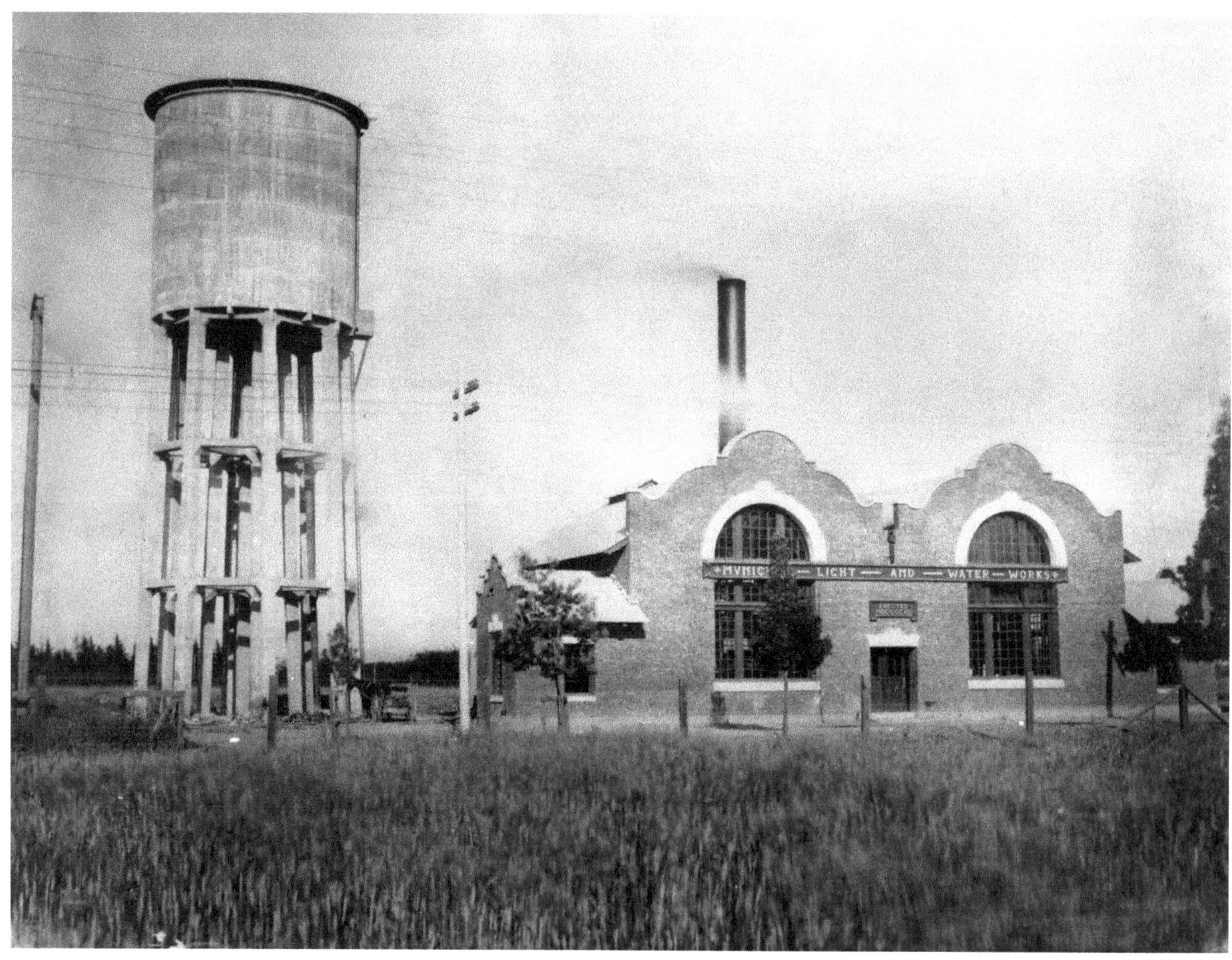

Around 1908 on Broadway at Los Angeles Street stand the large home of Dr. Herbert A. Johnston on the southeast corner and the home of Dr. William Wickett, just behind. In addition to being neighbors, both doctors were partners in the Anaheim Sanitarium, later named the Johnston-Wickett Clinic.

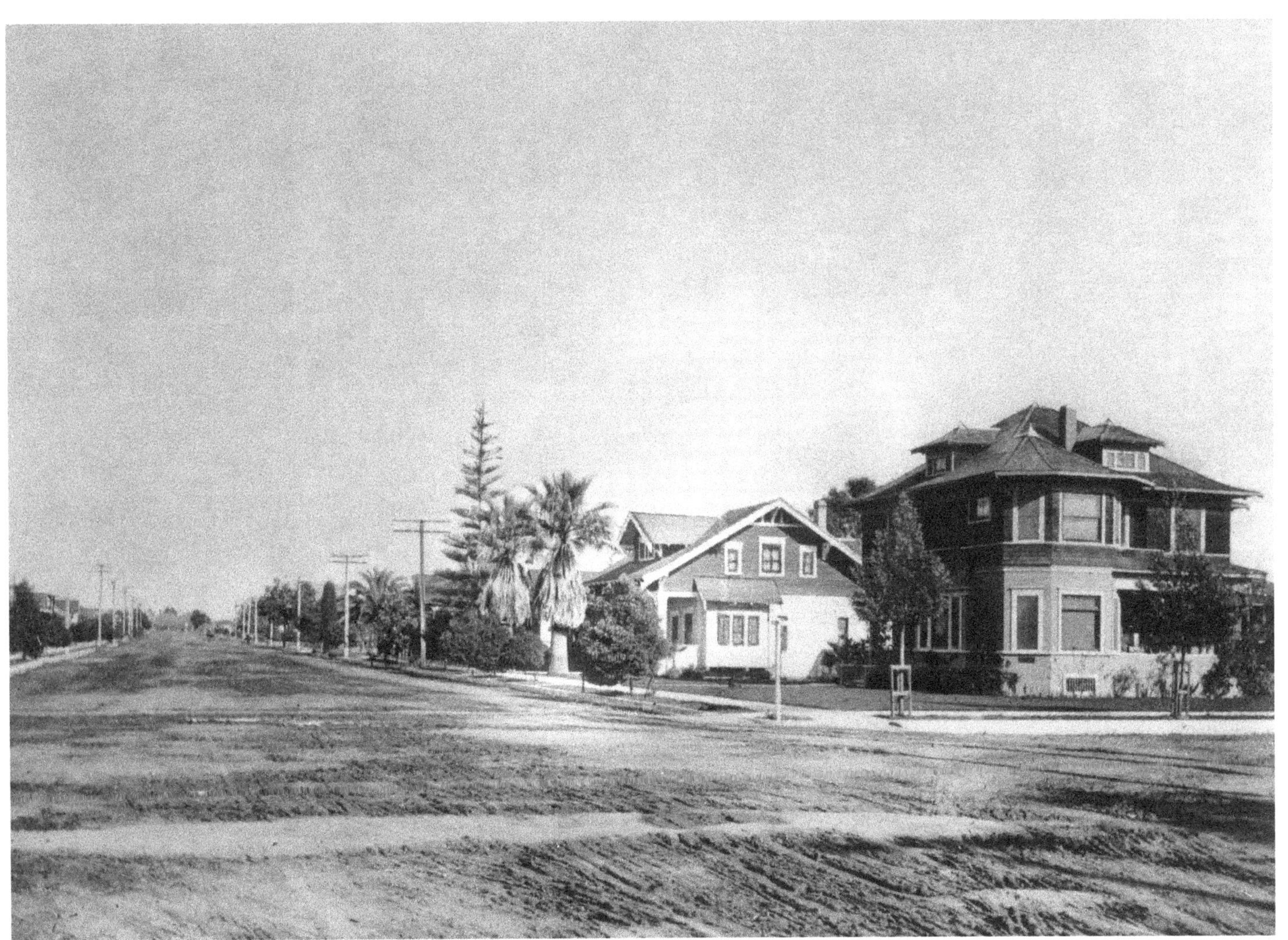

Shown here in the early twentieth century is Napoleon Hart's Place, located at 117 East Center Street. Dee Jackson stands behind the ornate bar, and Anaheim's Duke Paschall stands on the left. Hart's Place kept an interesting stock of spirits, wines, and cigars for patrons.

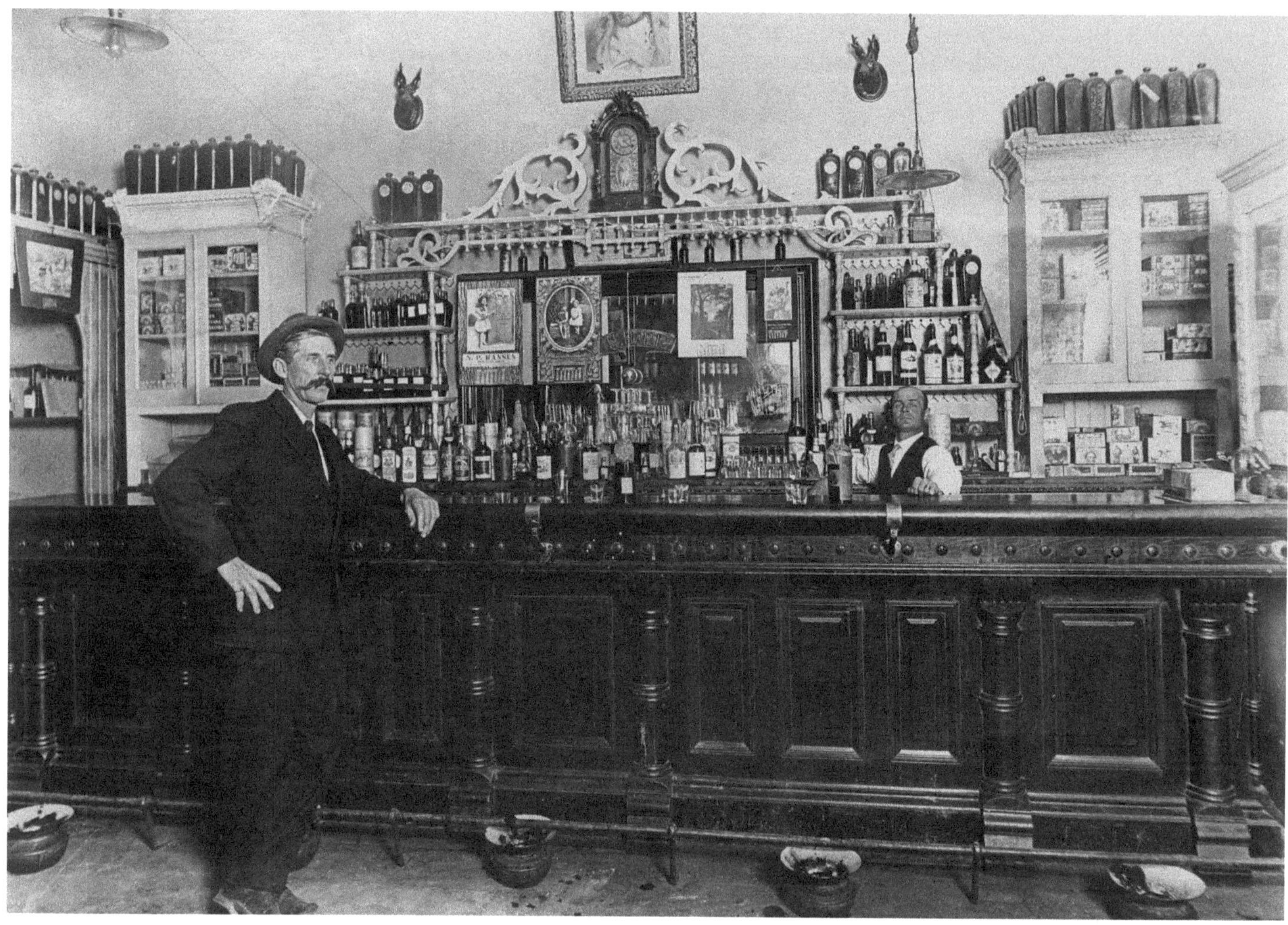

The Anaheim Knights of Pythias Lodge No. 105 chartered this Santa Fe train on February 13, 1910. The special train brought 1,500 brother Knights members from Los Angeles to Anaheim for an initiation of 118 new members into the Anaheim Lodge. A local Knight is seen greeting the train while riding a goat.

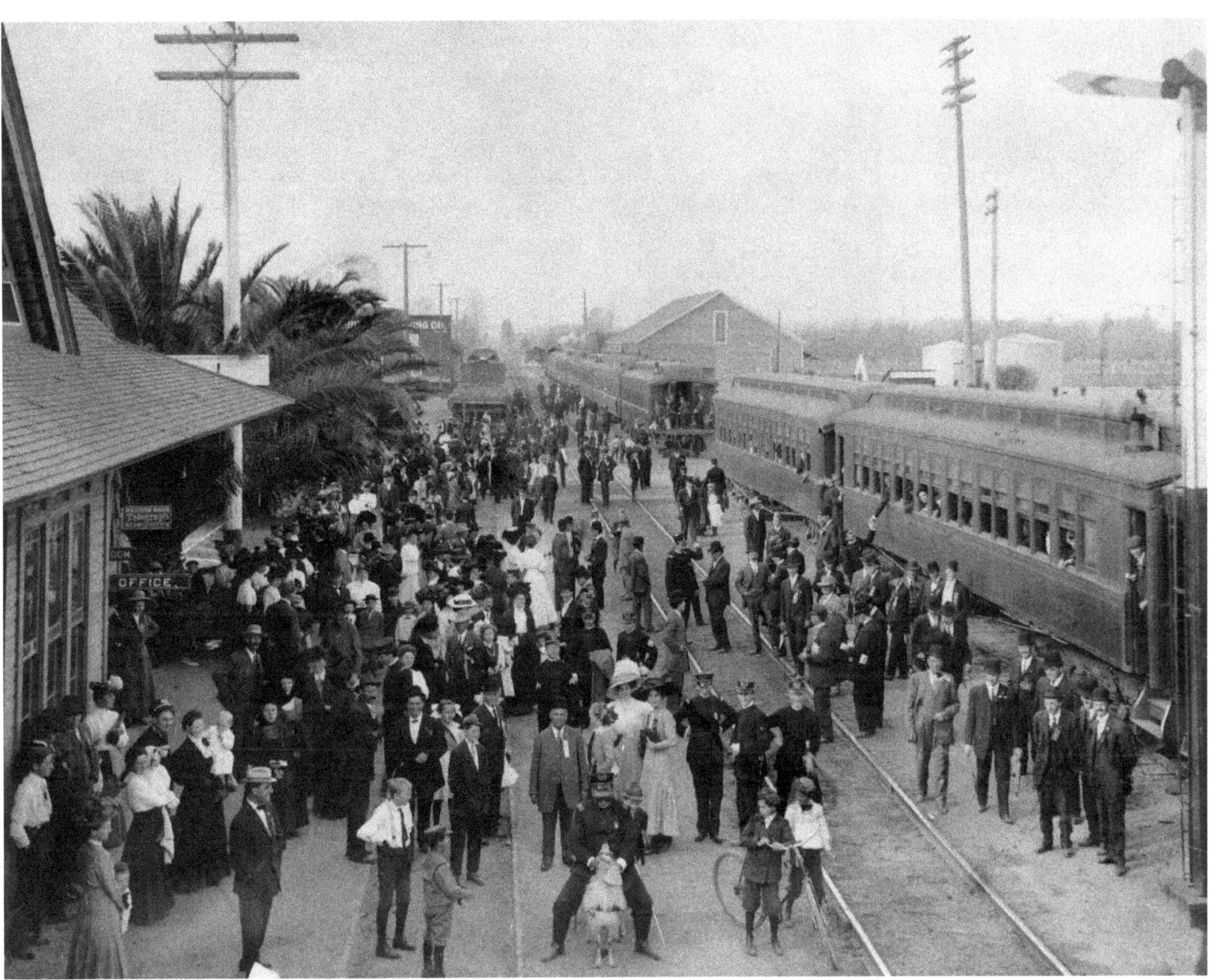

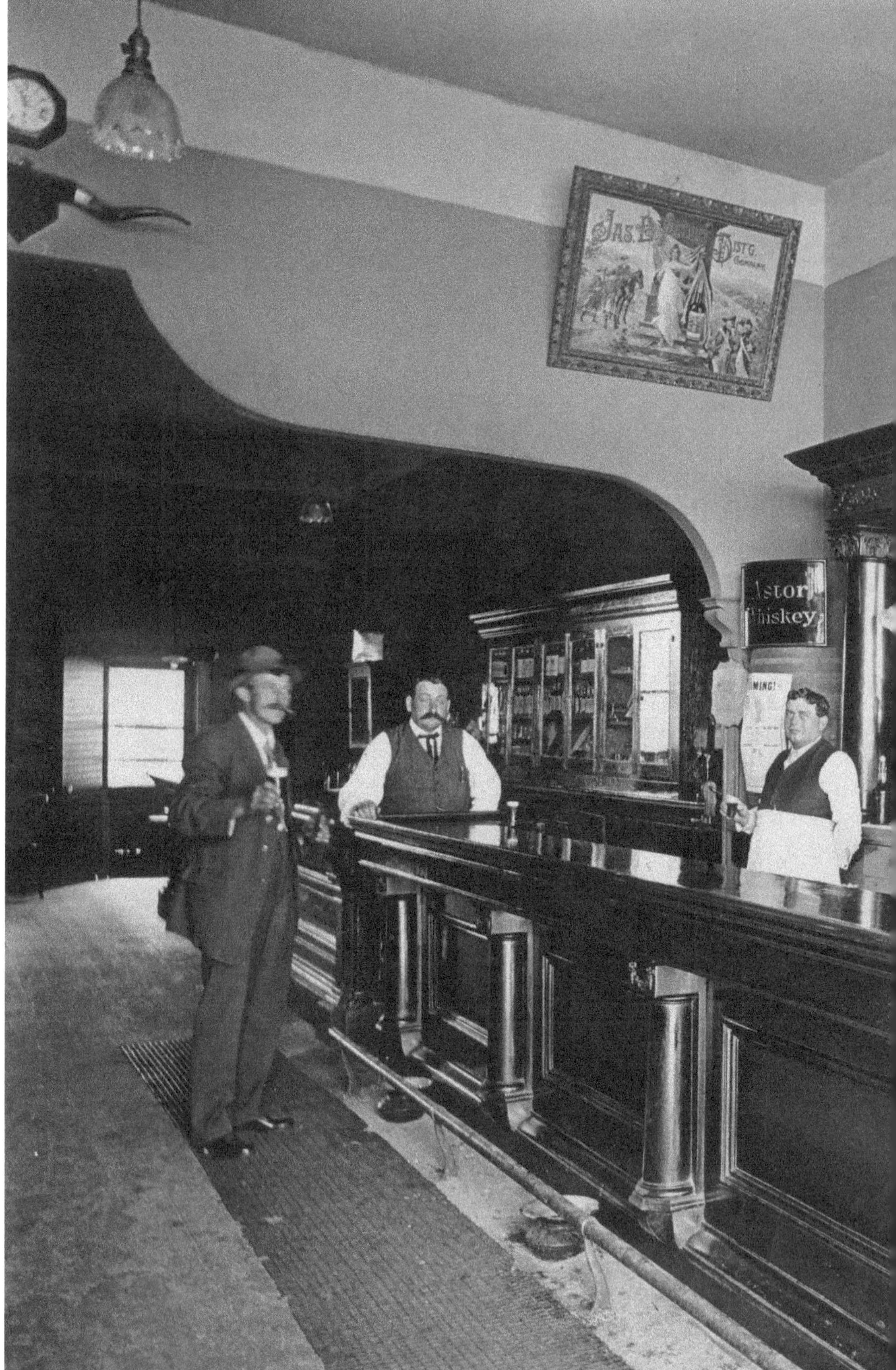
Astor
Whiskey

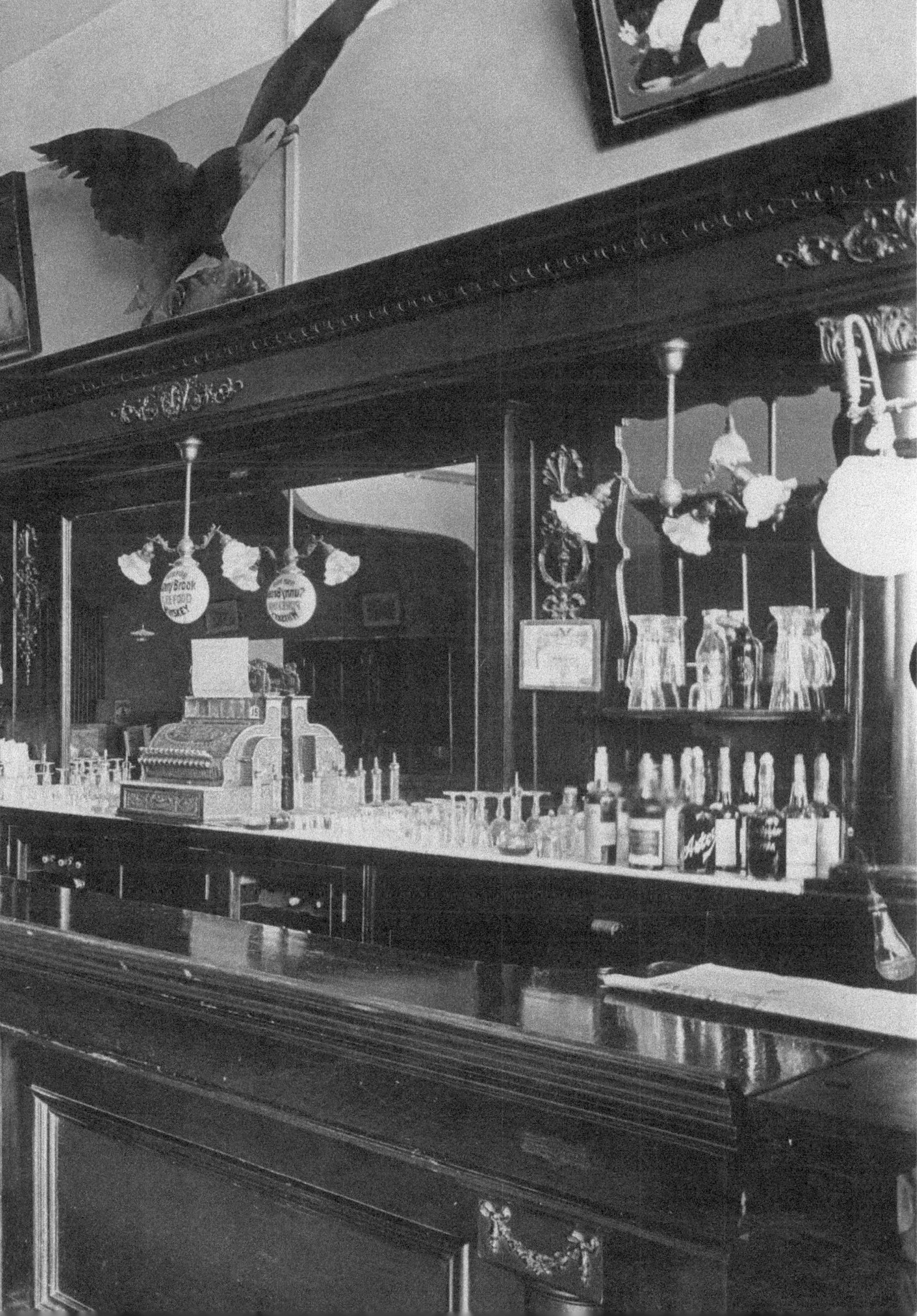

The interior of the Exchange Bar, located at 132 West Center Street, in 1908. Identified left to right are Sam Morningstar at the bar, William F. Stark, proprietor and mayor of Anaheim from 1920 to 1923, and A. L. Walter behind the bar. Anaheim's early German heritage ensured that wine and spirits were never far from hand. The coming of Prohibition in 1920 would close this interesting chapter of Anaheim businesses for many years.

By all accounts, Anaheim's favorite saloon was Roman Wisser's "Favorite Saloon" located on West Center Street. Lucien "Pete" Wisser, Roman's son, ran the business after Roman's death. The advent of Prohibition in 1920 forced the family to establish a new business. Wisser's Sporting Goods became an Anaheim landmark, supplying the town's children with their first bicycle, pocketknife, or baseball mitt.

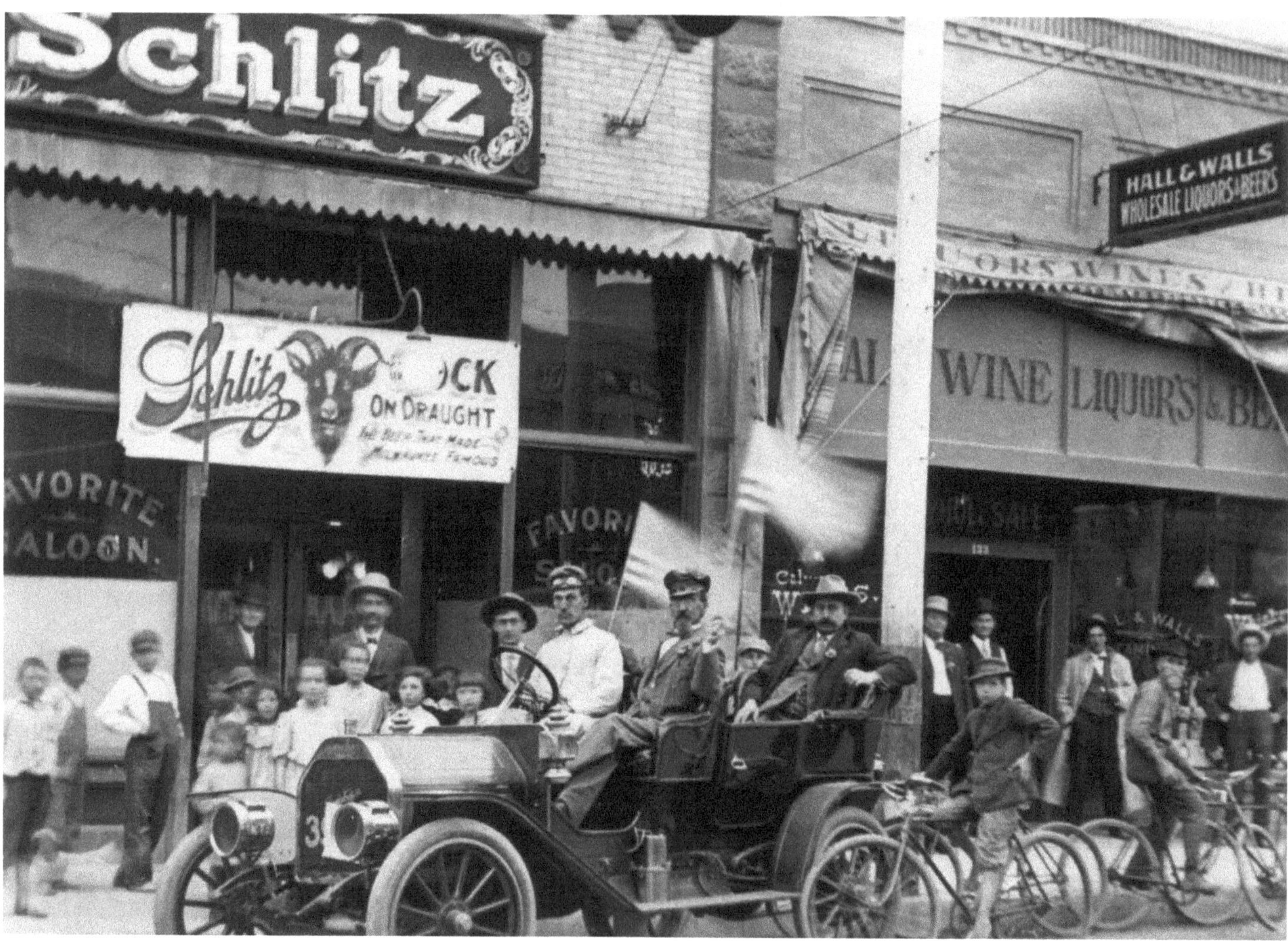

Buster Brown Shoes holds a promotion day at the William Falkenstein Store ca. 1910. Falkenstein's, located at 101 West Center Street, was for many years considered the town's premier department store where the town's businessmen would buy their Florsheim shoes, Hart Schaffner and Marx suits, and Arrow dress shirts.

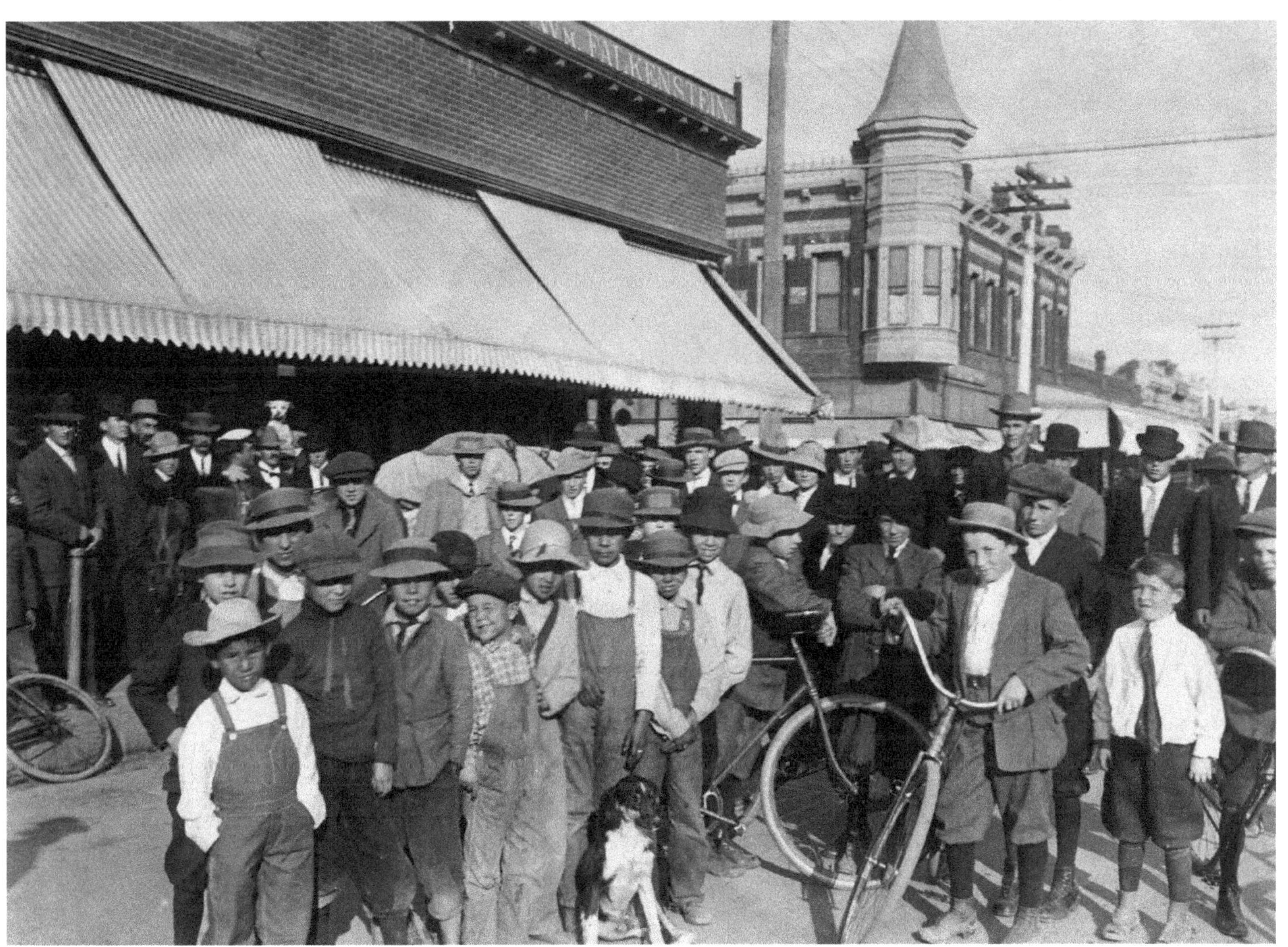

Horseless carriages appear on Anaheim's Center Street in 1910. By this time, the town's population was approaching 3,000 and the downtown streets were considered by some to be metropolitan. Horse and mule power was still in evidence and the streets still dusty, with paving still several years away.

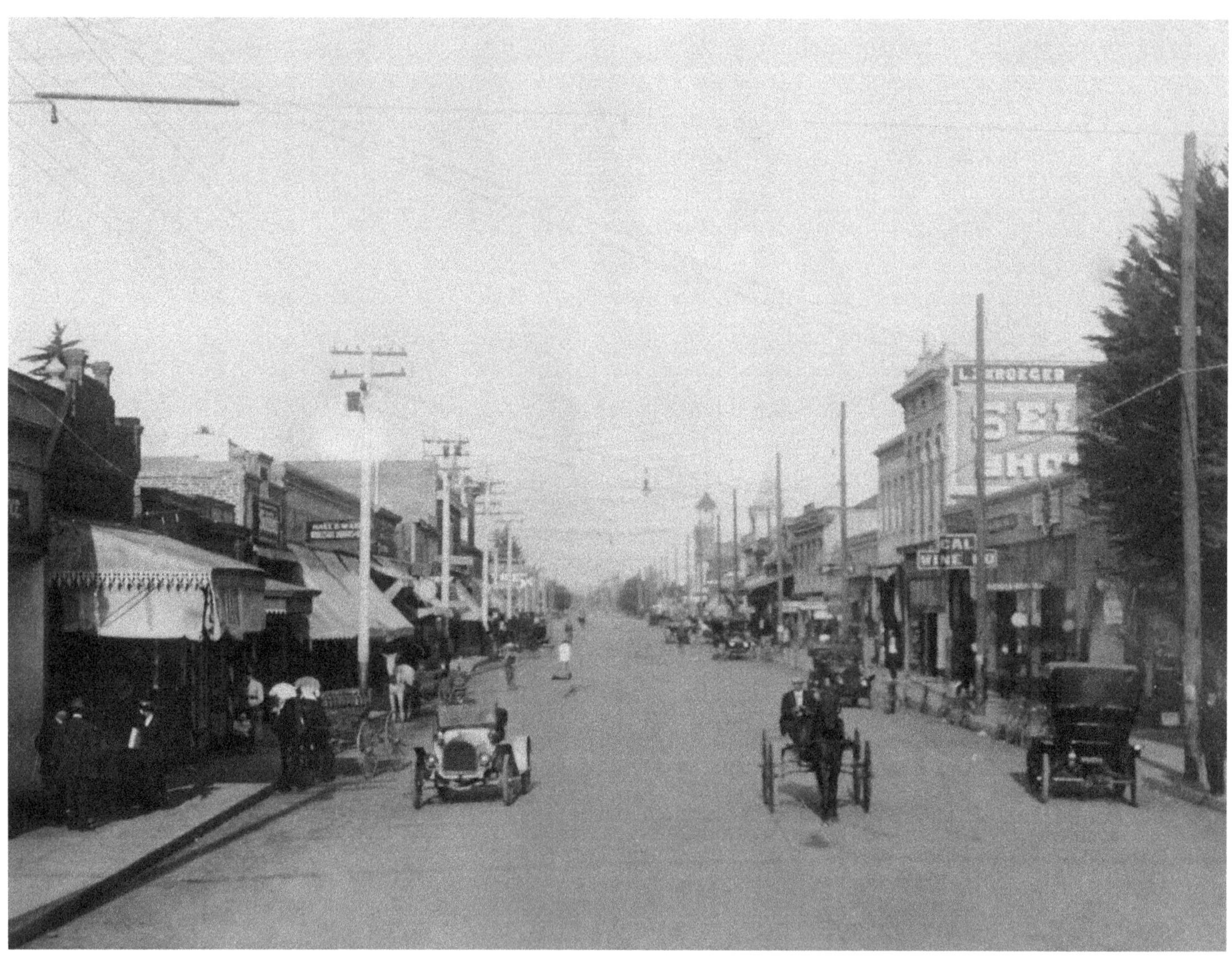

Broadway School was built in 1908 at the corner of East Broadway and South Olive streets. The building was enlarged in 1914 to accommodate kindergarten and additional students. The stately building appears here around 1910 as originally constructed.

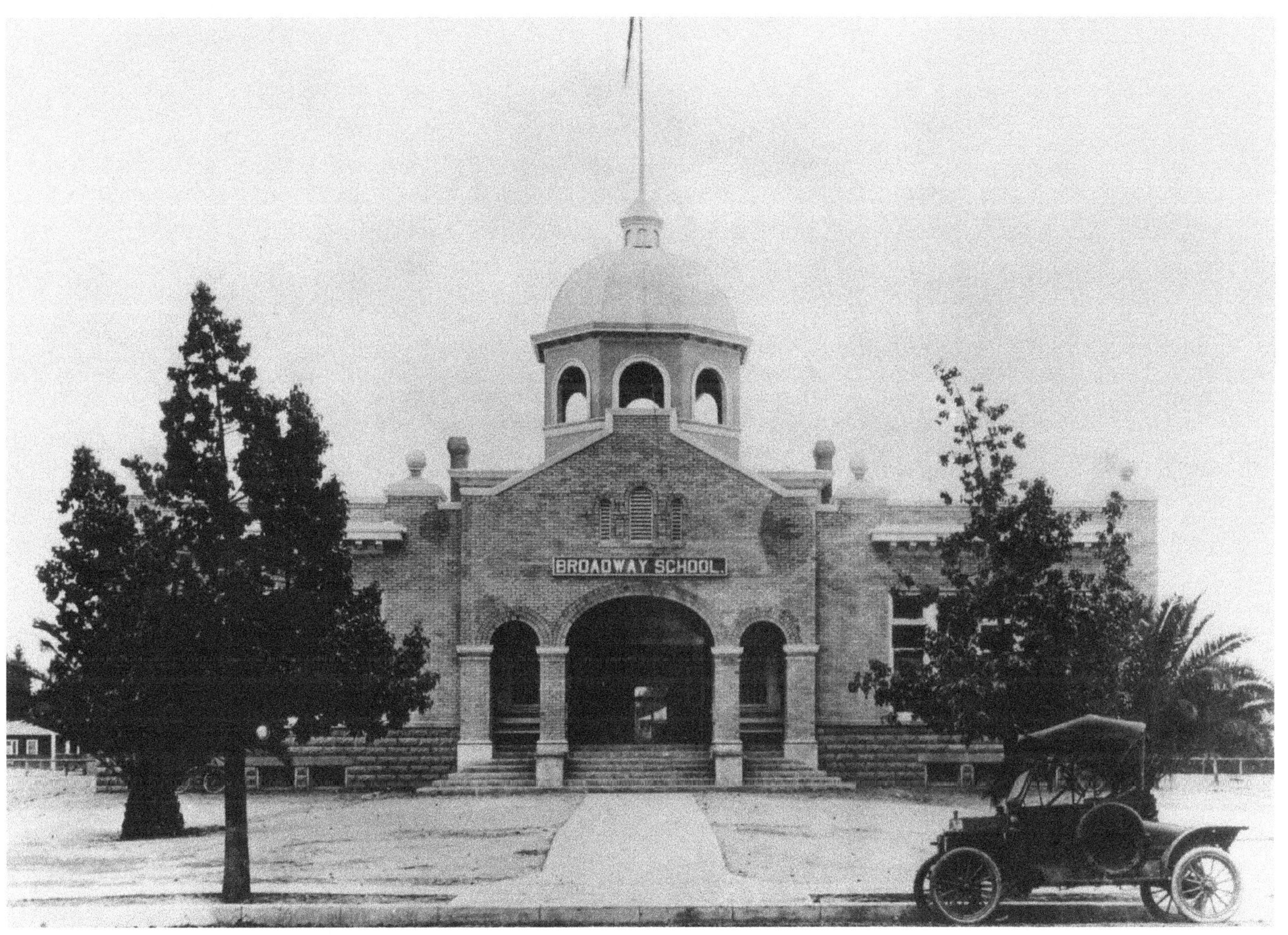

Another Fourth of July parade down Center Street around 1910 shows the Union Brewing Company float pulled by four horses. Although walnuts and citrus had replaced wine and spirits as the town's most important products, Union Brewing hearkened back to Anaheim's earlier age.

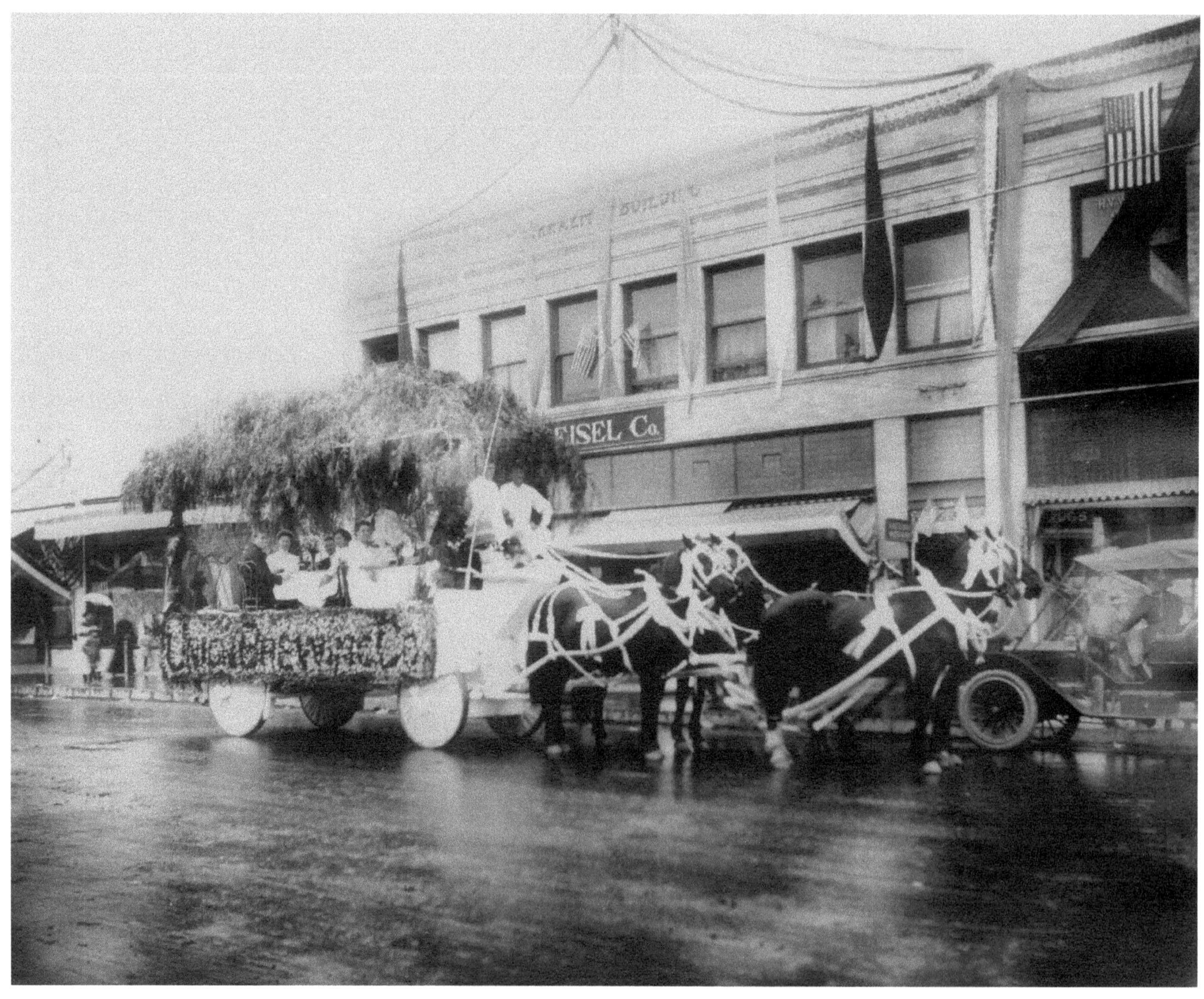

May Day in Anaheim in 1911 was celebrated in front of the high school building. Built in 1901 at 608 West Center Street, this structure was Anaheim's first high school and the third built in Orange County. It was sold to the elementary school district in 1911 when a new larger high school building was constructed one block west. This proud structure served the educational needs of the growing town until demolished in 1937 to make way for the new Fremont Junior High School.

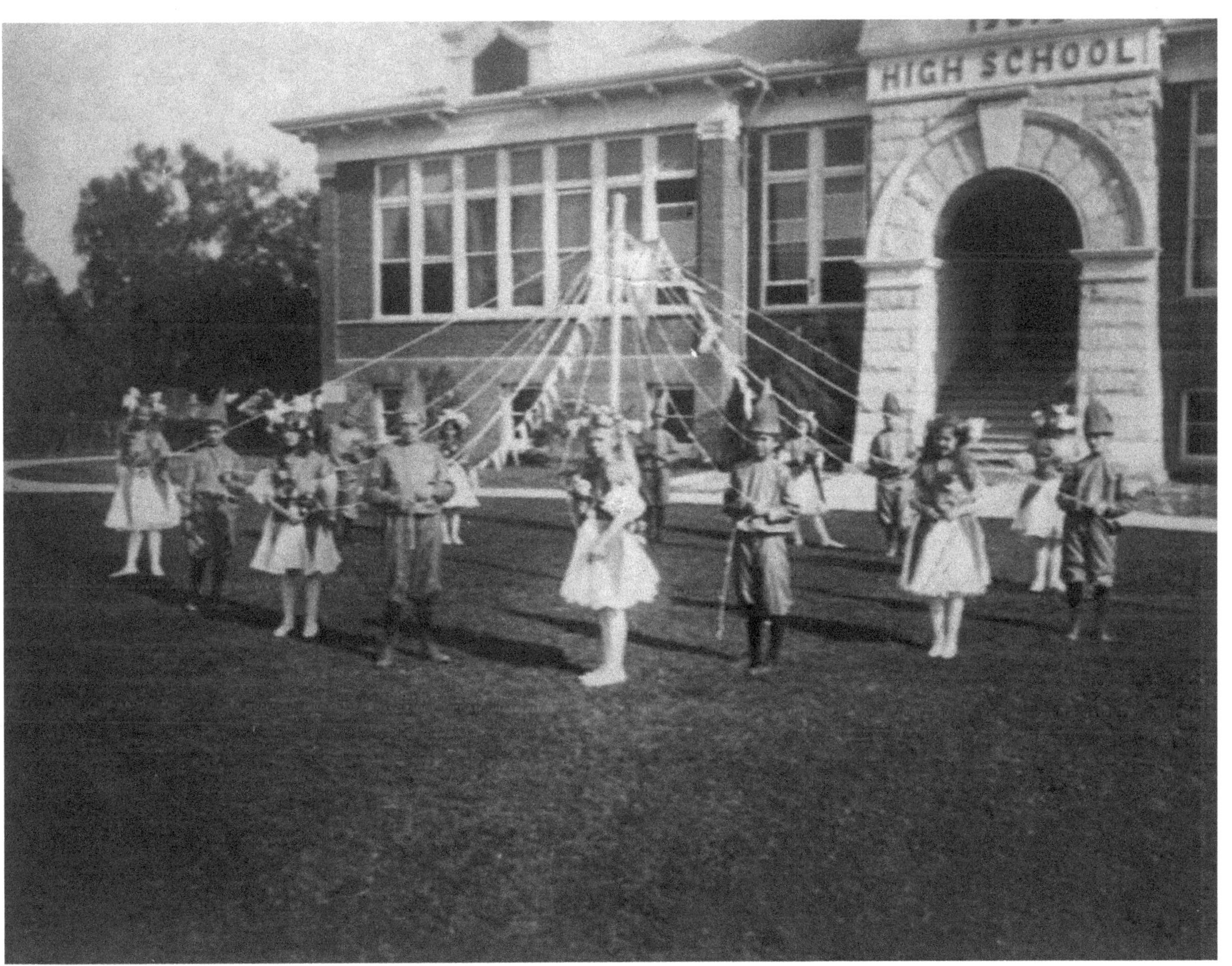

On February 5, 1911, Anaheim's first El Camino Real bell was blessed and dedicated in front of the Adelheid Steam Mineral & Electric Bath Parlor at 212 South Los Angeles Street. These bells were installed throughout California to signify the route of the Padres as they established the early Mission system in the Spanish-controlled California of the late 1700s. The El Camino Real (Kings Highway) passed through Anaheim from San Diego to Los Angeles. Mrs. Adelheid Koenig sponsored the bell to commemorate this early trail.

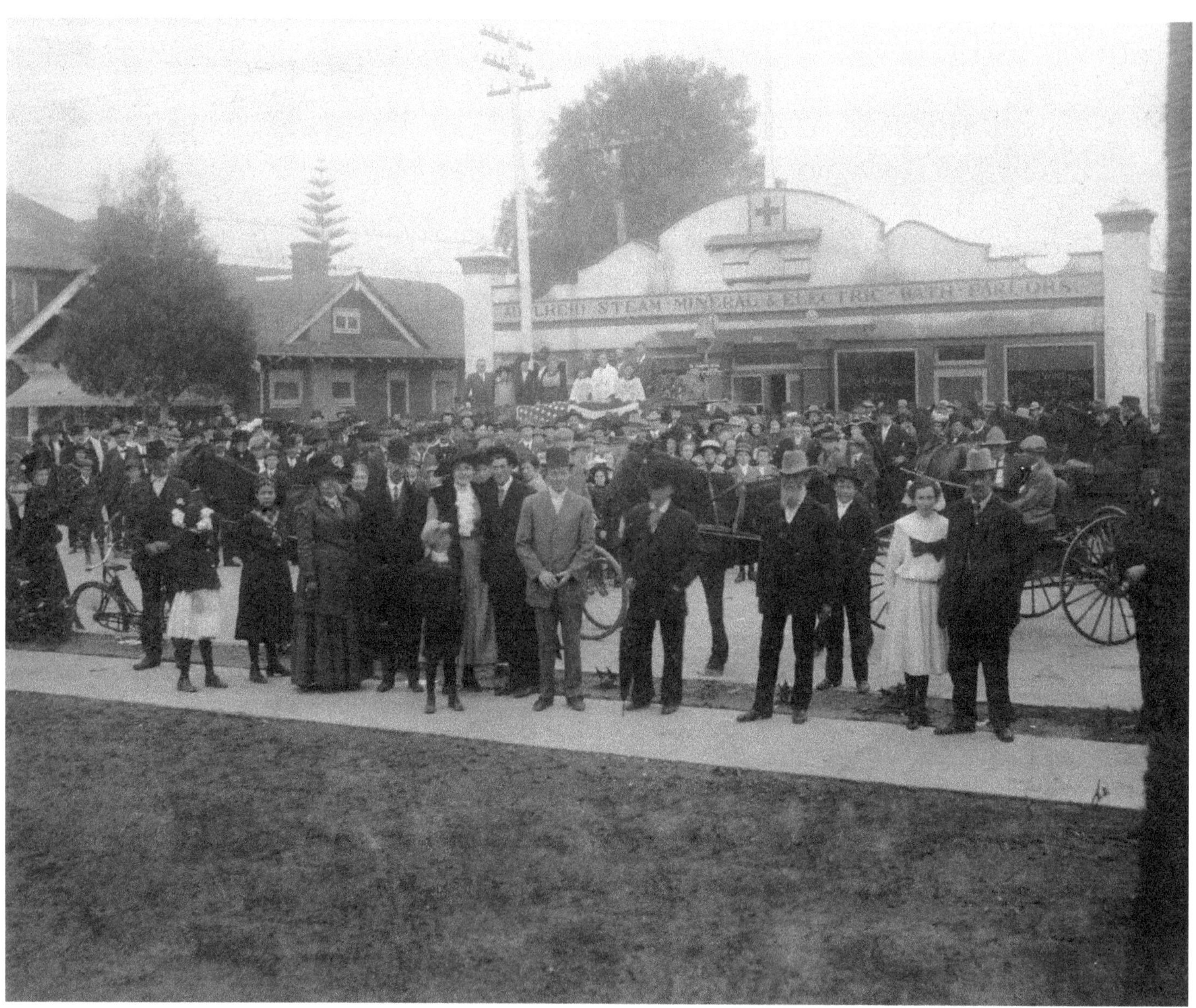

The interior of Richard Fischle's Mission Ice Cream Parlor in 1911. Located at 124 East Center Street, it was a very popular stop for the young and old alike in early Anaheim. A public-spirited person, Fischle served as the city's fire chief in 1924.

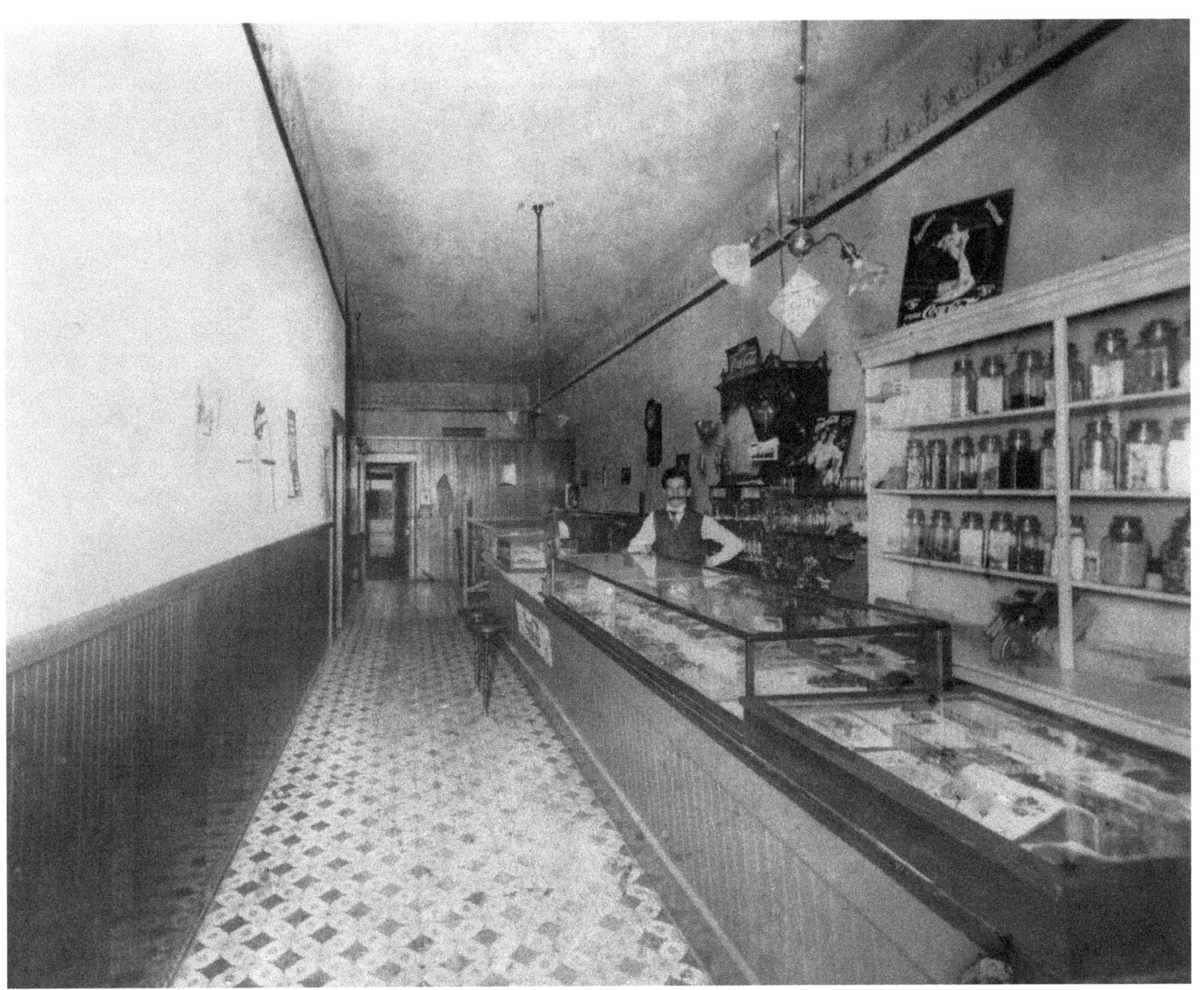

On April 6, 1911, the local Knights of Pythias marched in funeral procession down a drizzly West Center Street for their beloved member, Herman Kruger. Pallbearers included Herman A. Dickel, John W. Duckworth, Henry M. Adams, Clemens Amberg, John Hahn, and N. J. Kuhlman. Kruger was the promoter and builder of the Anaheim Sugar Factory, one of the town's early industrial firms.

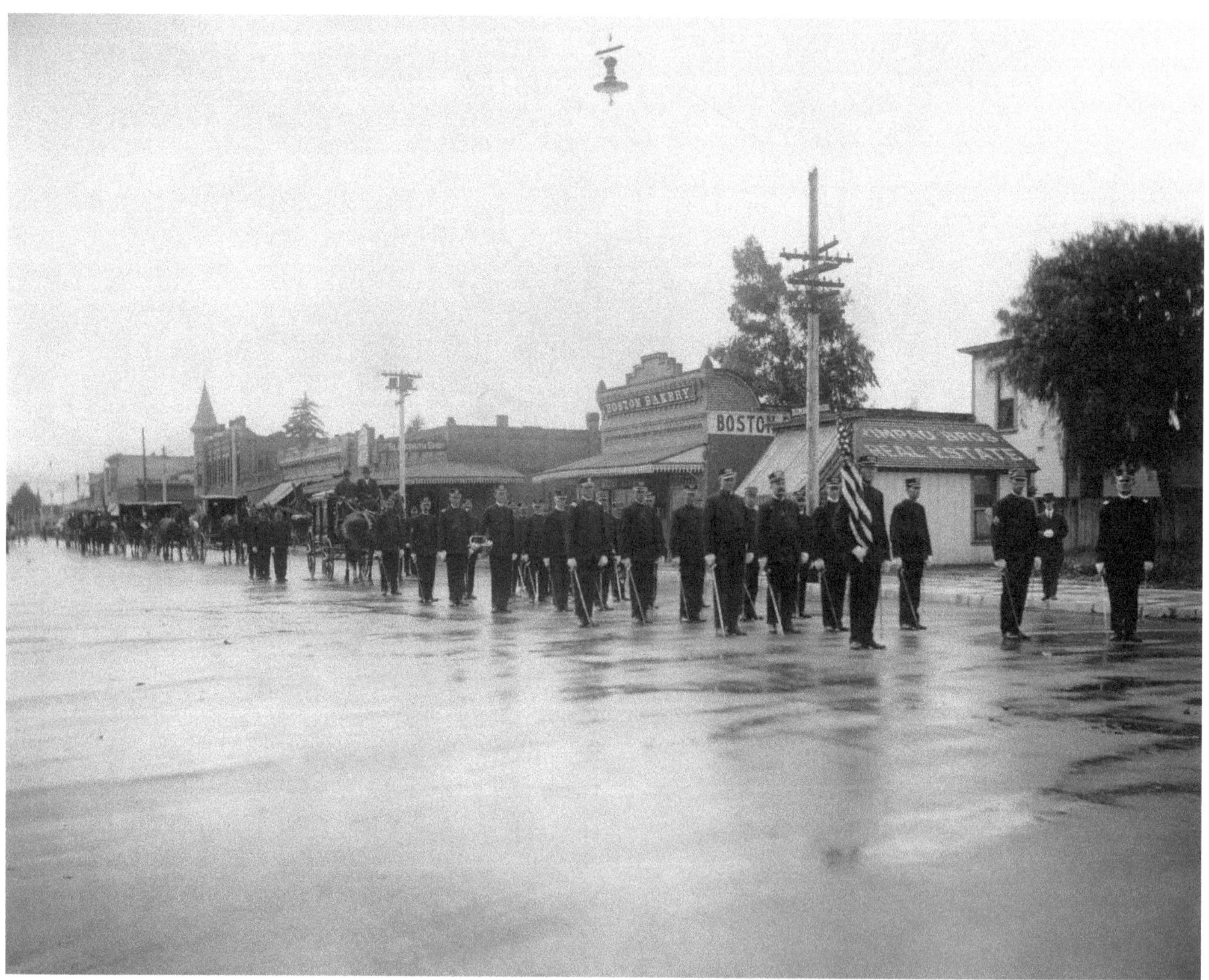

Visitors to the 1911 Anaheim Carnival are preparing to ascend in the Balloon Ride. Once airborne, they will see the roughly one-square-mile town surrounded by walnut and Valencia orange tree groves.

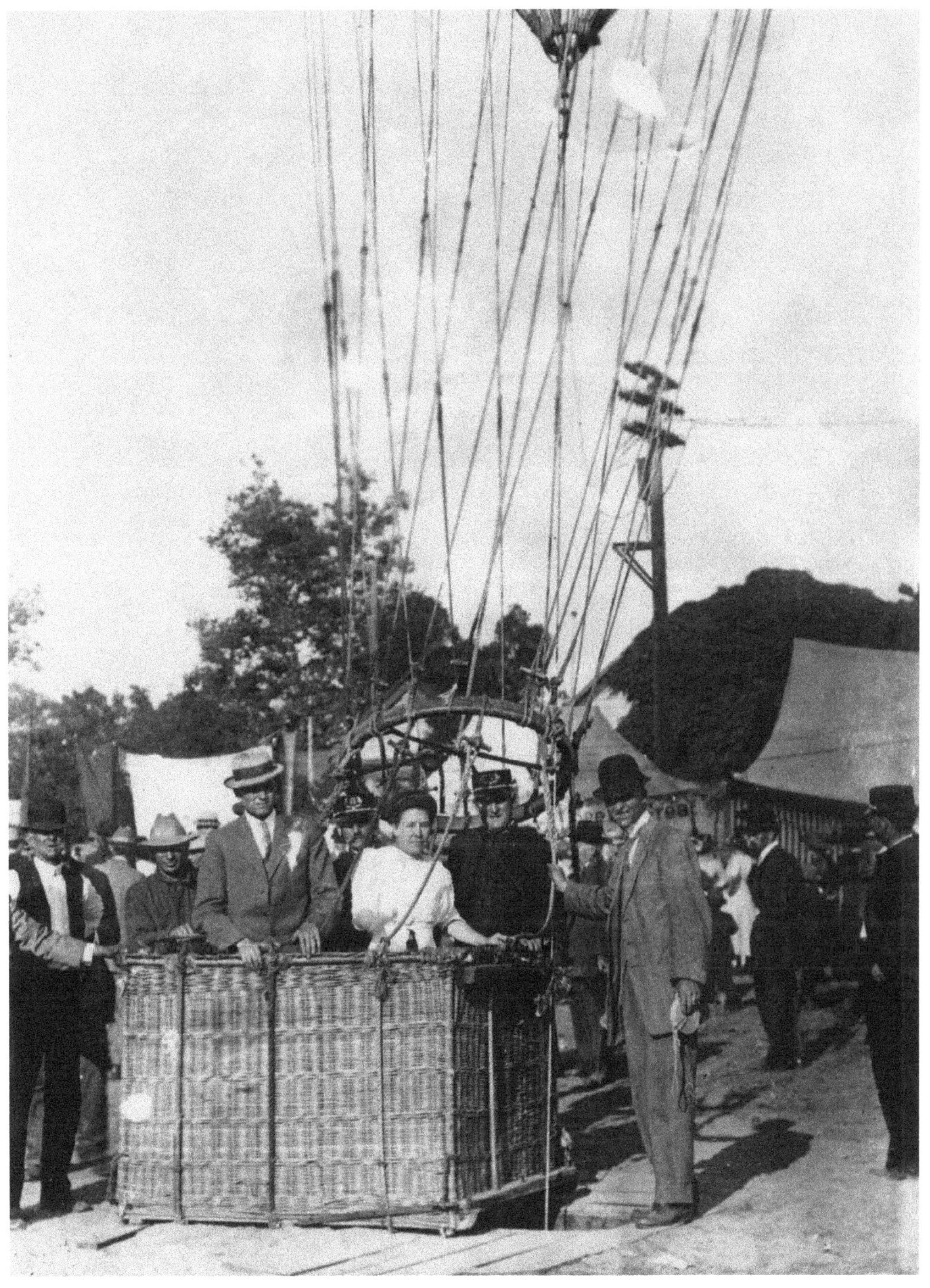

In 1911, the Anaheim Carnival ran from September 29 through October 1 and attracted visitors countywide. Anaheim, as the oldest and one of the larger towns in the county, was already known for its many forms of entertainment. For those who could manage the 10-cent admission, food booths, a balloon ride, and a sideshow featuring "Dirty Dora" were offered.

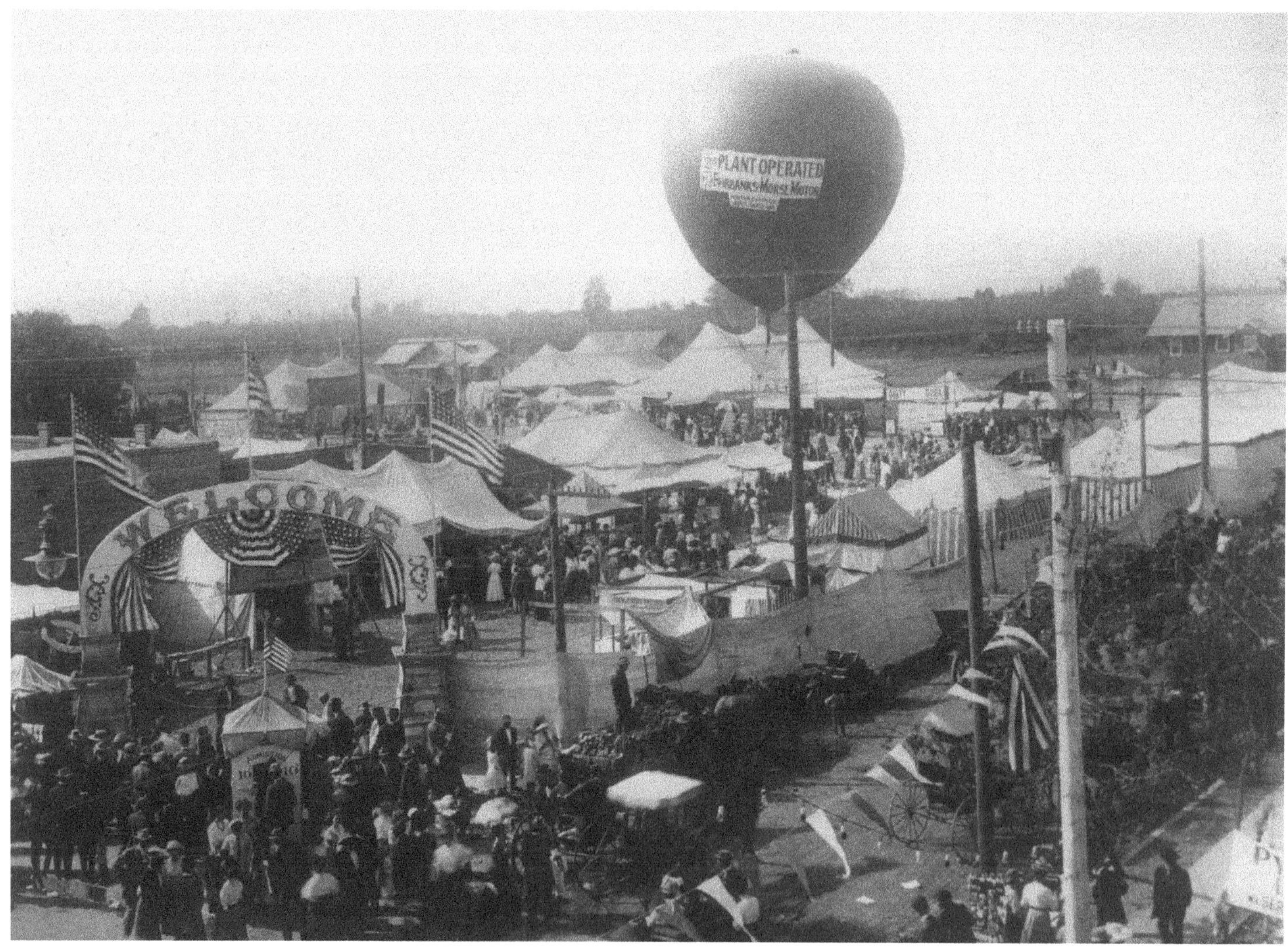

Budd McAlvay, an employee of P. J. Weisel's automobile dealership, won the Medium Car Road Race held as part of Anaheim's 1912 Fourth of July celebration, driving this Studebaker. For the three laps around town, his record time was 18 minutes, 36 seconds.

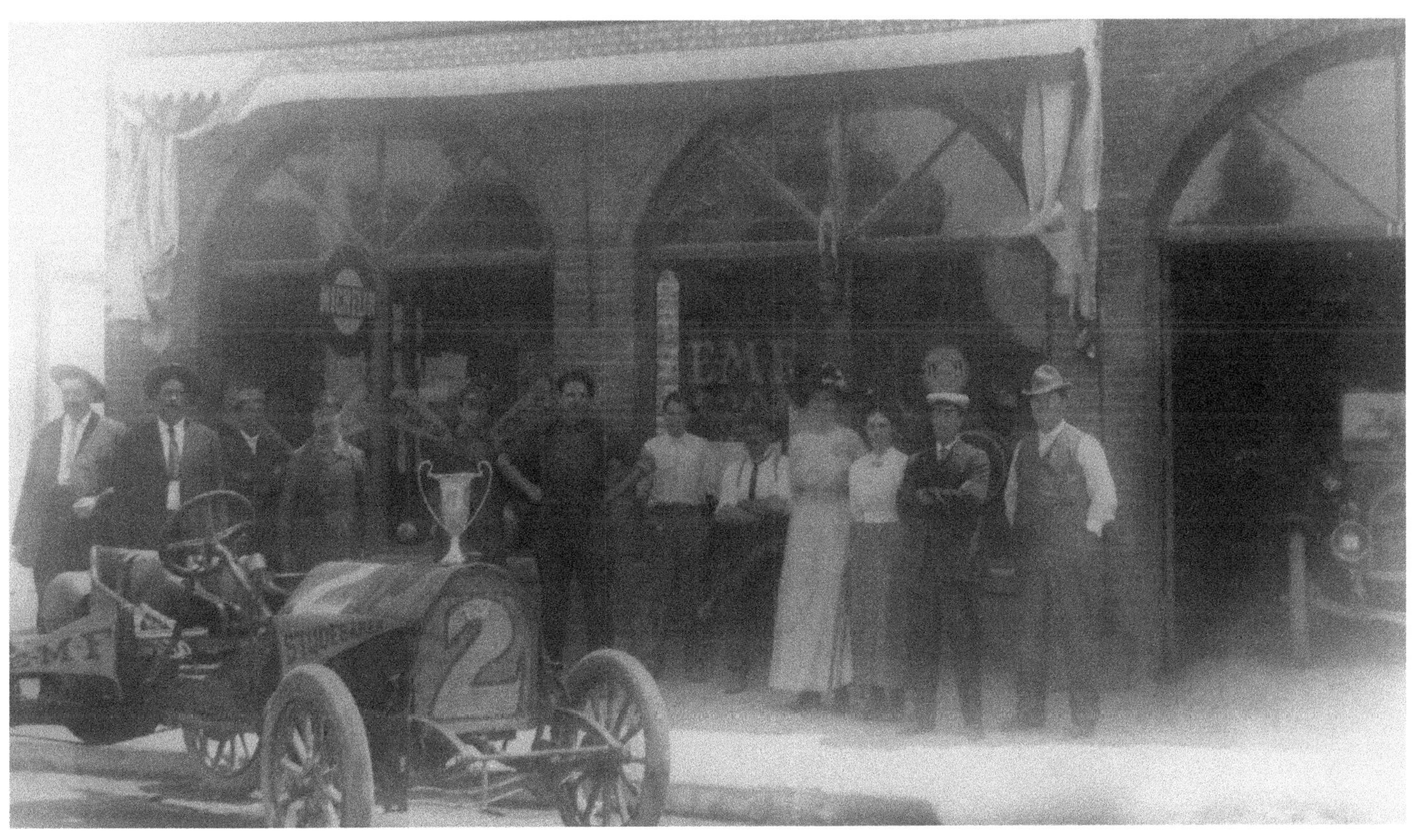

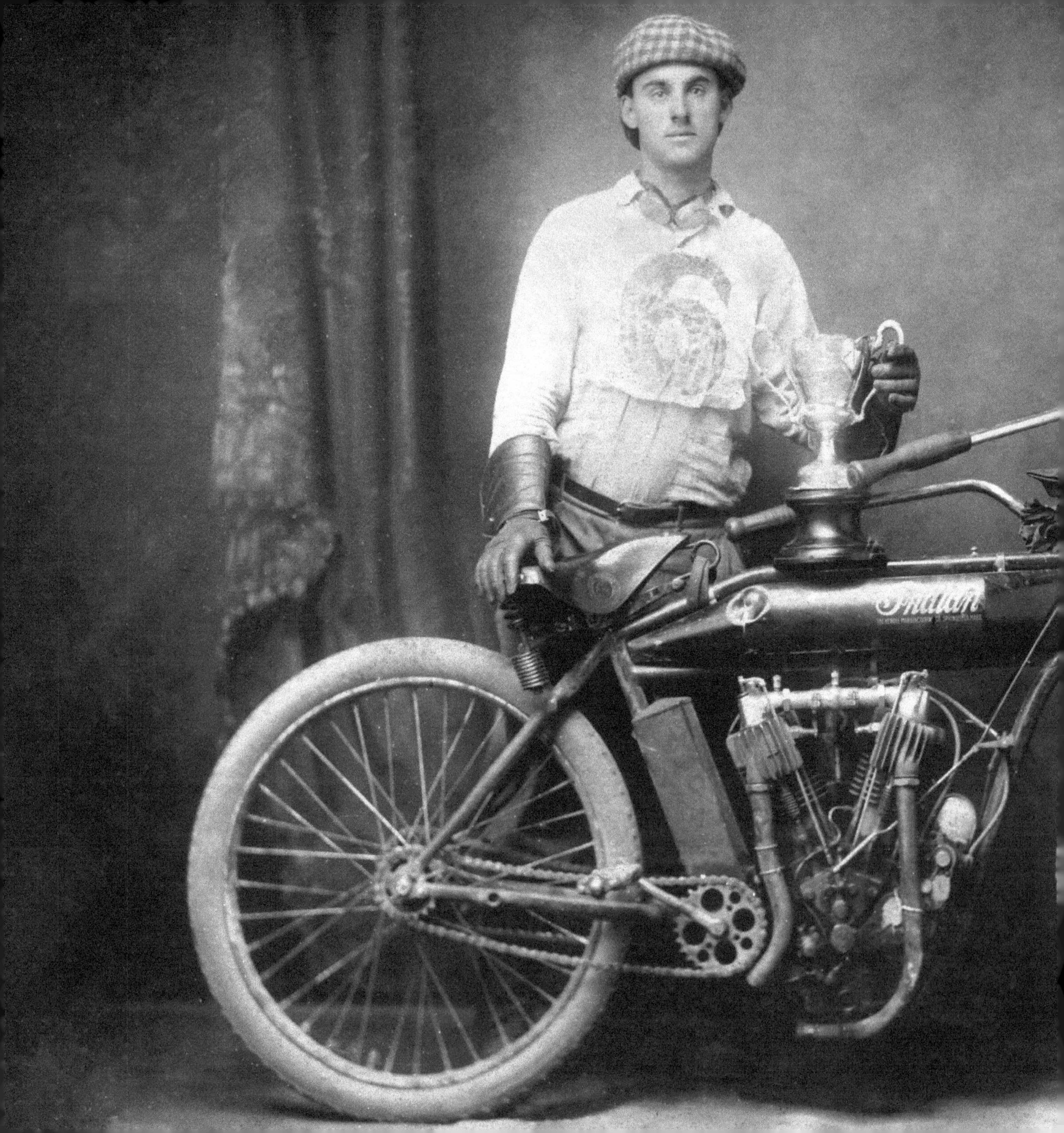
Indian

Anaheim's 1912 Fourth of July celebration included both automobile and motorcycle races in addition to the usual parades. Alfred "Butch" Bittner won his "Fine Silver Loving Cup" for completing the 20-mile motorcycle race in 24 minutes, 6 seconds. Butch is standing behind his winning 7-HP, 2-cylinder Indian Twin motorcycle.

Judge James Solomon Howard, Anaheim's popular photographer, captured this view ca. 1913 of the first building constructed in 1894 for Anaheim's First Christian Church. Located at 349 West Center Street this edifice featured two large rose windows over eight-paned stained-glass windows.

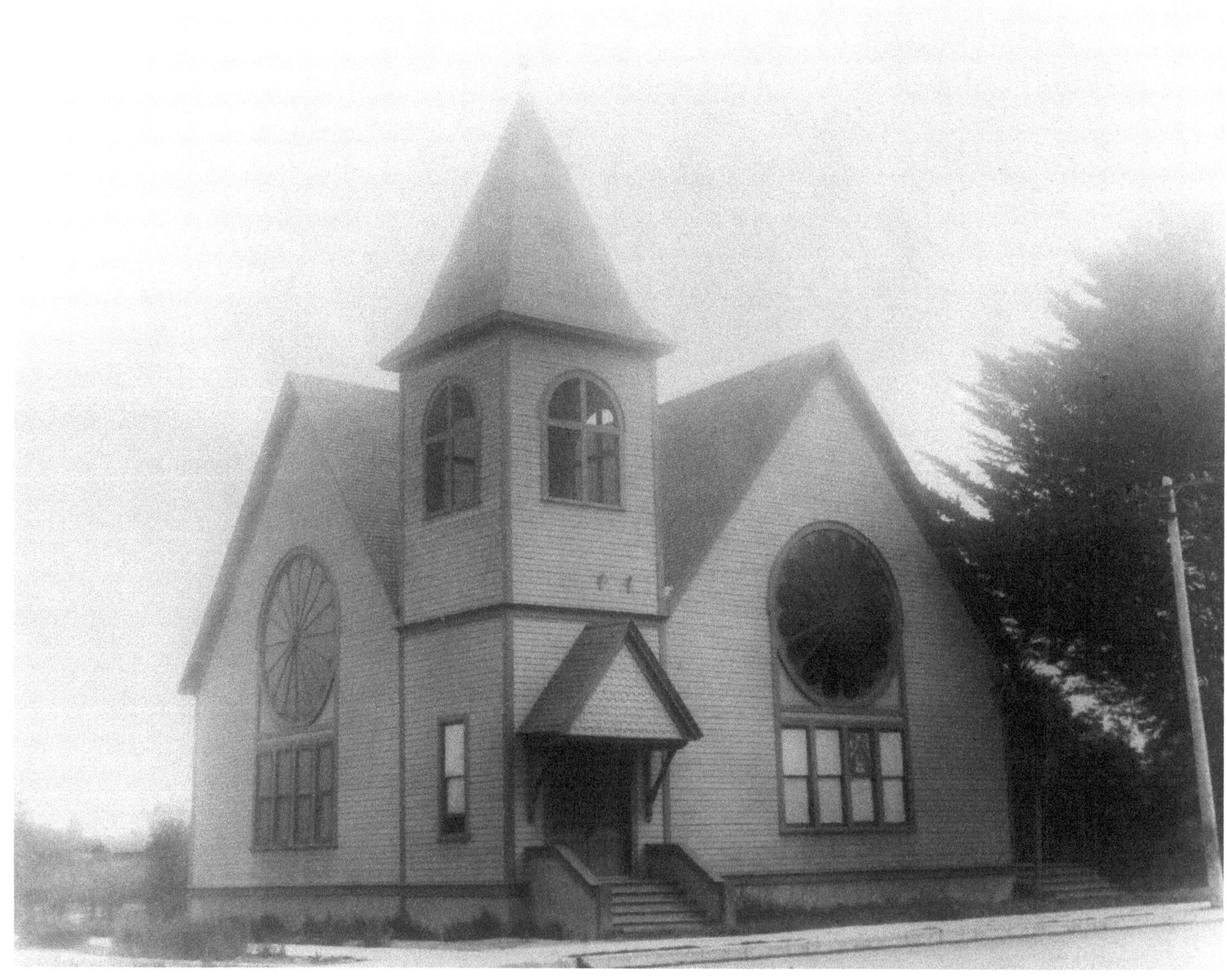

Anaheim's frugal trustees began to pave the city's streets by the mid teens, finally realizing a long-held dream of the street-side merchants. In this 1914 photograph Anaheim's city fathers are showing off the city's new Elgin Motor Sweeper in front of City Hall. From left to right are Bill Sackett, Mayor John Cook, Councilman John Brunsworth, and Charles Mann. Bud Sackett, Street Superintendent, is at the controls and Bill Stark is sitting forward.

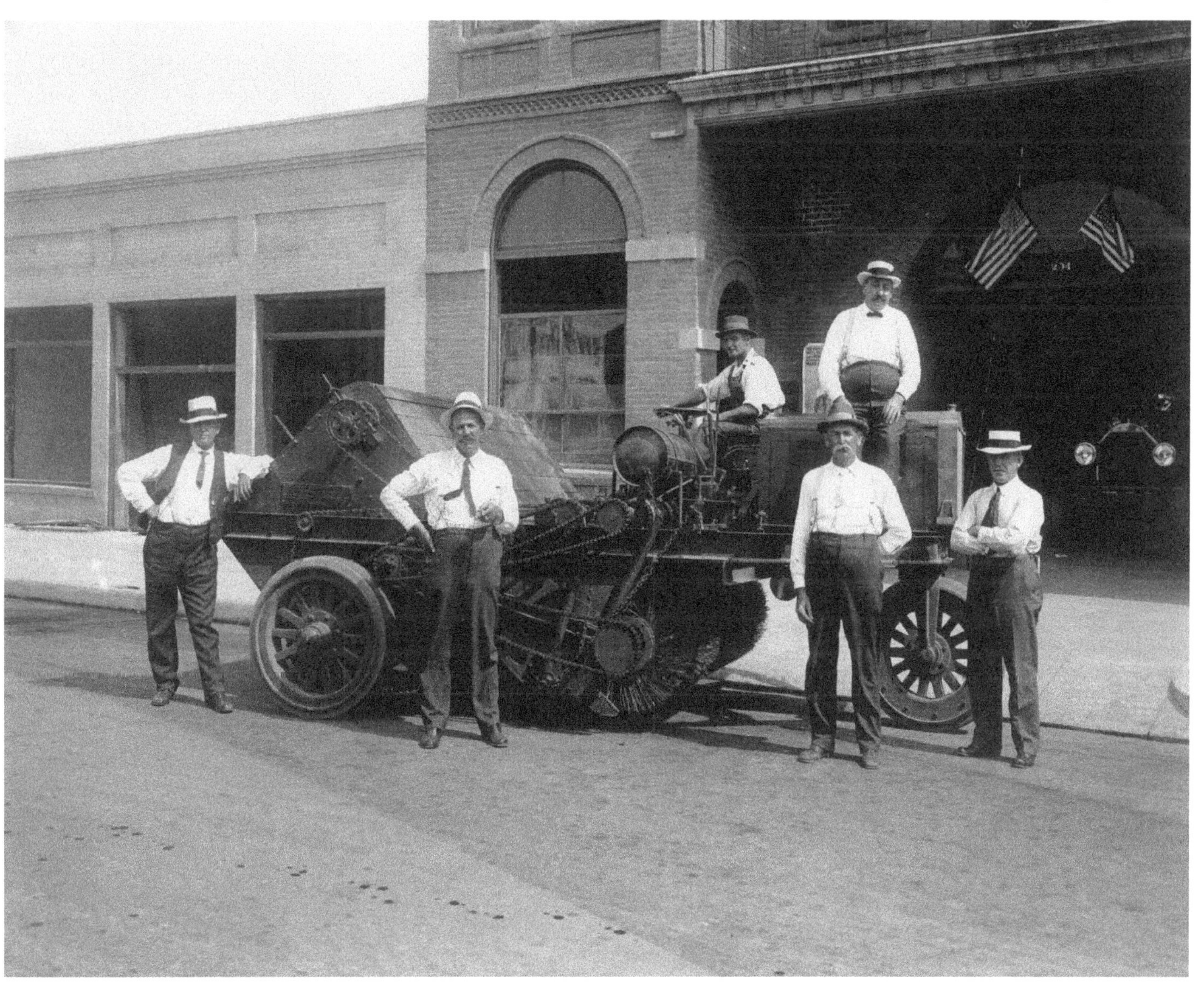

A new 1914 Studebaker automobile is decorated for Anaheim's carnival parade. The revelers in the car are left to right: (front seat) Lucy Ziegler Anderson and driver Arthur Ackerman; (back seats) Henrietta Schindler Sims, Sadie Friend, Elsie Mieneke Schindler, and Olivia Smith.

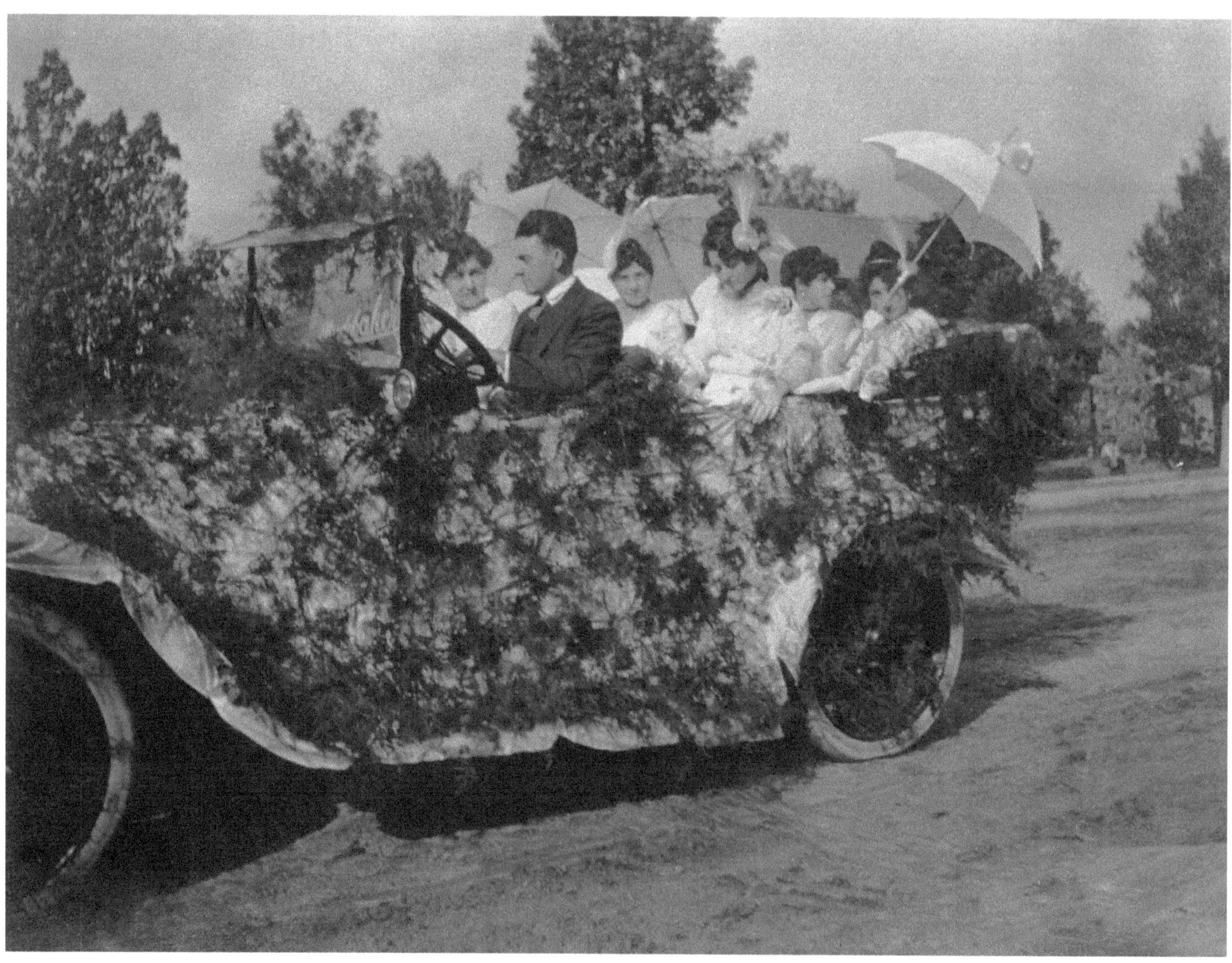

With the advent of paved streets, the pollution emitted by horse-powered transport was ever the more conspicuous. Fritz Stolt, here at work on East Center Street ca. 1914, was employed by the City of Anaheim to keep the thoroughfares free of the hazard.

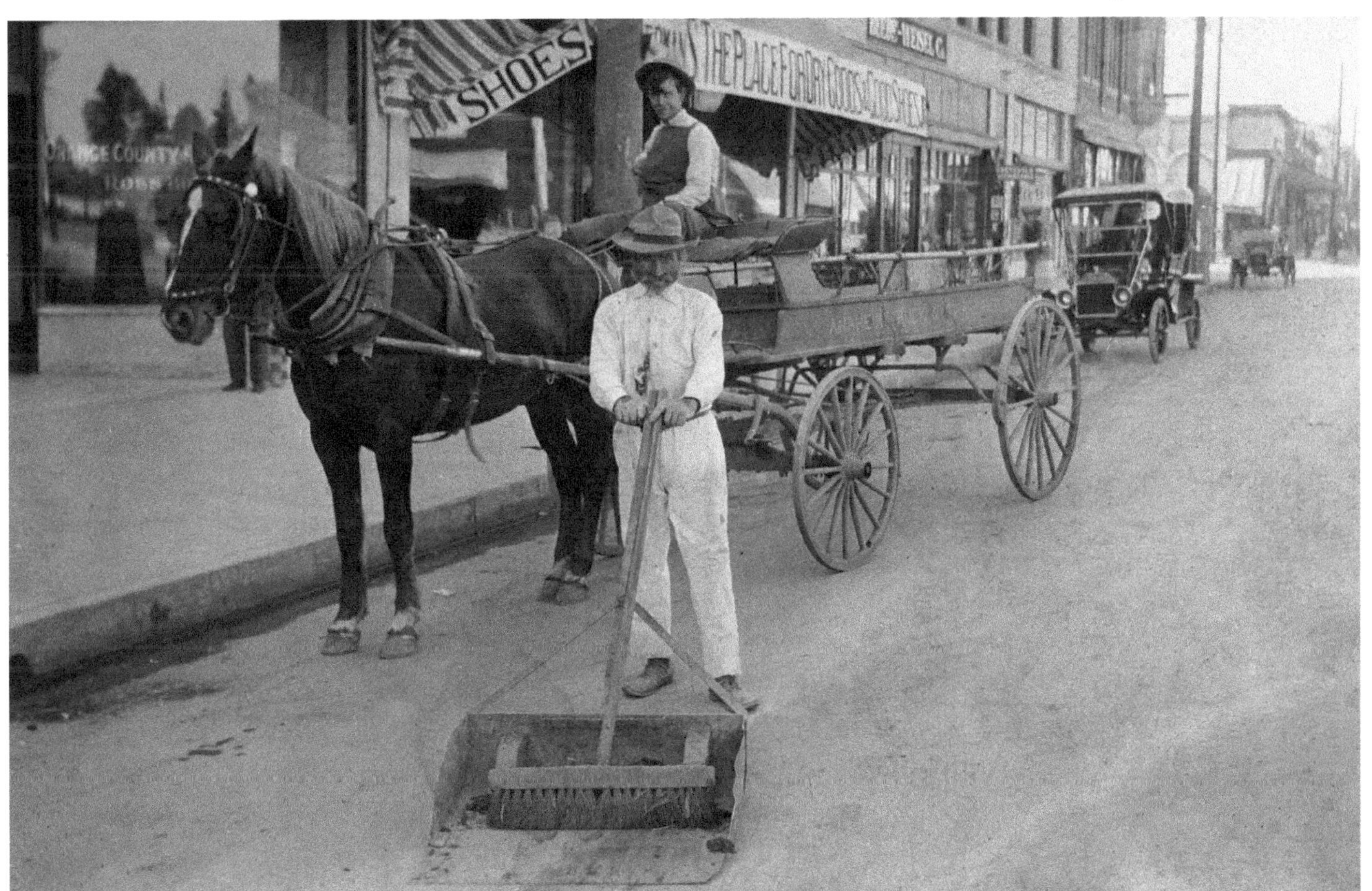

Morris Wampler Martenet, Sr., started his hardware store in downtown Anaheim in 1910. This 1915 view shows the interior of the store at 125 West Center Street. Martenet poses in the background at right, behind a row of wood-burning stoves. His store was known as the place to buy the heavy stoves and other hardware needs the growing town required. Martenet's son Morris "Morrie" Martenet, Jr., later inherited the business and served as a city councilman from 1932 through 1942.

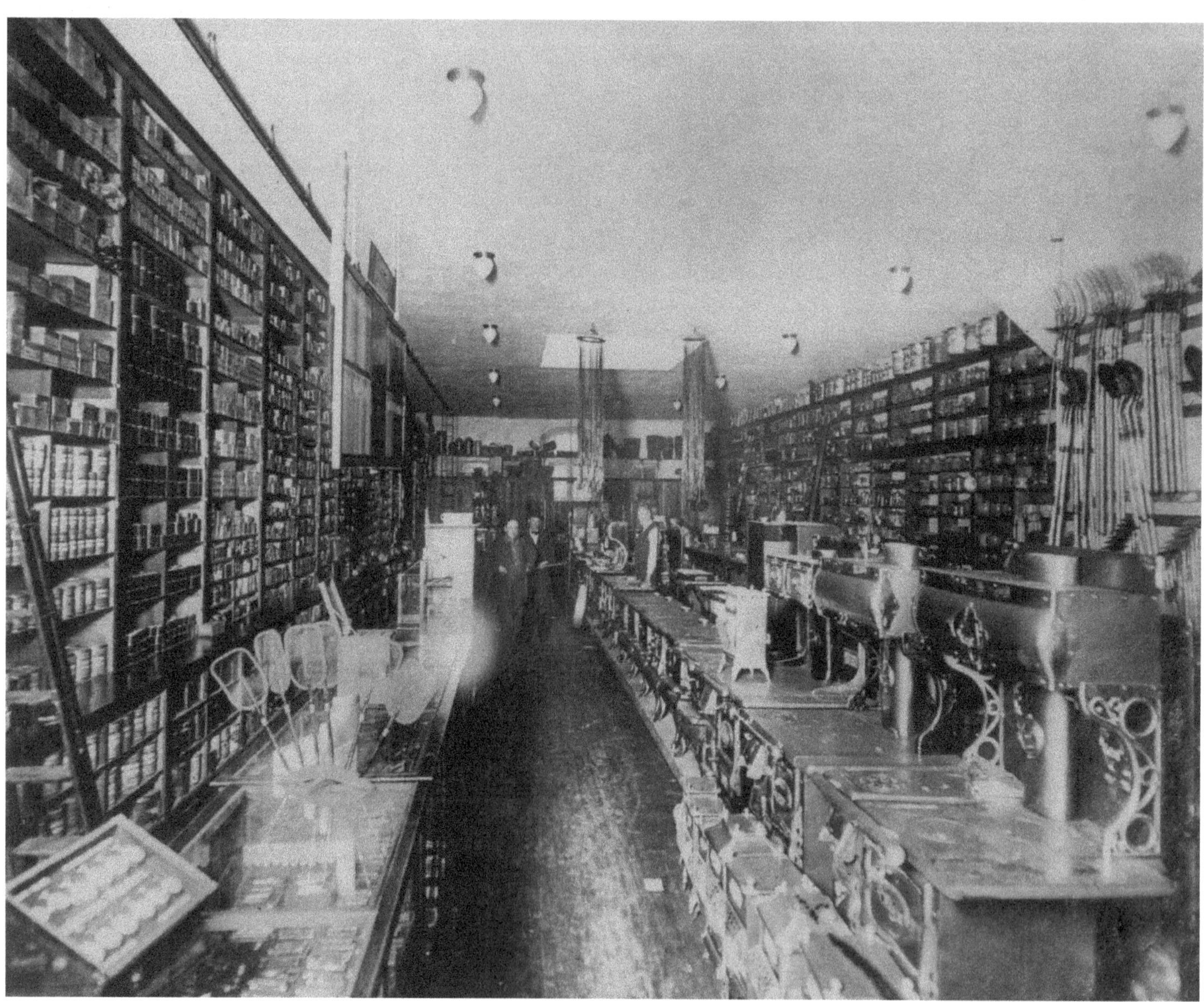

Anaheim's Salem Evangelical Church was located at 400-402 West Center Street in 1915. This impressive brick and stucco structure served the congregation into the mid twentieth century.

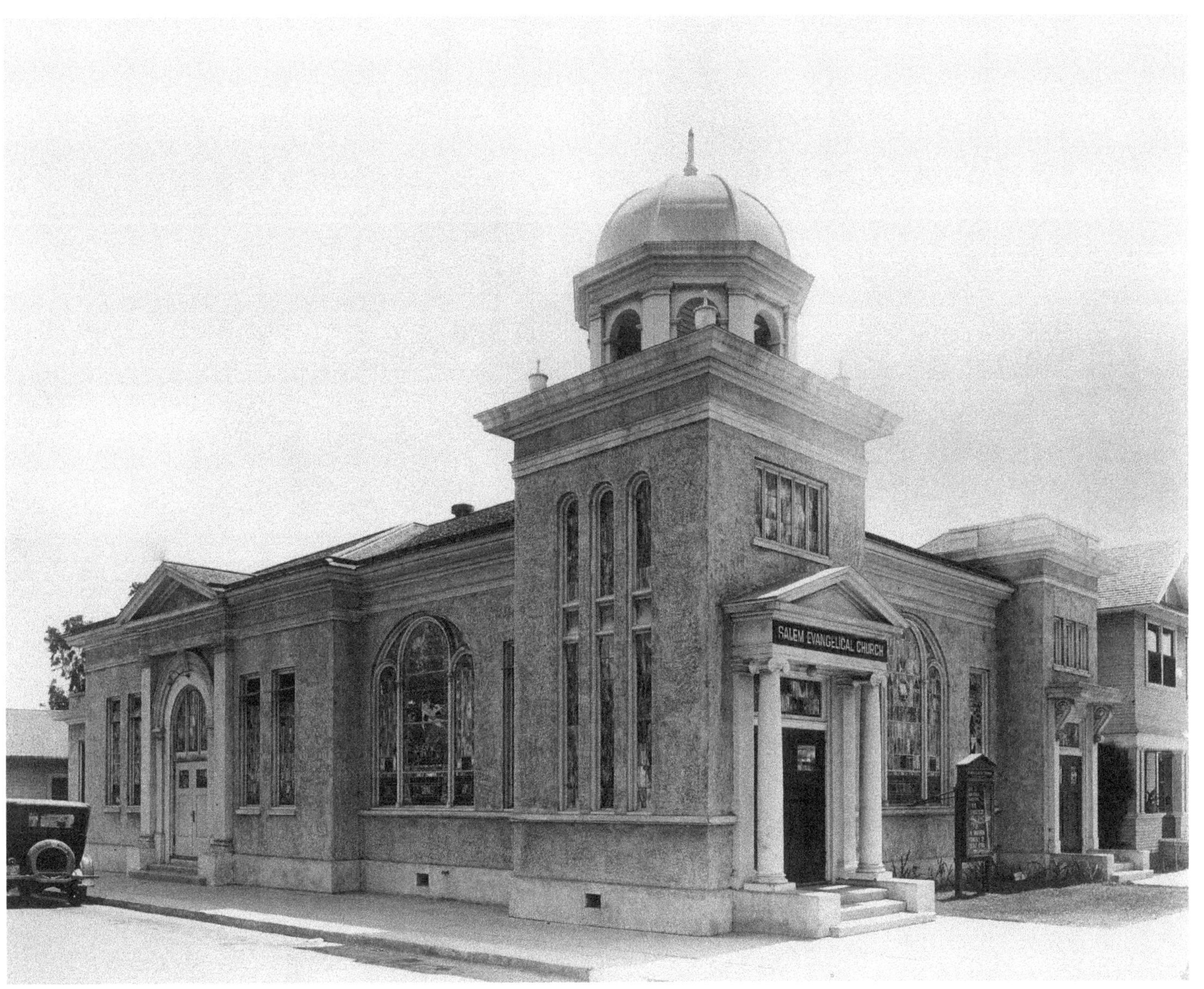

After Anaheim lost its grape industry in the late 1880s to blight, the propagation of the Valencia orange became the town's most important concern. The Anaheim chamber of commerce took every opportunity to promote Anaheim as the "Capital of the Valencia Orange Empire." In this 1915 view, two boosters are promoting "Anaheim California, Home of the Finest Sunkist Valencia Oranges."

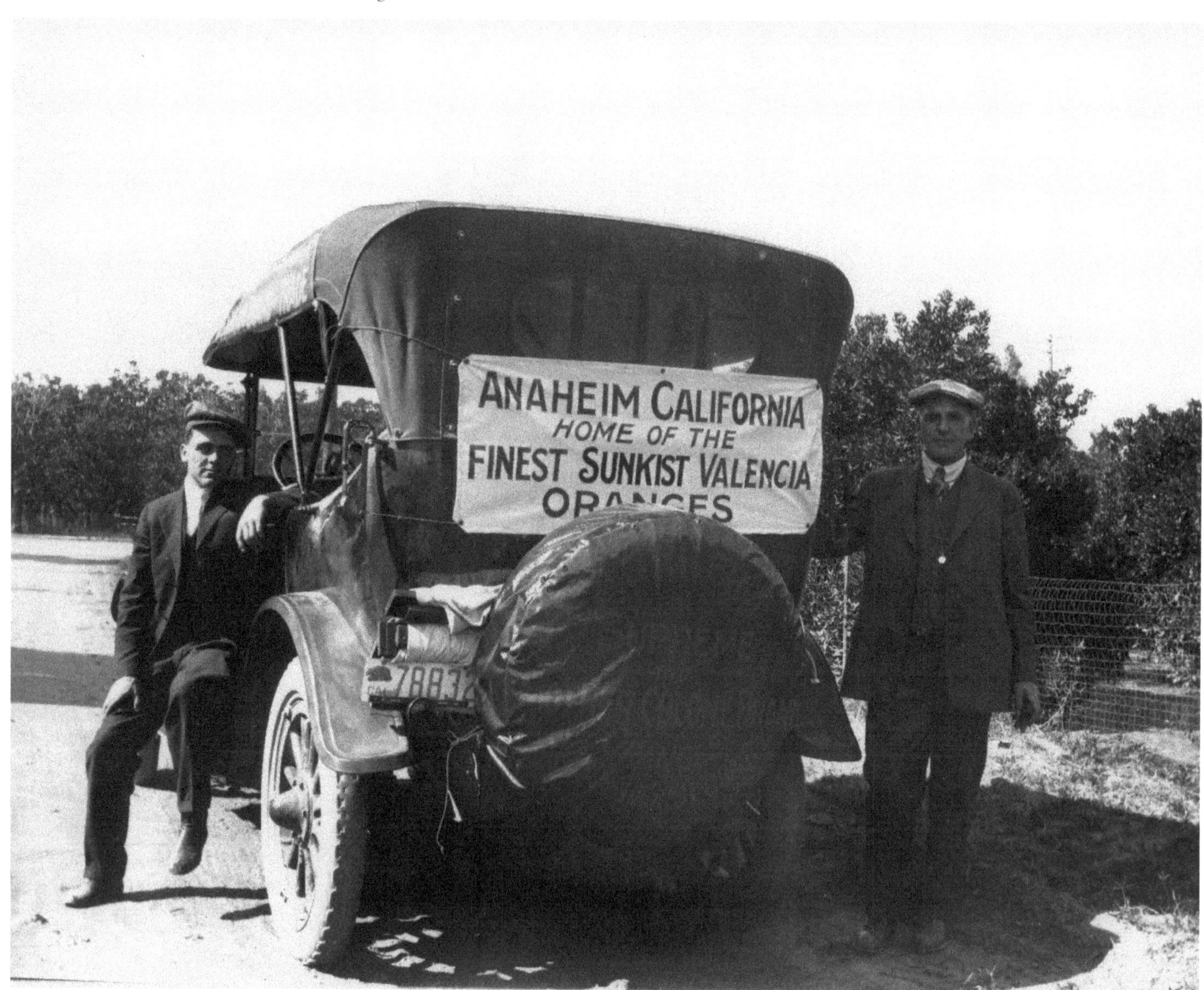

The 1915 Anaheim Central School faculty has boarded a truck for a picnic, presumably to Orange County Park (now Irvine Park), a regular destination for such relaxing events.

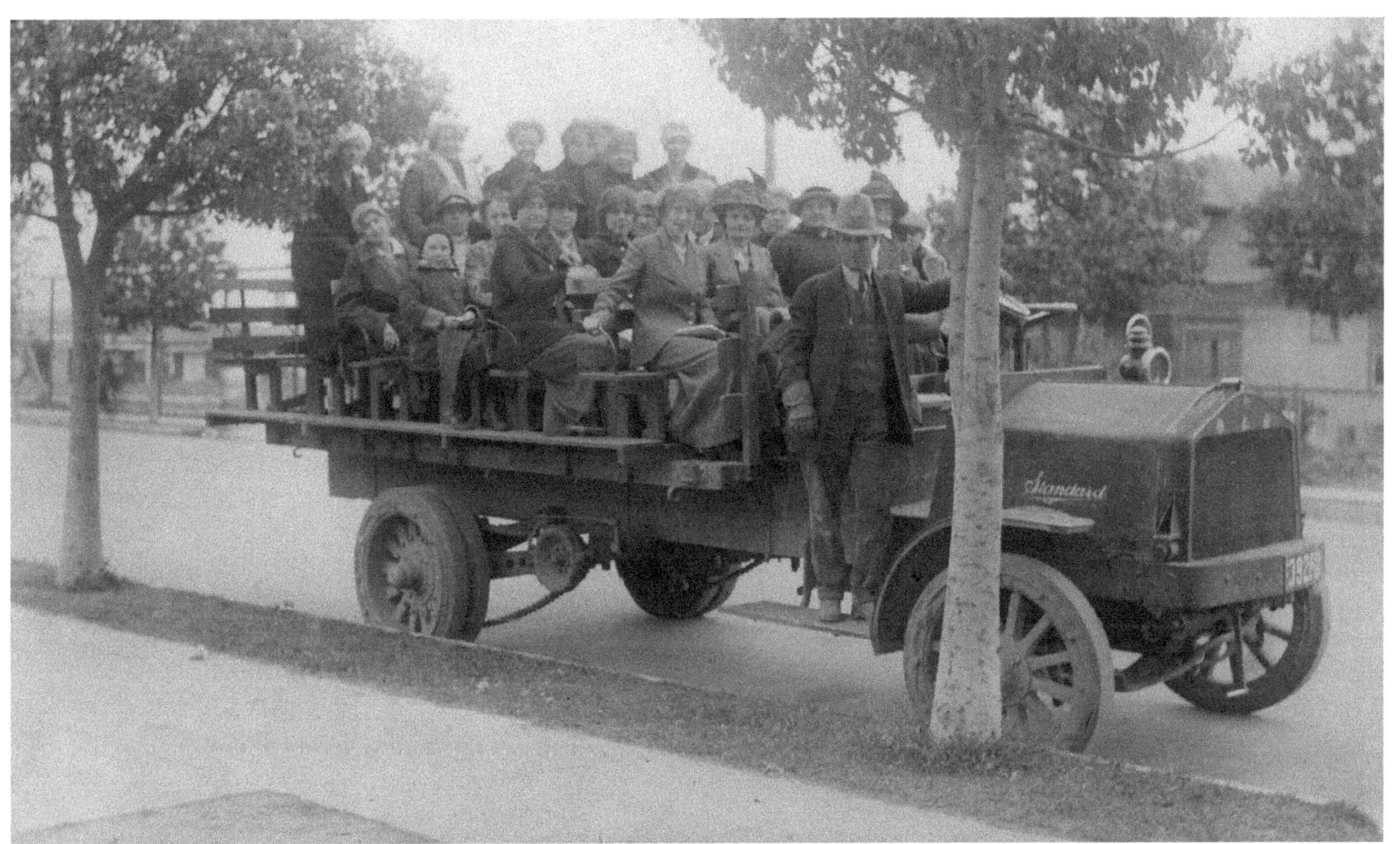

Ensconced in his stylish roadster, John Dwyer and his cousin Bee Conner are taking in the sights at Anaheim Landing (now Seal Beach) ca. 1915.

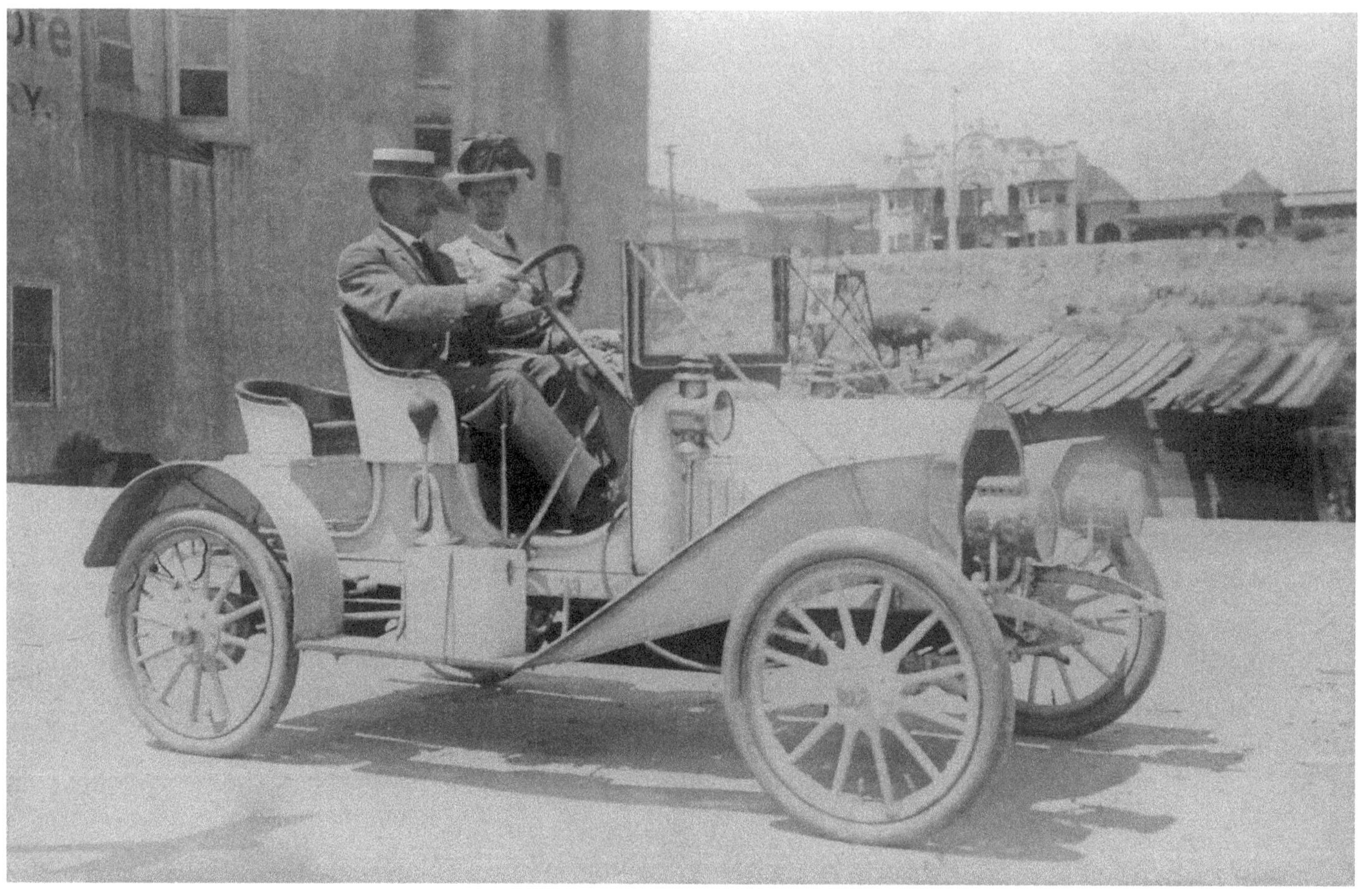

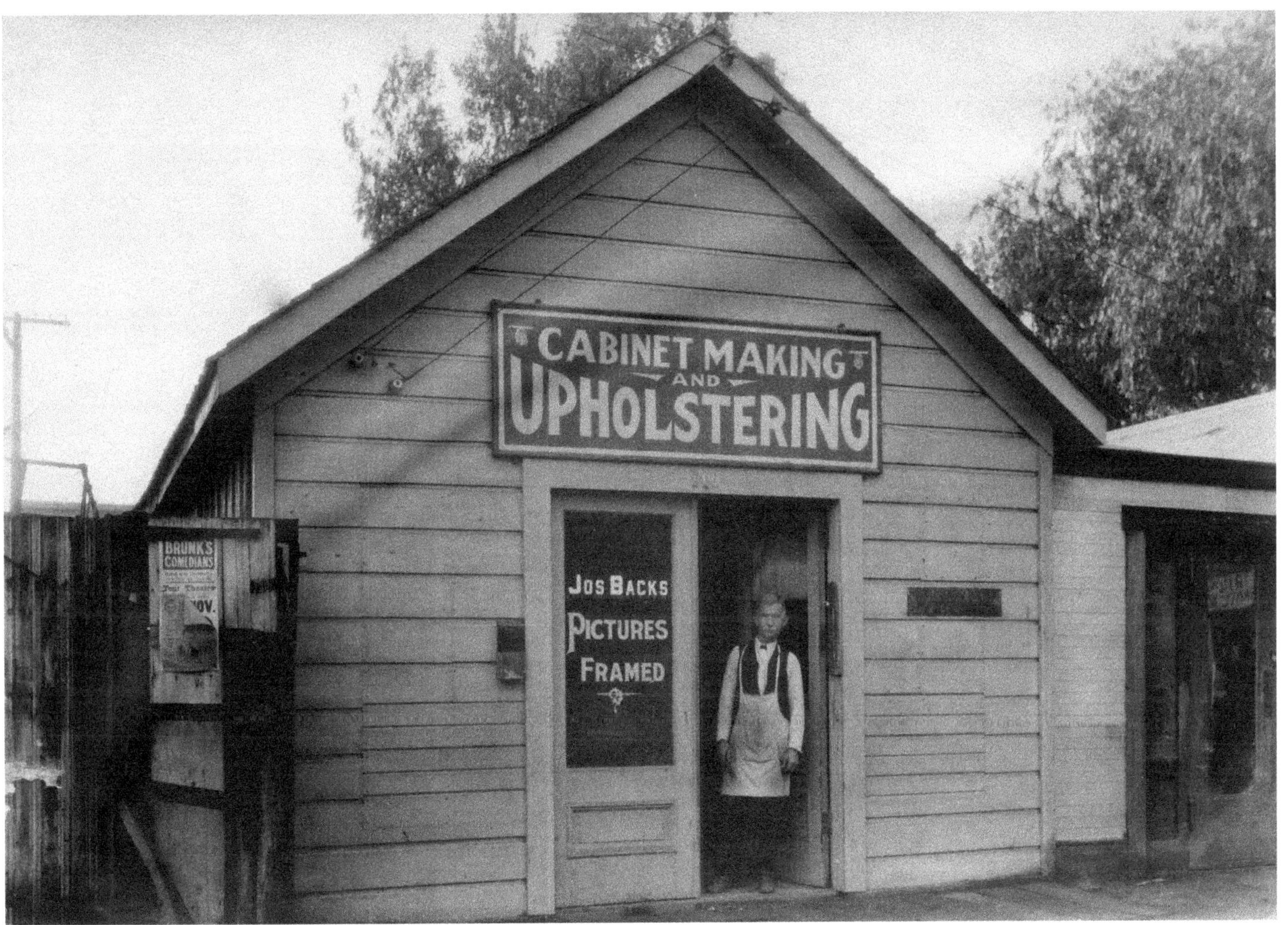

Joseph Backs is seen in the doorway of his upholstery shop at 112 West Chartres in this view from ca. 1915. Joseph's brother Frederick was the town's undertaker.

The Ingram Brothers Ford Motor Cars Garage and Sales Room was located at 228 North Los Angeles Street (now Anaheim Blvd.) in 1916. A variety of models are advertised from $665 to $765. By this time, the horse and buggy was losing out, although citizens of lesser means would keep their stables for some years to come.

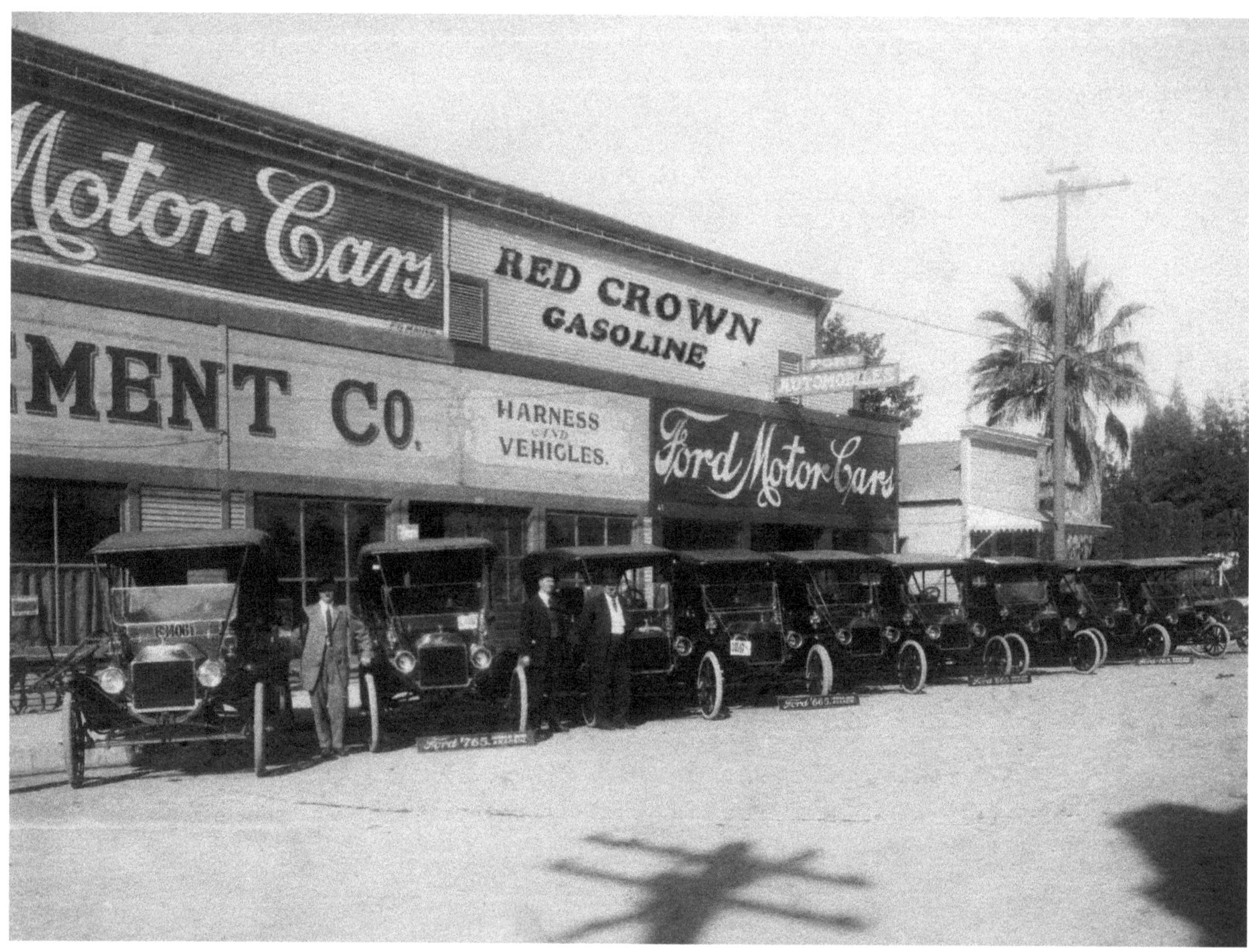

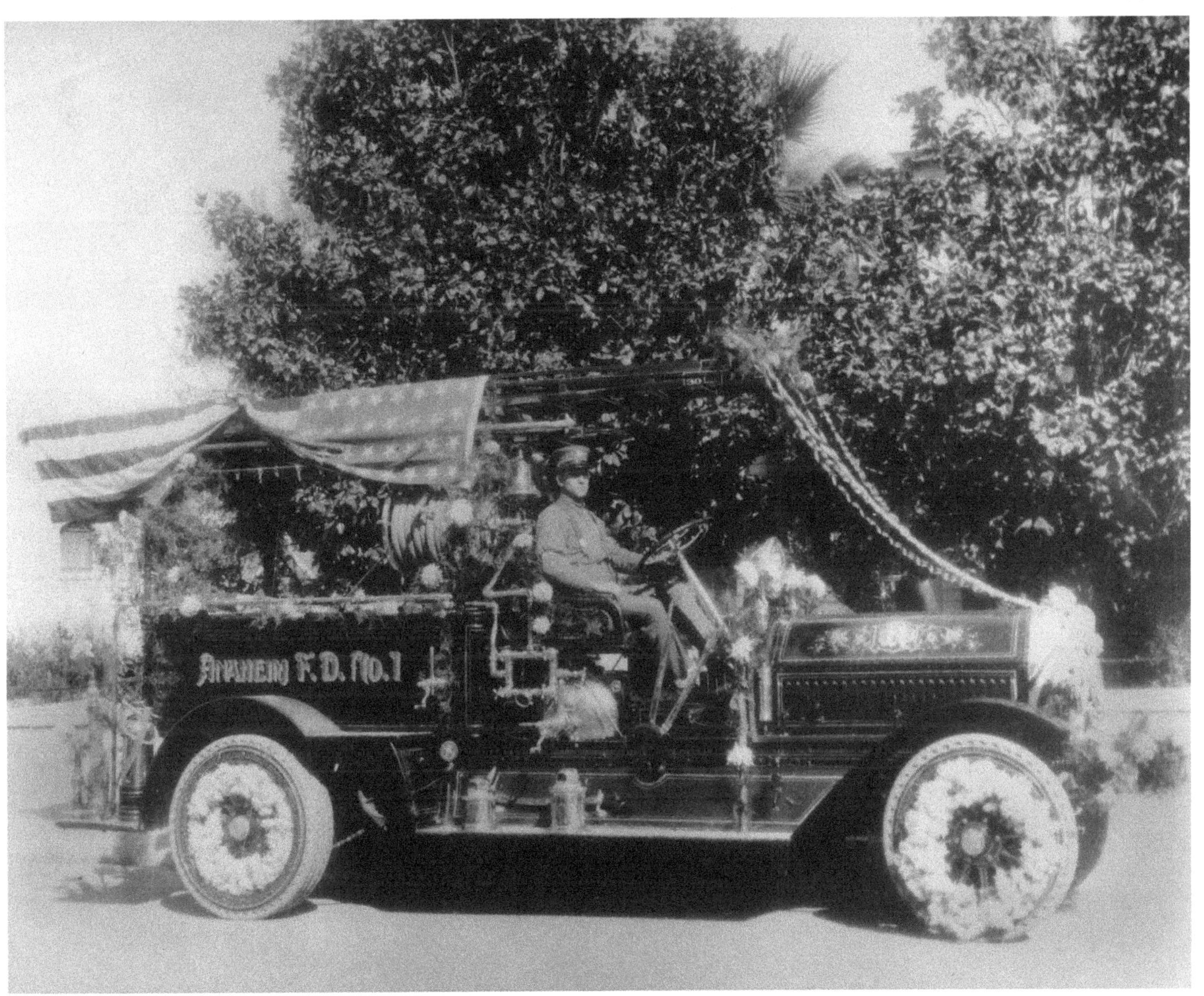

Conrad "Cooney" Mauerhan is seen driving the Anaheim fire department's truck No. 1 in the Fourth of July parade, ca. 1916. Anaheim took delivery of this modern pumper in 1915, replacing the early hose cart the town's "Fire Laddies" used for many years.

High water is seen in the West Anaheim area during the 1916 flood. The Santa Ana River, Anaheim's main source of irrigation water, was frequently a dry, sandy waste but would often flood during a long rainy season. This view taken at the corner of Magnolia and Lincoln (the county road west of Anaheim's downtown) reveals the expanse of the water in the area. Another, more devastating flood would arrive in Anaheim in 22 years.

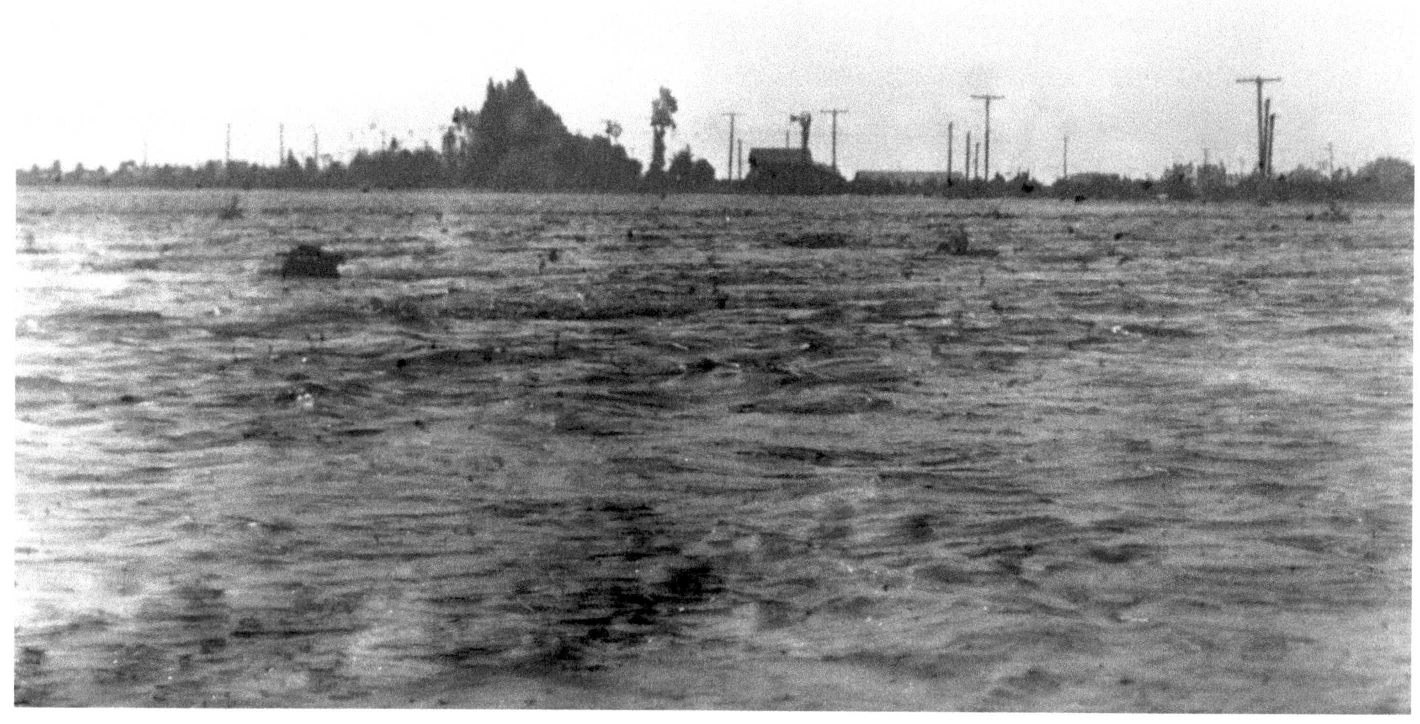

The Anaheim Cemetery, the first public cemetery in Orange County, was established by the Los Angeles Vineyard Society in 1866. Anaheim's F. A. Hartman, nephew of original colonist Theodore Reiser, donated this Pioneer Memorial Archway in 1917, which marked the original entrance off Center Street. At this time "Gottes Acker" (God's Acre) was in very poor condition; Hartman offered the arch as an incentive for other community leaders to restore the important Anaheim site.

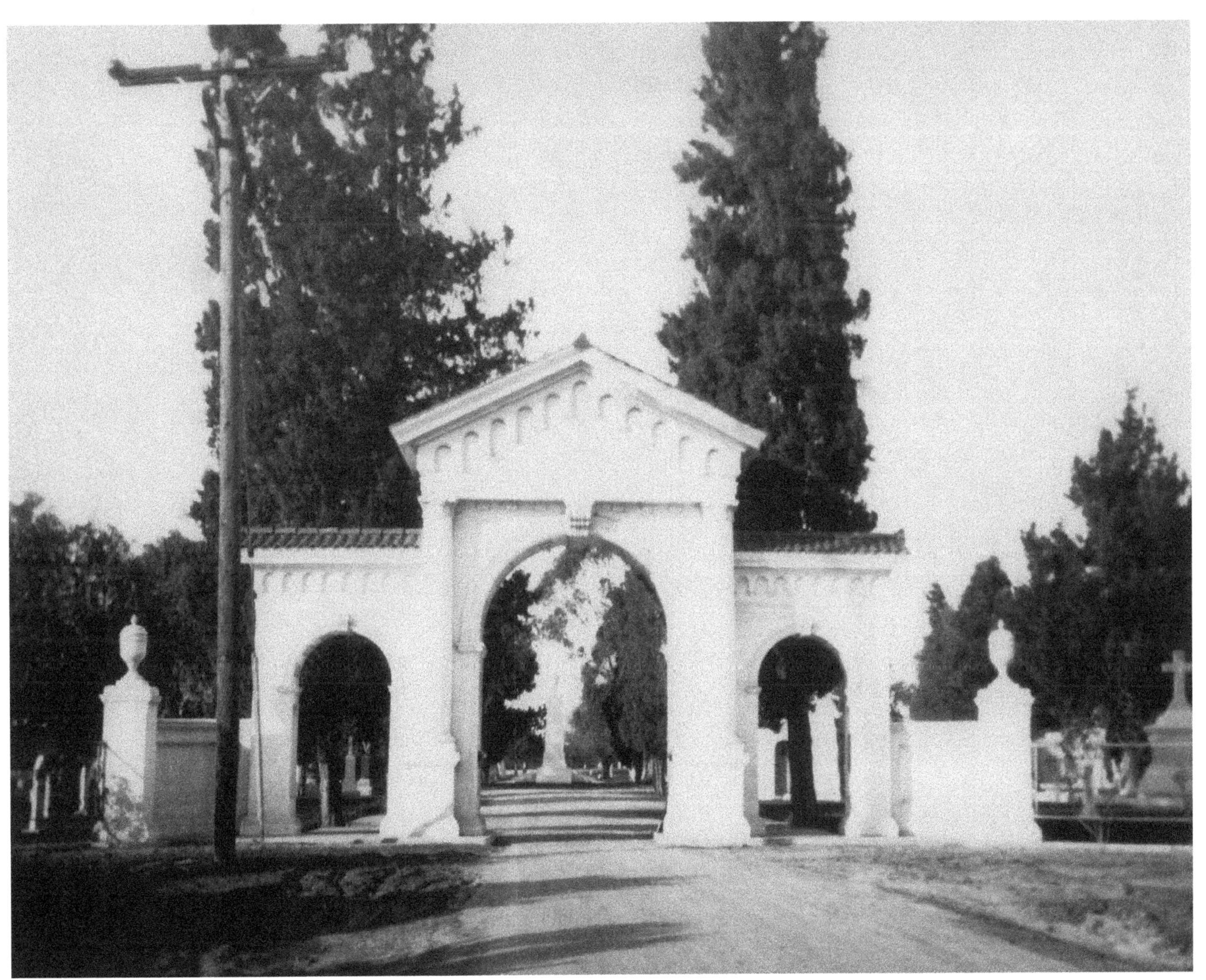

At the Anaheim Steam Laundry employees pose for the camera on a portrait day in 1917. Located at 412 South Lemon Street, the two-story building was a landmark for many years. It was sold to the Theodore Brothers in 1918, who constructed a new building, which later burned.

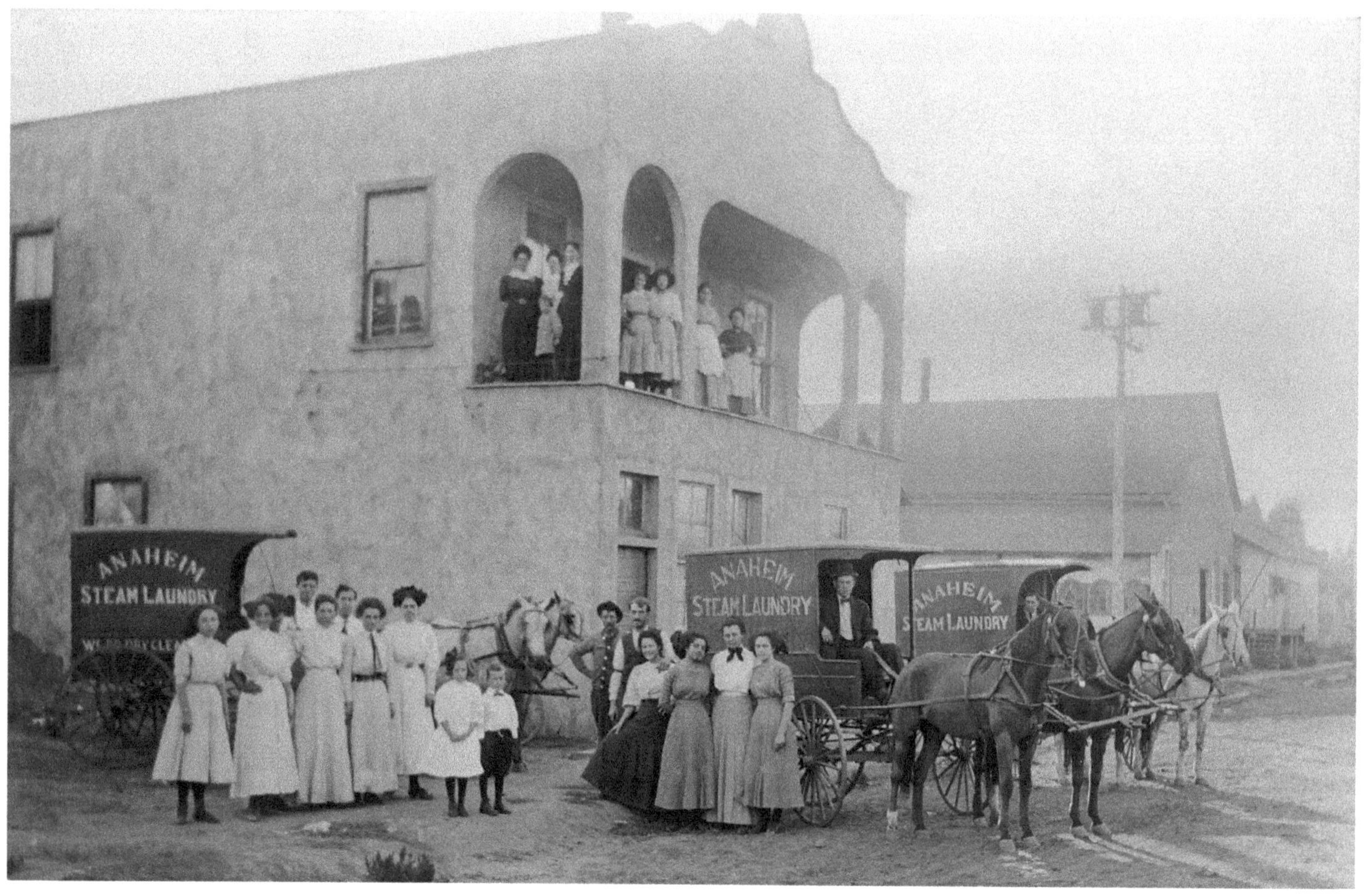

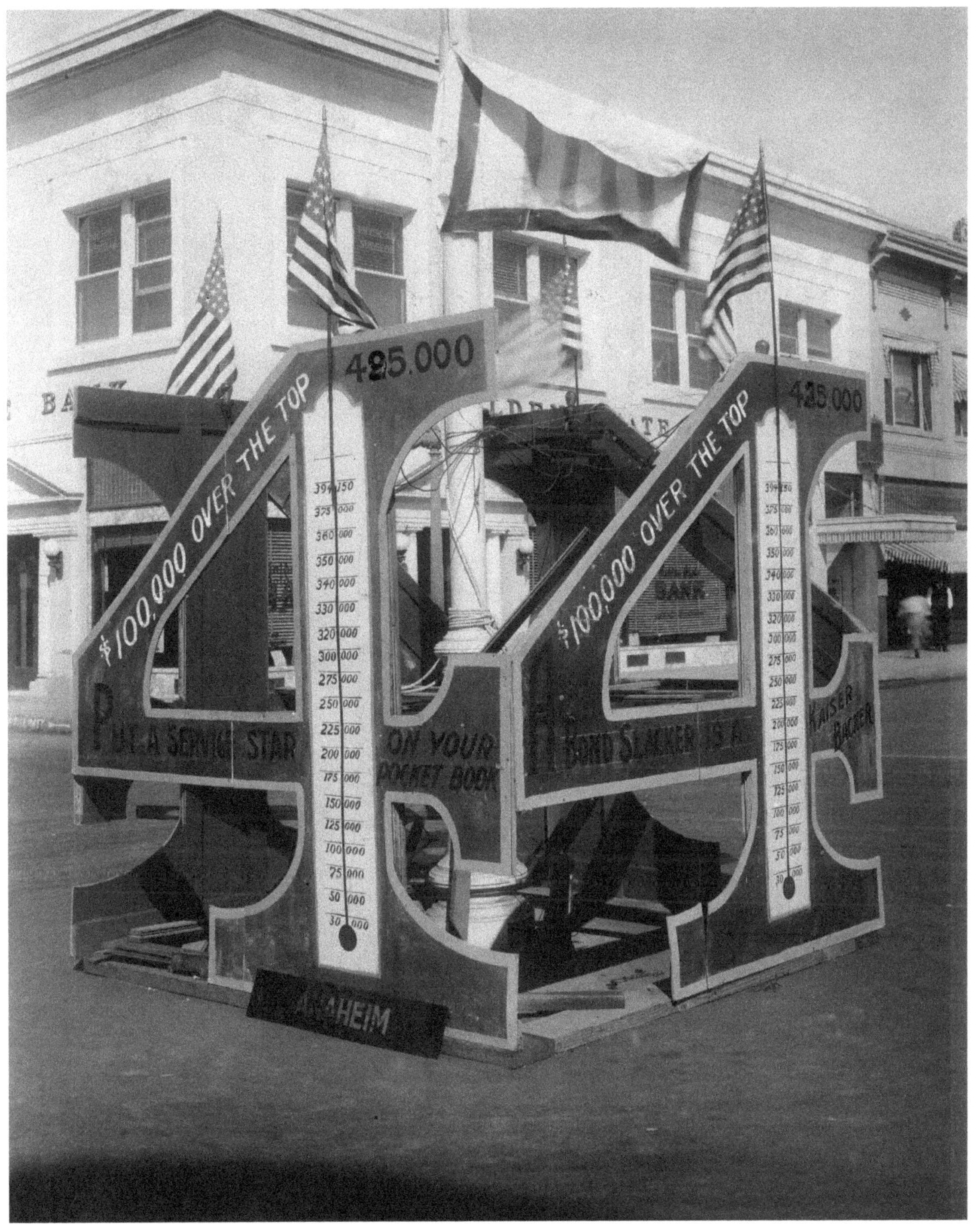

During World War I, the patriotic citizens of Anaheim contributed $425,000 to the fourth Liberty Bond Drive, $100,000 more than the goal. This four-sided sign was placed at Anaheim's main intersection of Center and Los Angeles streets.

Soshi Kusumoto was the owner of a barbershop in 1918 Anaheim. His wife, Ito, ran a small seamstress shop. Although founded by German immigrants, Anaheim had a significant Asian population that also contributed to the growth and success of the community.

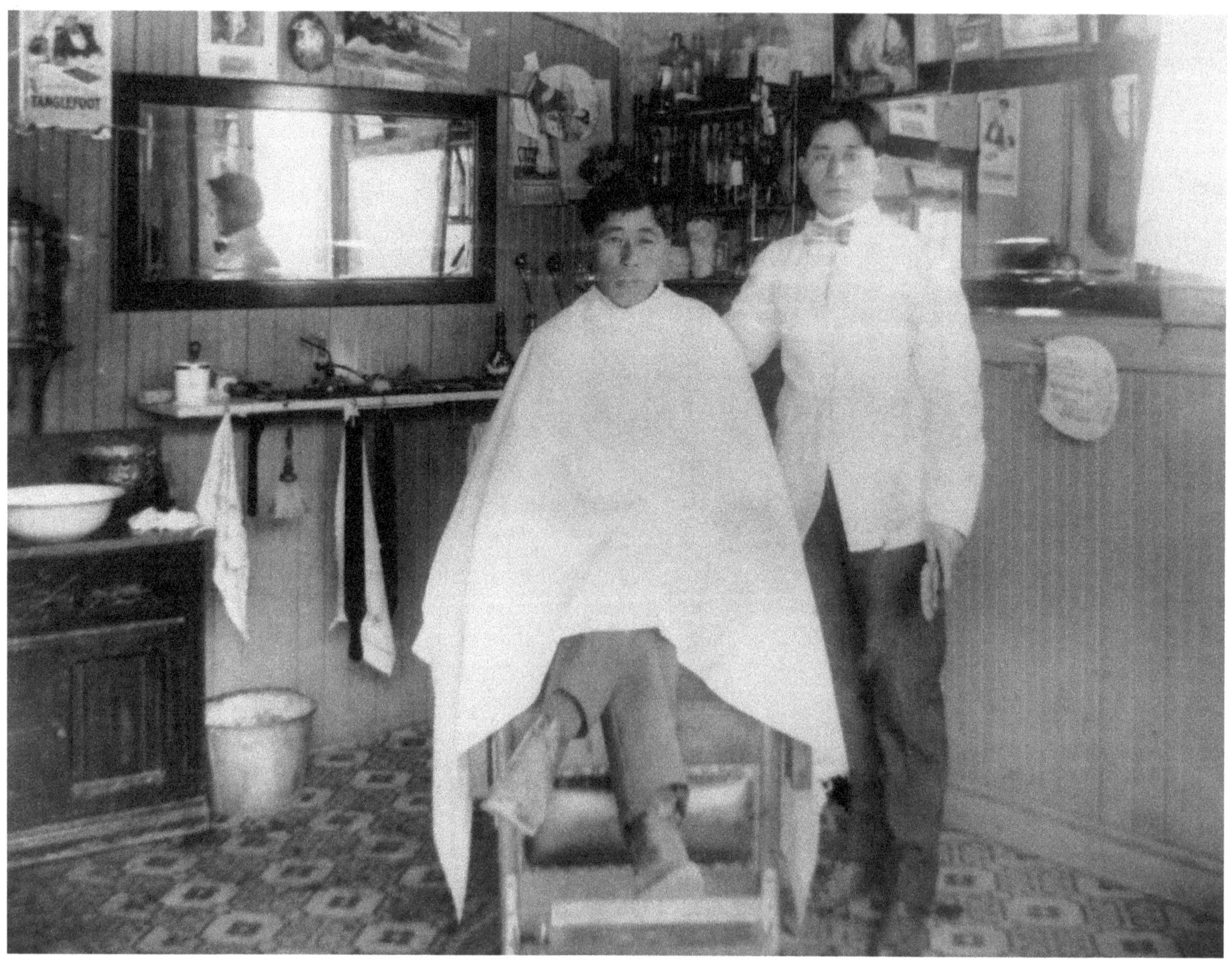

Lee's Service Station at 604 East Center Street was the first individually owned service station in Anaheim. Built and operated by Lee Geiselman, it featured Ventura Gasoline. Here in 1920 (left to right) are Ralph Maynard, Harold Ritchie, and the proprietor, Lee Geiselman.

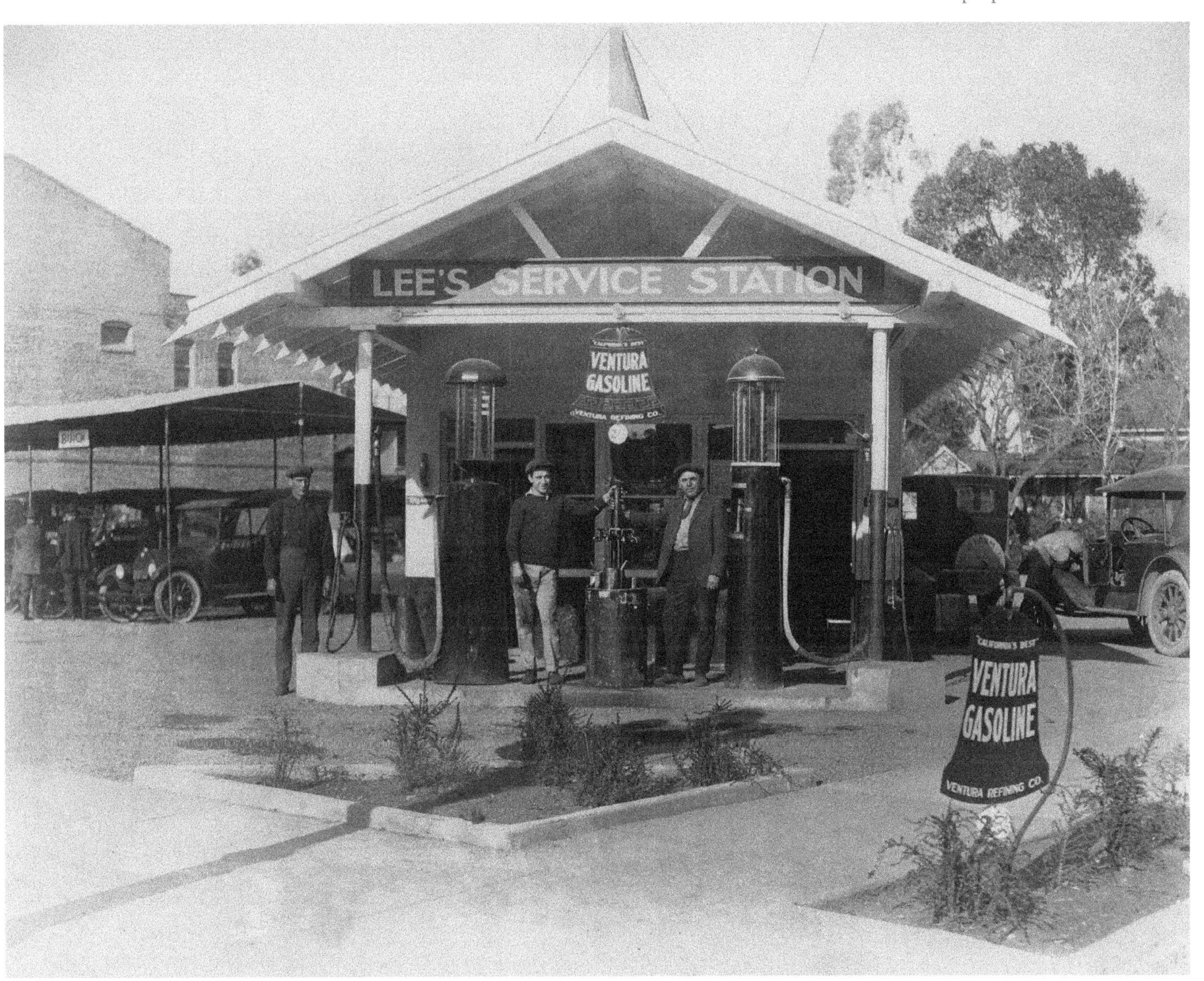

Following Spread: The May 30, early 1920s, Memorial Day parade float features a Salvation Army hut in the Argonne Forest. A number of Anaheim boys had seen service overseas in "the War to End All Wars" and this float was very meaningful.

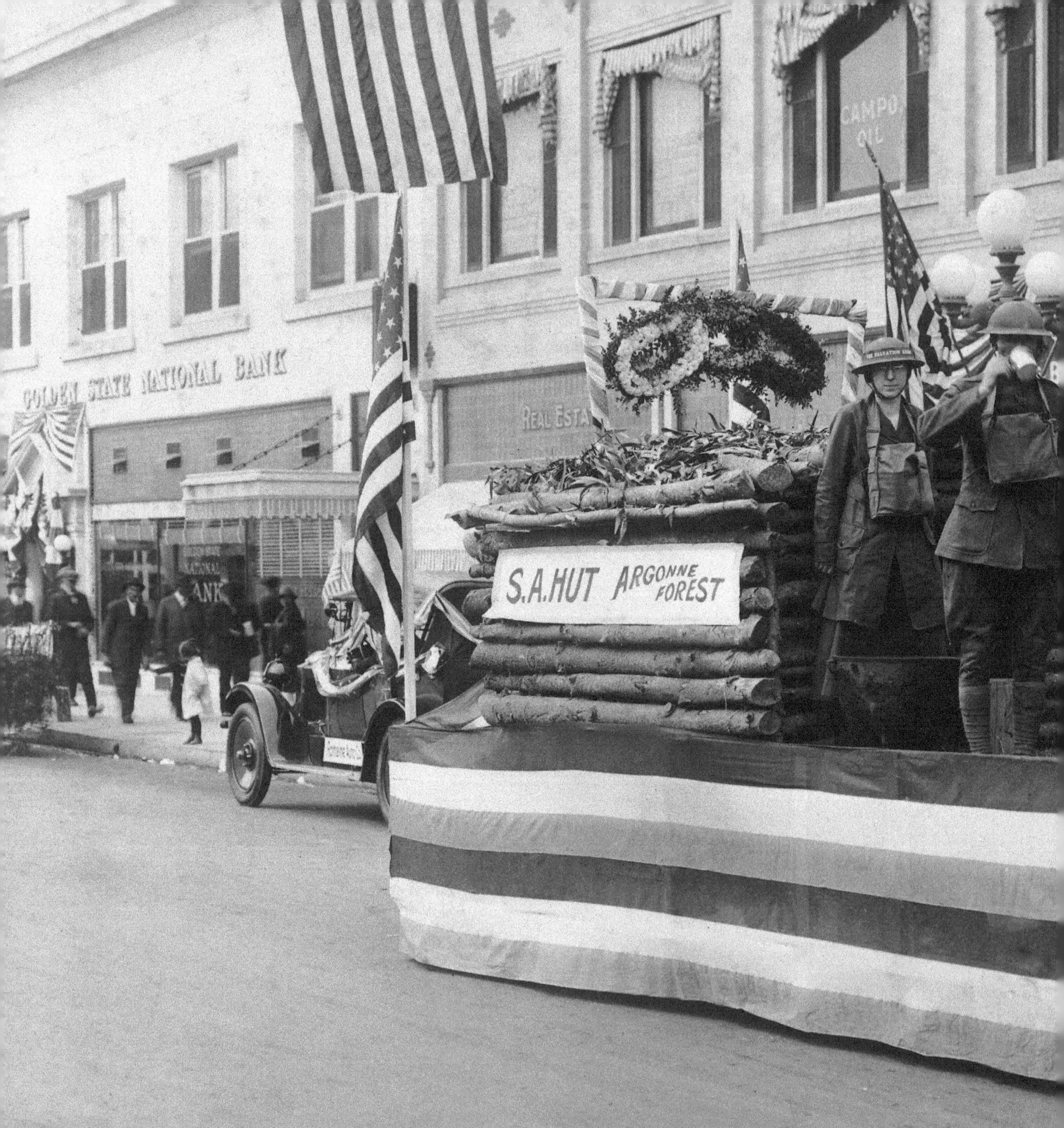
GOLDEN STATE NATIONAL BANK
CAMPO OIL
S.A.HUT ARGONNE FOREST

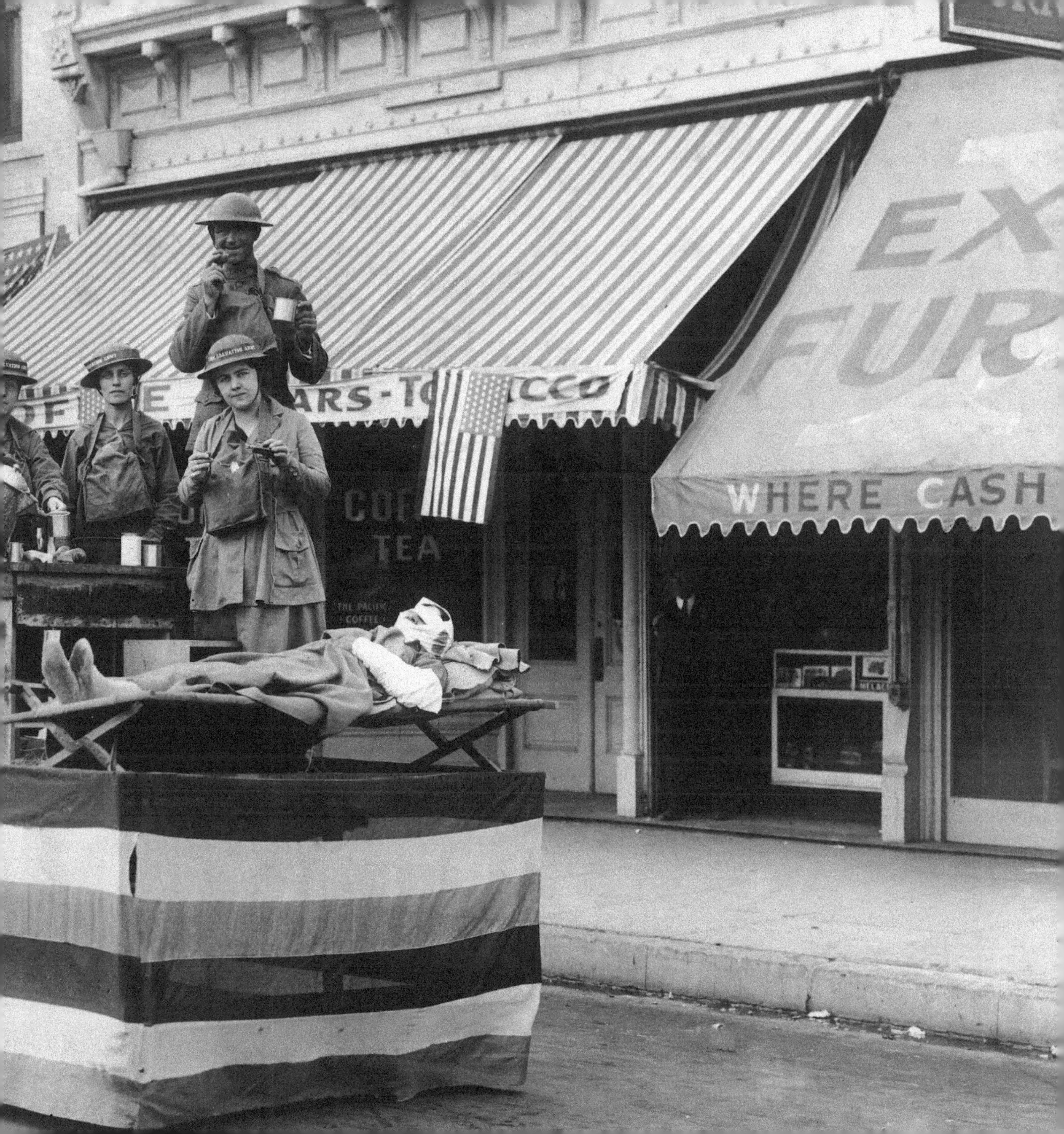
TEA
WHERE CASH

The marquee of the California Theater at 231 West Center Street announces a "World Premier Tonight Only" of the Los Angeles Orpheum's popular vaudeville act, April 11, 1923. Silent screen star Norma Talmadge was also starring in the *Voice from the Minaret* the same week.

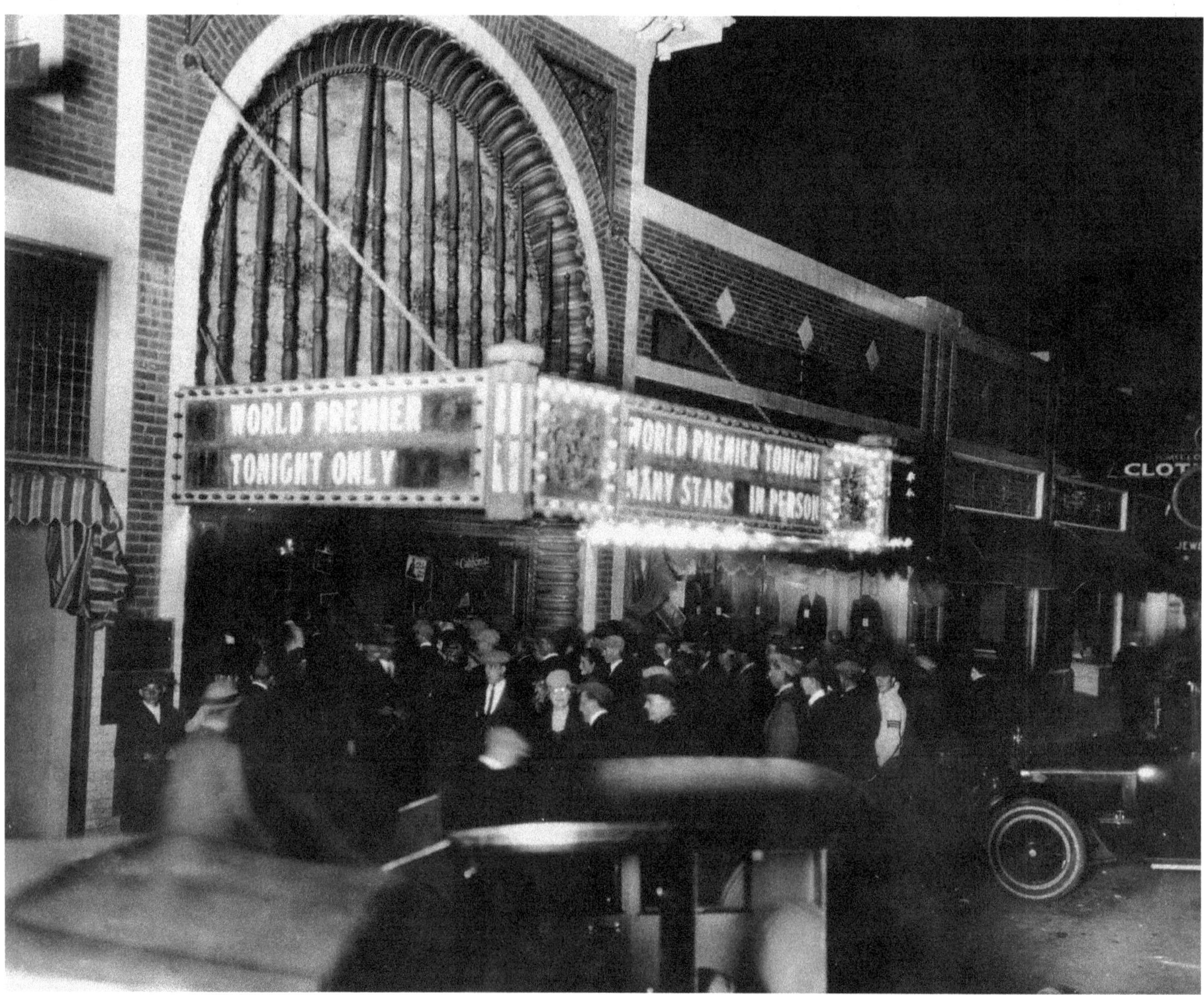

The Gerrard Brothers & Hanson Grocery Store was located at 249 East Center Street at North Emily Street. This store opened in 1923, before the partnership was incorporated as Alpha Beta Markets. Lars Hanson was manager of the chain's Anaheim store No. 12.

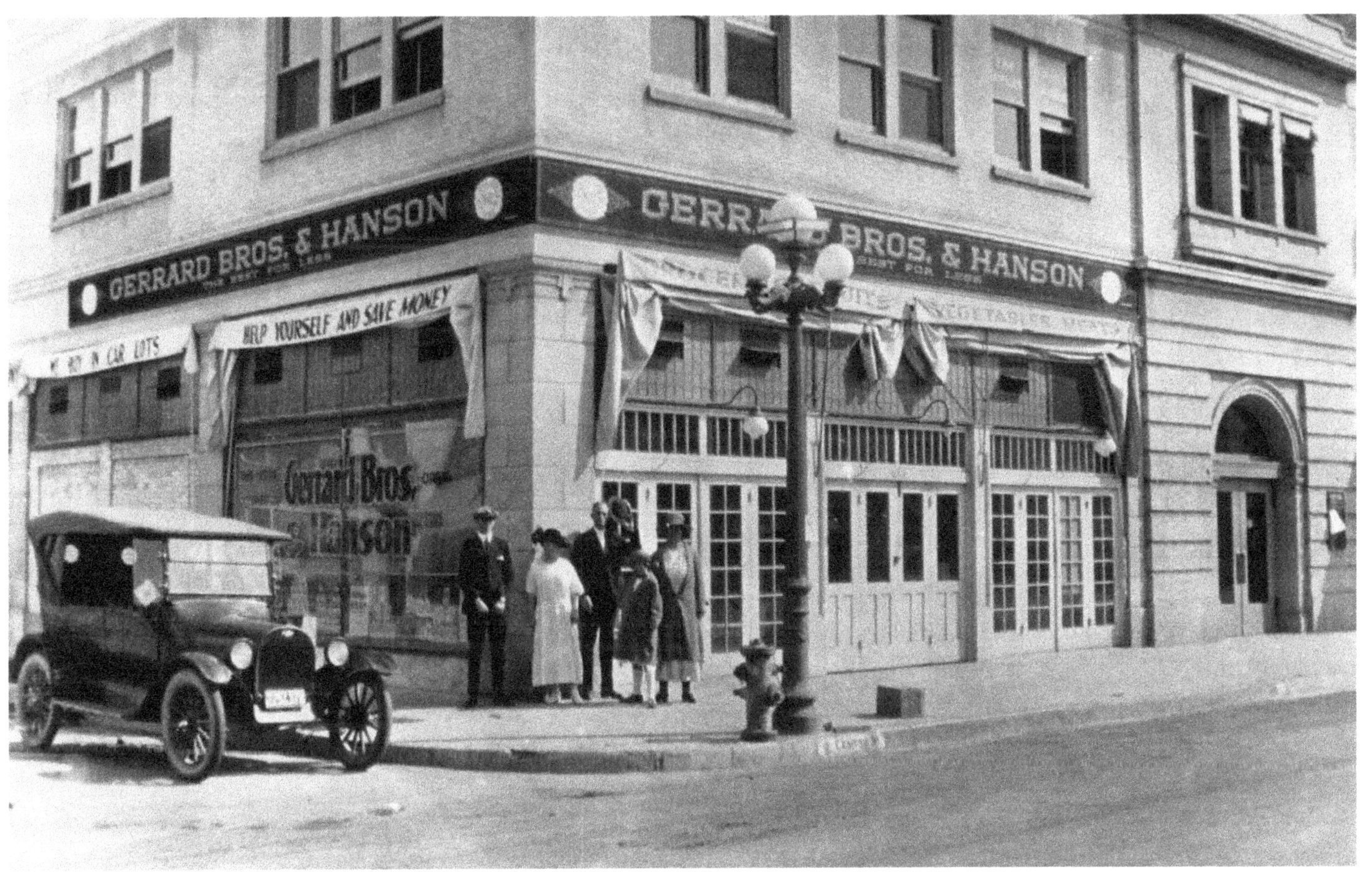

Excavation for the basement of the new Angelina Hotel is under way in 1923. Completed in 1924, the Angelina was one of Anaheim's better hostelries. Alex's Tamale Factory and the Anaheim Union Water Company offices are visible along Philadelphia Street in the background.

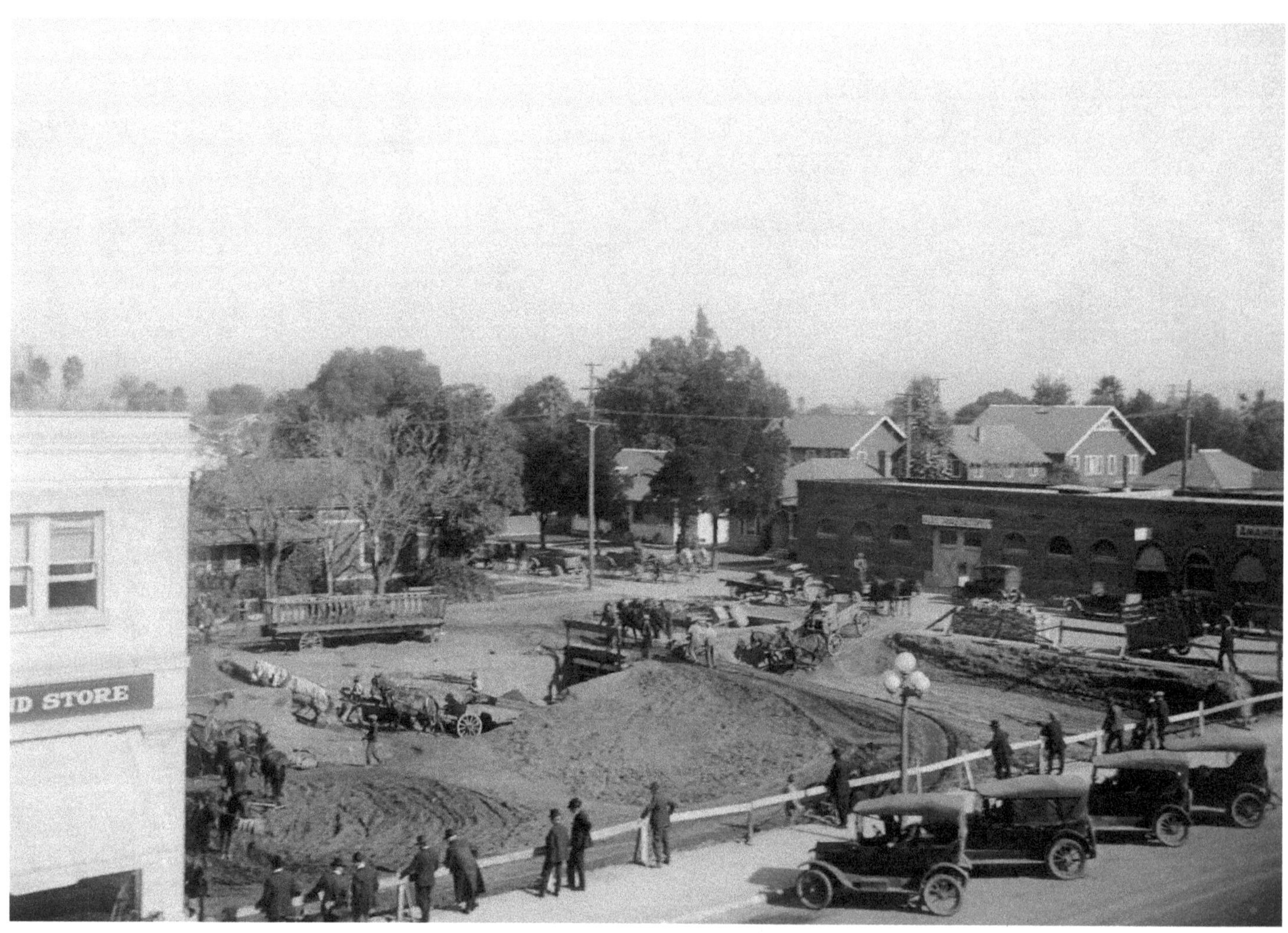

The three-story American Savings Bank Building (formerly the First National Bank Building) was located at the Southeast corner of Center Street and Los Angeles Street. Conspicuous in this image from ca. 1923 is Anaheim's landmark flagpole, in the middle of the intersection.

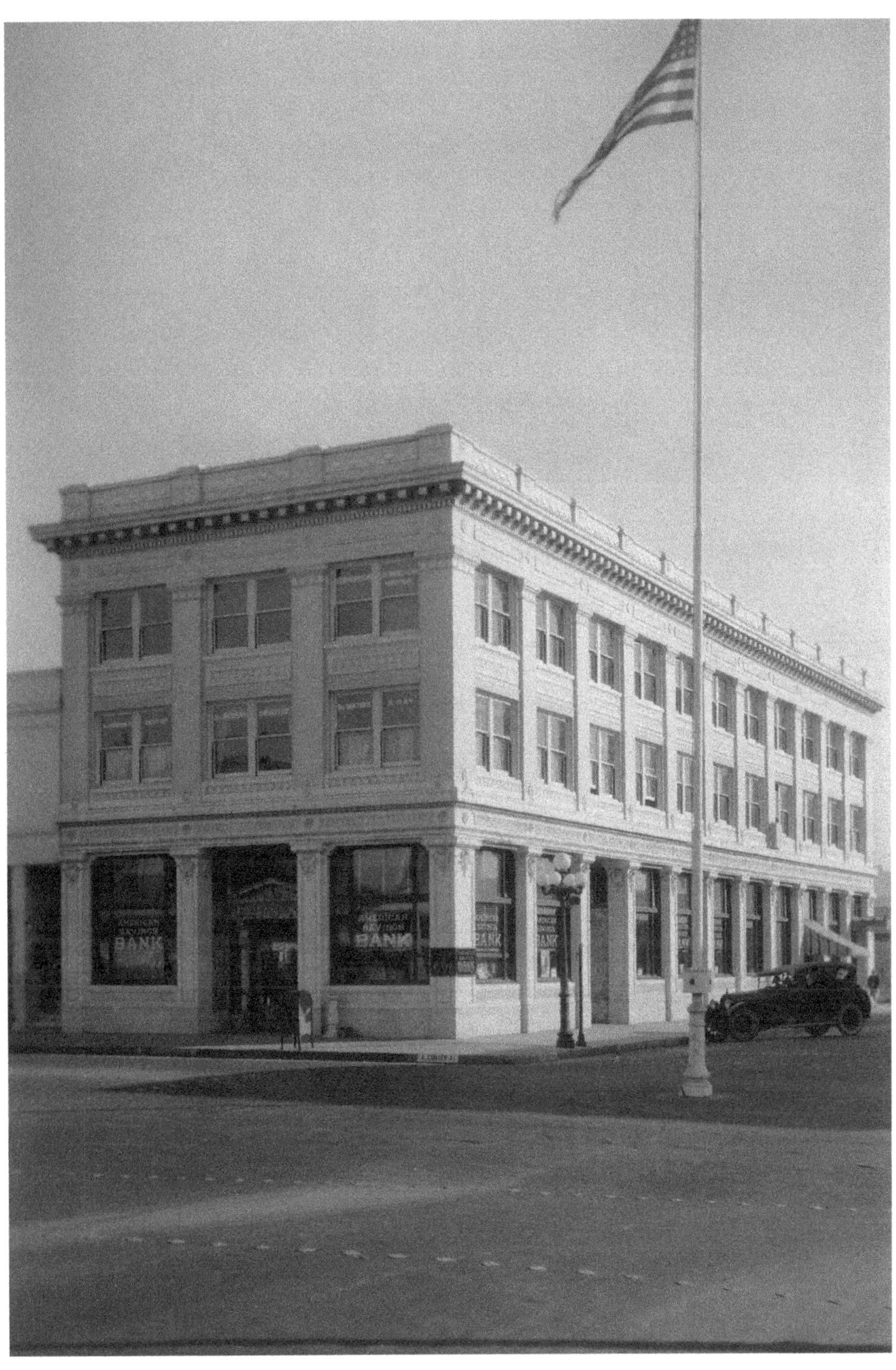

The Anaheim chamber of commerce, along with other local organizations, produced the California Valencia Orange Show in Anaheim from 1921 through 1930. The show was designed to "spread the fame, beauty, and richness of the Valencia Orange." By the turn of the century, citrus had become an increasingly important crop for the area. The inaugural show opened on May 17, 1921, with a long distance call from the President, Warren G. Harding, whose sister lived in neighboring Santa Ana at the time. The 1921 show filled a 50,000-square-foot tent and enjoyed more than 20,000 visitors (Anaheim's population was a mere 5,526).

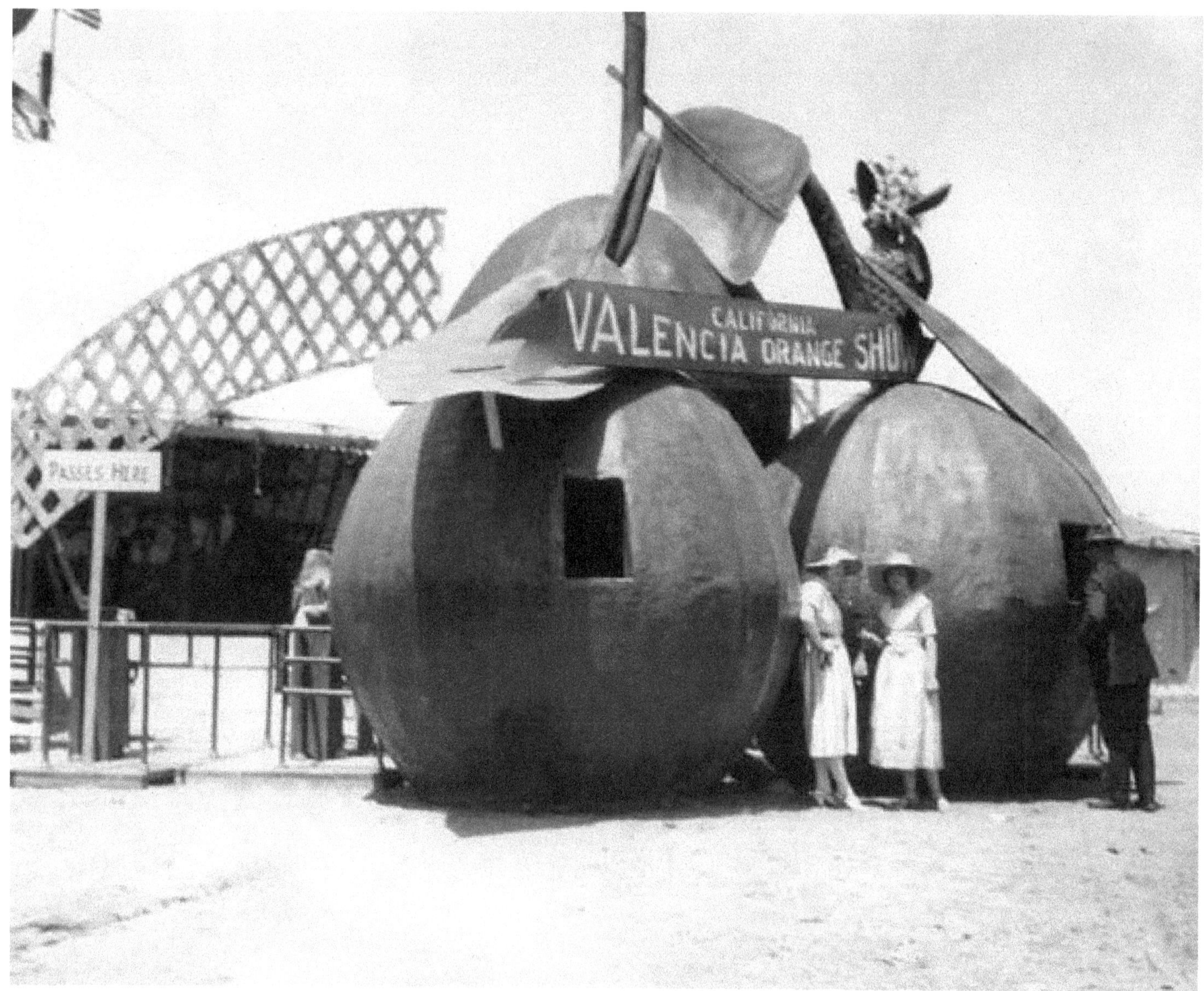

Anaheim's 1923 California Valencia Orange Show had by this time found a permanent home at the future site of Anaheim's La Palma Park. This year's theme was "Egyptian Settings" attributable in part to the recent discovery of King Tut's tomb and the high interest it had created.

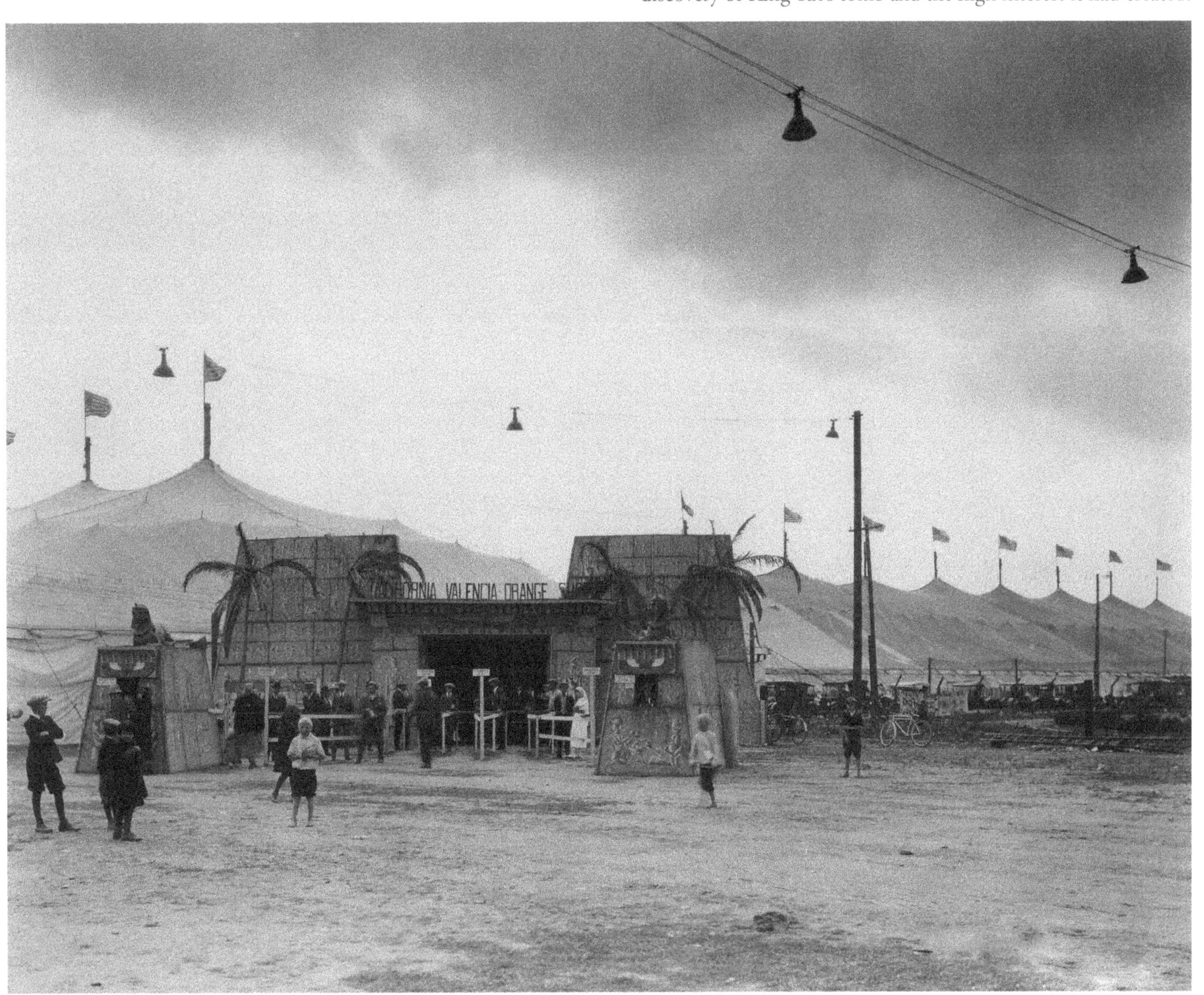

The interior of the 1923 California Valencia Orange Show offers a glimpse of the Egyptian theme for this year's event. The large tent included all kinds of displays, each centered on the Valencia orange, the region's most important agricultural product. Contests were held at these events and prizes were given for the best exhibit, as well as to the local orange packinghouse with the fastest packer.

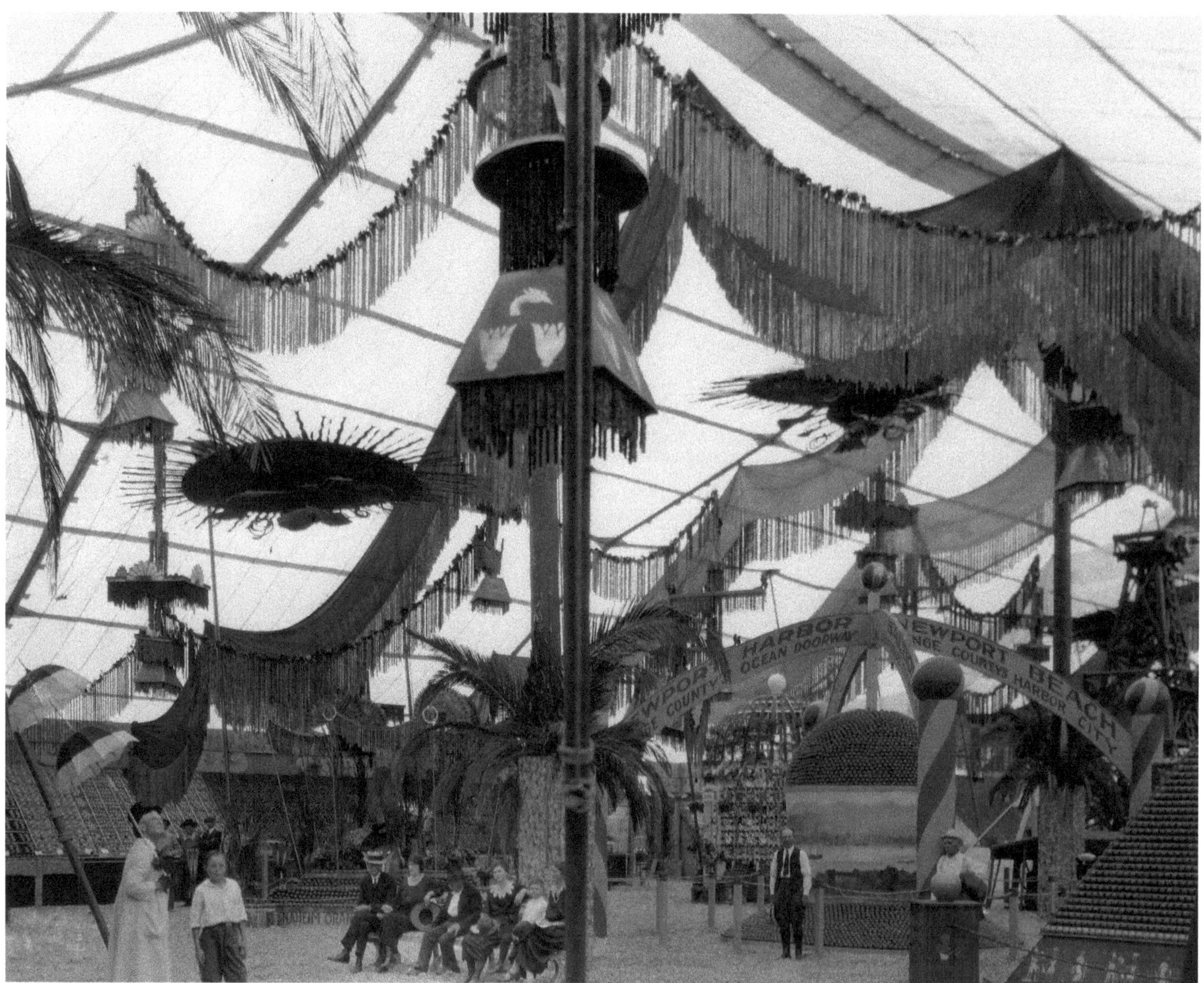

In 1925, this "permanent" Moorish arch entrance to the California Valencia Orange Show was built, featuring an 85-foot tower that contained a searchlight. The French Renaissance was this year's theme, and exhibits filled a 200-foot by 400-foot tent. The shows held four exhibits: Citrus, Automotive, Industrial, and Amusement.

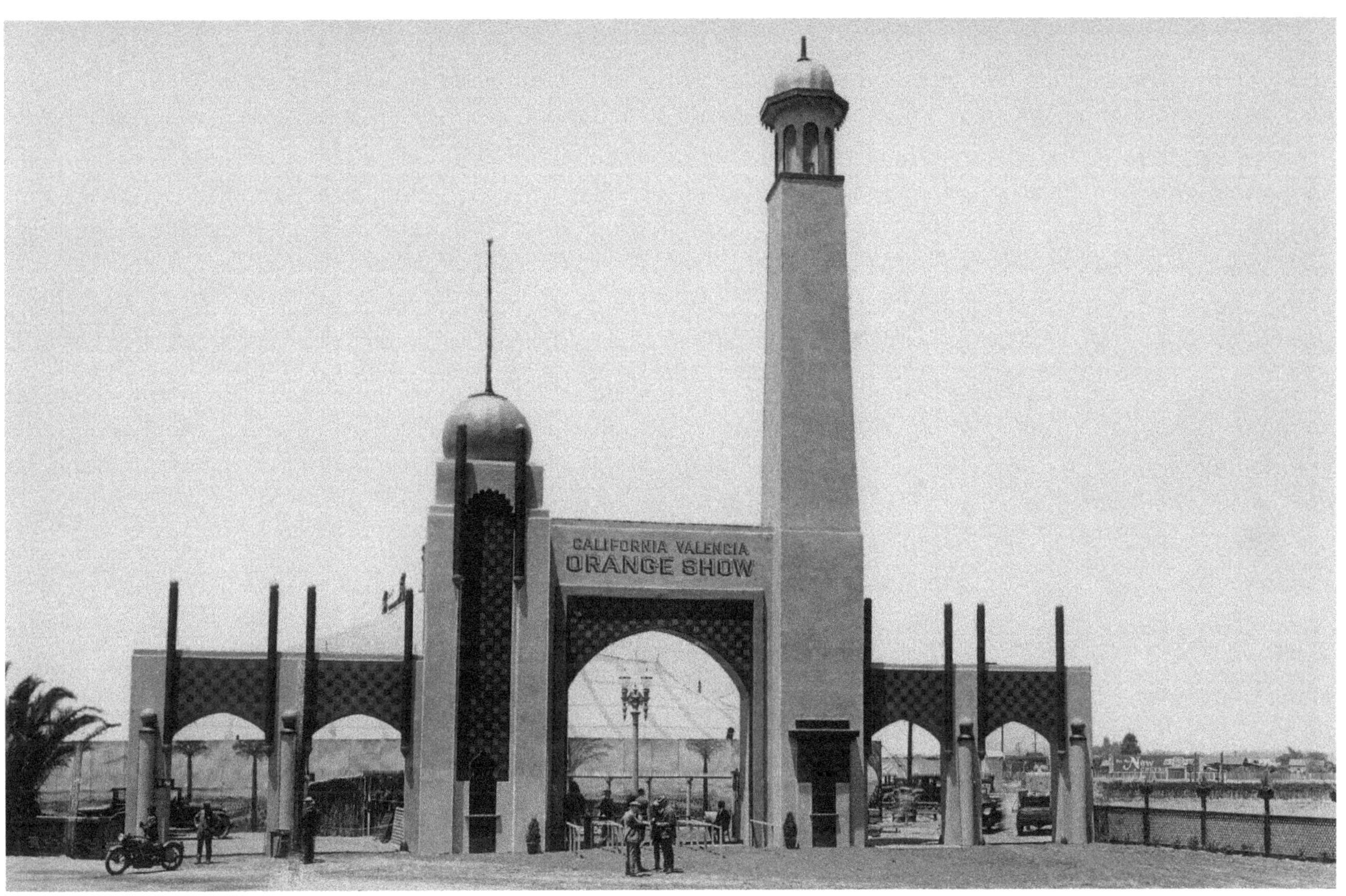

A parade through downtown Anaheim opened the 1928 California Valencia Orange Show. The theme was Aladdin's Lamp and the Anaheim float was decorated accordingly. More than 85,000 visitors attended the event, which filled a tent covering 400,000 square feet—reportedly, the largest tent ever erected in the country.

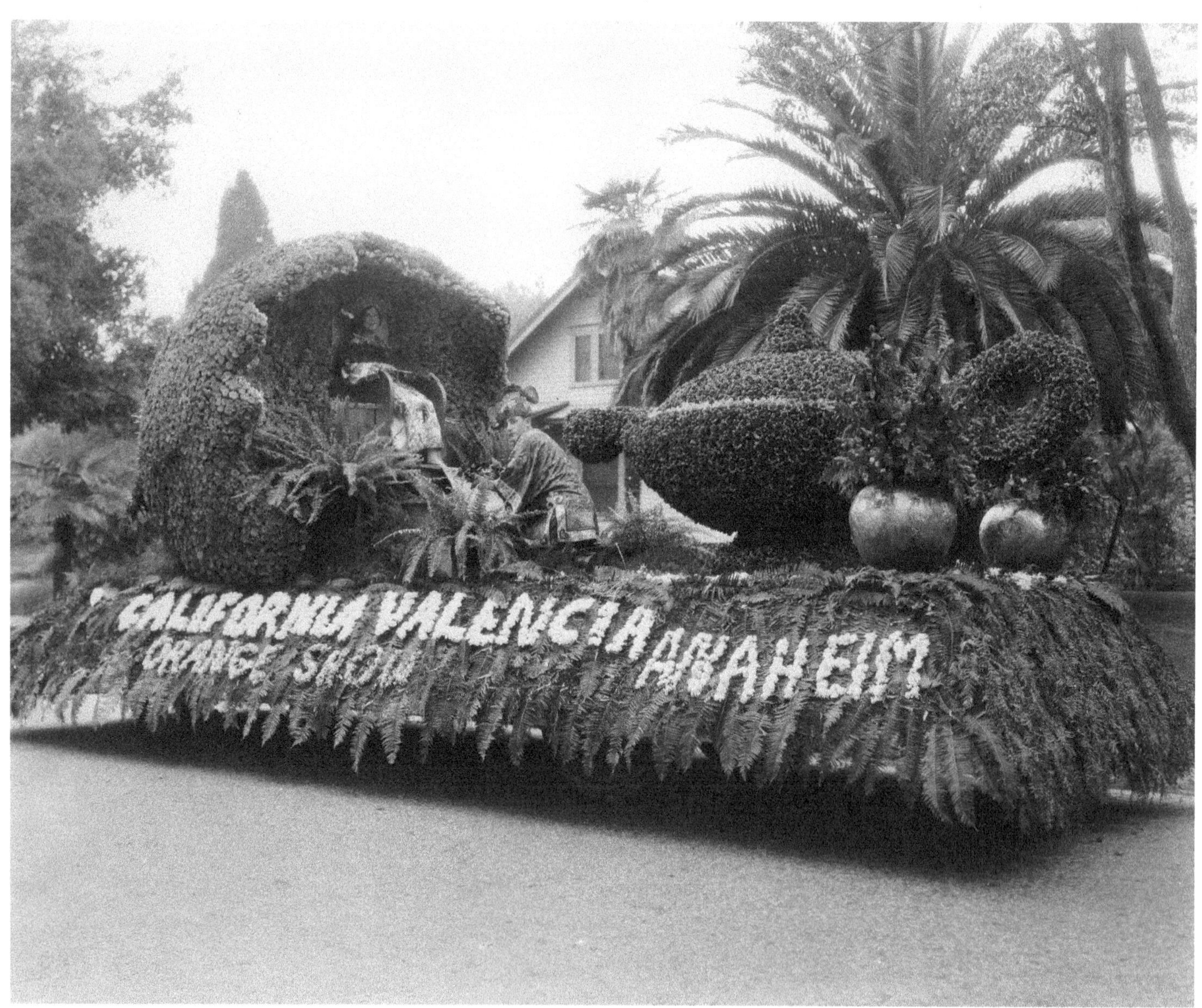

Anaheim's Boston Bakery had moved into more substantial quarters by 1924. Located at 201 East Center Street, the popular store would soon be razed for the construction of Samuel Kraemer's new American Savings Bank of Anaheim.

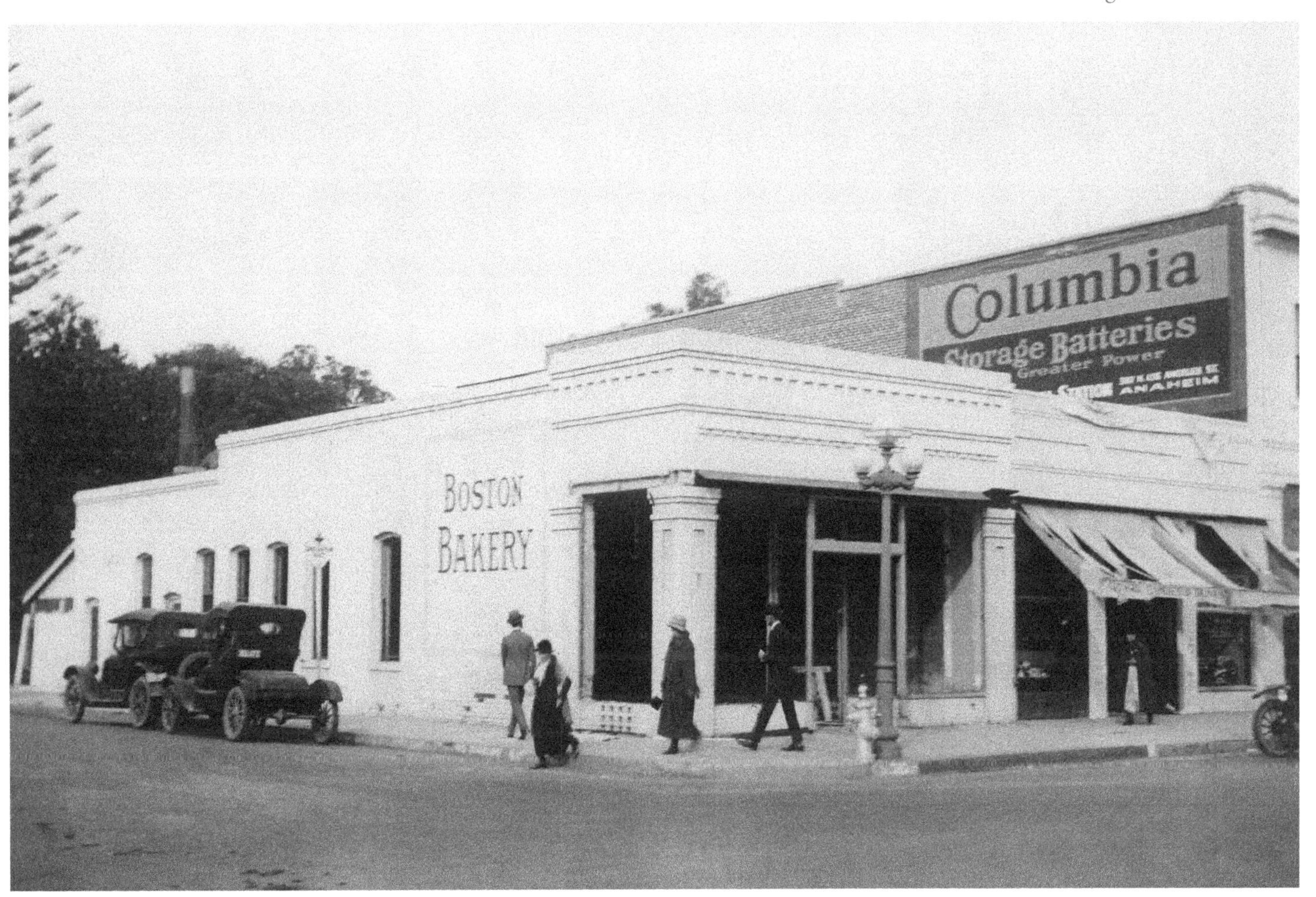

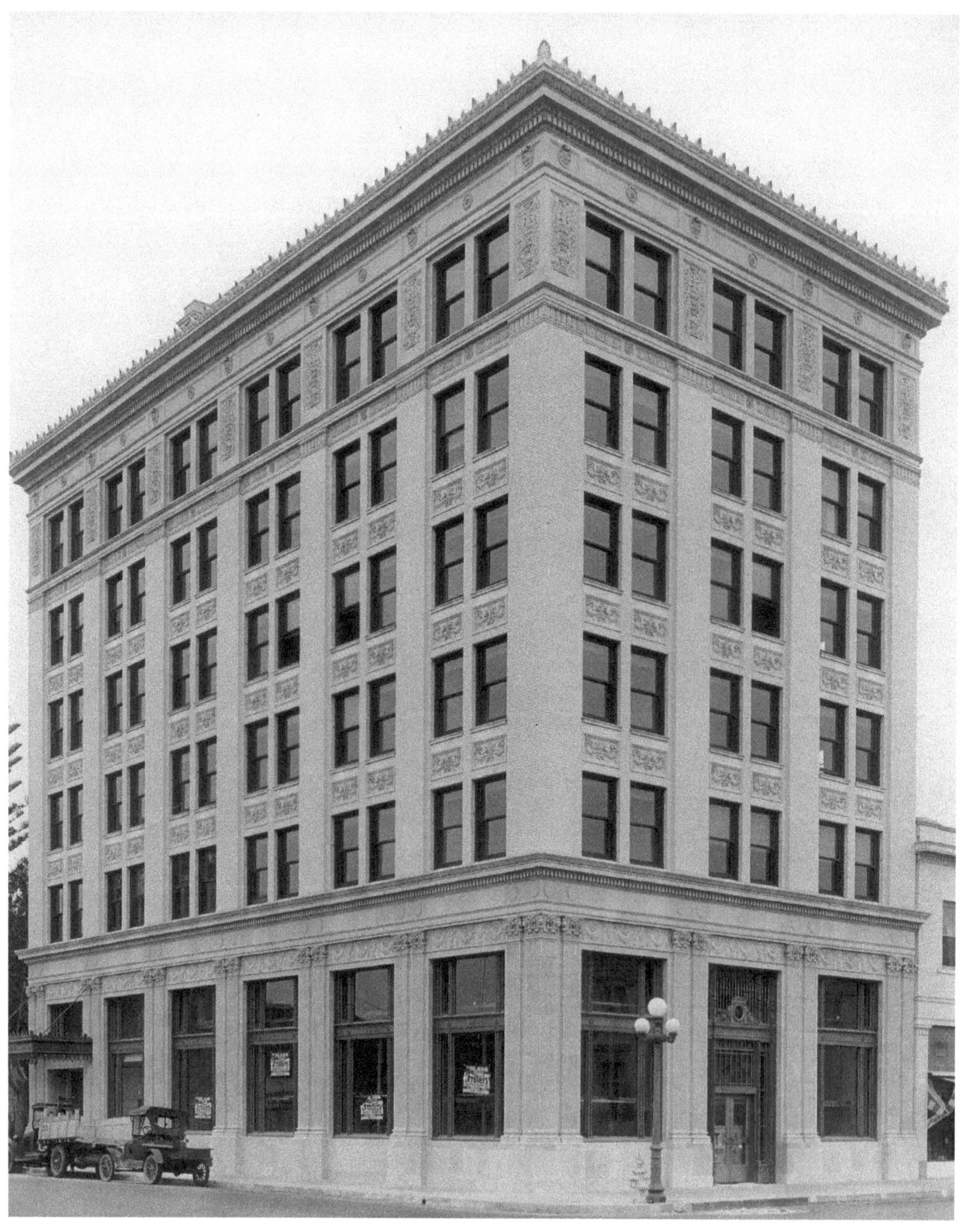

After the turn of the century, Anaheim businessmen were beginning to replace their lightly built downtown buildings with more substantial structures. Samuel Kraemer, one of the county's most successful citizens, developed much of downtown Anaheim in the 1920s. His six-story American Savings Bank was built at the same time Charles C. Chapman was building his new "skyscraper" in nearby Fullerton. After Kraemer heard that Chapman's building was to be five stories, he had an additional story and penthouse added so that his building would be the tallest in Orange County. And so it remained for more than four decades. The Kraemer Building is Anaheim's last surviving example of the building boom of the twenties.

In 1890, Anaheim's early brick mason contractor, Charles Schindler, built this imposing house at 422 West Center Street. By 1928, the home had been converted to the "Orange County School of Fine Arts" depicted here. The Queen Anne Victorian structure suffered extensive damage in the March 10, 1933, Long Beach earthquake and was the first building scheduled for demolition.

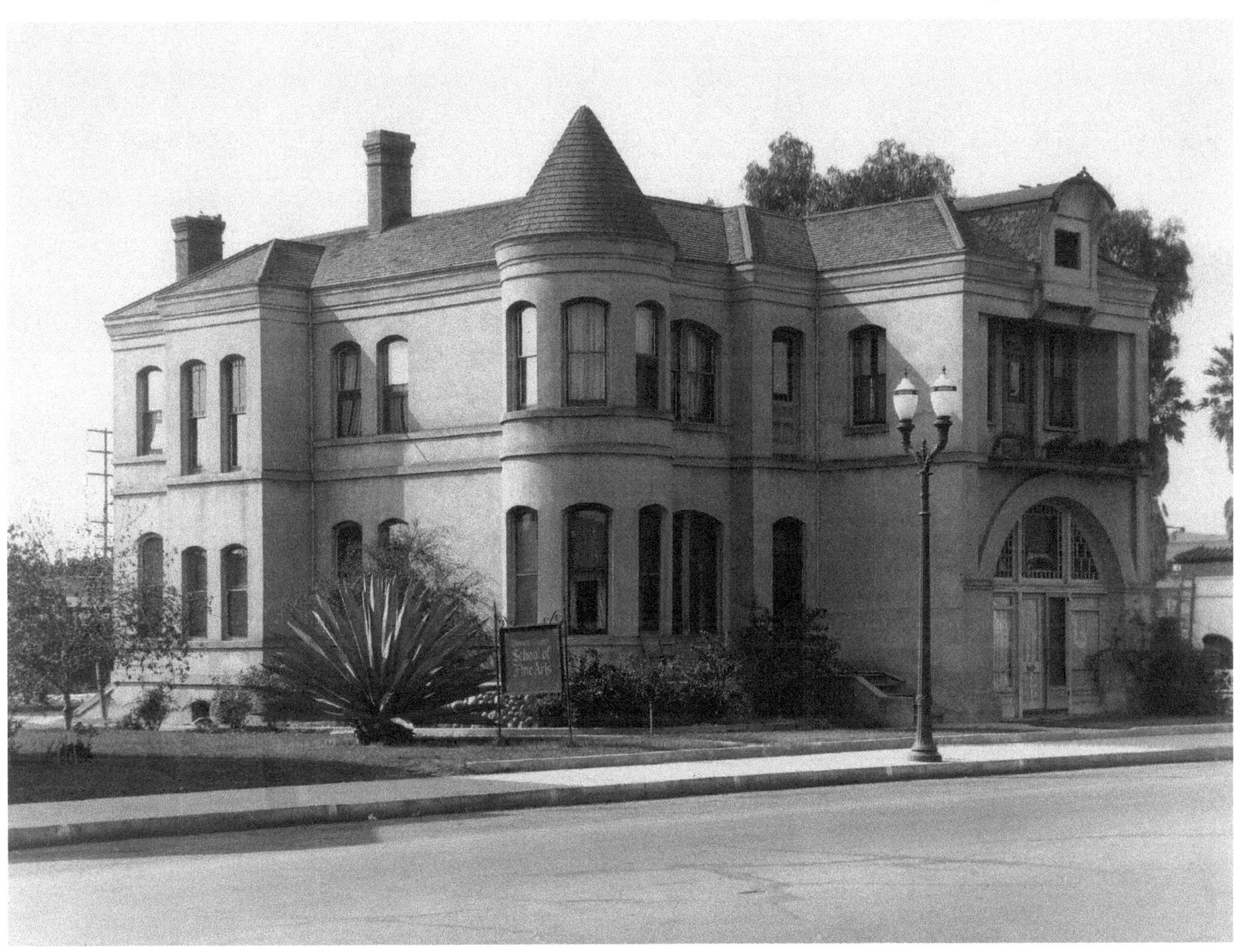

Following Spread: Warren Hodges at left and Frank Dotts are shown standing in their garage business at 306 North Los Angeles Street in the 1920s. The partners had a reputation with fast cars, much to the dismay of the Anaheim police force.

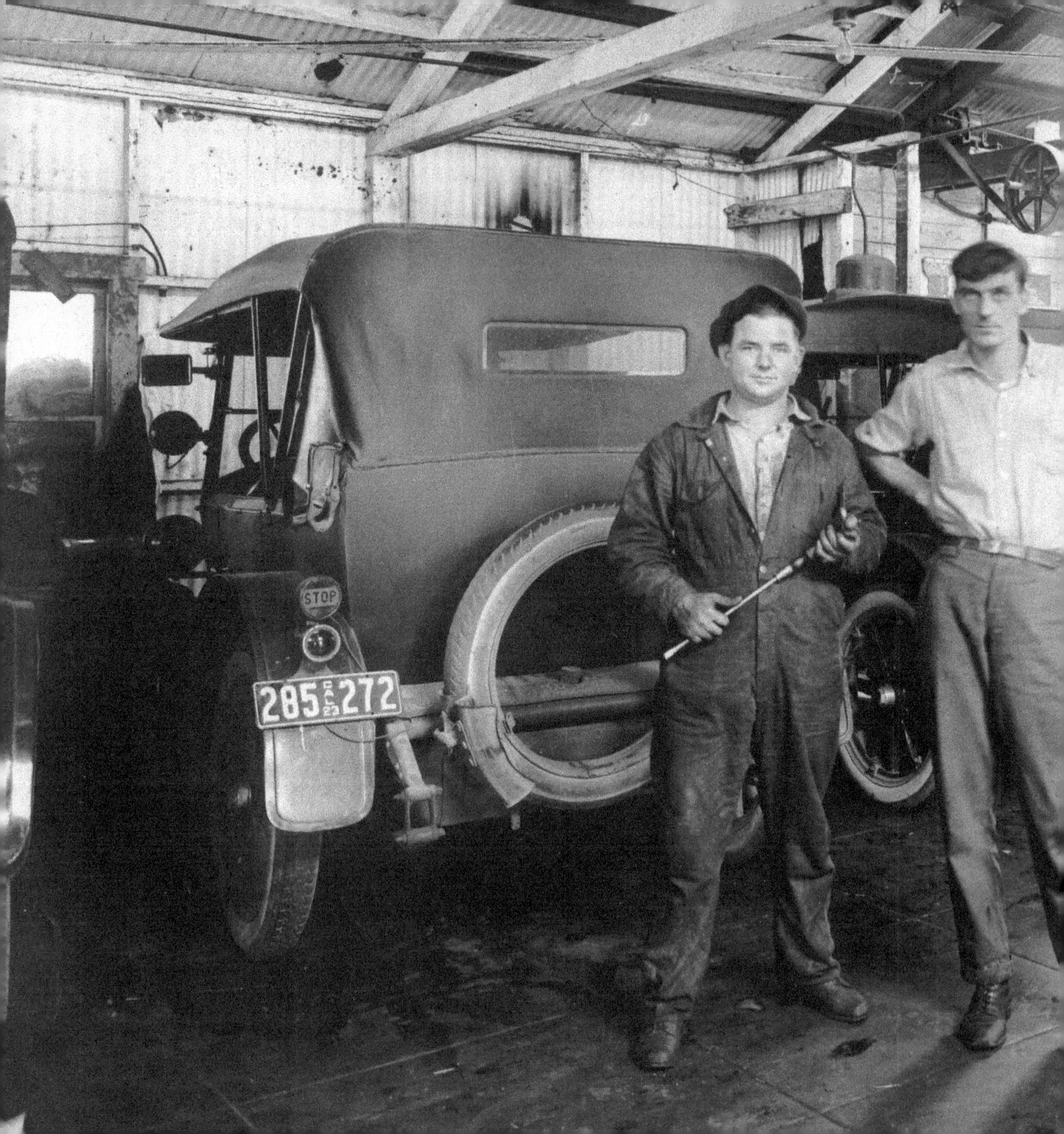
STOP
285 CAL 23 272

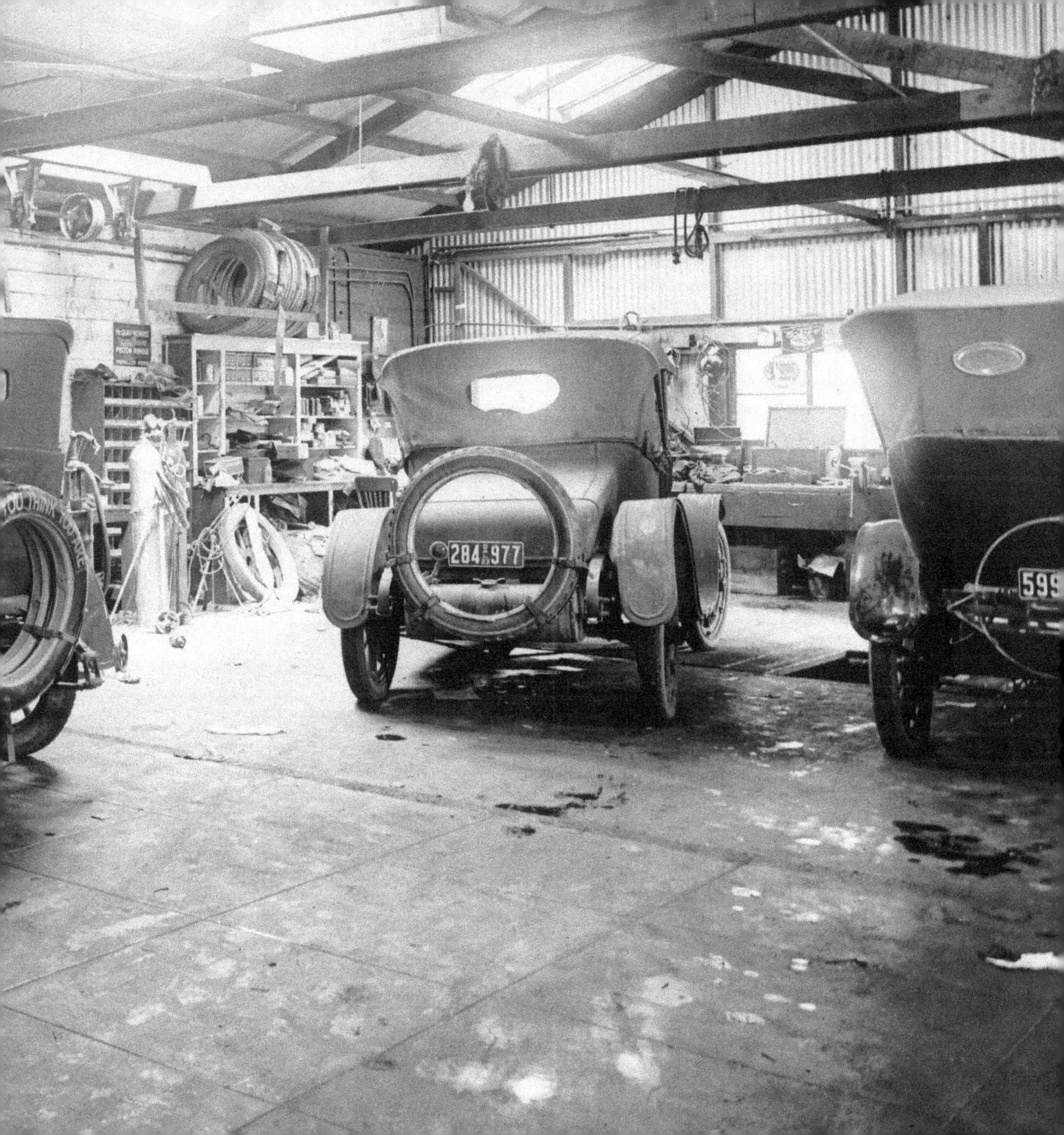
284 977

Picking time at Theodore Rimpau's orange grove, at 309 South Palm Street (now Harbor Blvd.). In 1962, this became the site for Anaheim's new central library. In this view are (left to right) George Wells, Wells's son, Frank Jennings, Wells's younger son, Frank Clark (on ladder), Archie Cadman, George McAuley, William T. Wallop, and Billie Cooper.

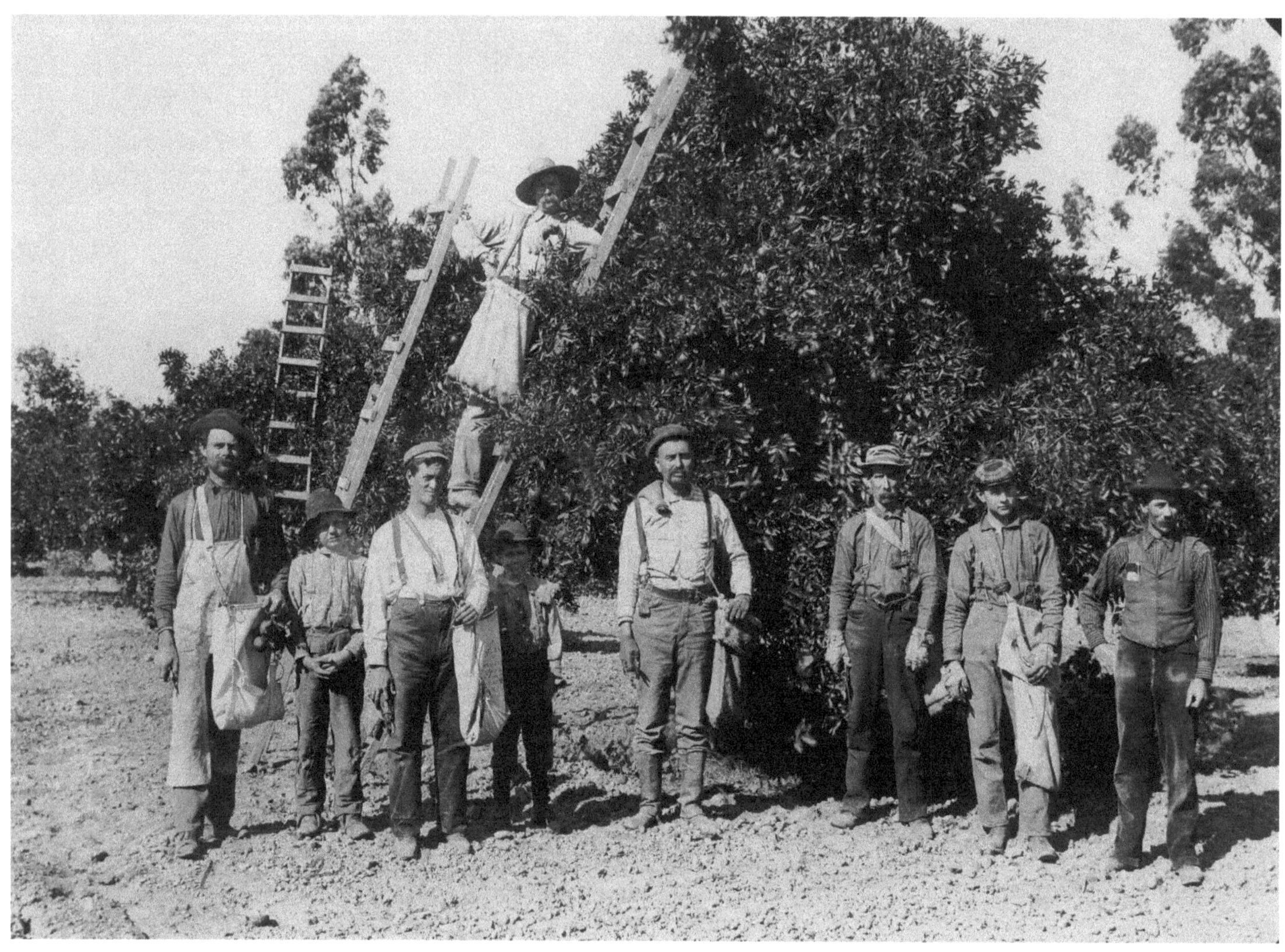

Baseball greats Walter "Big Train" Johnson (pitcher for the Washington Senators) and Babe Ruth of the New York Yankees, played an exhibition game at the Brea Bowl on October 31, 1924. The teams were playing a benefit game for the Anaheim Elks Christmas Charity Fund. Later in the evening, both players served as grand marshals of Anaheim's inaugural Halloween parade.

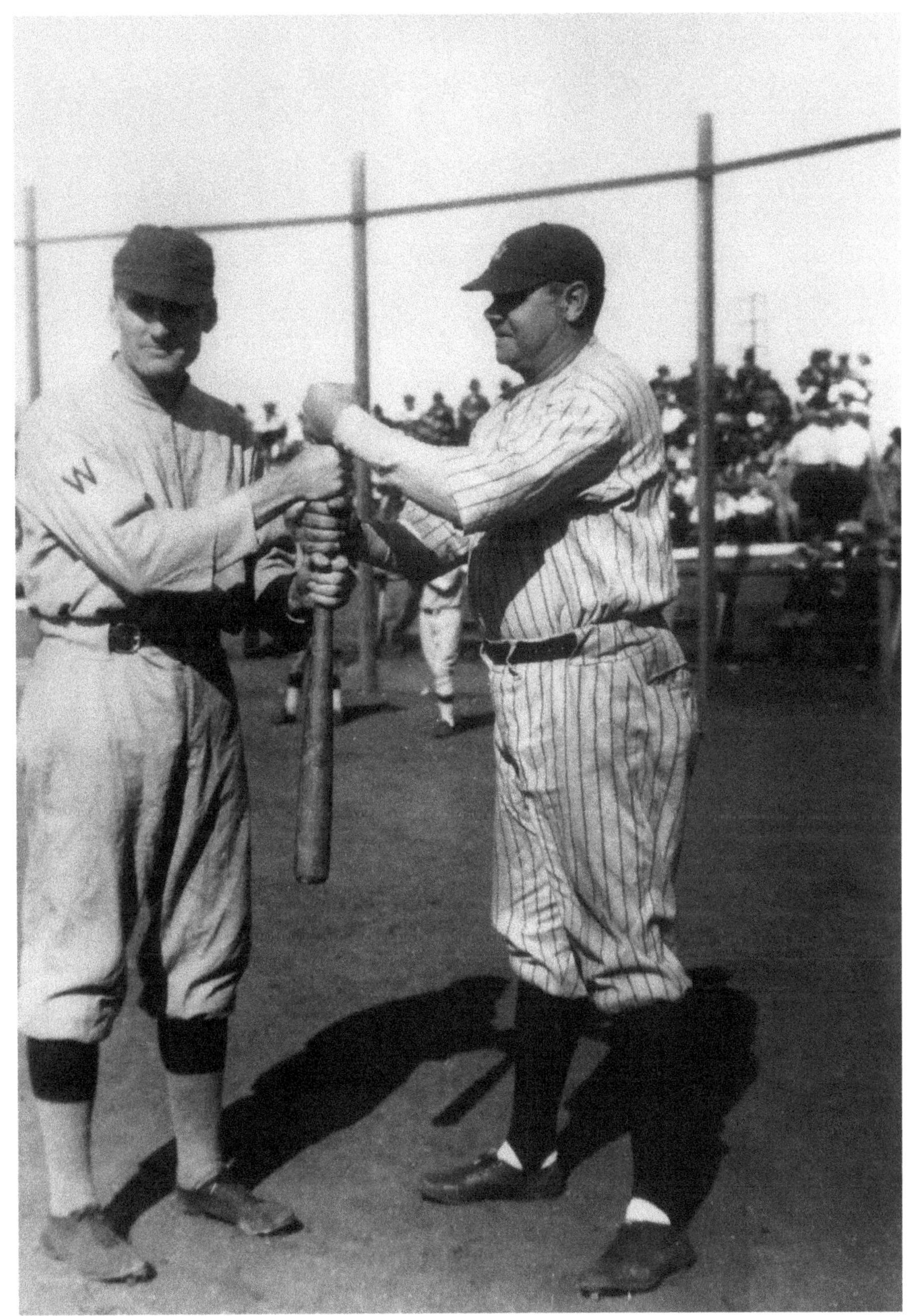

Seven friends are driving their 1917 Jordan Touring car around Anaheim streets, advertising the 1924 silent movie *Sea Hawk* previewing at the California Theater that evening.

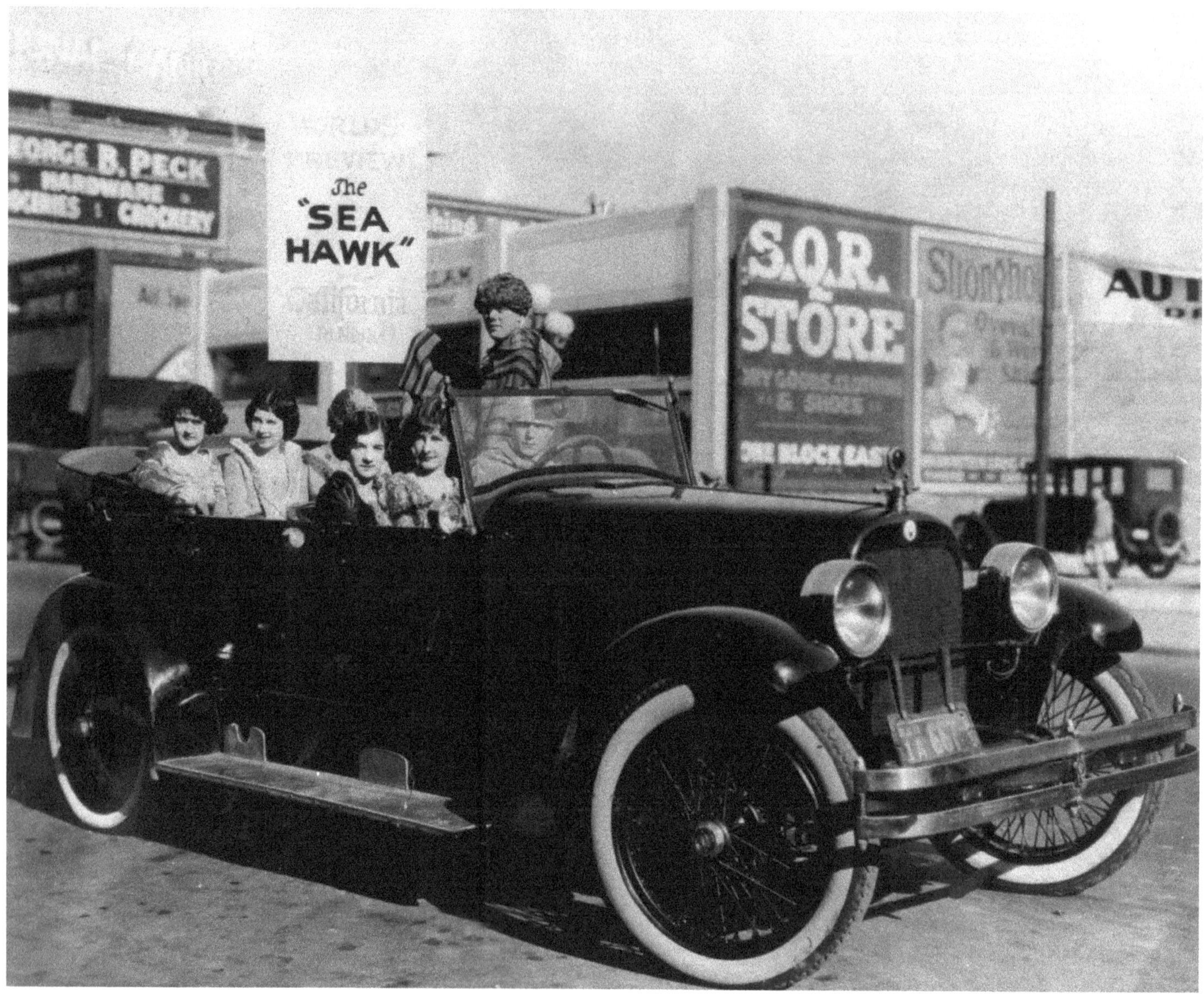

The Anaheim city band is playing in the street at the corner of North Emily and East Center Street in the 1920s. Anaheim had several community bands over the years that were popular for many occasions and celebrations, from hotel openings to Fourth of July parades. Anaheim's 1913 Masonic Lodge building is visible in the background.

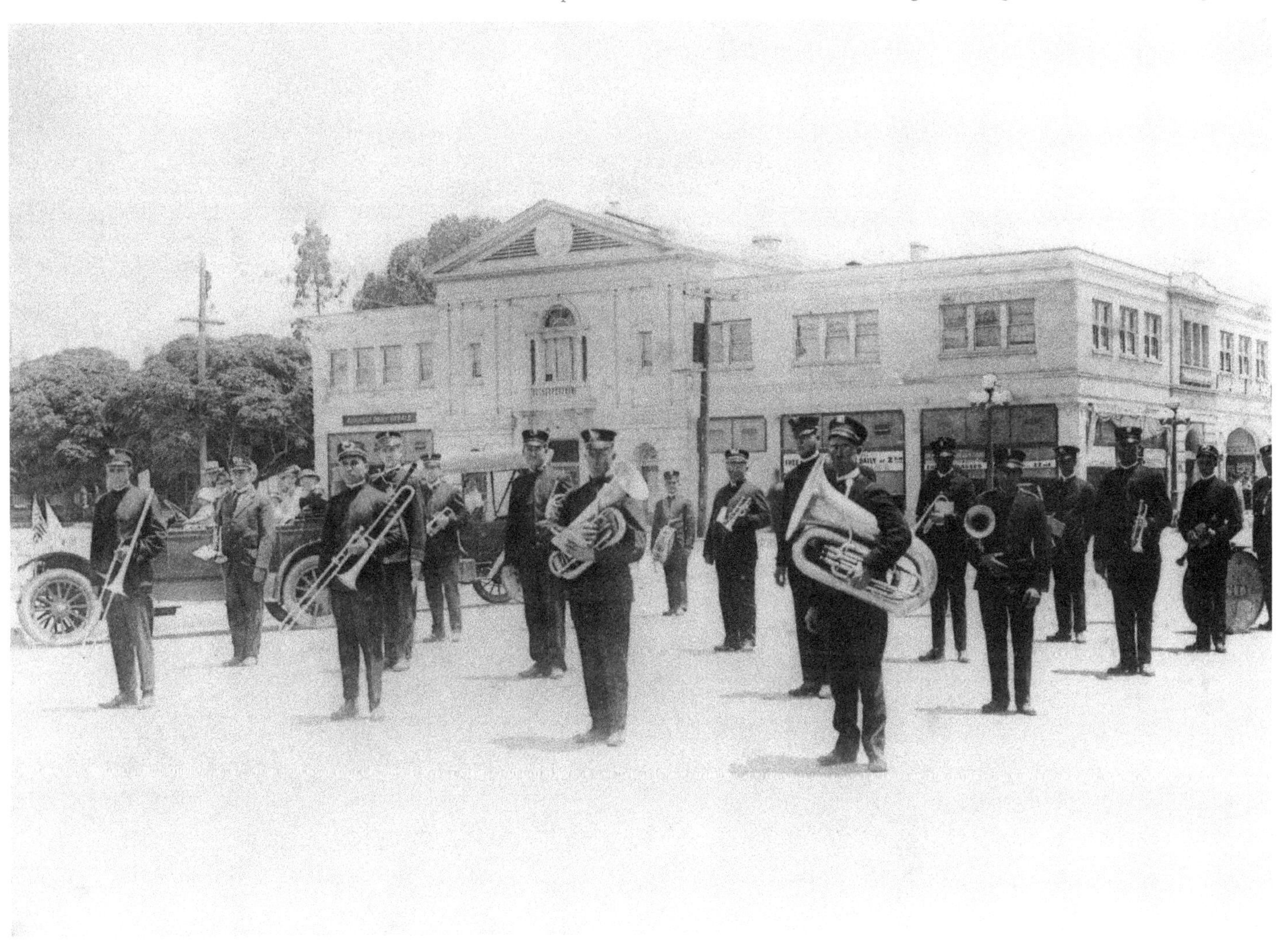

In 1925, the streets of downtown Anaheim are sporting new five-globed ornamental streetlights, concrete sidewalks, and paving, much to the relief of the street-side merchants. Automobiles have now completely replaced the horse and mule as the preferred mode of transportation, and brick and tile buildings have replaced the lightly built downtown of years past.

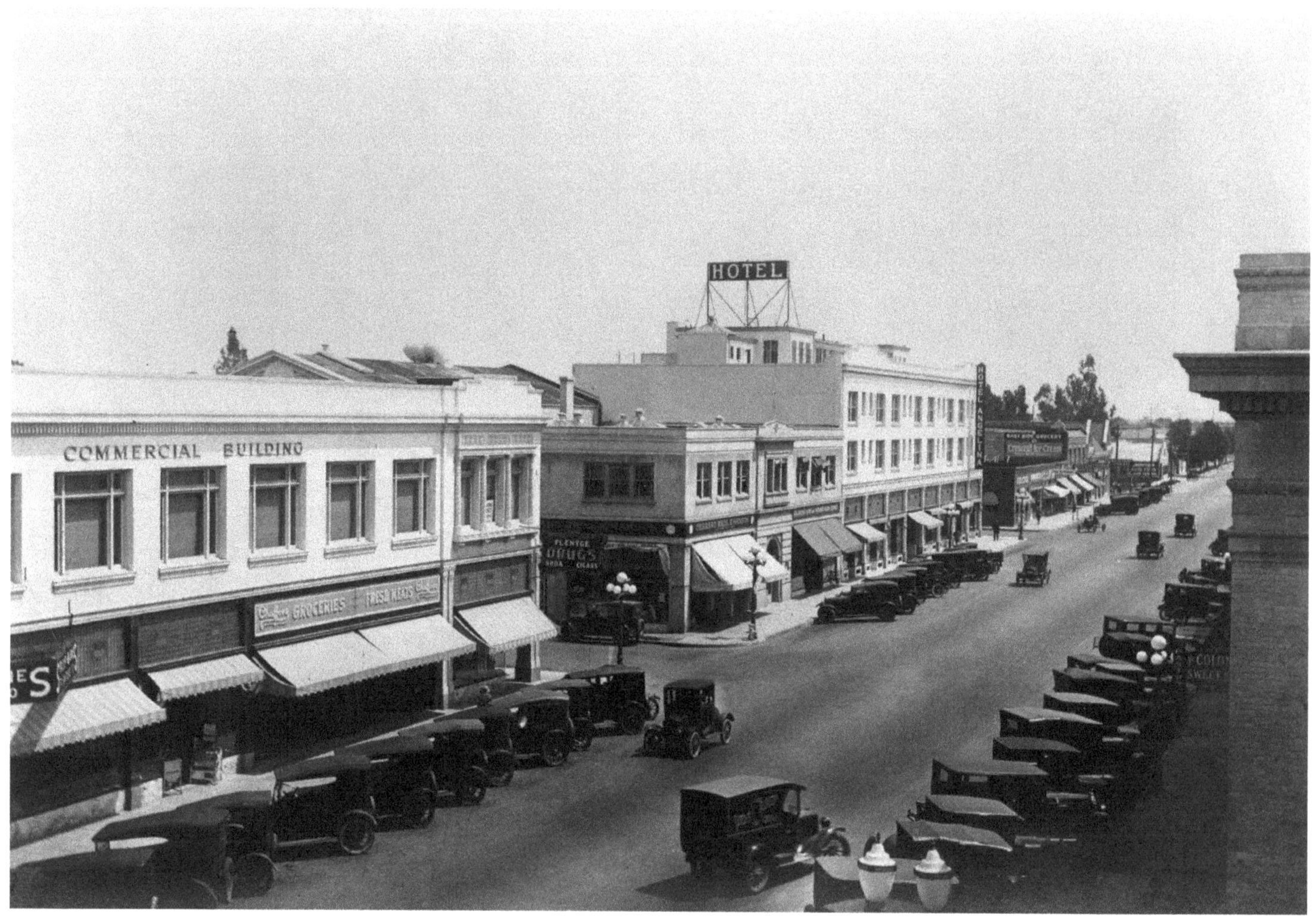

The Bethel Baptist Church at the corner of South Broadway at Lemon Street was dedicated in 1927. It replaced the original 1903 German Baptist wood-framed church built on this site.

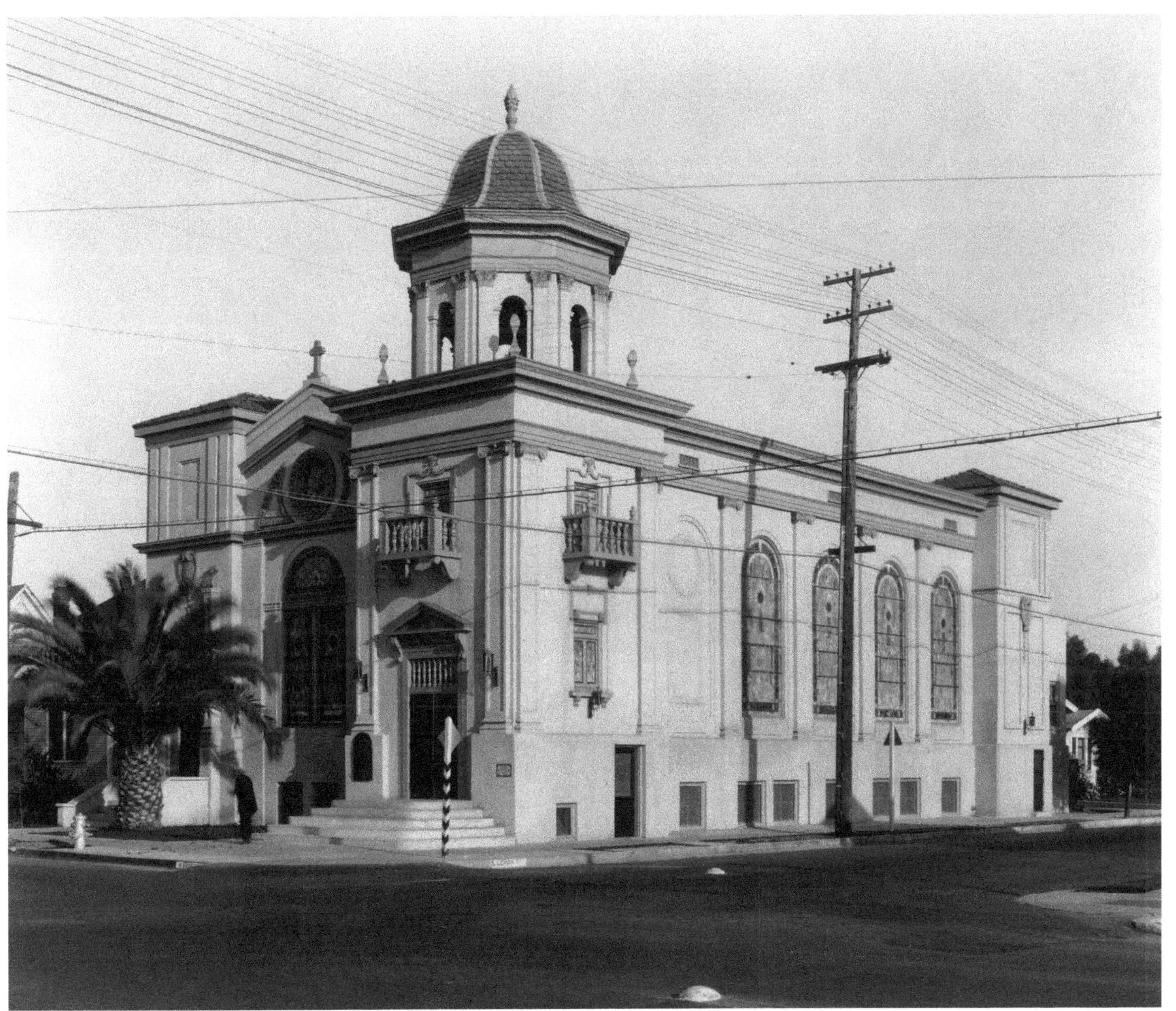

Anaheim's German Methodist Episcopal Church was established in 1881. Located on West Broadway at South Clementine Street, it was later known as the Free Methodist Church. Shown here in 1930, its two arched stained-glass windows illustrate "Christ in the Garden of Gethsemane" and "the Good Shepherd."

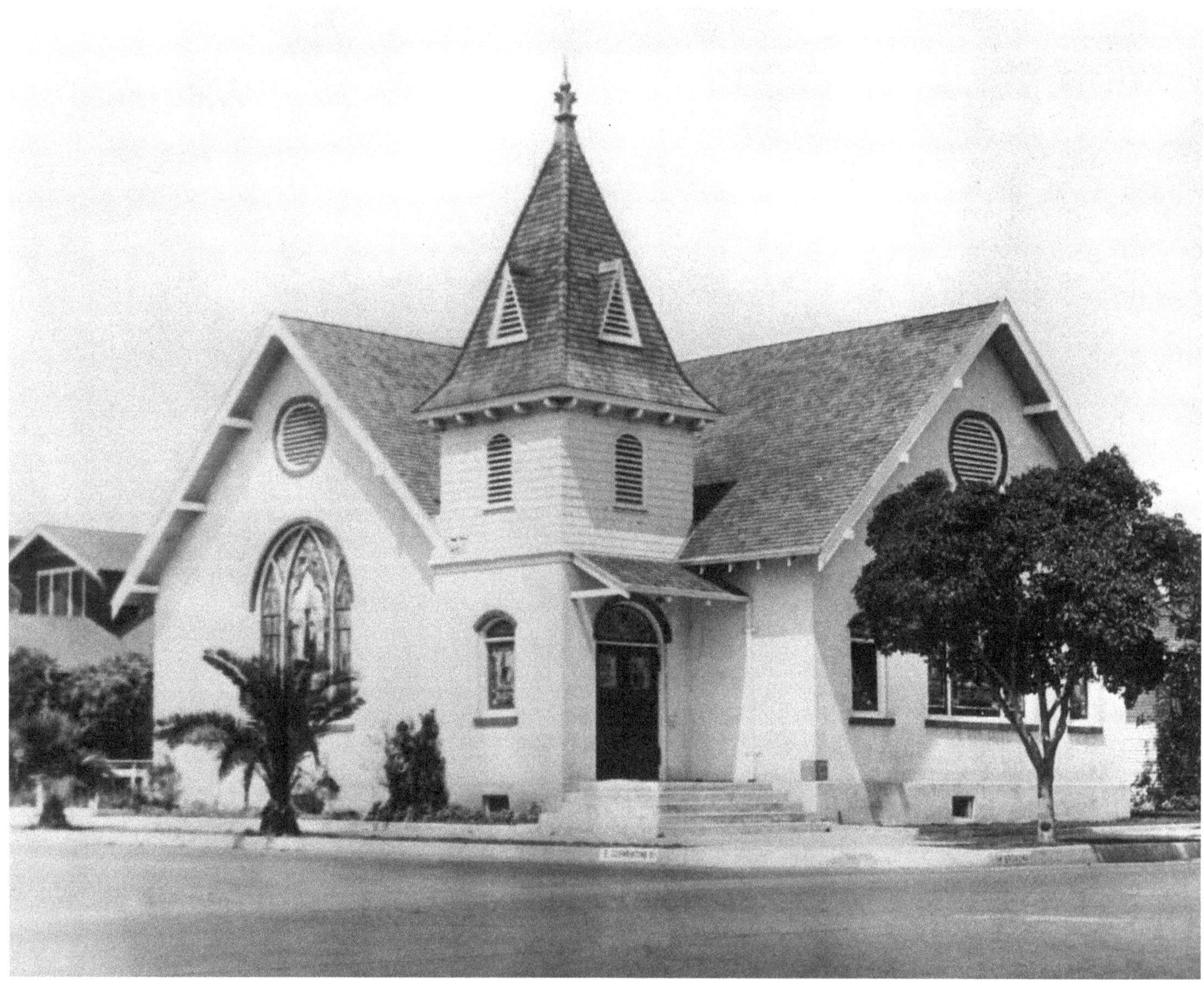

Anaheim's annual Halloween parade was inaugurated in 1924 and became a favorite regional civic event. Although Anaheim's population was just under 10,000 in 1928, that year's parade was seen by several times that number. Here the parade makes its way through the center of town at Center and Los Angeles streets.

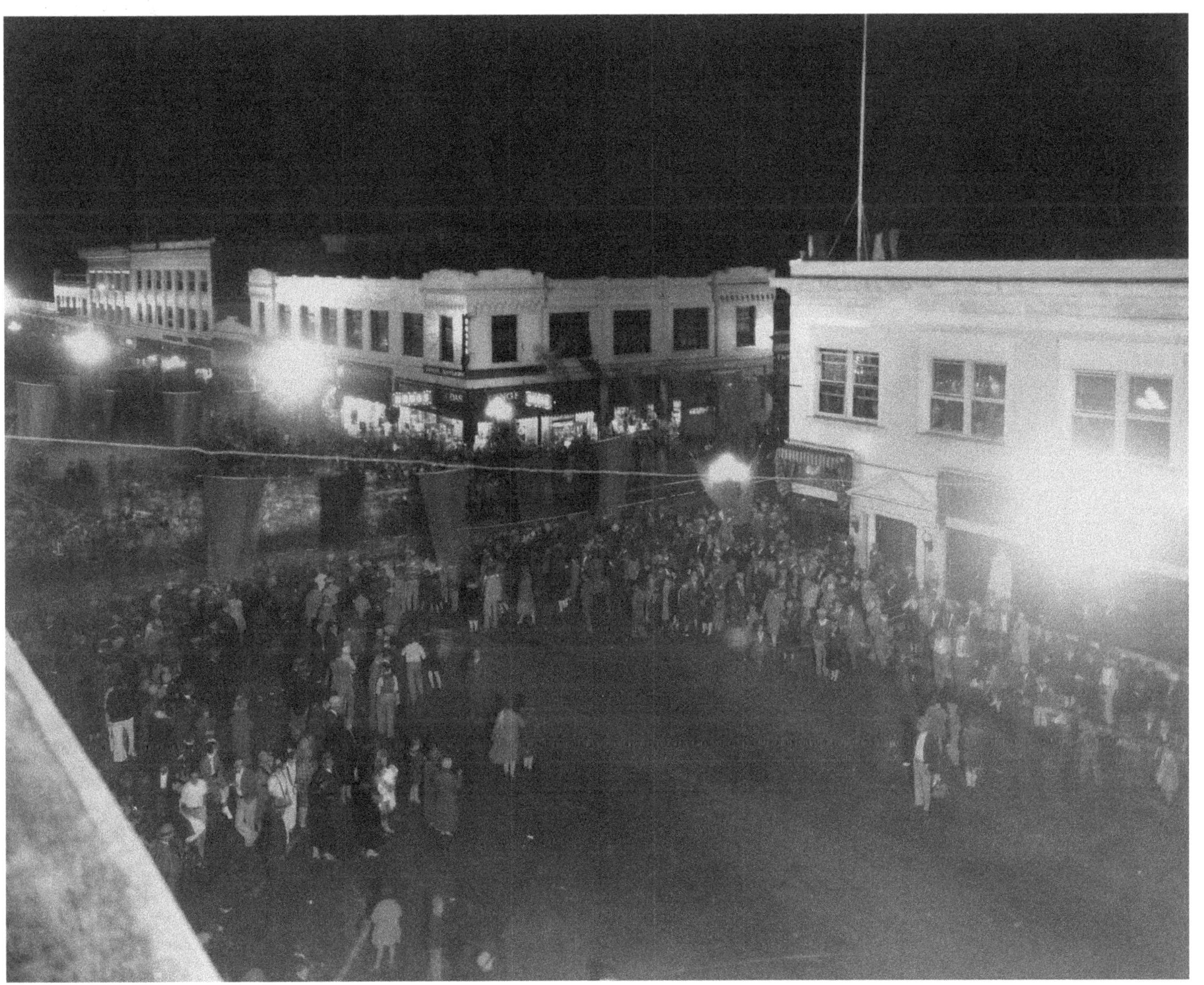

Anaheim's American Legion "40 & 8" Post members march alongside their horse-drawn float in a 1920s Armistice Day parade.

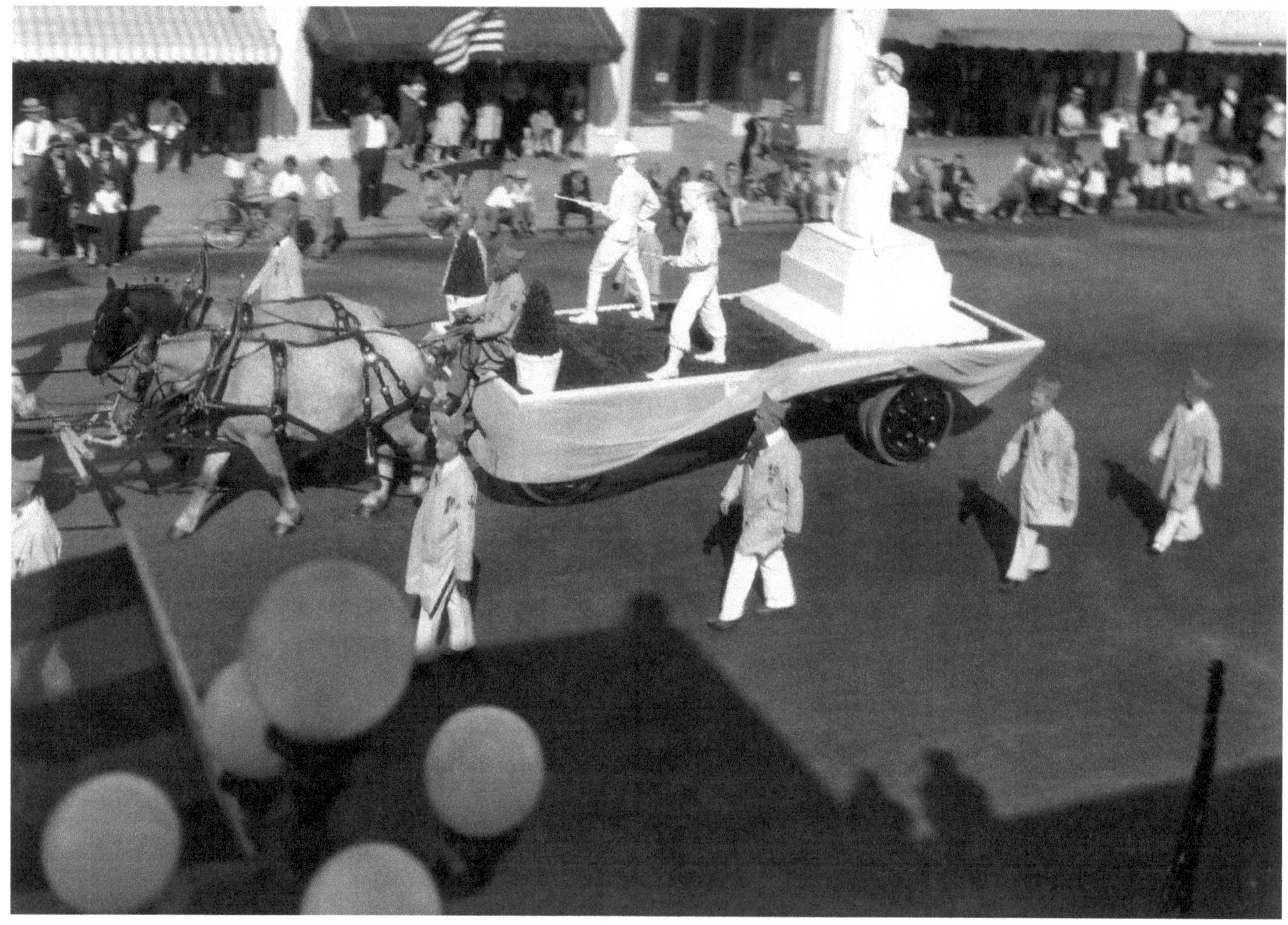

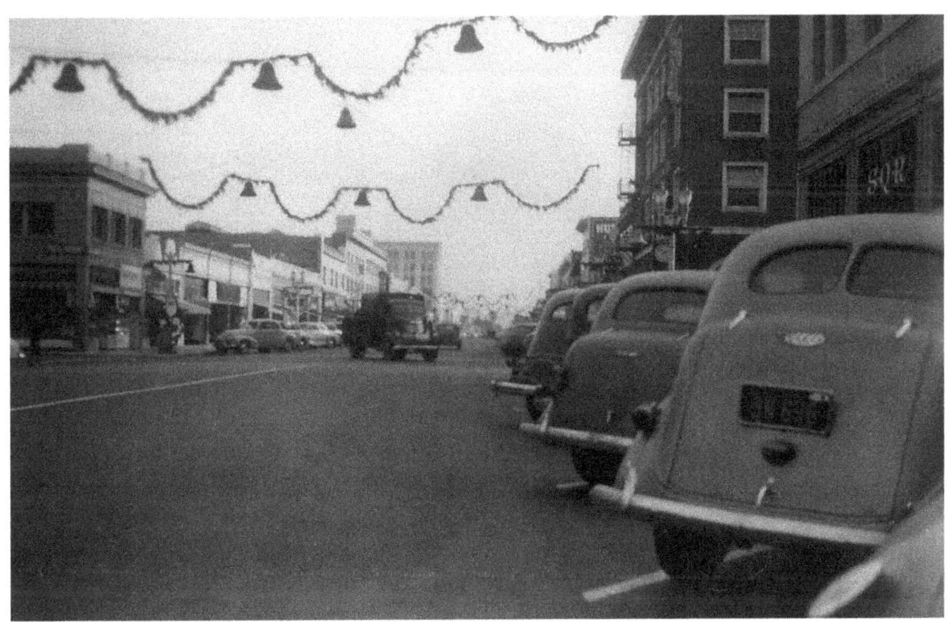

Center Street Christmas decorations are now hung, calling Anaheim families to purchase their gifts before Santa's arrival. Downtown stores would stay open in the evenings to accommodate local shoppers in this era before regional malls. Anaheim's well-loved S.Q.R. department store is on the immediate right and the Hotel Valencia is across South Lemon Street.

In 1857, George Hansen, the surveyor who laid out the town of Anaheim for the Los Angeles Vineyard Society, built this pioneer home, the first "modern" home in what would later become Orange County. On March 14, 1929, the "Mother Colony House," as it became known, was dedicated as the county's first museum. Donated to the city of Anaheim in 1954 by the Daughters of the American Revolution, the house remains today a beloved tie to the community's past.

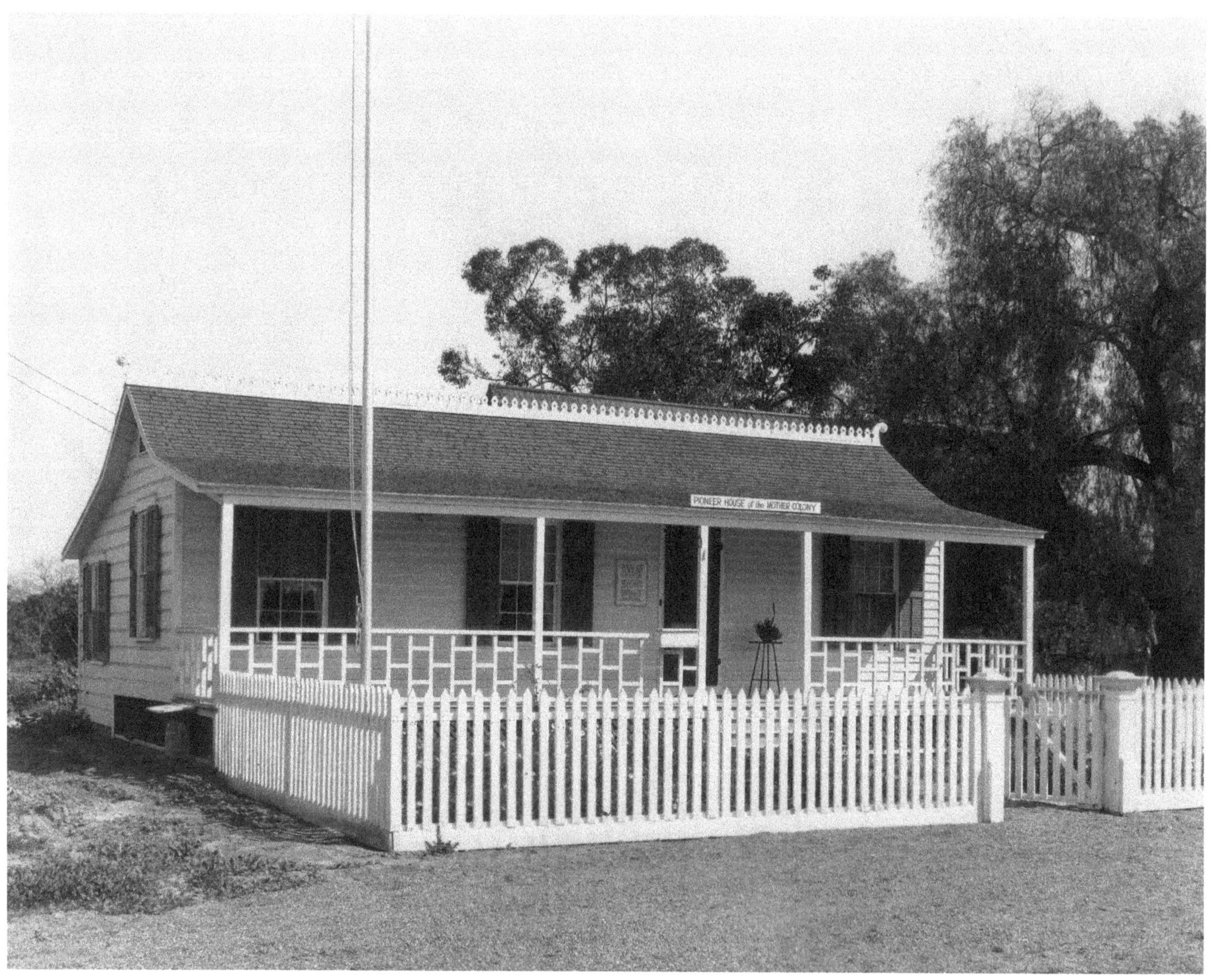

What became known as the Long Beach Earthquake severely shook the southland at 5:55 P.M. on March 10, 1933. A number of local cities recorded deaths; Anaheim, however, suffered no loss of life. A number of un-reinforced brick buildings in the downtown area did incur significant damage, as is visible here on West Center Street. California's National Guard was called to patrol the streets of many communities to protect the residents from falling materials.

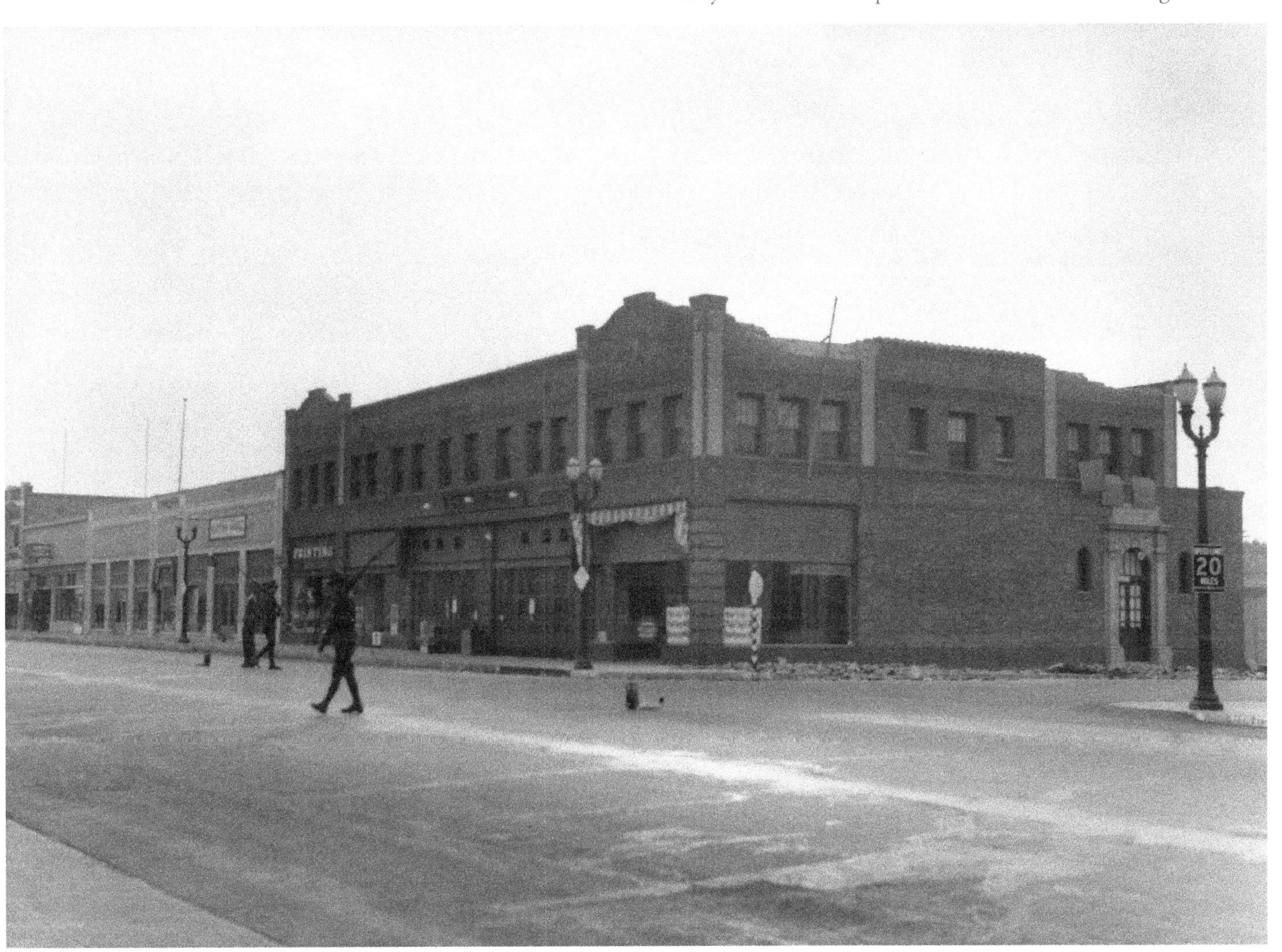

After many years of debate and two unsuccessful trips to the polls, the community finally voted in 1920 the $100,000 of bonds required to purchase land for the city's new public park. Another $100,000 park construction bond followed two years later, resulting in Anaheim's new moniker the "City with the Beautiful Park." This major civic improvement included goldfish-filled lagoons, a lighted softball diamond, picnic grounds, tennis courts, an Olympic-sized pool, and an amphitheater that could seat 2,000. This was a remarkable commitment to local recreation by a community that numbered less than 6,000 residents.

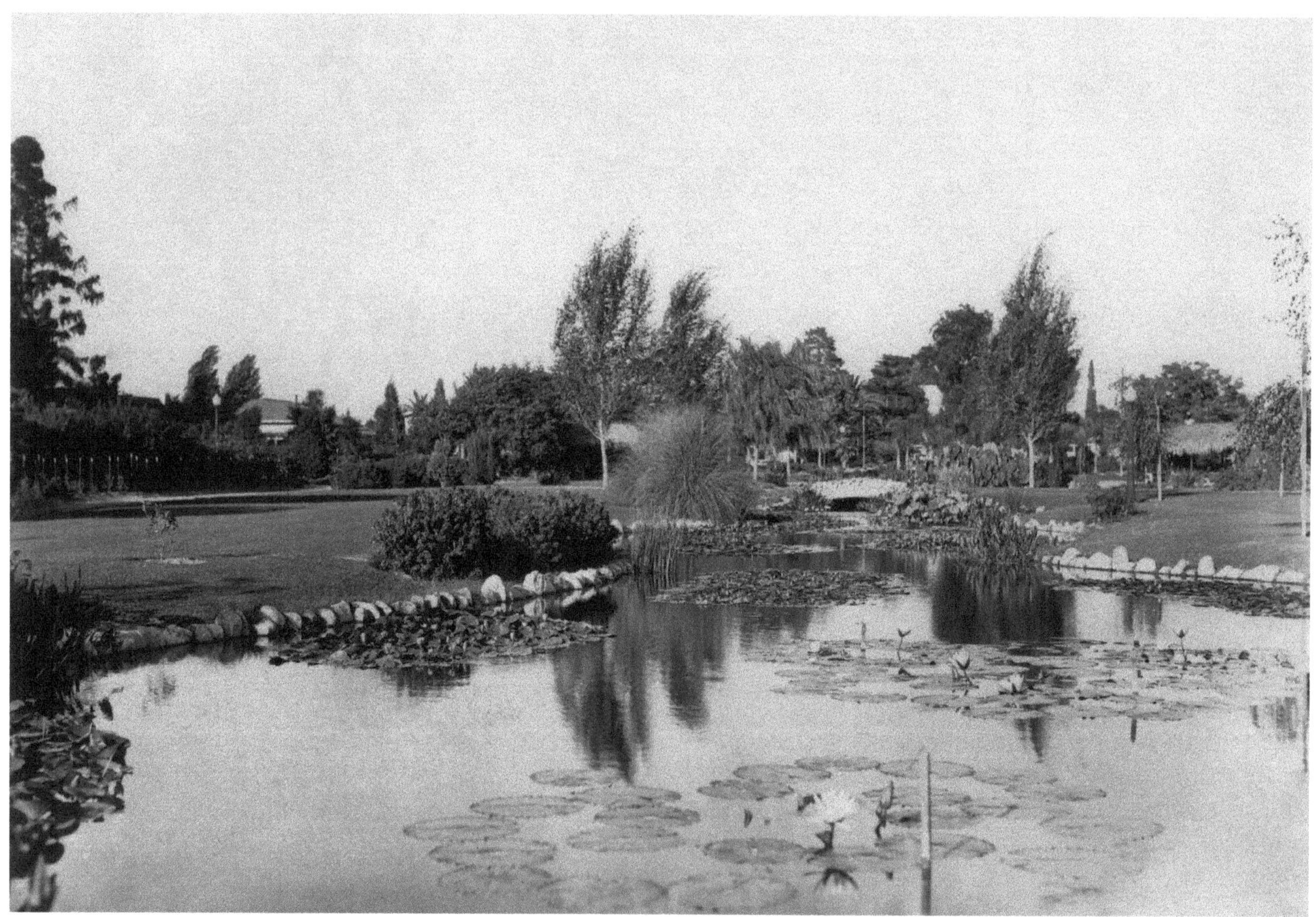

On July 15, 1927, the city fathers formally dedicated City Park's new $35,000 amphitheater. This scene shows the still-unfinished building draped in patriotic bunting in preparation for the opening ceremonies. Now called the Pearson Park Theater in recognition of the park's renaming in 1960 for longtime mayor Charles A. Pearson, it continues today to serve as Orange County's oldest cultural arts venue.

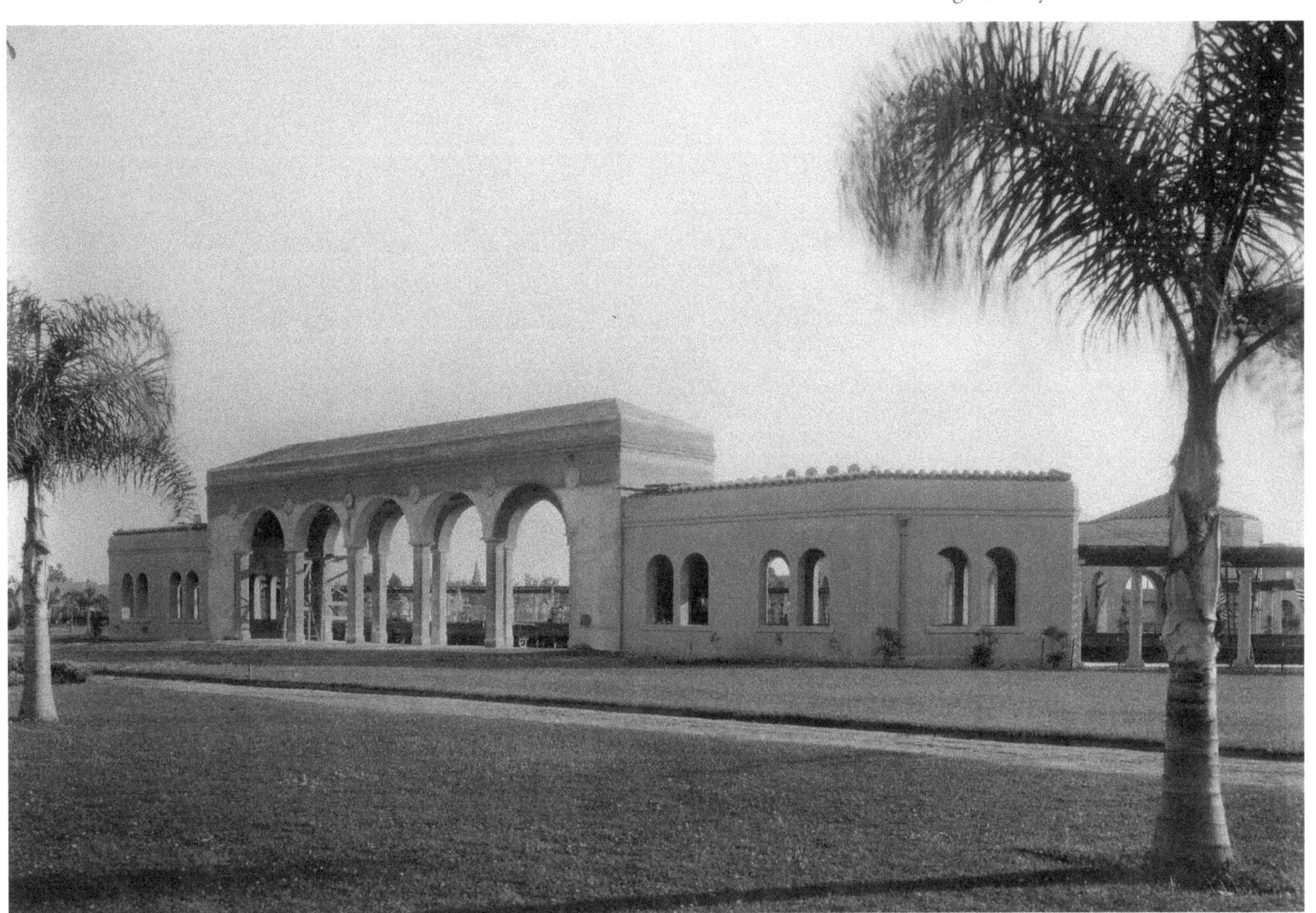

The Hotel Valencia, at the corner of Lemon Street and West Center Street, was built in 1916 by John B. Ziegler. It occupied the same corner where both the original Anaheim Hotel and the Commercial Hotel had stood. Designed by Anaheim architect M. Eugene Durfee and costing a formidable $40,000 to build, it was one of Anaheim's premier hotels for many years. This mid 1930s image shows both the First National Bank and the Oyster Loaf Café as first-floor tenants.

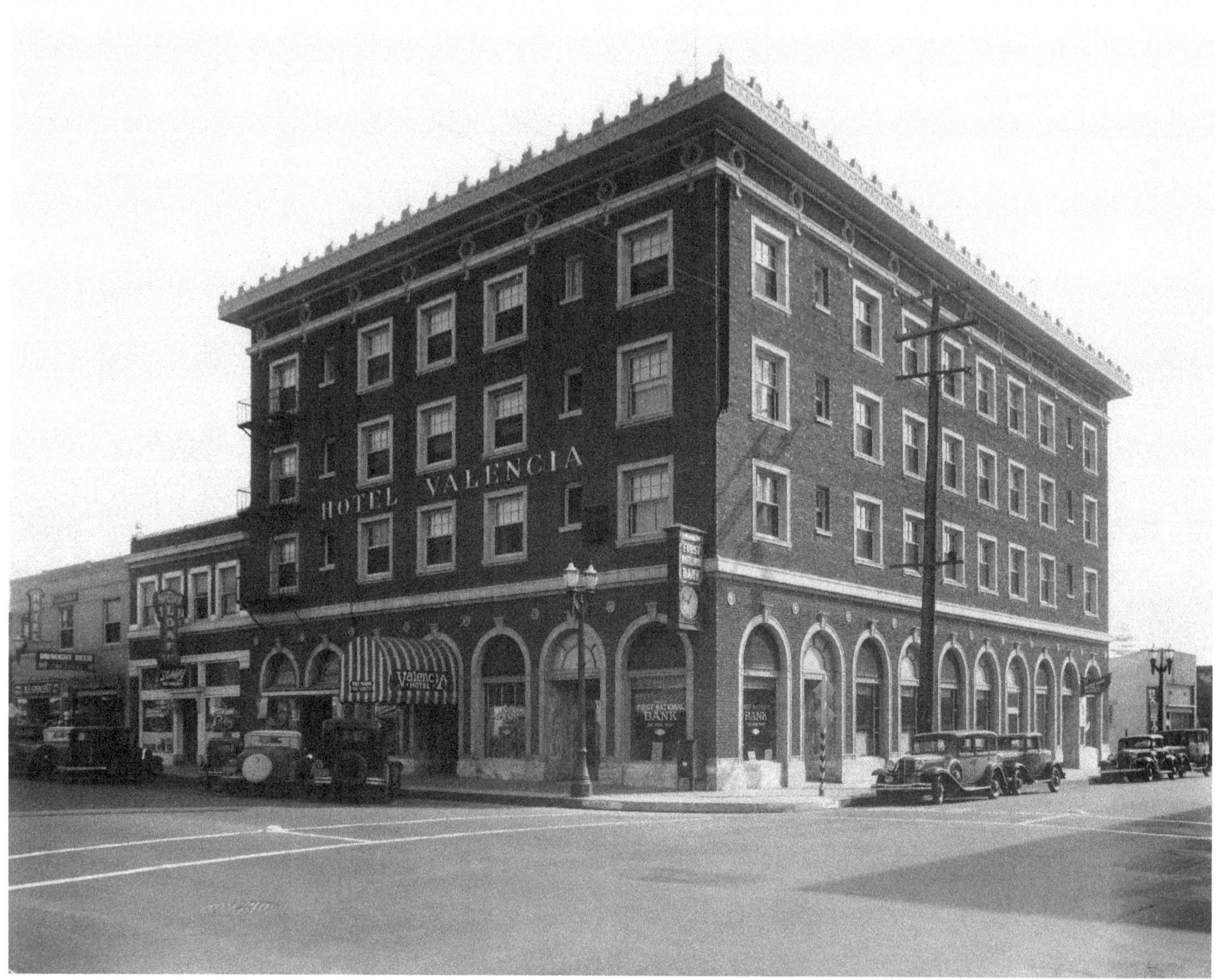

After a number of years of discussion, negotiating, and political wrangling, ground was finally broken for Anaheim's new post office on May 29, 1936. Eventually built for $86,000 and located at 121 West Broadway, this federal station continued to serve the postal needs of the community until its demolition in 1996. Here the officers of Anaheim's Masonic Lodge #207 officiate at the ceremony.

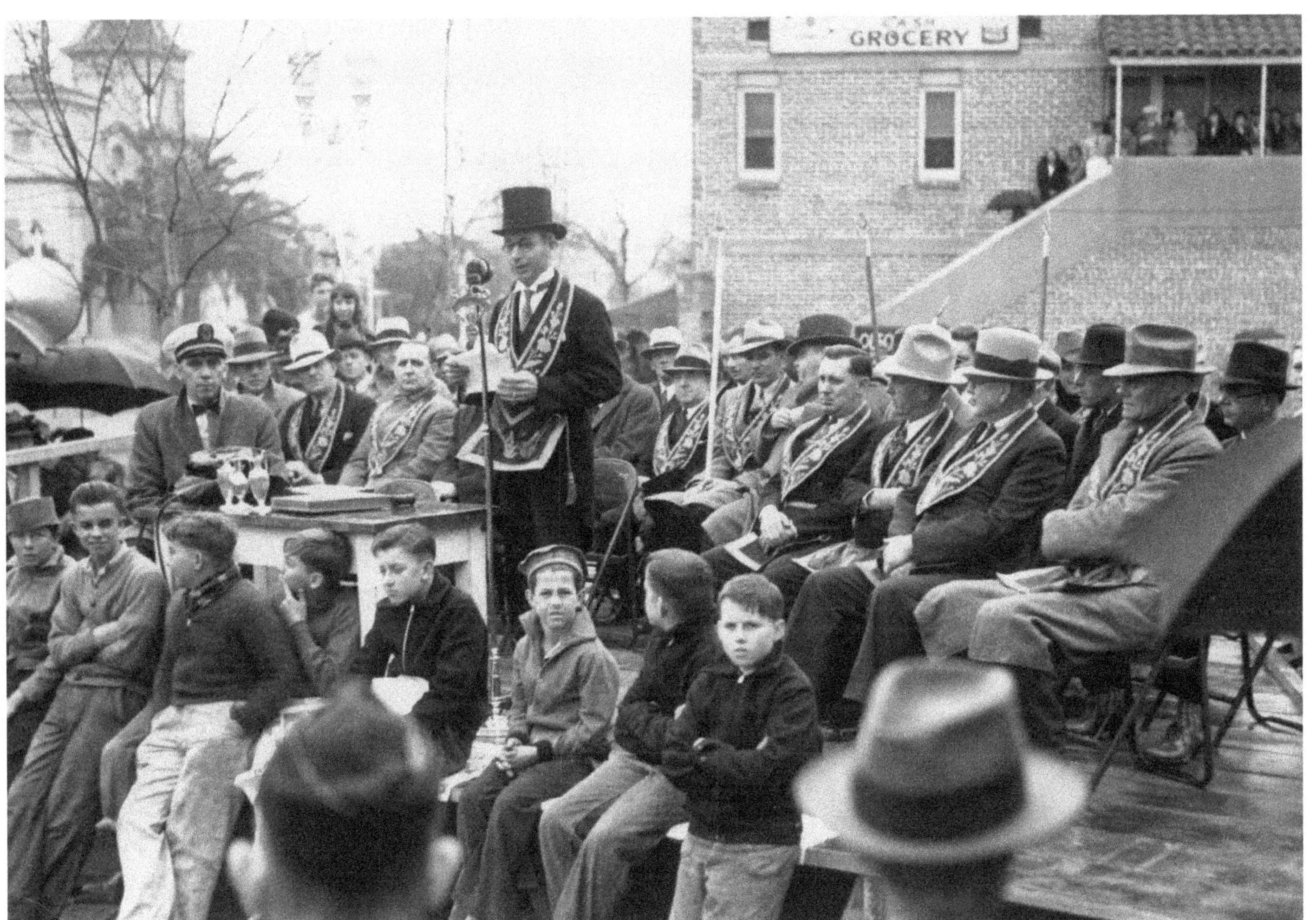

The packinghouse for the Anaheim Orange and Lemon Association, later renamed the Anaheim Valencia Orange Association, was built at 424 South Los Angeles Street in 1919. Anaheim's chamber of commerce boosted the area's Mediterranean climate as the "frostless belt." Anaheim citrus growers had packed more than 5 million boxes of Valencia oranges by 1930.

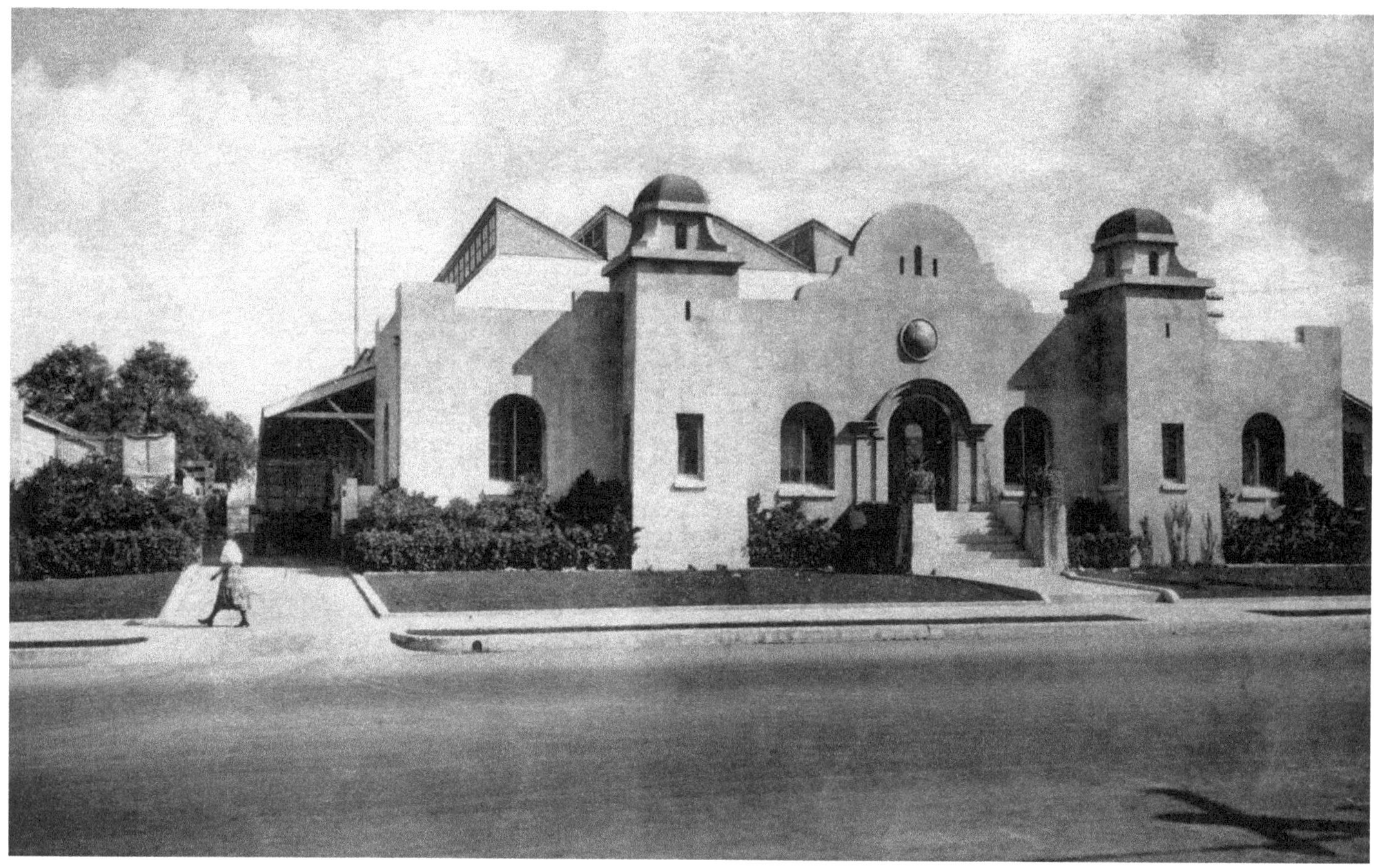

Around 1936, the chamber of commerce's latest publicity idea was to send one of the area's famous Valencia orange trees directly to New York City. This image of the truck and its precious cargo was recorded outside Anaheim's 1923 city hall building. Mayor Charles Mann (in the dark suit at doorway of the truck) is surrounded by local residents, who are wishing the truck and its important cargo good luck.

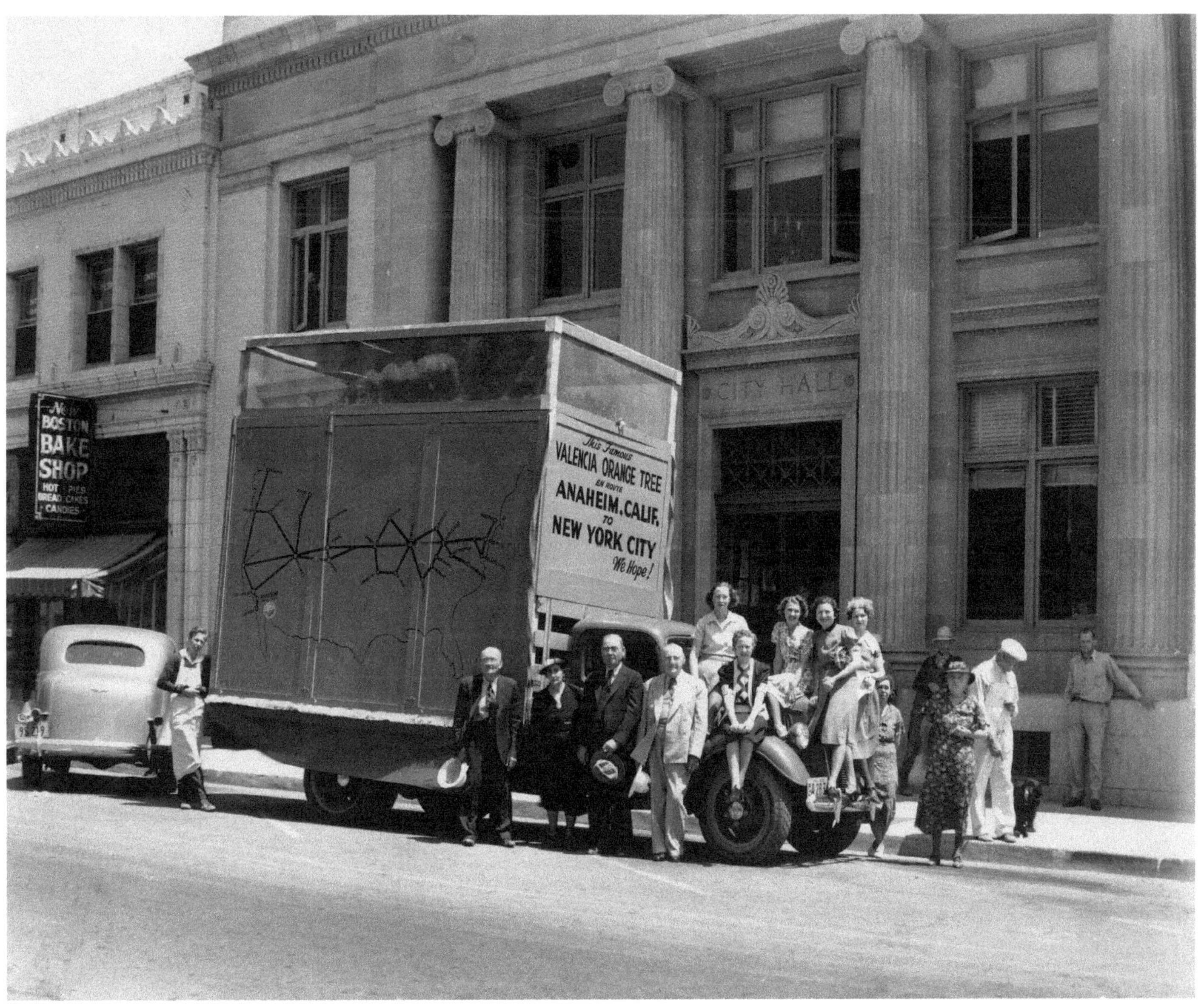

After several days of heavy rain, on the morning of March 3, 1938, the Santa Ana River broke through its banks and flooded most of northern Orange County. Anaheim was especially hard hit owing to its proximity to the river. This view captured the morning of the flood shows South Los Angeles Street from Broadway. In the background is the municipal water tower adjacent the powerhouse, where operator Oren Morey sounded the first warning whistle at 4:15 A.M., waking Anaheim's sleepy residents to the impending disaster.

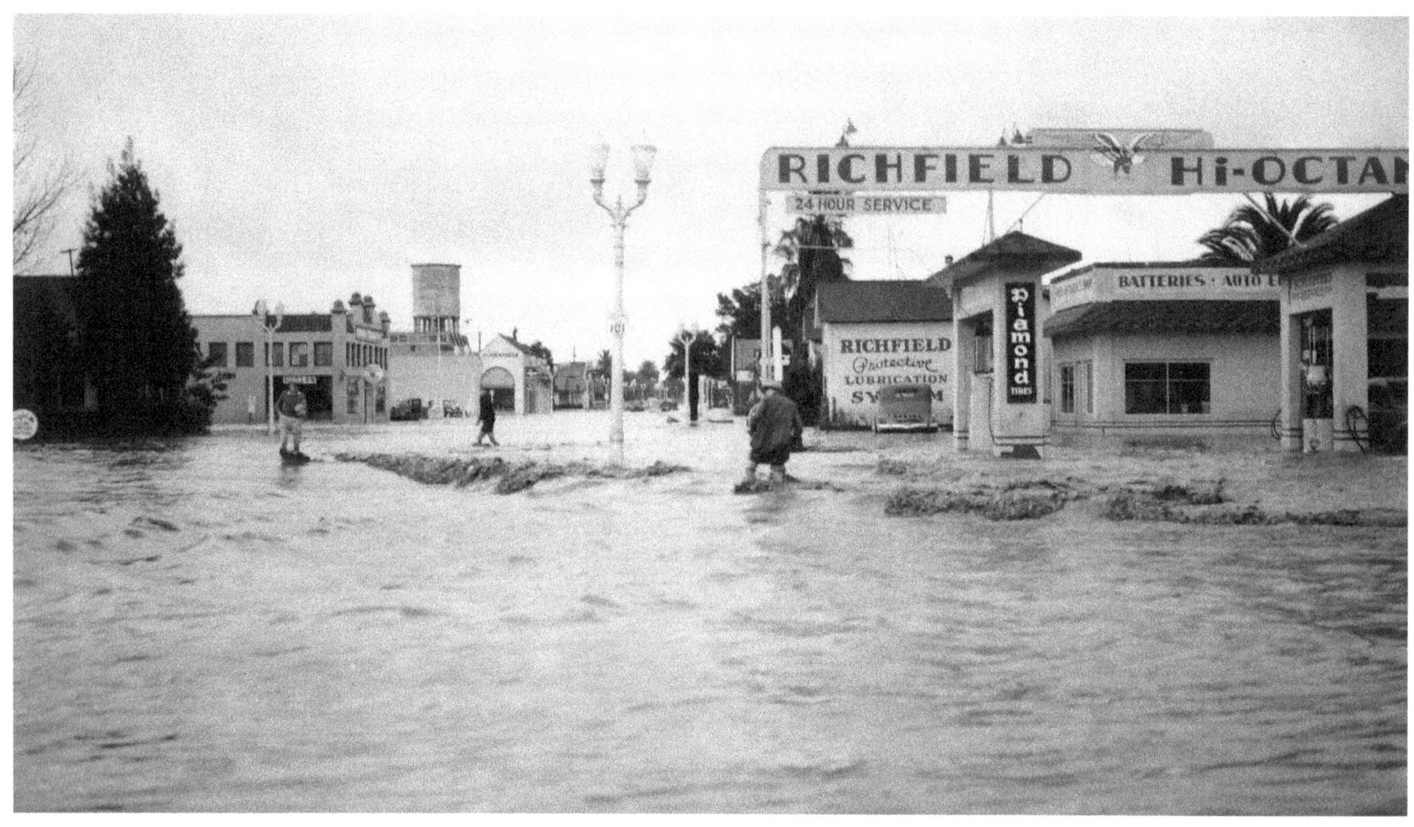

This view of North Los Angeles Street later the morning of the flood shows the receding floodwaters. Once the water drained away, storekeepers needed to deal with flooded basements and ruined merchandise. The basement of the telephone building on North Lemon was inundated, cutting off all phone service in the stricken community.

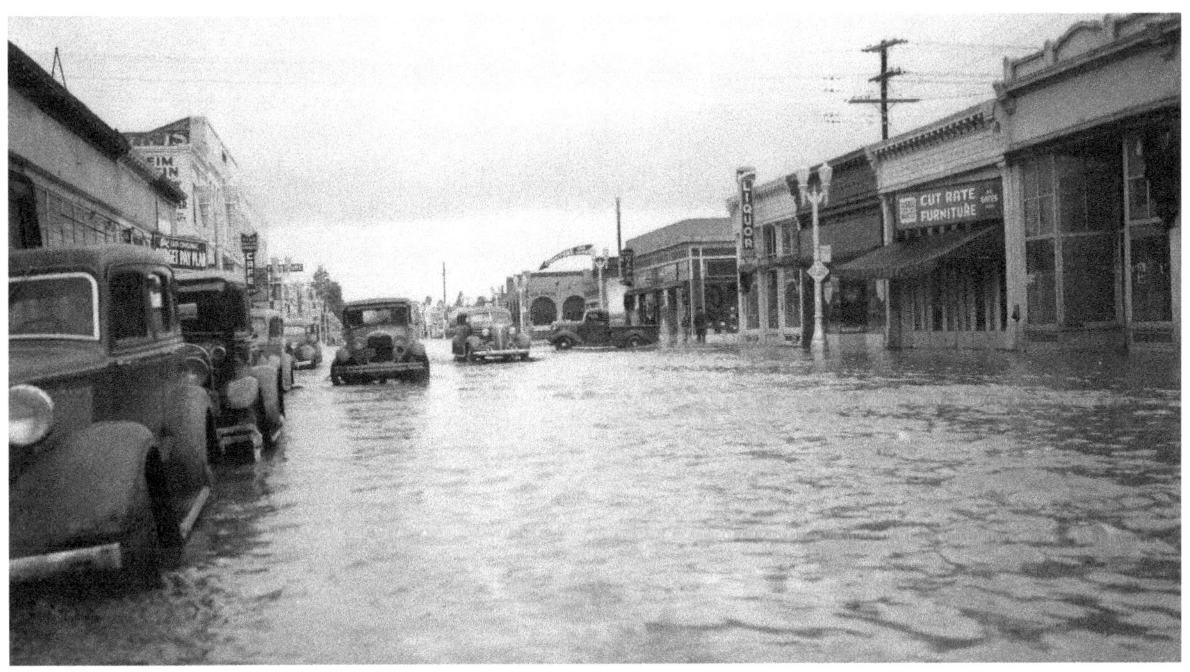

This bird's-eye view of East Center Street (now Lincoln Ave.) facing west shows the strong flood current as it passed through downtown. Center Street became a river, with wooden orange crates, lost pets, and other debris floating on the current. Debated for decades, the need for a flood-control dam in the Santa Ana Canyon was finally recognized after this catastrophe claimed 45 lives in the county.

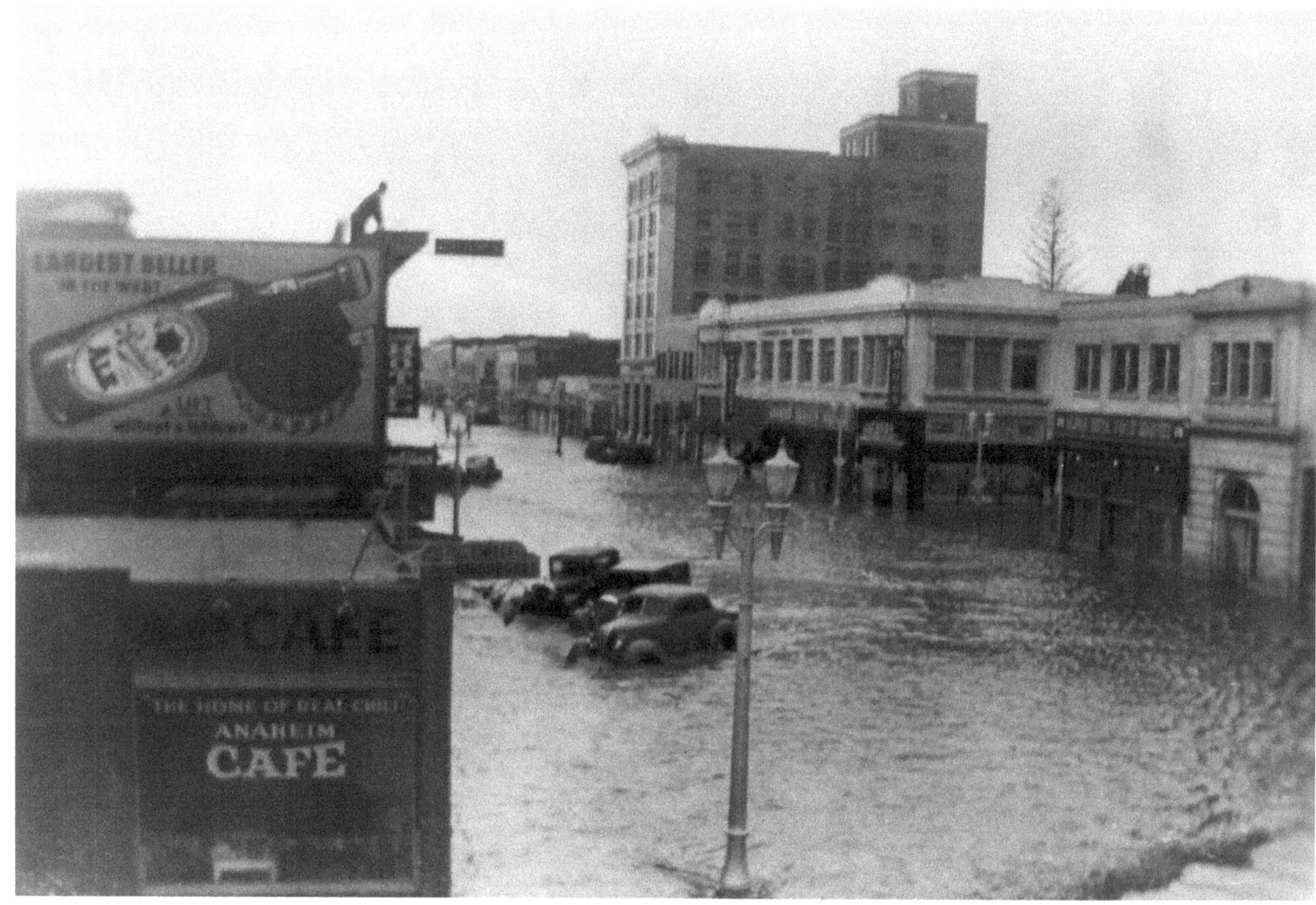

The name of Anaheim's second public park, located at the north entrance to the community, was chosen by public lottery. La Palma Park was dedicated as the city's newest public asset on Saturday, August 4, 1939. The park included a nicely arranged hardball diamond and would serve as the spring training grounds for the Philadelphia Athletics (1940–1943), and the St. Louis Browns (1946) professional baseball teams.

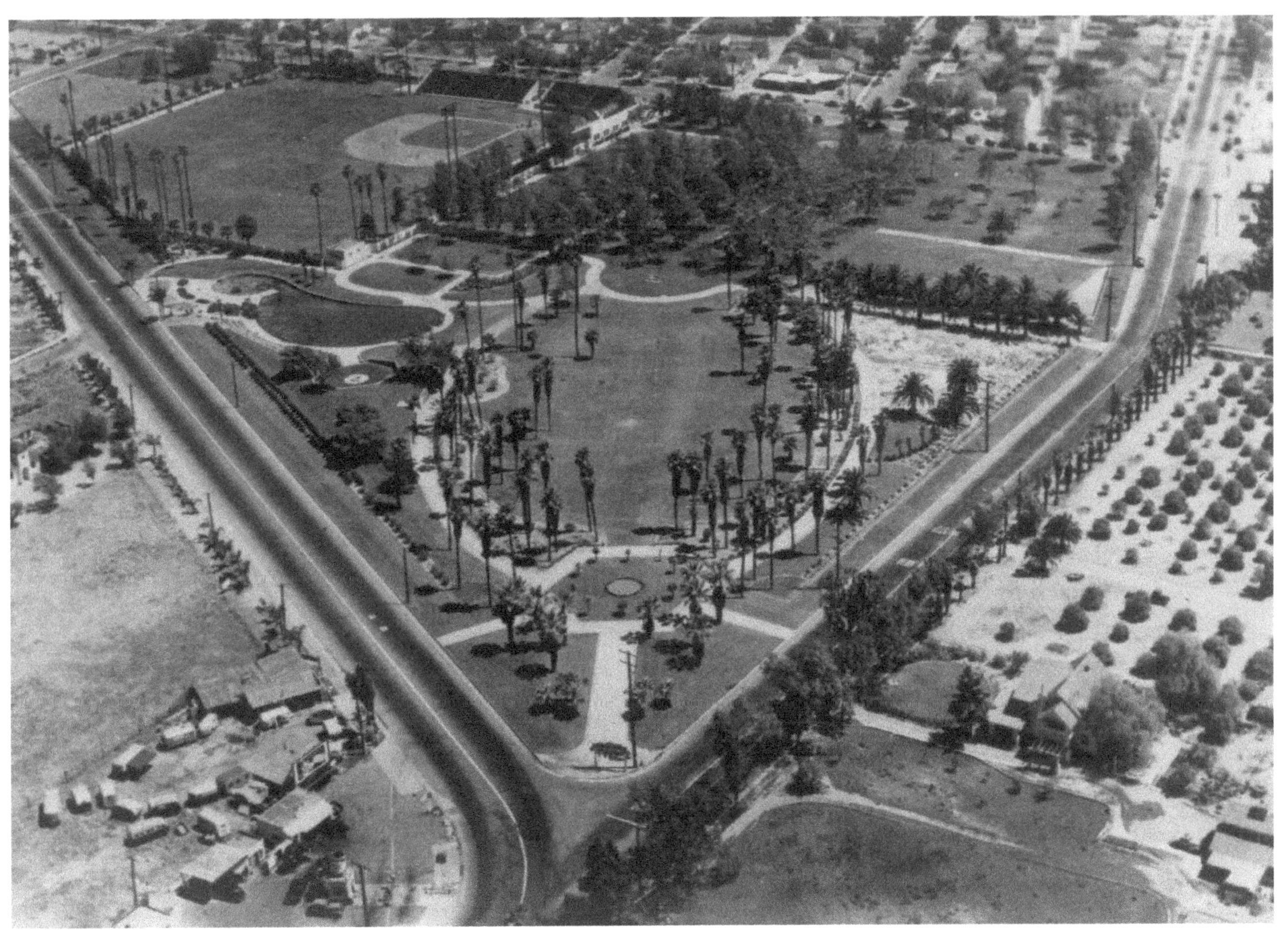

Anaheim's annual Halloween parade one year included this float, sponsored by the Anaheim chamber of commerce. A small model of Anaheim's original home, the Mother Colony House is accompanied by Miss Kathleen Burkhard and two-year-old Donna Reafsnyder.

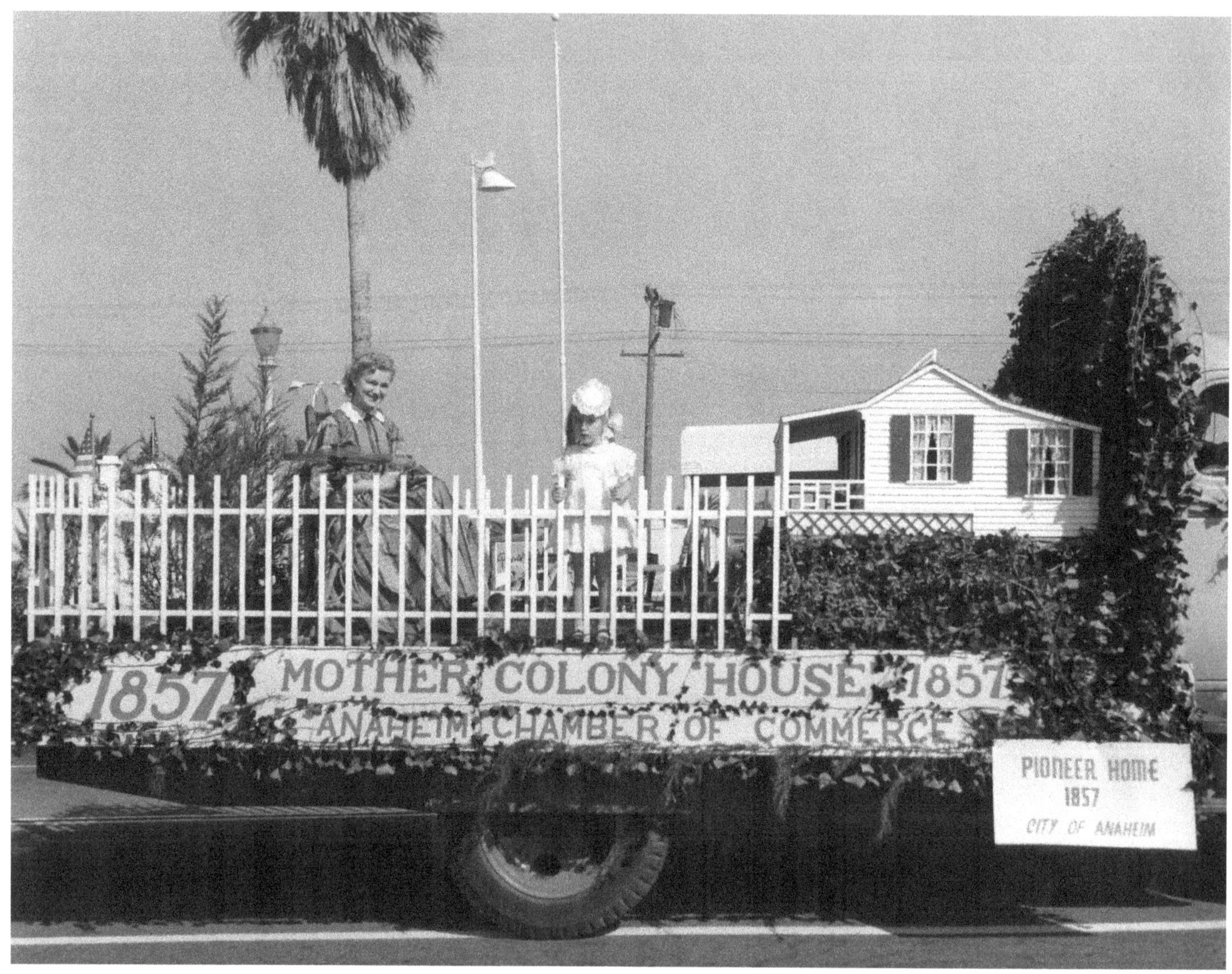

A City Is Born

(1940–1953)

Anaheim's elected leaders recognized as early as 1928 that for the town to flourish a dependable water supply was required. Located on the dry Southern California desert plain, the inconsistent flows from the Santa Ana River were always of concern. Once aquifer levels began to drop in the 1920s, Anaheim took a bold step and voted to join the Metropolitan Water District of Southern California with the hope of tapping the Colorado River, nearly 300 miles distant. This new water source arrived in late 1941, in time to benefit World War II Anaheim and the postwar development that followed. This move, perhaps more than any other, ensured Anaheim's, as well as Orange County's, growth well into the twenty-first century.

The city's new public asset, La Palma Park, would welcome two professional baseball teams for spring training in the early 1940s, presaging the arrival of the Los Angeles Angels twenty-five years later. Anaheim's mention on national radio as part of a Jack Benny radio gag fired up the local boosters, who made the most of this promotional opportunity. While the war years were generally quiet for Anaheim, the community leaders' insistence on developing local industry would pay big dividends in the post World War II era. Light manufacturing would join and eventually replace the citrus industry that had made Anaheim the "Capital of the Valencia Orange Empire."

Anaheim's population of just over 11,000 in 1940 would grow to nearly 30,000 by 1954 as many returning war veterans found the area's modest housing prices and the many jobs attractive. Anaheim's city limits would grow from a scant 3.7 square miles in 1940 to more than ten square miles by 1954 as the city annexed new and potential residential and commercial sites.

Just as a blight had forced the early colonists to change from the propagation of the grape to the Valencia orange in the 1880s, so again did the onset of a citrus disease in the late 1940s, called Quick Decline, coupled with increasingly expensive irrigation water and property taxes force another change on the growers. Few citrus ranchers in the post World War II era could deny that the profits made by selling their long-held properties to residential subdividers far exceeded any current income they derived from citriculture. One by one the groves were lost as were the many packinghouses that served them. Anaheim would now enter a time of change so dramatic the look of not only the community, but Orange County as a whole, would change forever.

Anaheim's new La Palma Park featured a full-size hardball diamond and concrete bleachers. The chamber of commerce strongly promoted the facility, which, together with the area's mild winter climate persuaded Connie Mack's Philadelphia Athletics to make Anaheim their spring training grounds from 1940 to 1942. An exhibition game held in 1940 shows Anaheim police chief James Bouldin trying his luck in the batter's box.

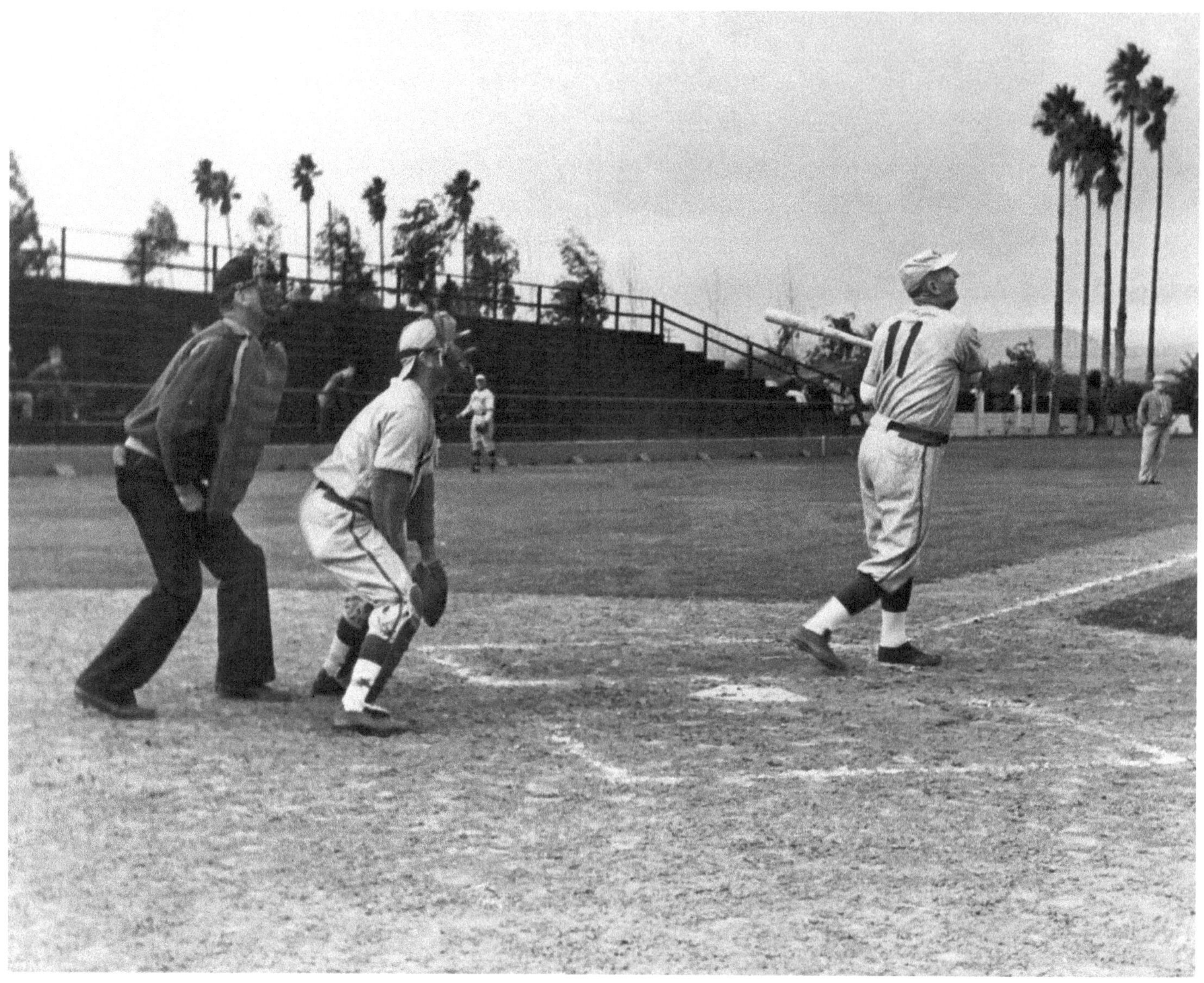

Anaheim survived the World War II years well although a number of its sons and daughters were lost to the conflict. In order to provide nighttime safety, the city built this air raid lookout tower behind the city powerhouse on South Claudina Street. Manned by local "wardens," the facility served to protect loved ones at home from surprise aircraft raids.

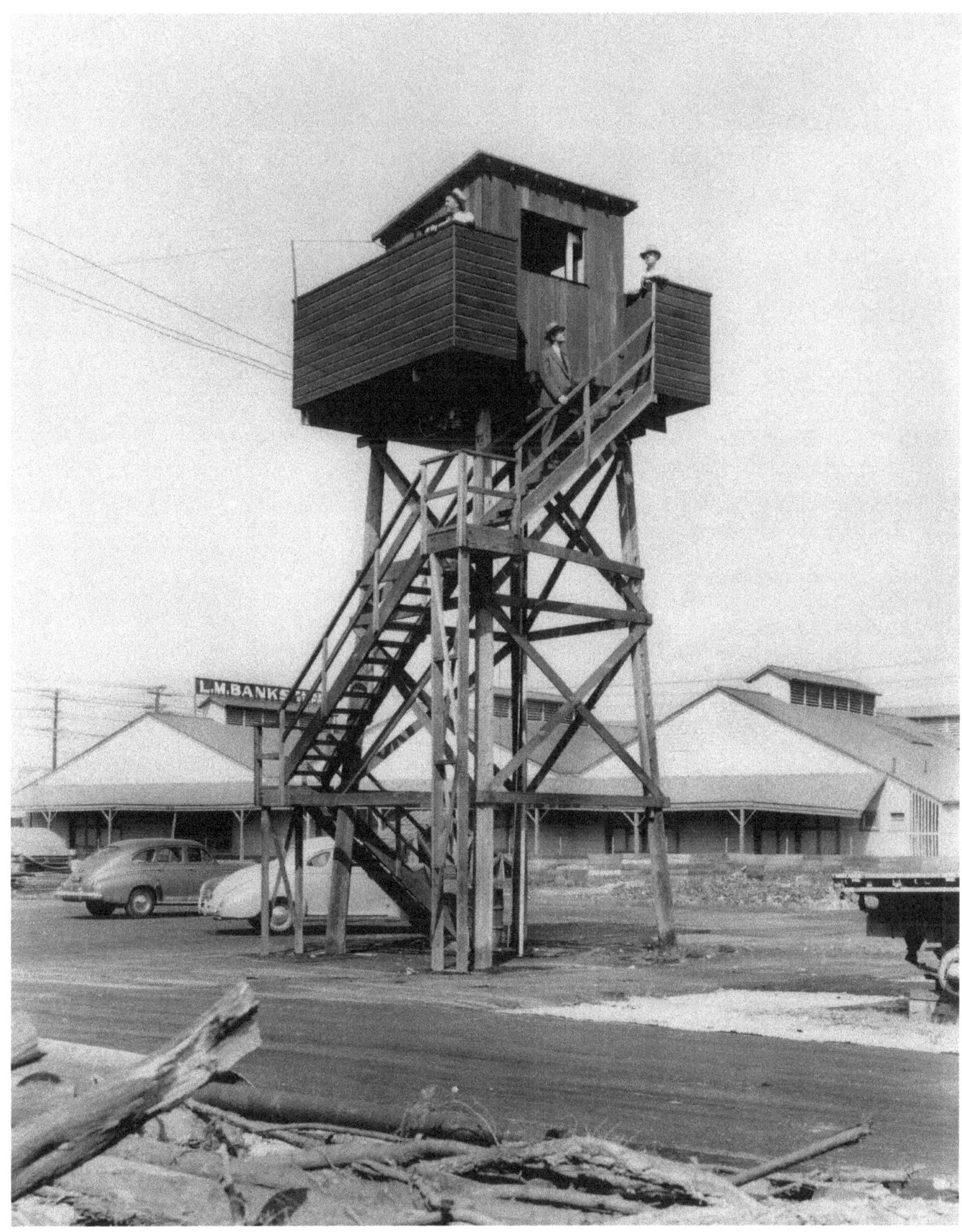

Orange County production of the Valencia orange peaked in 1938 when more than 9.3 million boxes, worth $16.9 million, were shipped from local packinghouses. Anaheim's Mediterranean-like climate, dubbed the "frostless belt" by local boosters, was ideal for the propagation of this kind of citrus and was home to a number of citrus packers. The interior of Orange Belt Fruit Distributors at 805 East Center Street is pictured here in 1940. Local women worked seasonally and handled the actual grading and packing of the fruit. Pictured from left to right are Marcella Gomez, Chonita Veyna, and two unidentified women packing Orange Belt's Three Star brand.

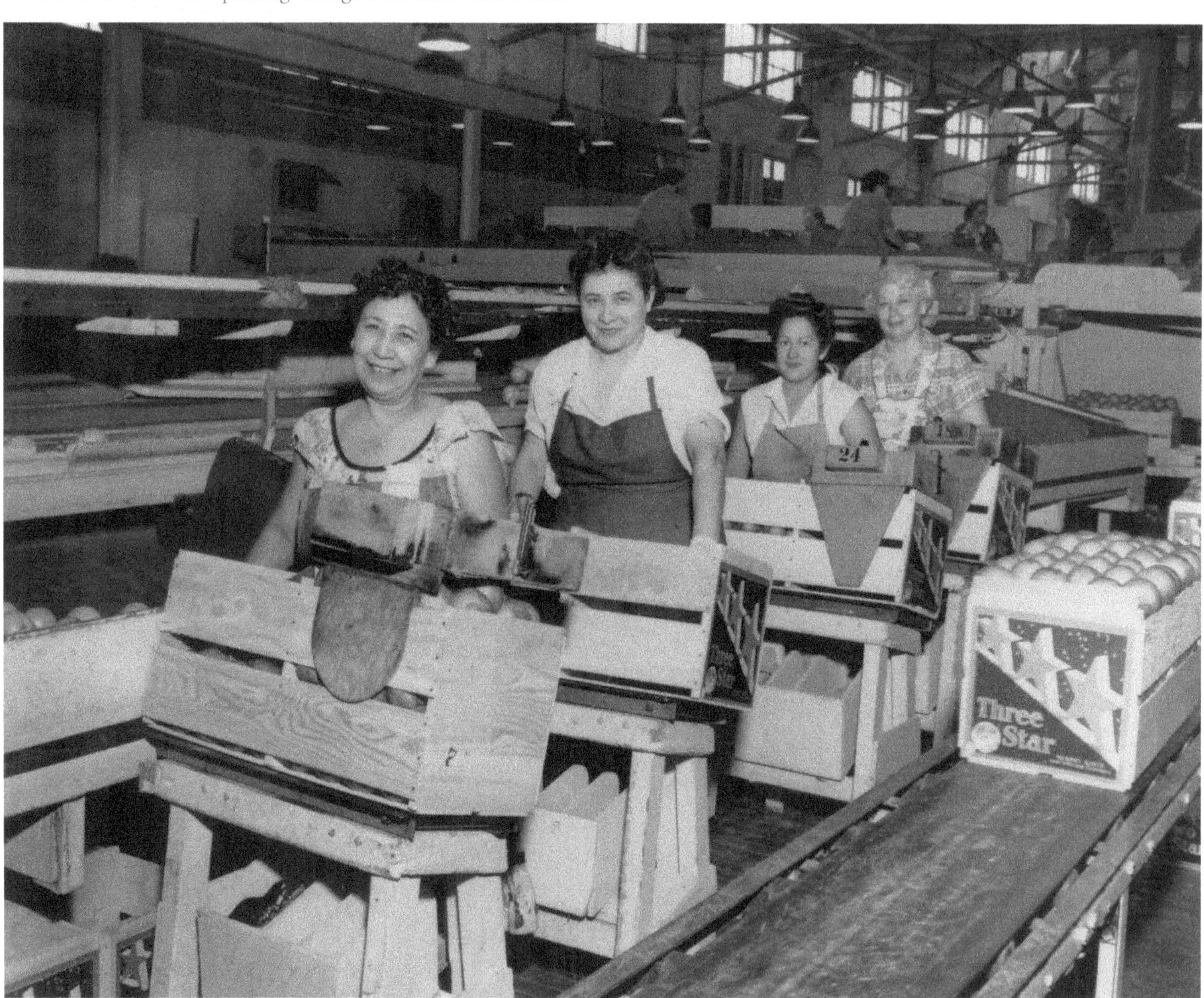

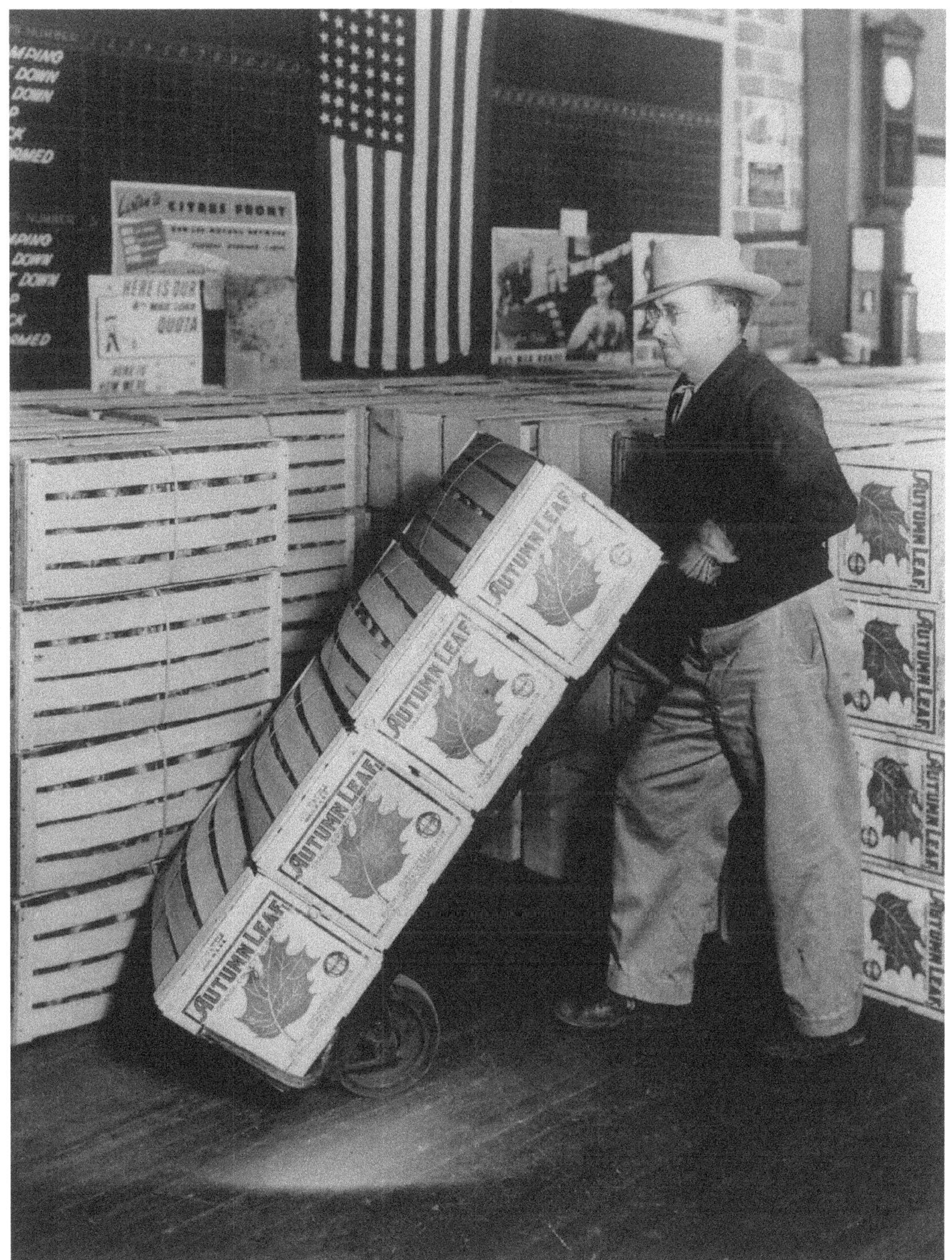

One of several local orange packinghouses in town, the Anaheim Cooperative Orange Association was owned by the fruit growers themselves. Their large modern facility was located at 1530-1540 West Lincoln Ave. This 1943 image (including a patriotic American flag in the doorway) shows Charles Reynolds loading crates of the co-op's Autumn Leaf brand.

As the "Capital of the Valencia Orange Empire," Anaheim was in the center of a large citrus-producing area. Its mild climate was especially important to the frost-sensitive citrus, as well as to prospective snowbound residents the chamber of commerce continued to woo. This view from ca. 1948 shows Frank Belmont's new Granada Fruit Company facility at center with the Borden Fruit Company at right facing East Center Street (now Lincoln Ave.). Although still dependent on citrus for its livelihood, several new industrial businesses were beginning to locate in postwar Anaheim.

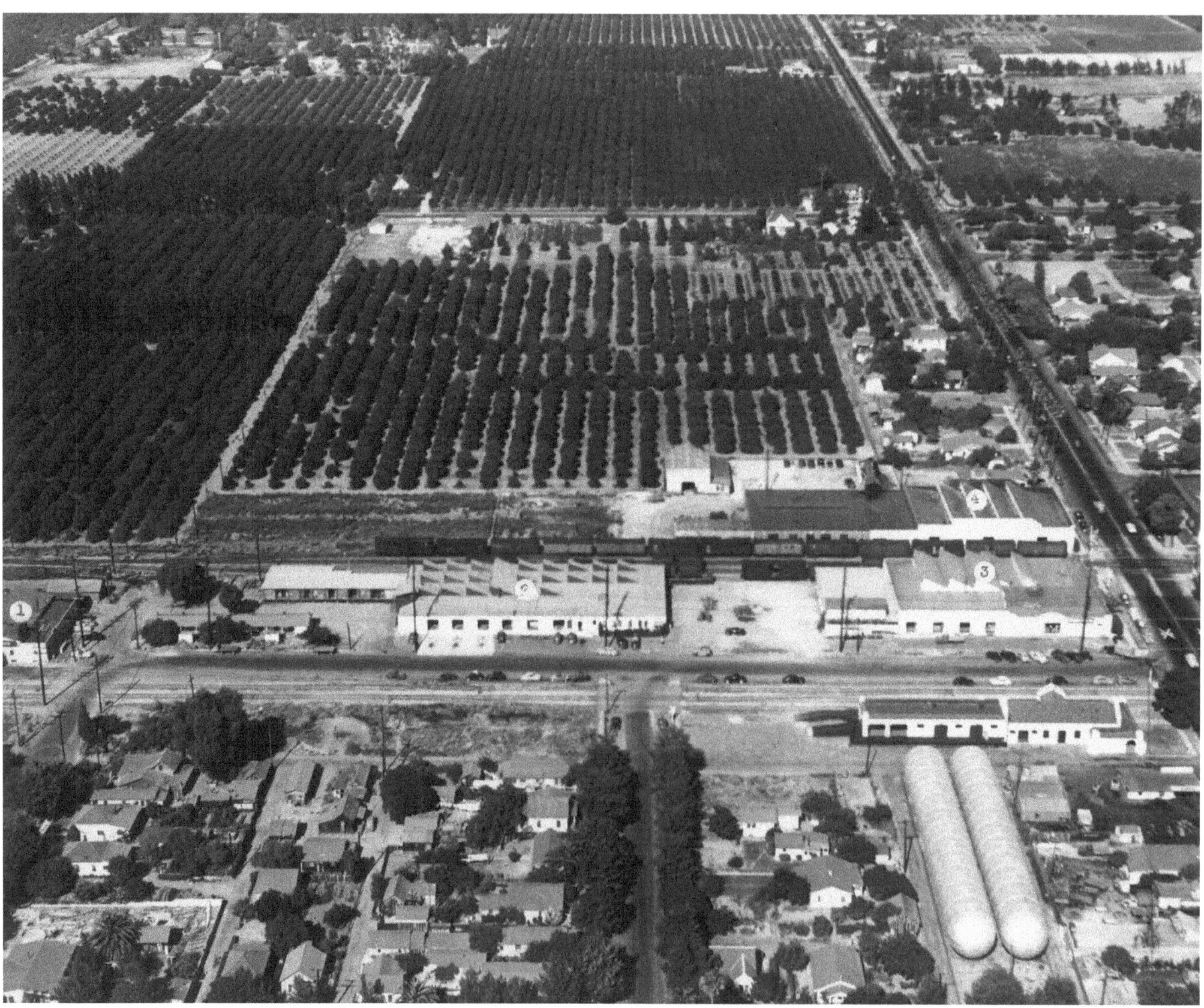

Much of Anaheim's citrus industry was located around the Santa Fe Railroad station on East Center Street. This 1953 view shows the Santa Fe depot at left-center, the Orange Belt Fruit Distributors across Center Street, the Anaheim Citrus Fruit Association across the tracks, and juice processor E. A. Silzle Corp. at the corner of Broadway and Atchison streets. Orange groves still surround most of the community, some to the northeast visible here.

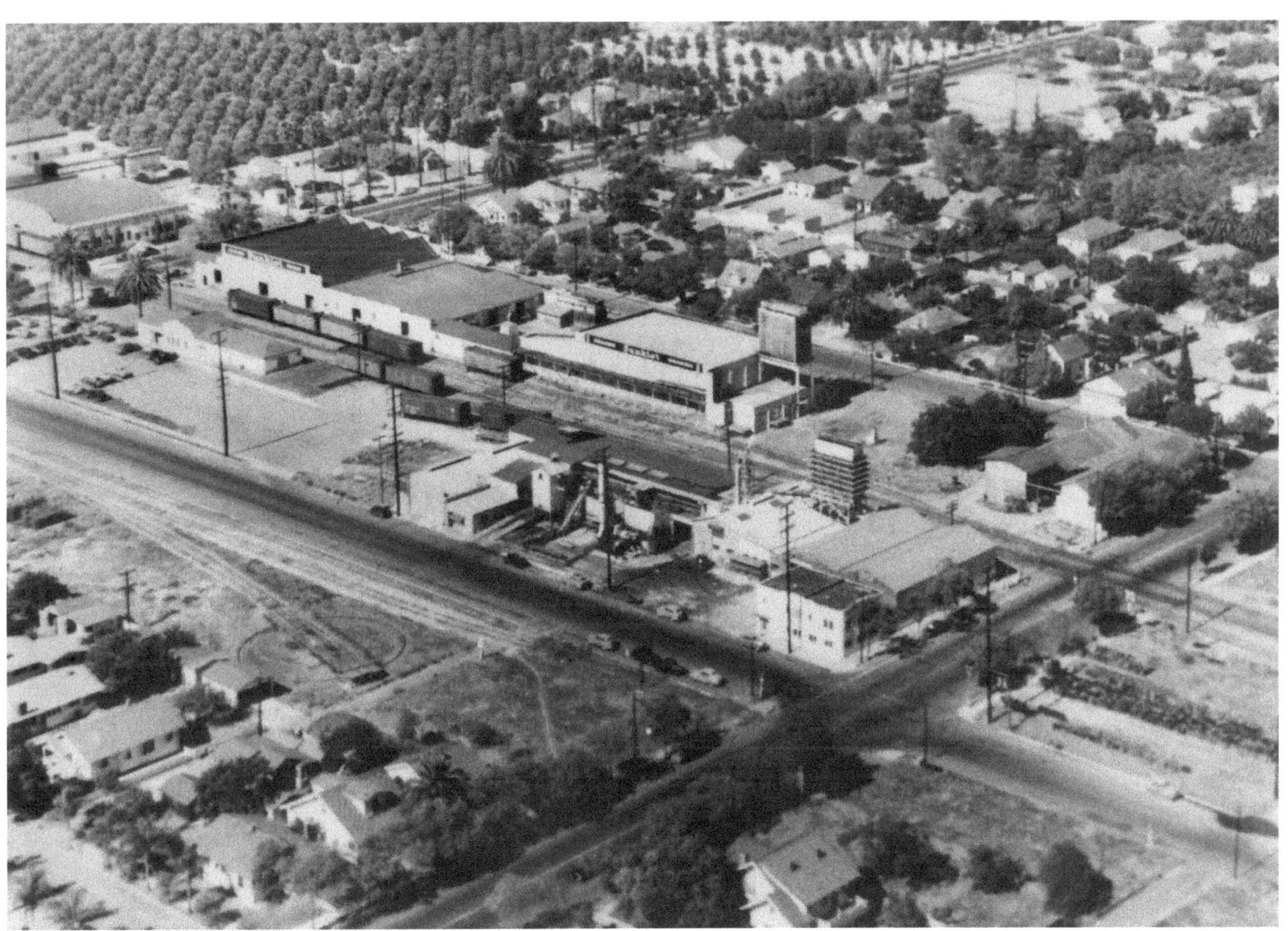

This 1946 aerial view facing east on Santa Ana Street shows a number of firms along Atchison Street (at center) including Winckler & Smith Citrus Products at 408 South Atchison Street and Mutual Citrus Products at 424 South Atchison Street. Within a few years, a newly reported citrus malady called Quick Decline and the high cost of irrigation water would devastate the local citrus industry. Coupled with a migration of returning World War II veterans seeking a milder climate and economical housing, ranchers would begin to sell off their long-held family farms for subdivisions, and the look of Anaheim as well as Orange County would change forever.

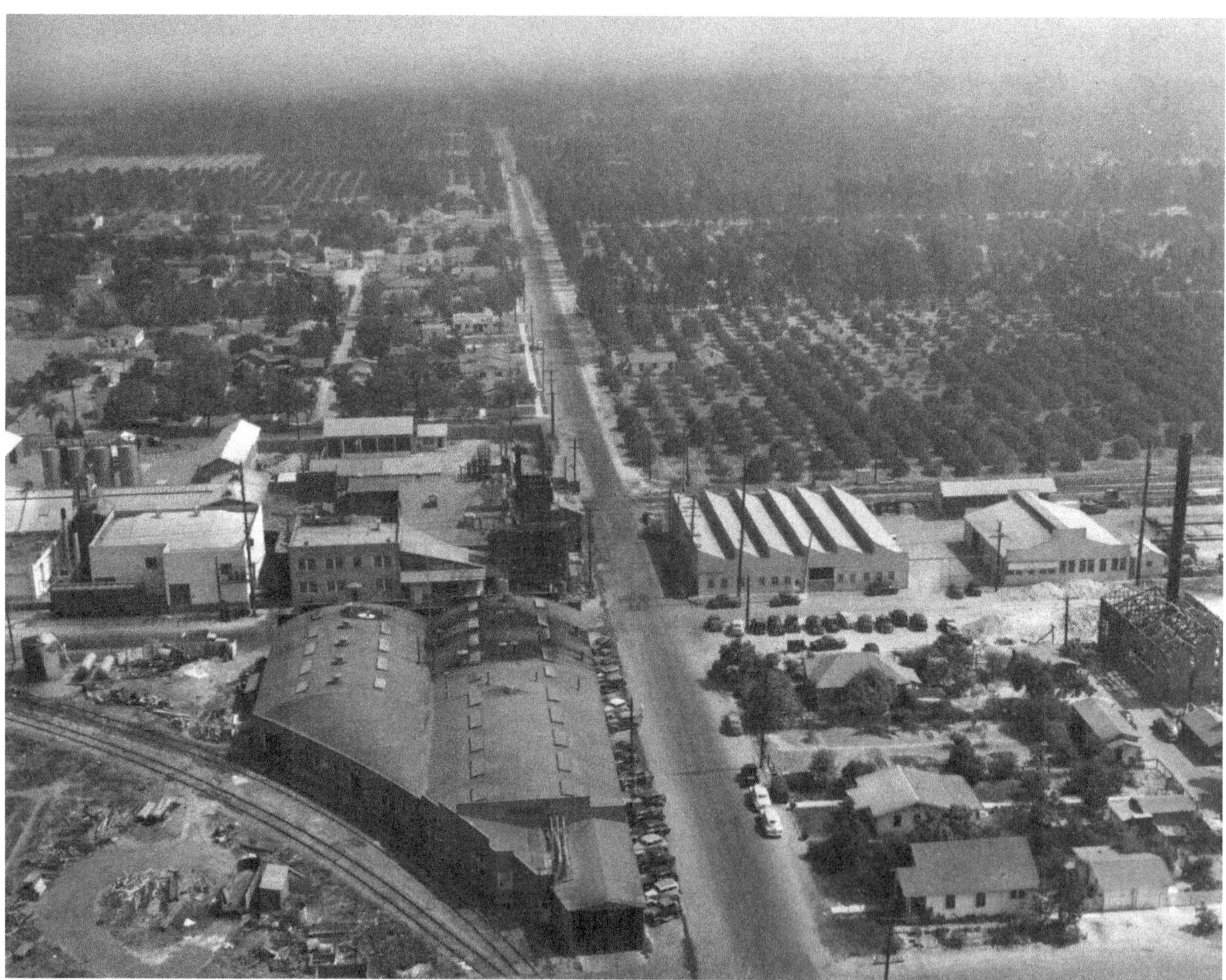

The Henry Brothers Drug Store is visible in this April 1946 view facing north on Lemon Street from Center Street. The upper floors of a number of downtown business buildings held apartments. The Roberts Apartments were located above the Henry Brothers store.

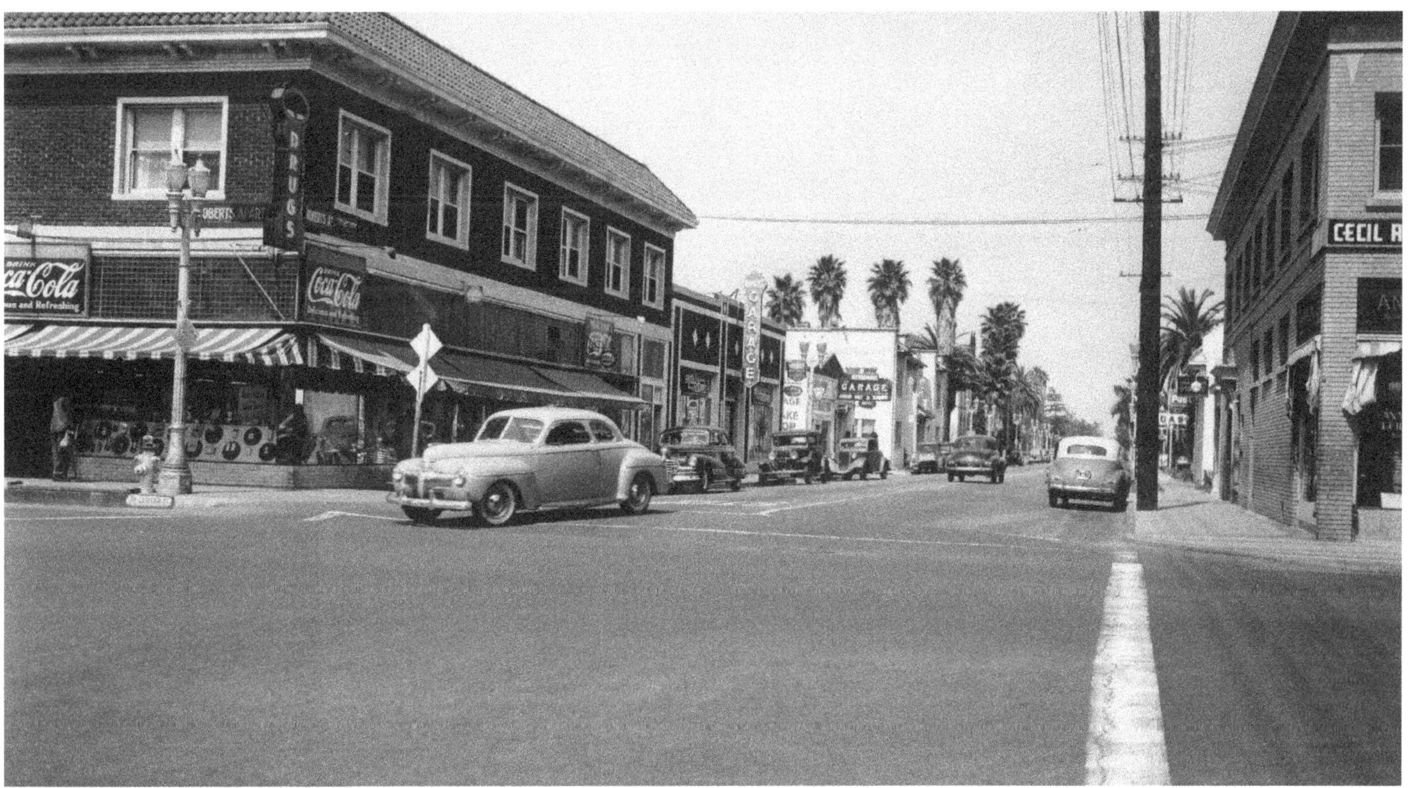

Facing east on Center Street across Lemon Street in April 1946. On the south (right) side of the street are the S.Q.R. department store at 202 West Center, the Southern County Bank at 184 West Center, the Hotel Valencia at 182 West Center, the Oyster Loaf Café at 174 West Center, and Rommel's Café at 170 West Center.

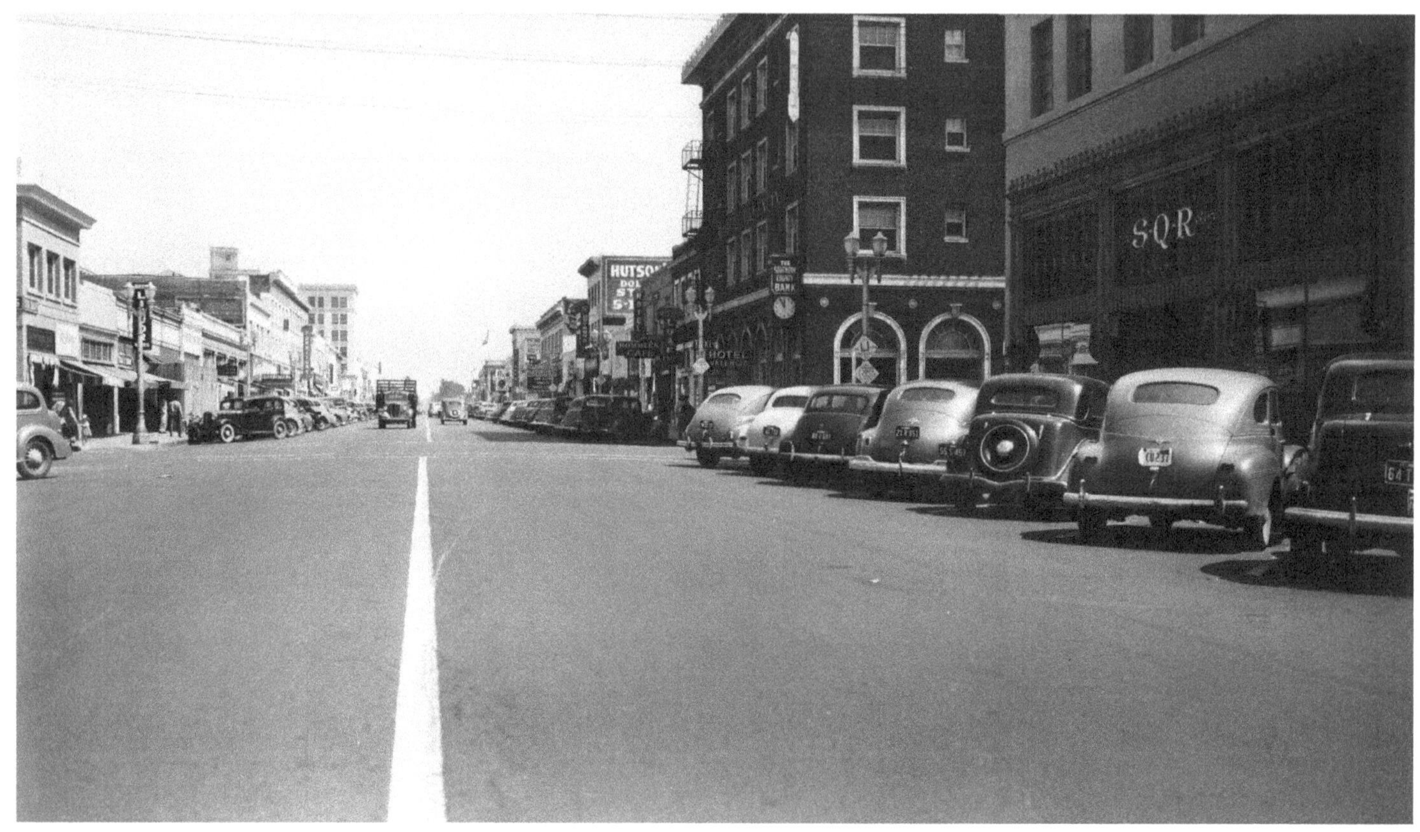

Comedian Jack Benny was the nation's most popular radio personality when on January 7, 1945, he included the name of the town in his famous "train leaving on track 5 for Anaheim, Azusa, and Cucamonga" comedy skit. Anaheim's chamber of commerce wasted no time proceeding to "adopt" Jack as their own native son. Plans were finally made to have Benny visit Anaheim during its Civic Progress Week celebration on April 21, 1947. The star arrived at the Anaheim Elks Clubhouse in a 1906 Maxwell driven by local Judge Raymond Thompson and surrounded by most of the community. Six-year-old David Faessel was surprised to see the famous radio voice in person.

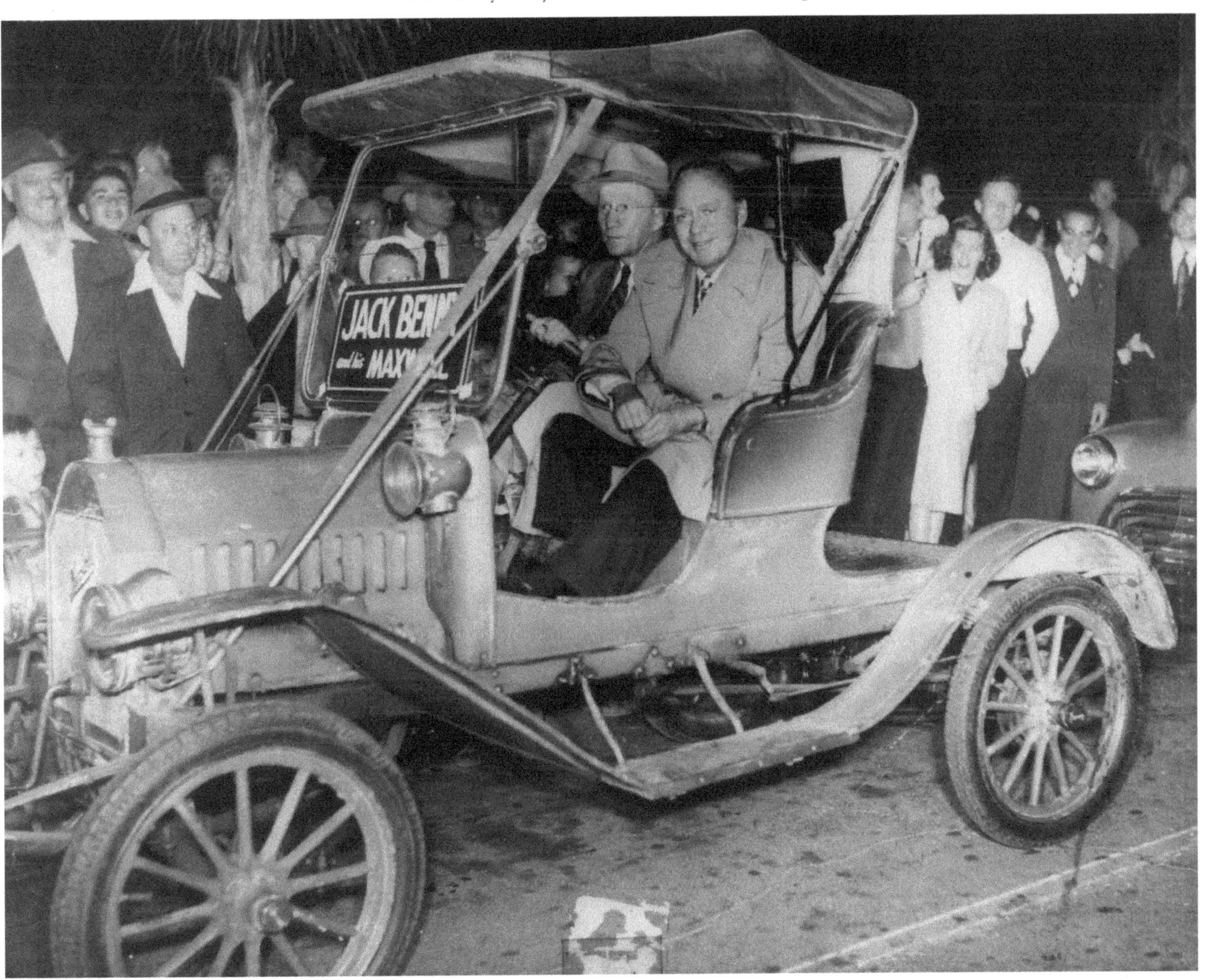

Anaheim's annual Halloween parade is marching west on Center Street here in 1947. The small float and costumed children illustrate the Hansel and Gretel story. By this time, Anaheim's old California Theater had been converted to a Fox Theater and featured a new, modern lighted marquee. The double feature today includes both Rex Harrison and Maureen O'Hara.

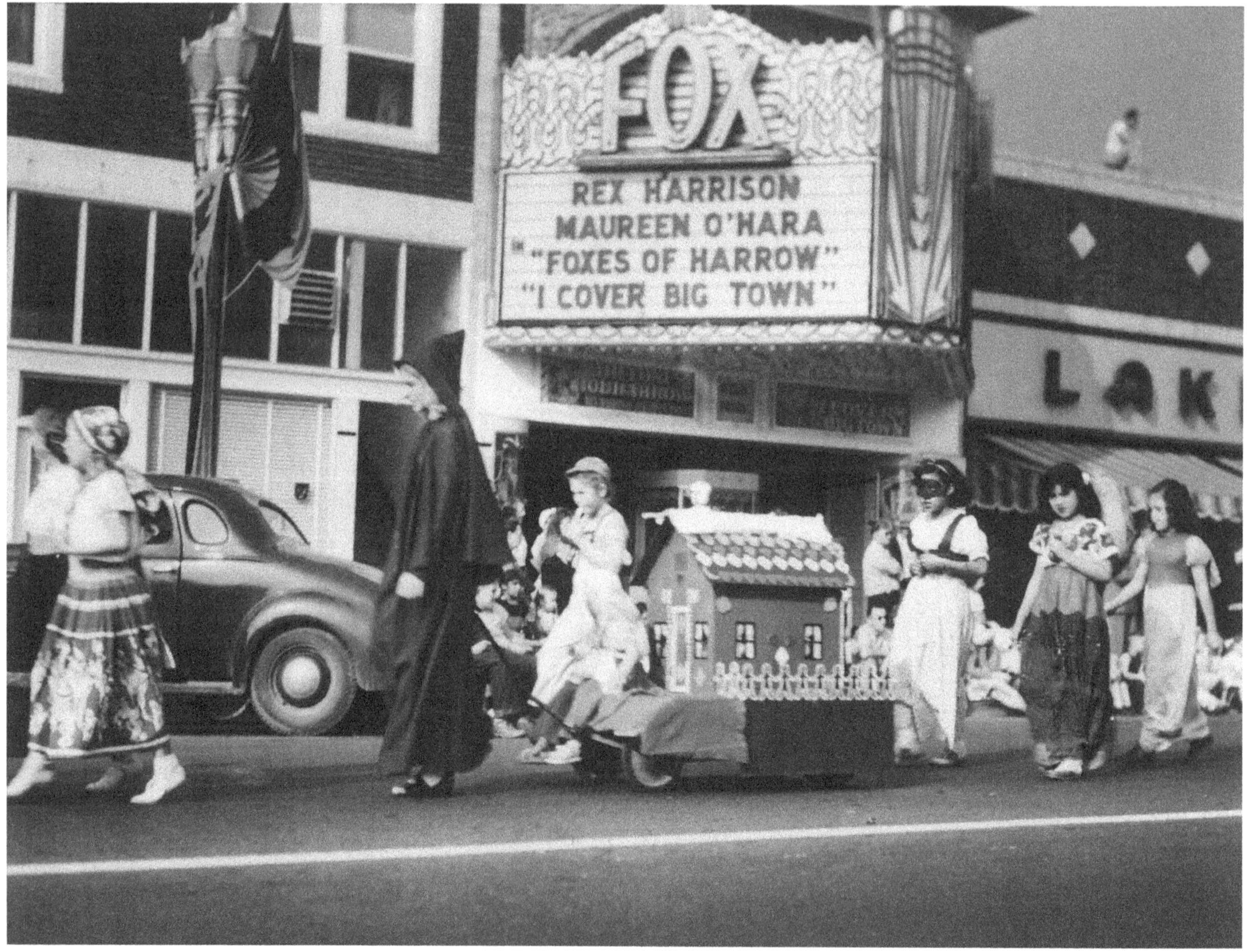

Anaheim's population was nearing 14,000 by 1948 and Center Street was its main thoroughfare. The county's tallest structure, the six-story Kraemer Building, is visible in this image of East Center Street. The F. W. Woolworth Store is also visible at 115 West Center as well as the Bank of America at 201 East Center Street. Urban redevelopment of the early 1980s would demolish all of these business buildings except the Kraemer, the last reminder of Anaheim's bustling post World War II downtown.

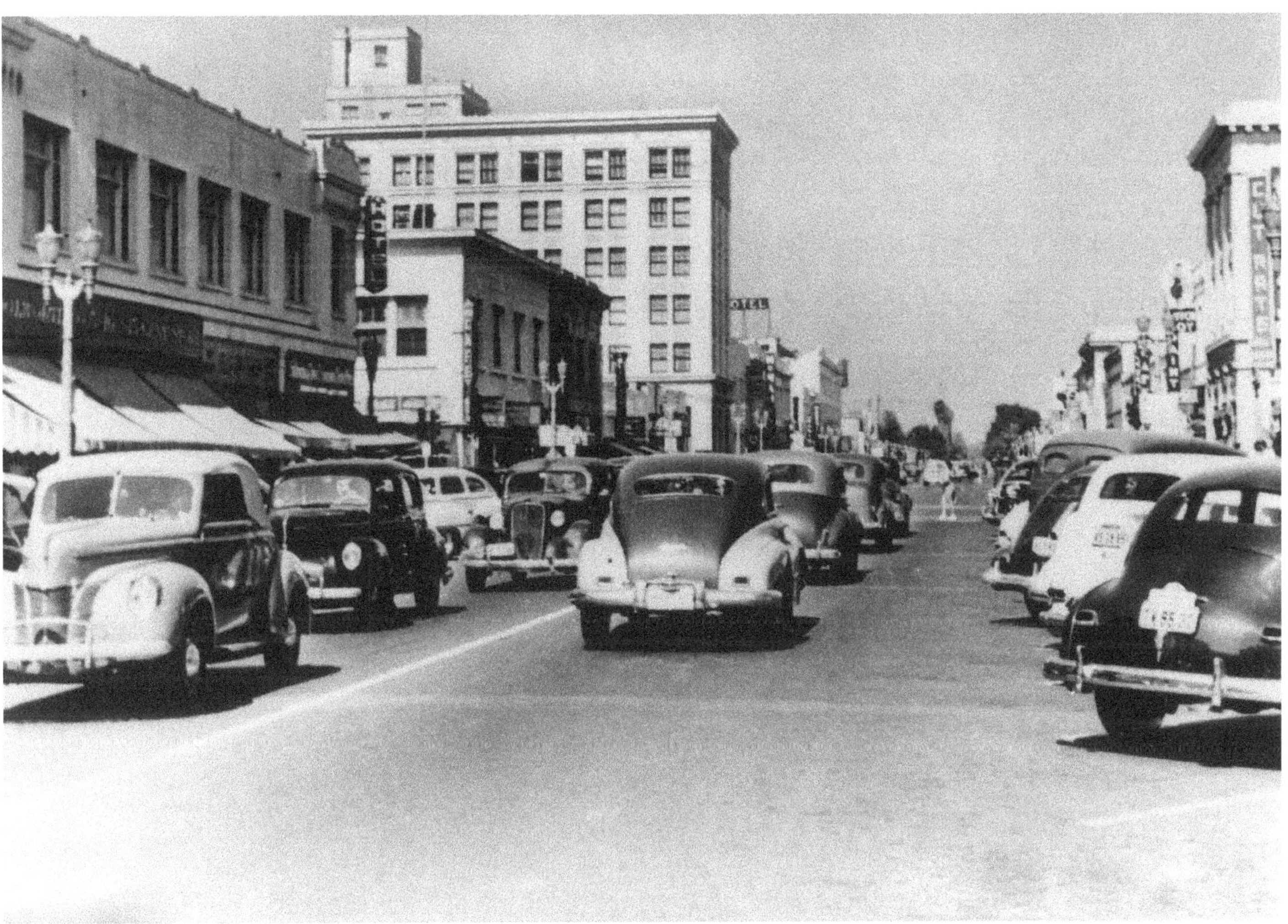

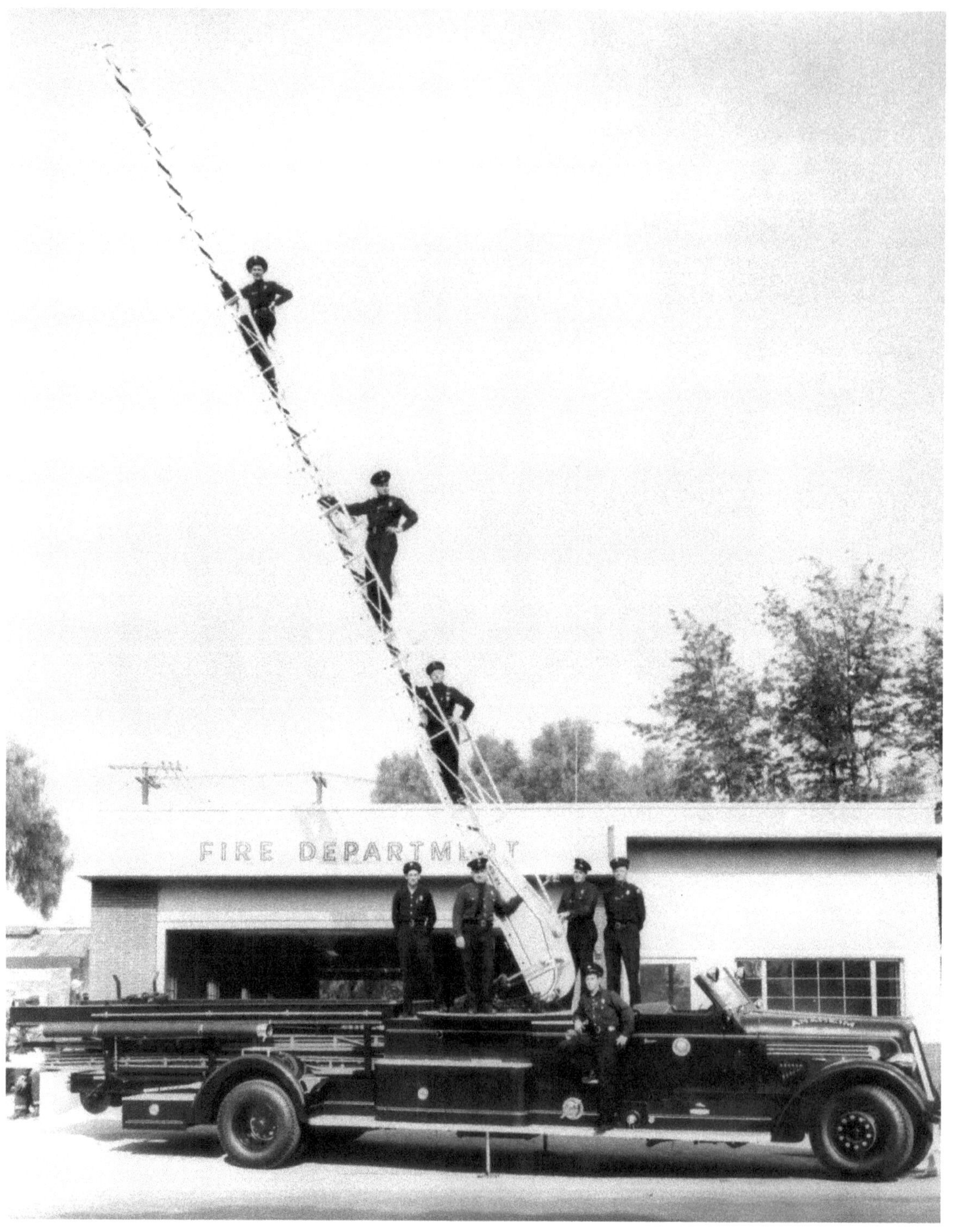

A growing city needs additional fire protection and when Anaheim took delivery of its new 1949 Seagrave city service fire truck, the department hammed it up for the photographer. From the top are James W. Wilson, James H. Gesler, John Saenger, Rex Bruhns, Fred Batenhorst, Chief Edward J. Stringer, Hubert Ladig, and George "Bill" Holden.

Anaheim's bustling downtown with its many shoppers in 1951. The 1950 census had just counted 14,522 noses, and records show that by this year the population ticked closer to 16,000. To the right is the S. H. Kress five and dime at 218 West Center Street, their large candy counter a favorite stop for parents with children in tow.

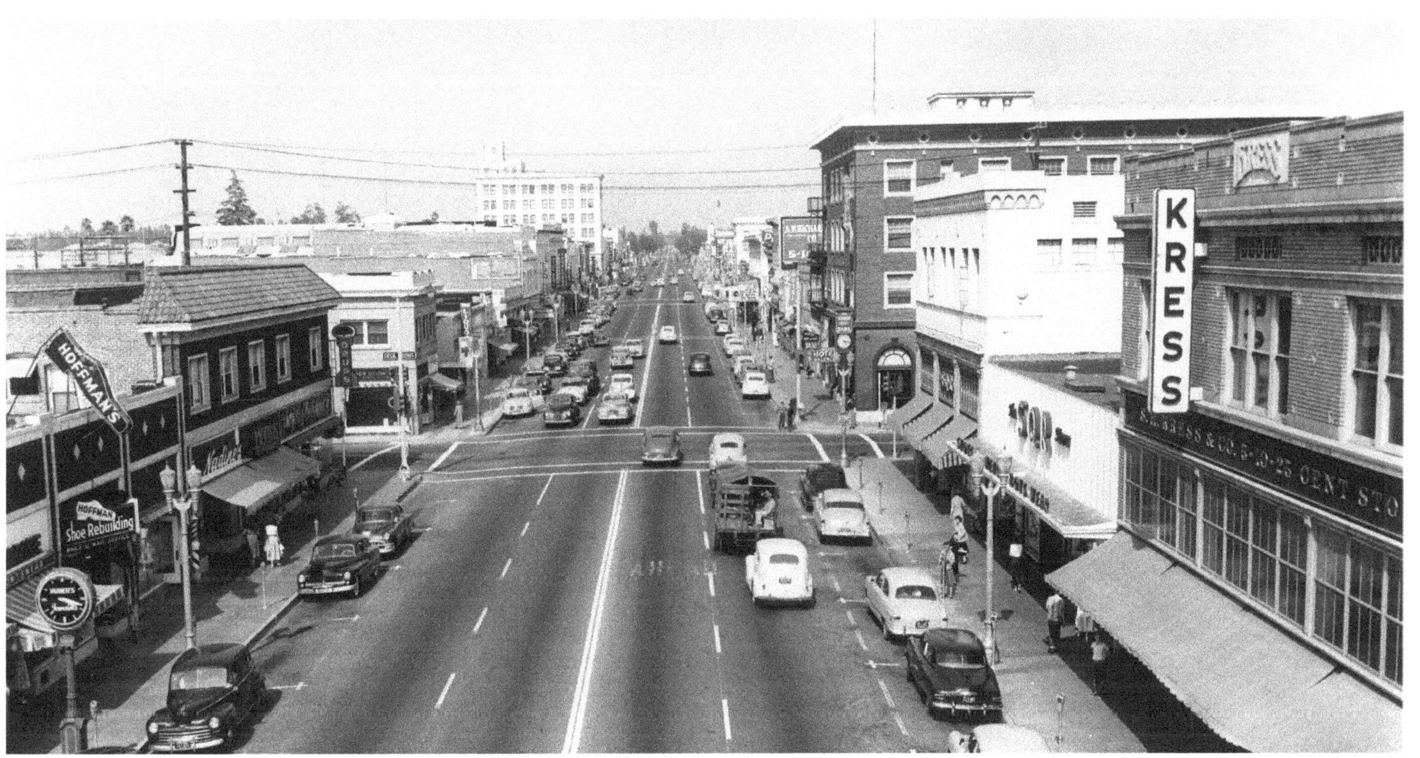

In August 1954, the McNeil Construction Company is preparing the grading for Disneyland. In just 11 months, Walt Disney's dream of a new kind of amusement park, for children and adults alike, would open in this dusty field, now devoid of the oranges and walnuts it produced for the old Anaheim families that had owned the land. Once the new "park" opened on July 17, 1955, Anaheim, and Orange County, would be forever changed.

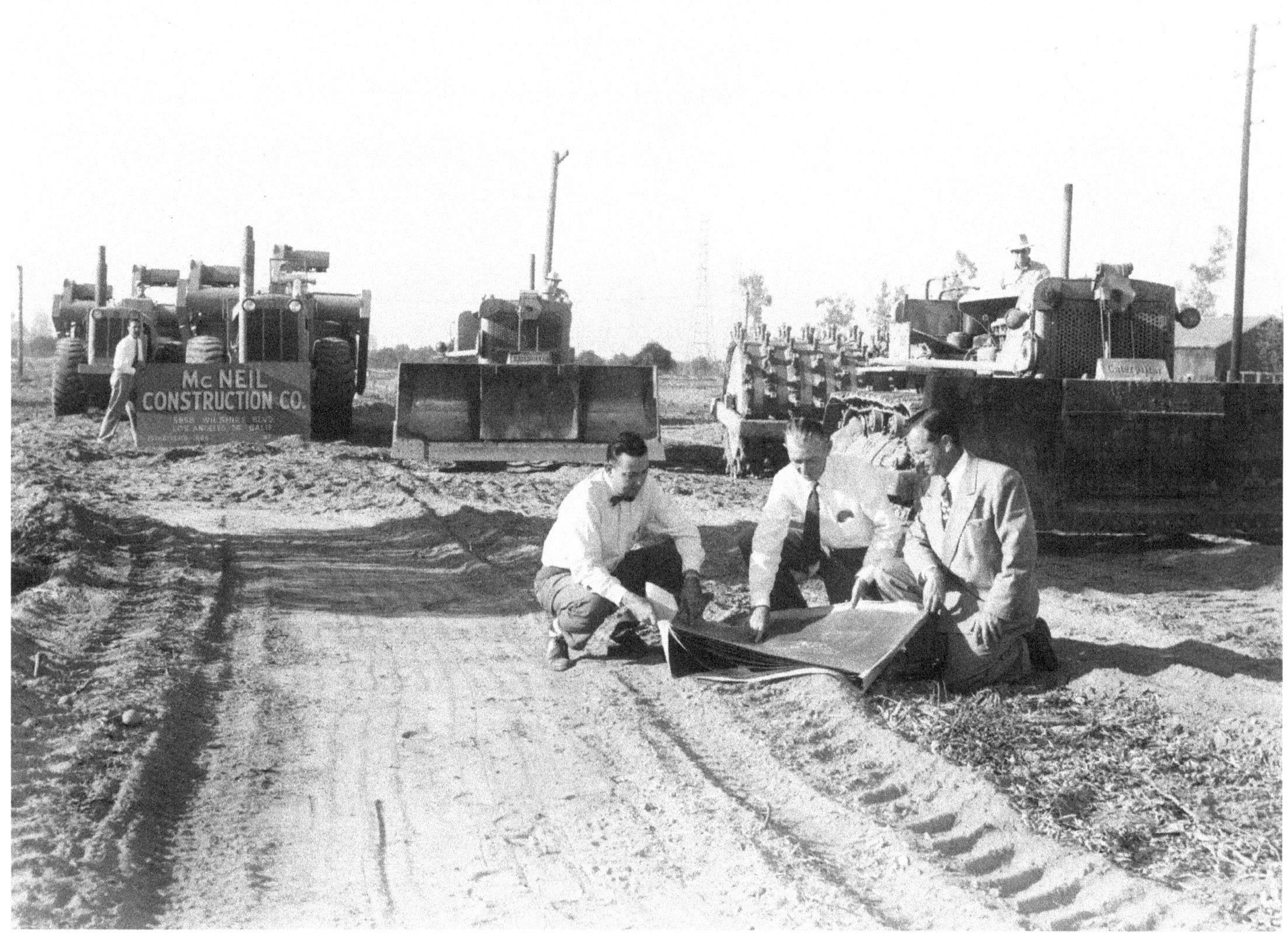

WHERE THE WORLD COMES TO PLAY

(1954–1970s)

In 1953, after a chamber of commerce meeting, Anaheim's city manager, Keith Murdoch, was quietly introduced to a representative of Walt Disney, and told that Walt was looking for a location in the area to build his newest dream, a new concept in amusement parks where children and adults together could enjoy themselves. It would be called Disneyland and a 160-acre location had so far eluded the designers. So began the partnership between a famous Hollywood animator and the city that would eventually host his dream.

Walt Disney had wanted to create a new format in family entertainment and had already surveyed much of Southern California for a suitable site. Armed with a highly detailed report from the Stanford Research Institute that suggested the center of growth in the southland to be an area just south of the Anaheim city limits, Disney began personally negotiating with Anaheim's mayor, Charles Pearson, and city manager, Keith Murdoch, known for his "can-do" ability. Soon the 160 acres of walnuts and oranges at the corner of Ball Road and South Palm Street (now Harbor Blvd.) would be changed into "the Happiest Place on Earth" and almost overnight propel Anaheim into the collective memory of every child in America. Anaheim's civic government took care of the many requirements that were posed, from annexing the 768 acres surrounding the proposed park to closing a little used road that crossed the property and for arranging the signature address of "1313" South Harbor Blvd.

Opening Day of Disneyland on July 17, 1955, was a nationally televised event and gave households across the nation a new vacation destination, Anaheim. Tourists need hotels, restaurants, and requisite services, and Anaheim dealt with all of these needs, some better than others. Disneyland was often just a summer destination. To encourage yearly use of the park and the many hotel rooms surrounding it, Anaheim leaders proposed a convention center. Groundbreaking in the middle of a cleared orange grove was accomplished in typical Anaheim style, with a charge of dynamite. Opened in 1967 across the street from Disneyland, the convention center is today one of the most popular venues of its kind in the nation and the largest on the West Coast.

Anaheim's elected leaders also moved decisively to attract Gene Autry and his California Angels professional baseball team to the city when an offer by nearby Long Beach faltered. Anaheim fast-tracked the Anaheim Stadium's $15.8 million construction so that an April 9, 1966, deadline could be met for an exhibition game.

By the middle of the 1970s, Anaheim's population had exploded to more than 200,000 residents and the city covered almost forty square miles. In 2007 with a population approaching 360,000, Anaheim has become California's tenth-largest city. Now an international sports and entertainment destination with several billion tourist dollars passing through the community each year, few reflect on Anaheim's inauspicious founding almost 150 years ago.

This north-facing aerial view of Disneyland recorded on June 7, 1958, shows the park surrounded by Walt's favorite attraction, his narrow-gauge steam railroad. The area around Disneyland retains the agricultural flavor of the region, now fast disappearing with the construction of motels, shops, and other tourist-oriented businesses. West Street is on the left side of Disneyland with the new Santa Ana Freeway, Interstate 5, running diagonally across the top.

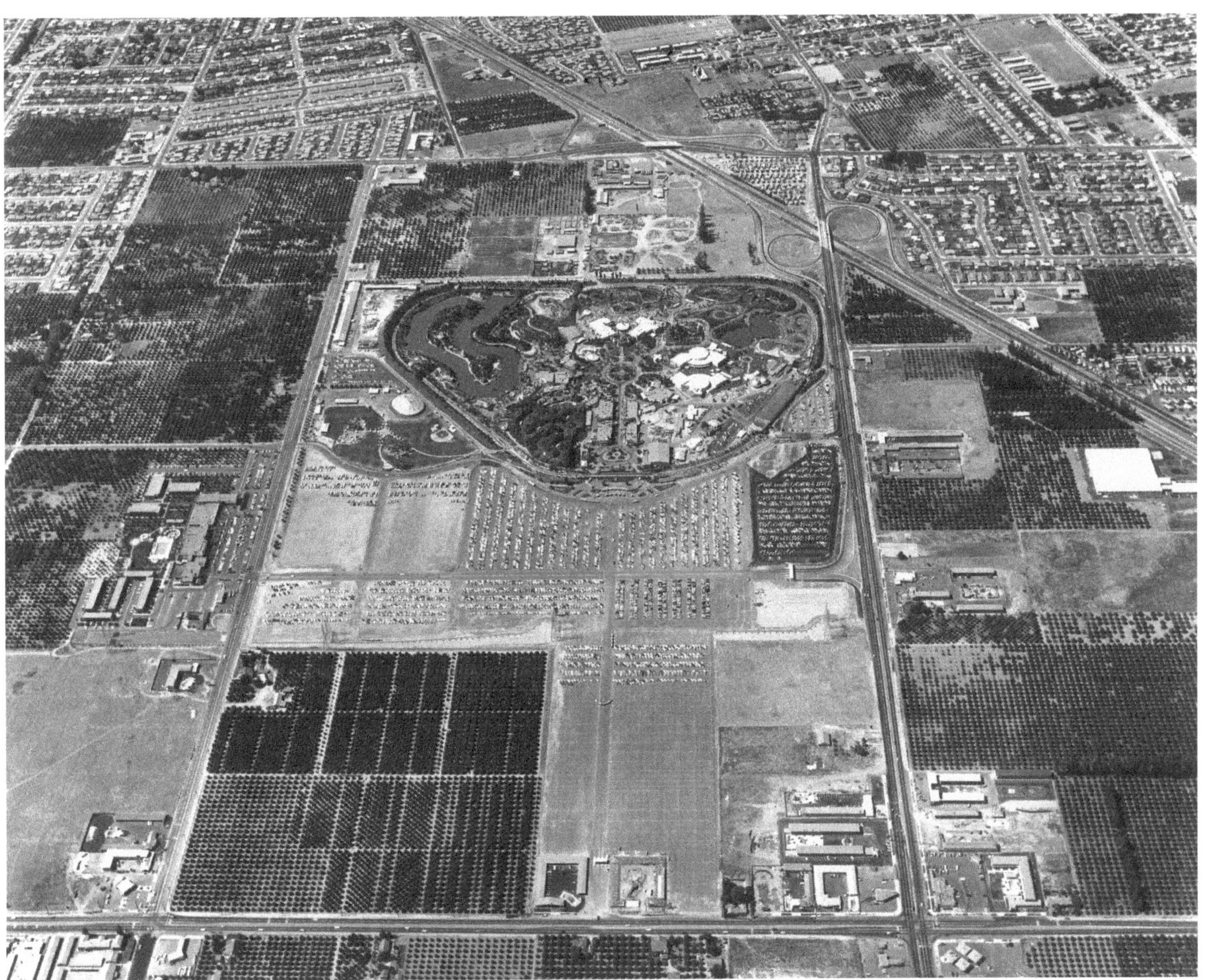

Shown here in 1967, Disneyland's Monorail has now connected the park to the Disneyland Hotel across West Street. Construction of the Haunted Mansion and the Pirates of the Caribbean rides is seen in this view. The few orange groves remaining around the park would soon disappear to make way for additional hotel rooms and restaurants.

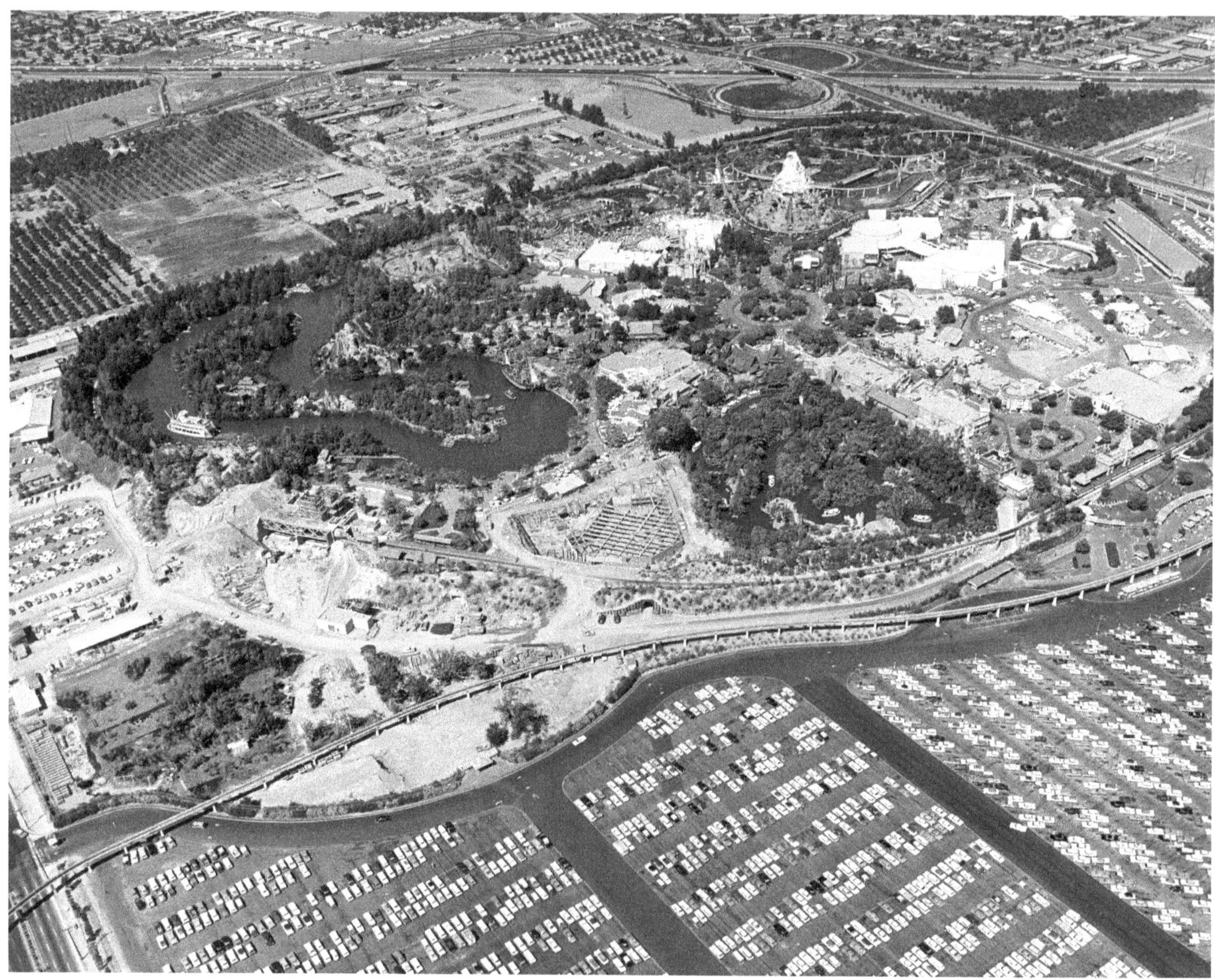

In view here in the 1960s are two of Disneyland's favorite early attractions. The Submarine Voyage opened June 6, 1959, featuring eight 52-foot submarines that took the visitor on a journey through "liquid space." The Monorail ride opened June 14, 1959, as the Disneyland-Alweg Monorail System, Alweg a Swiss firm that contributed to the design. When in 1961, the ride carried visitors to the Disneyland Hotel across West Street, it was the first time a monorail had crossed a public street in this country.

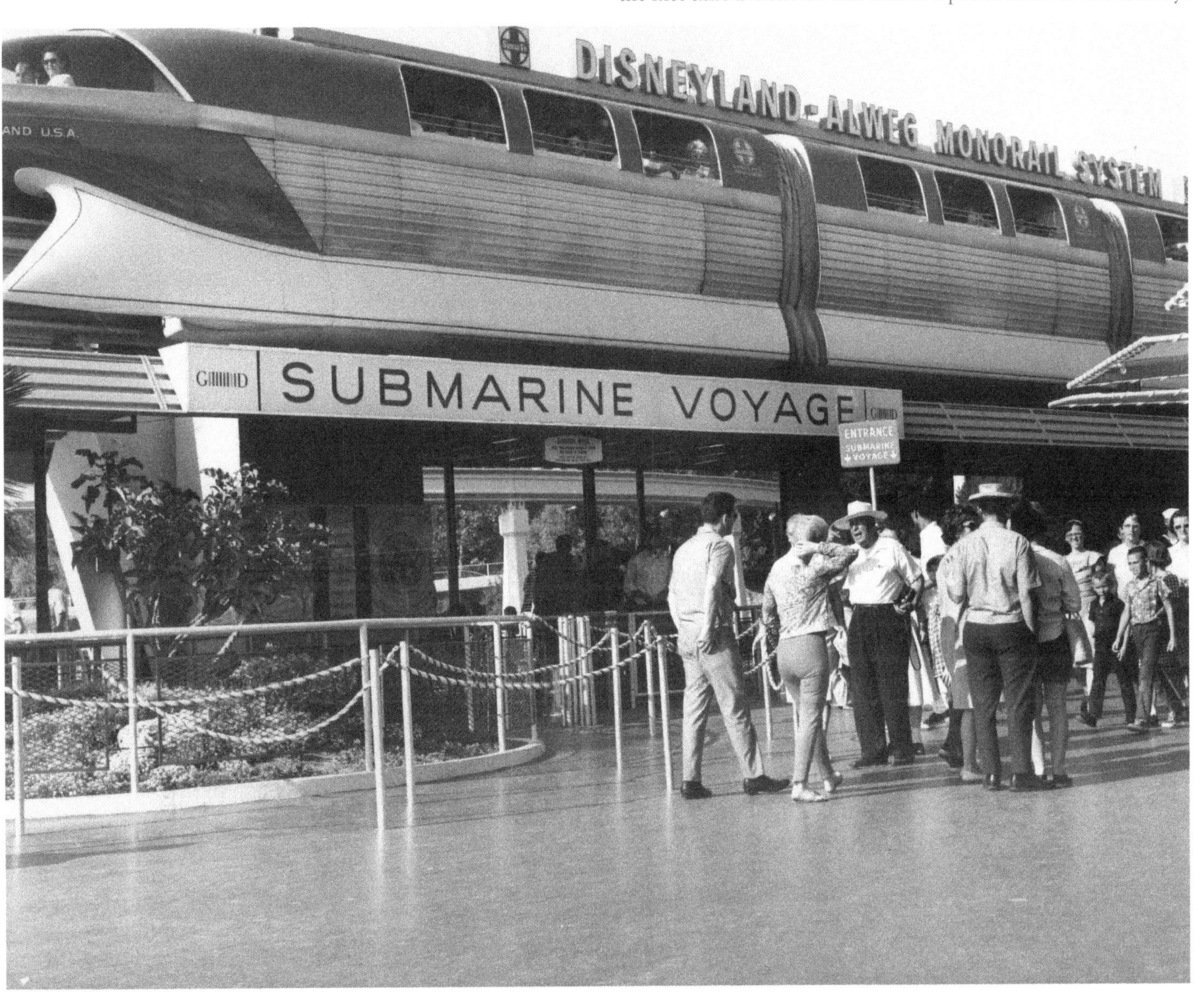

Anaheim's Halloween parade was begun in 1924 and by the 1950s was a leading civic event. The 1957 parade included a float from the S.Q.R. department store that featured three women dressed as witches in a haunted forest. By this time, the parade was beginning at La Palma Park, whence it proceeded down Los Angeles Street (now Anaheim Blvd.) to the downtown area.

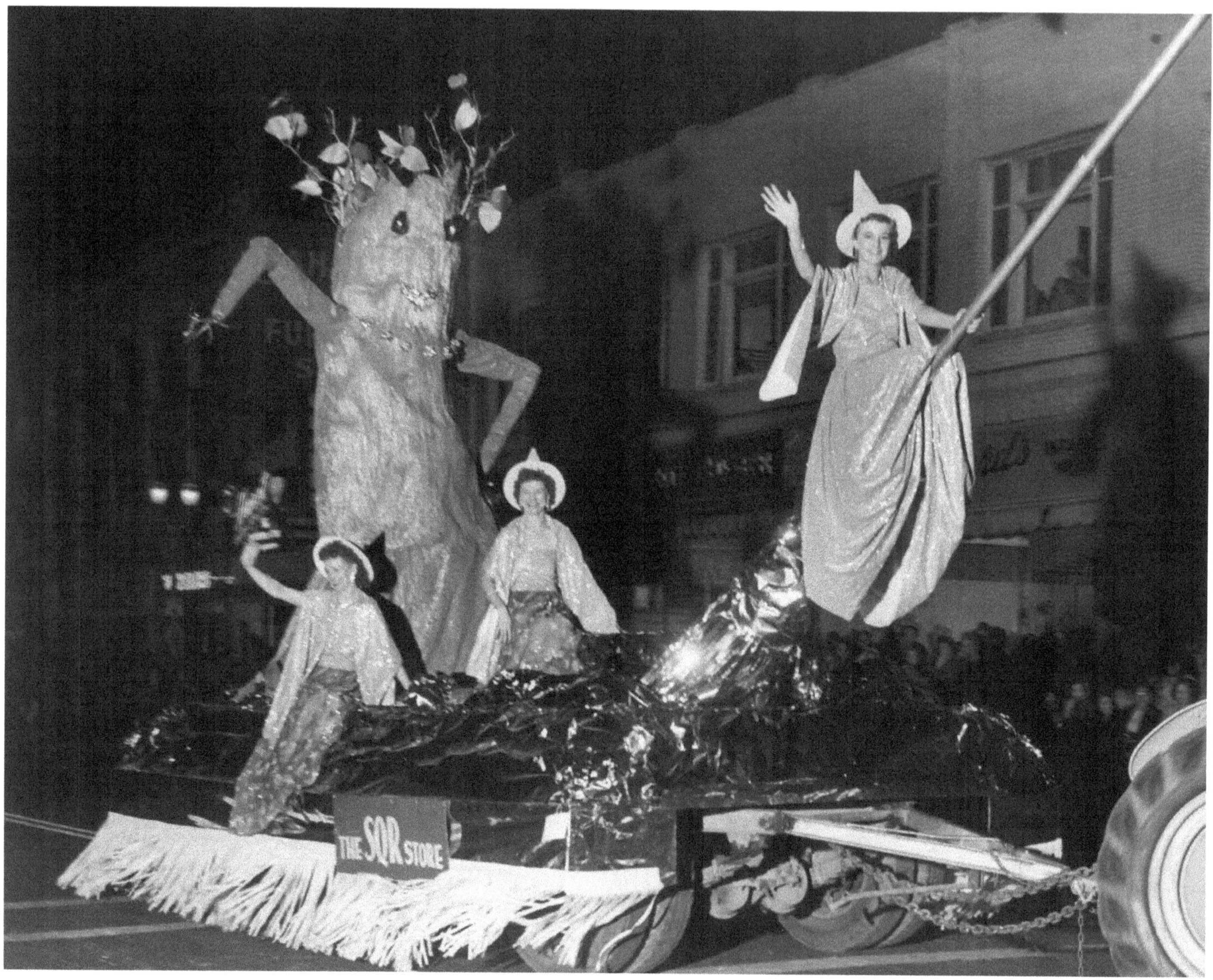

In order to meet the library needs of Anaheim's expanding community, a "Bookmobile" service was inaugurated in 1958. Making a regular route through the outlying parts of the city, it was a welcome addition to the city's literacy program.

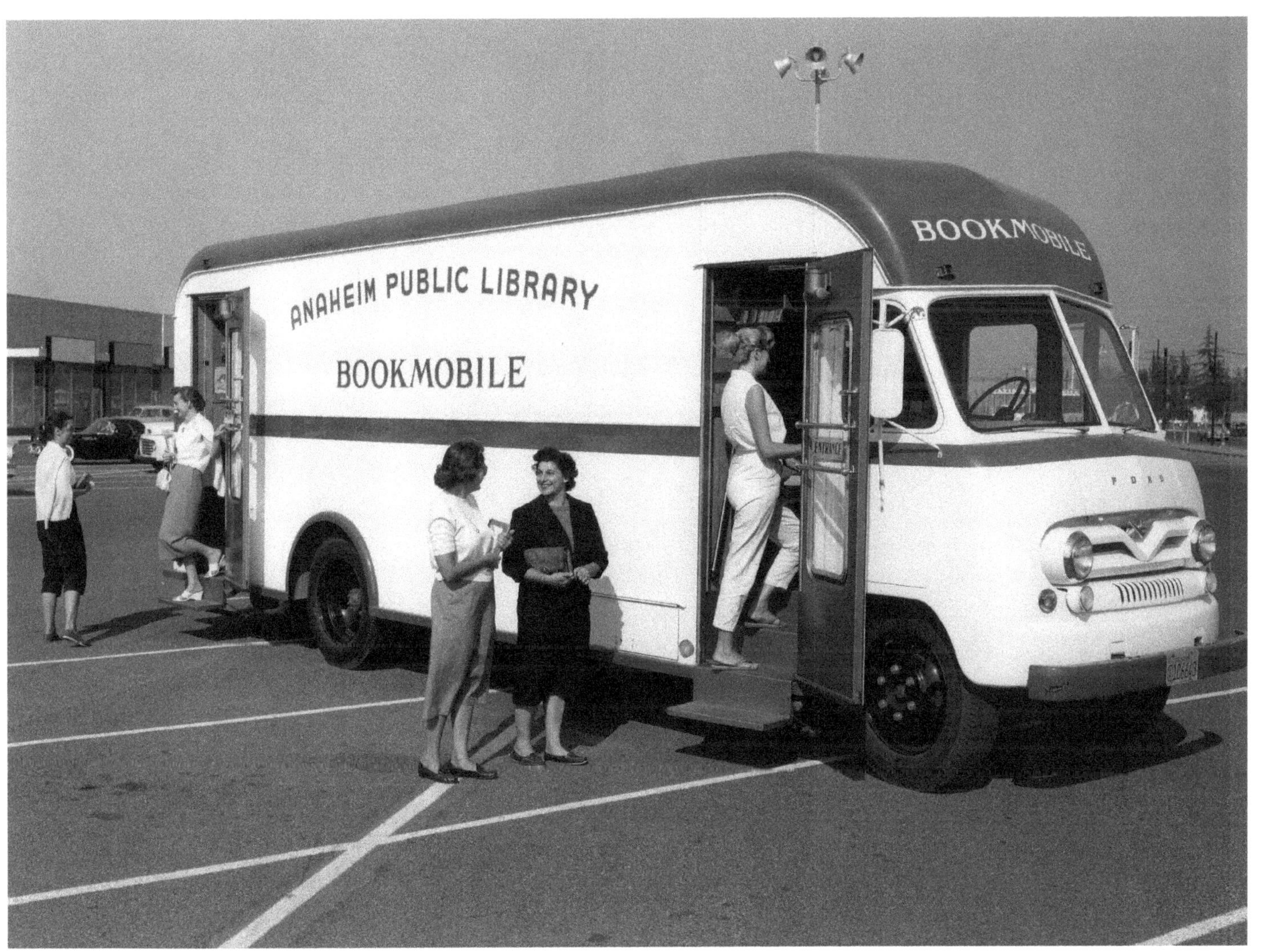

Anaheim's police department introduces its new roof-mounted-speedometer police car at La Palma Park in 1959. Designed to patrol the community, it reminded the residents to "Check Your Speed."

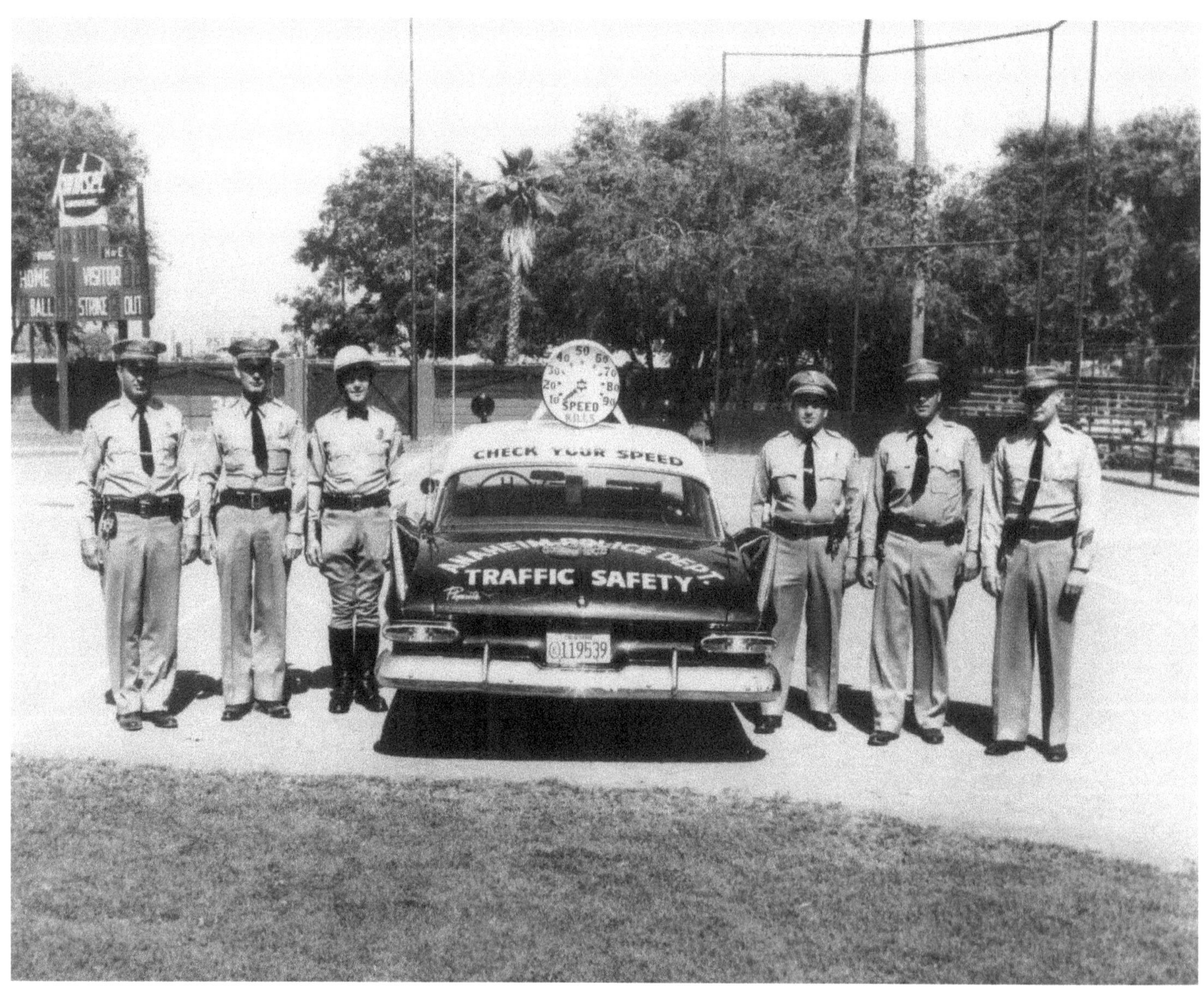

South Los Angeles Street (now Anaheim Blvd.) ca. 1960. In this view north from Broadway Street, Anaheim Pickwick Hotel at 225 South Los Angeles Street is visible at left. Built as the El Torre Hotel by the Pickwick Stage Lines in 1926, it served as the firm's bus station and also housed a number of small businesses. It served the community in a variety of roles until its demolition in 1988.

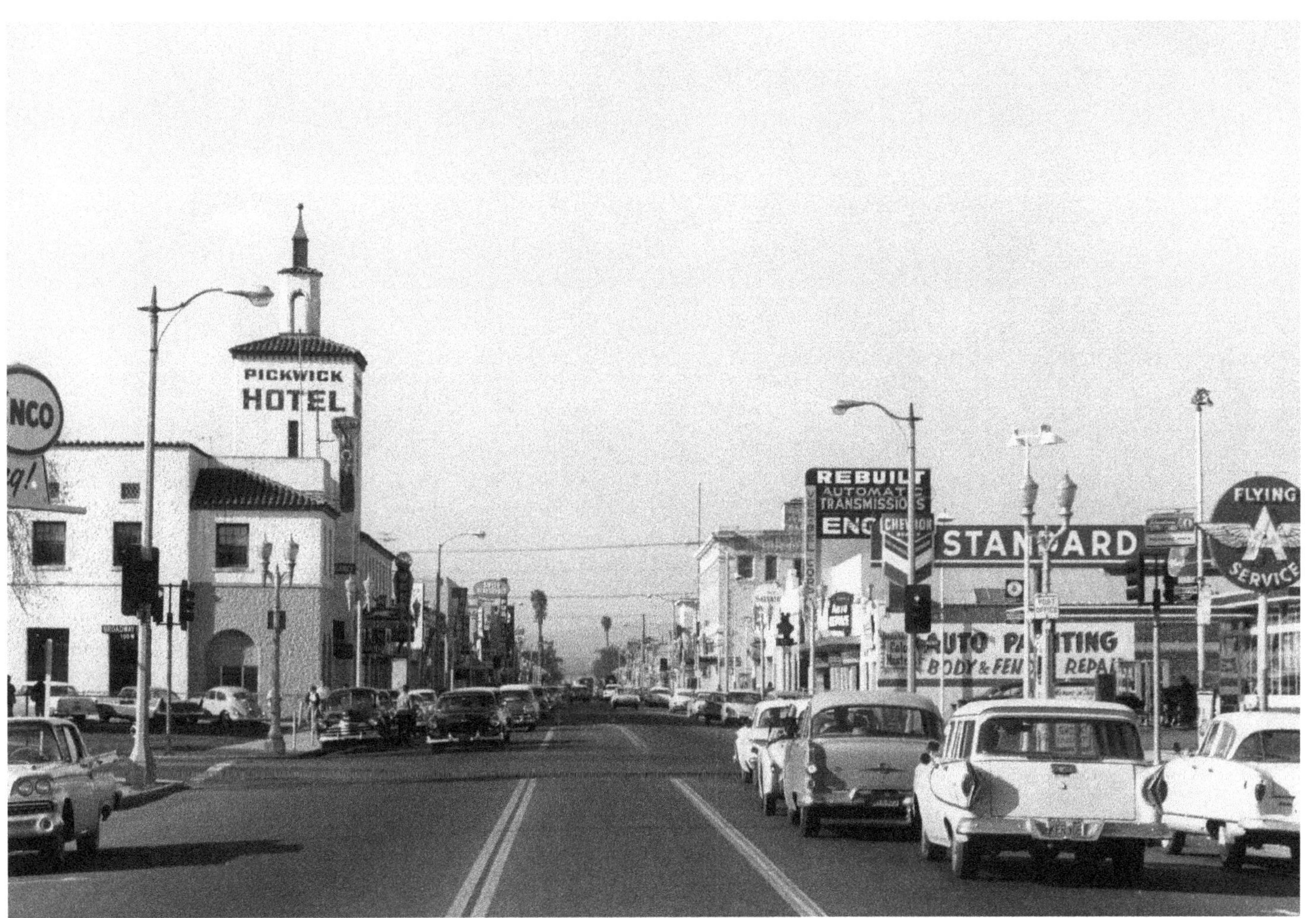

Sergeants 3 starring Frank Sinatra and Dean Martin and *G.I. Blues* with Elvis Presley are double-billed at the Anaheim Fox Theater in this 1962 view east on Center Street (now Lincoln Ave.). The Anaheim Plaza shopping mall had opened west of town in 1955 and the old businesses were beginning to suffer the loss of their customers to the early regional centers. This was the beginning of a downward spiral from which Anaheim's historic downtown would not recover.

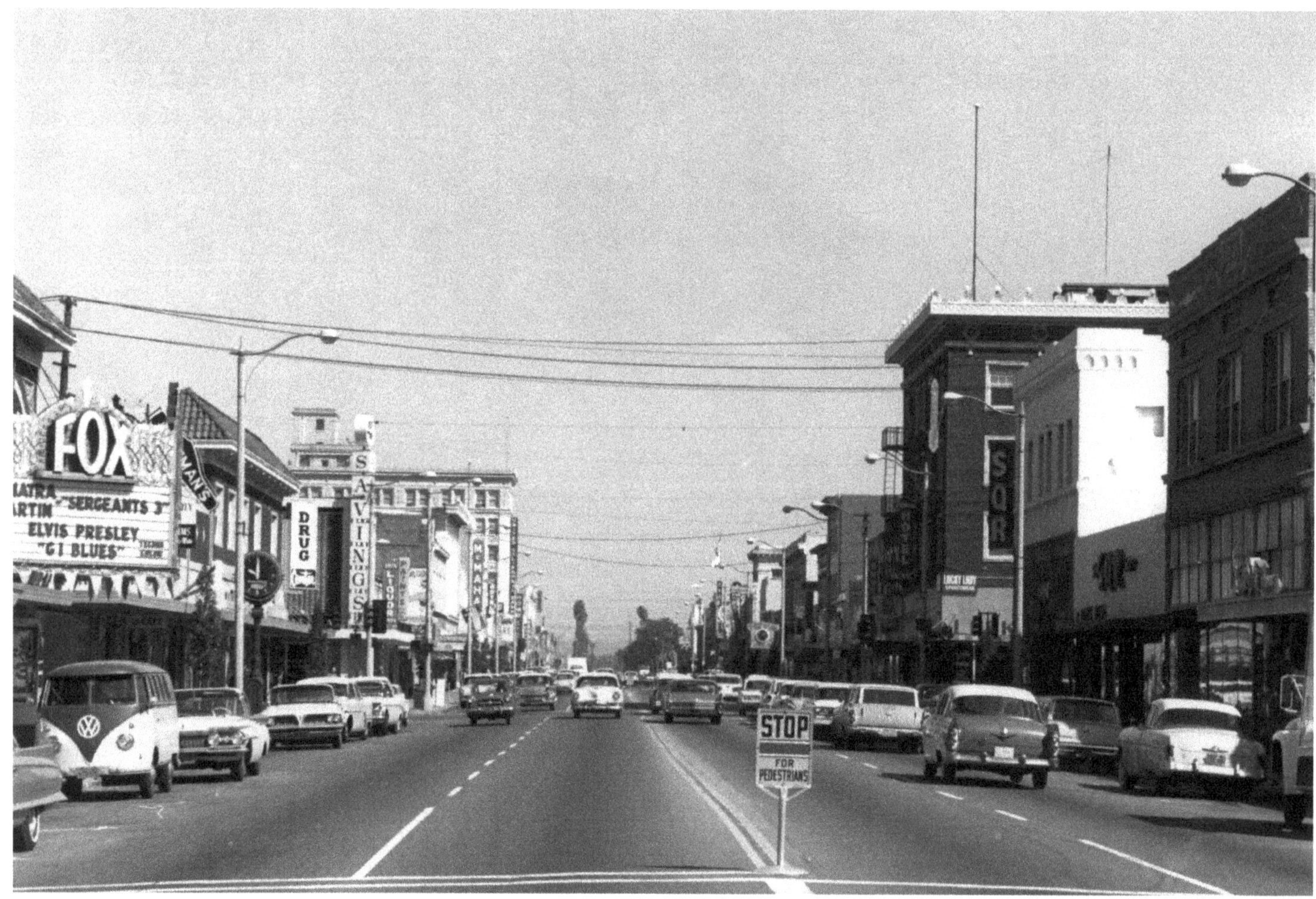

Recalling the 1940s when the Philadelphia Athletics called Anaheim home for their spring training, Anaheim embarked on a plan in 1964 to bring professional baseball to the community. The Los Angeles Angels, owned by cowboy star Gene Autry, were looking for a new home, and Anaheim promised a facility by opening day, 1966. Construction started immediately on 150 acres of orange groves adjacent the Santa Ana River, south of town.

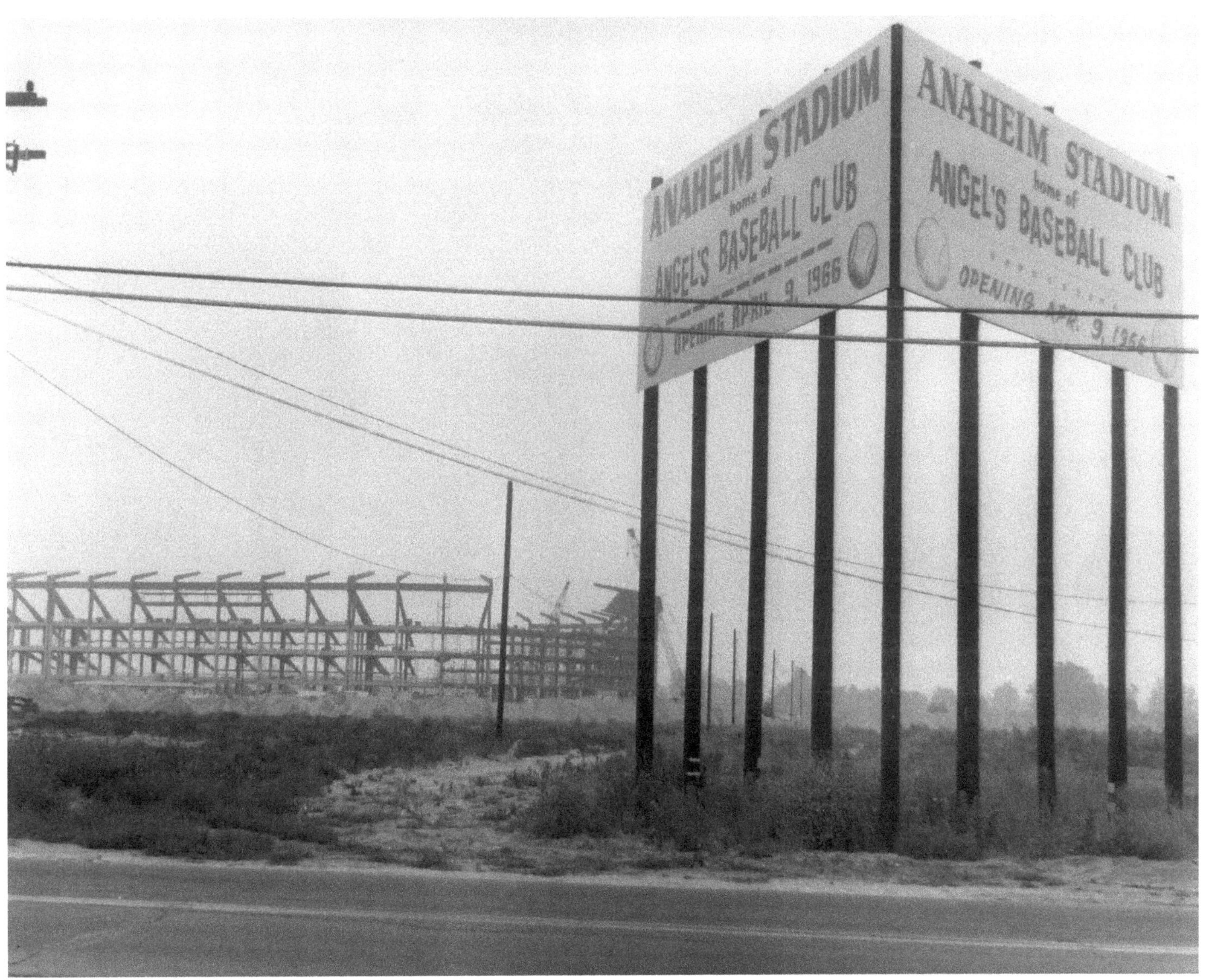

Dubbed the "Big A" for its landmark scoreboard, Anaheim Stadium appears soon after its completion in this aerial view. Costing $15.8 million and seating 43,204, the facility was formally dedicated on April 9, 1966, with an exhibition game with the San Francisco Giants that drew 40,735 fans.

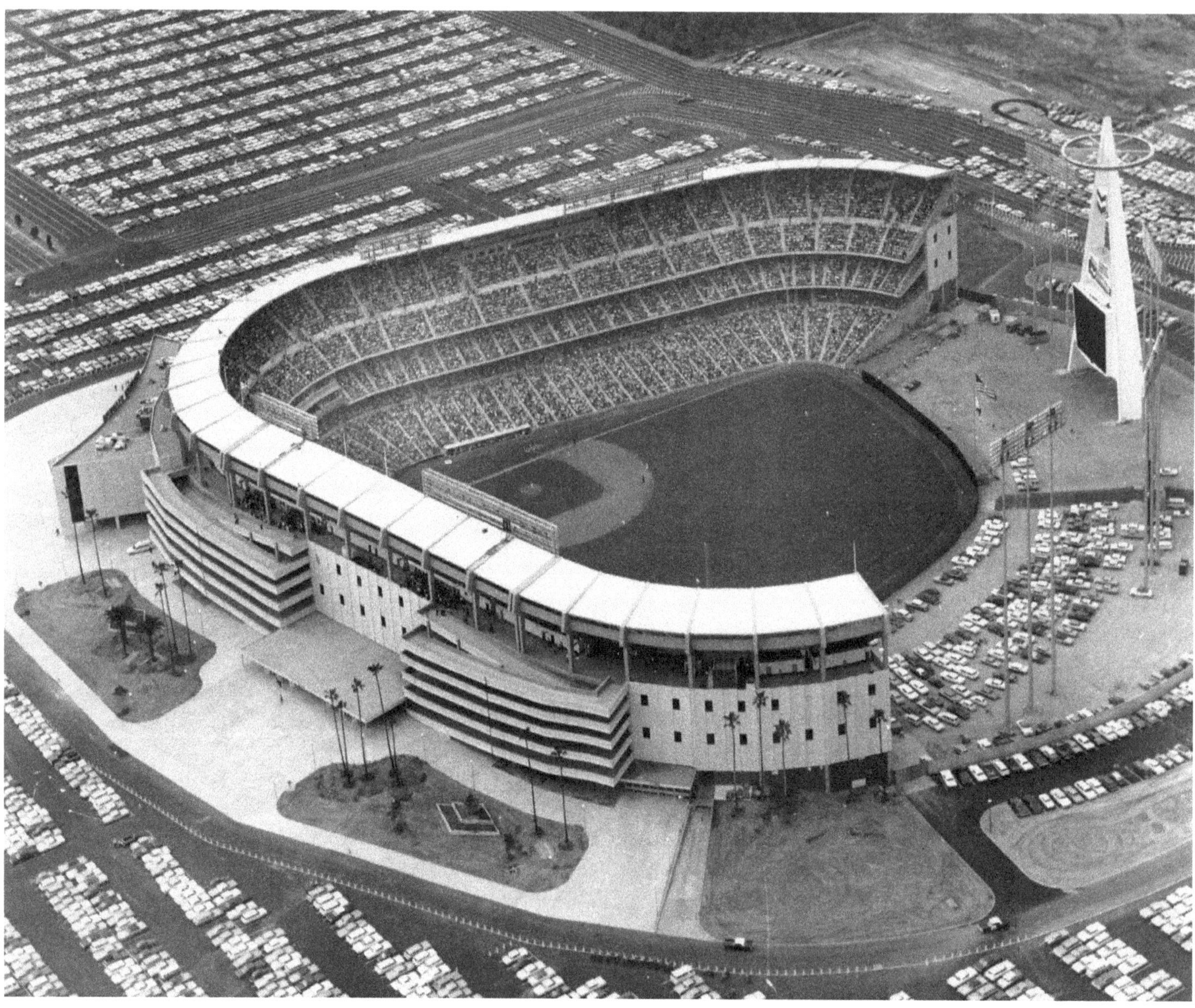

The Big-A's 230-foot-tall scoreboard towers above Anaheim Stadium in this 1960s view. Originally intended to be a joint city-county project, Anaheim built the stadium on their own once the county board of supervisors, believing the project to be too risky, backed out of the deal. A few of the county's remaining 20,000 acres of orange groves are visible across the Santa Ana River.

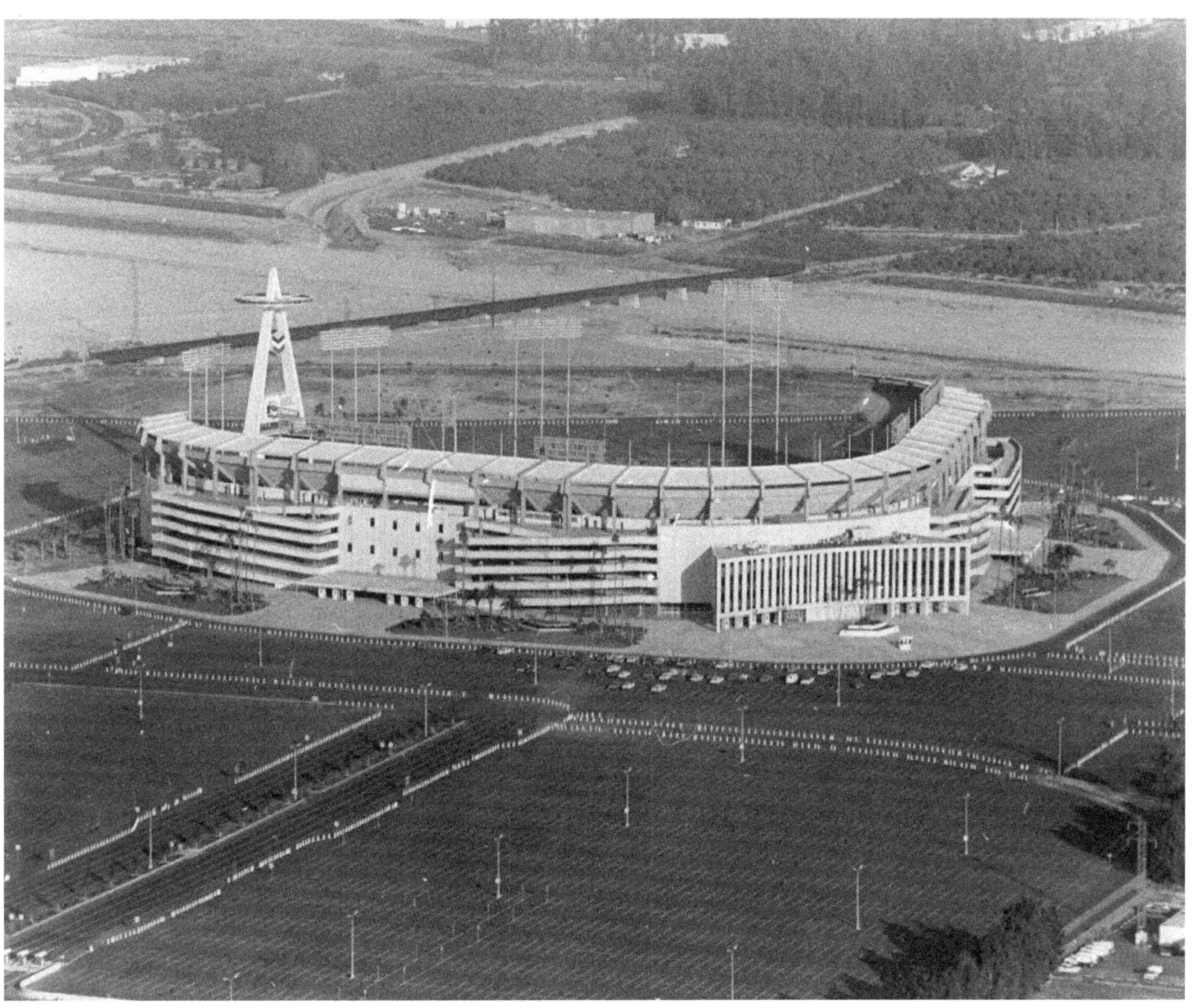

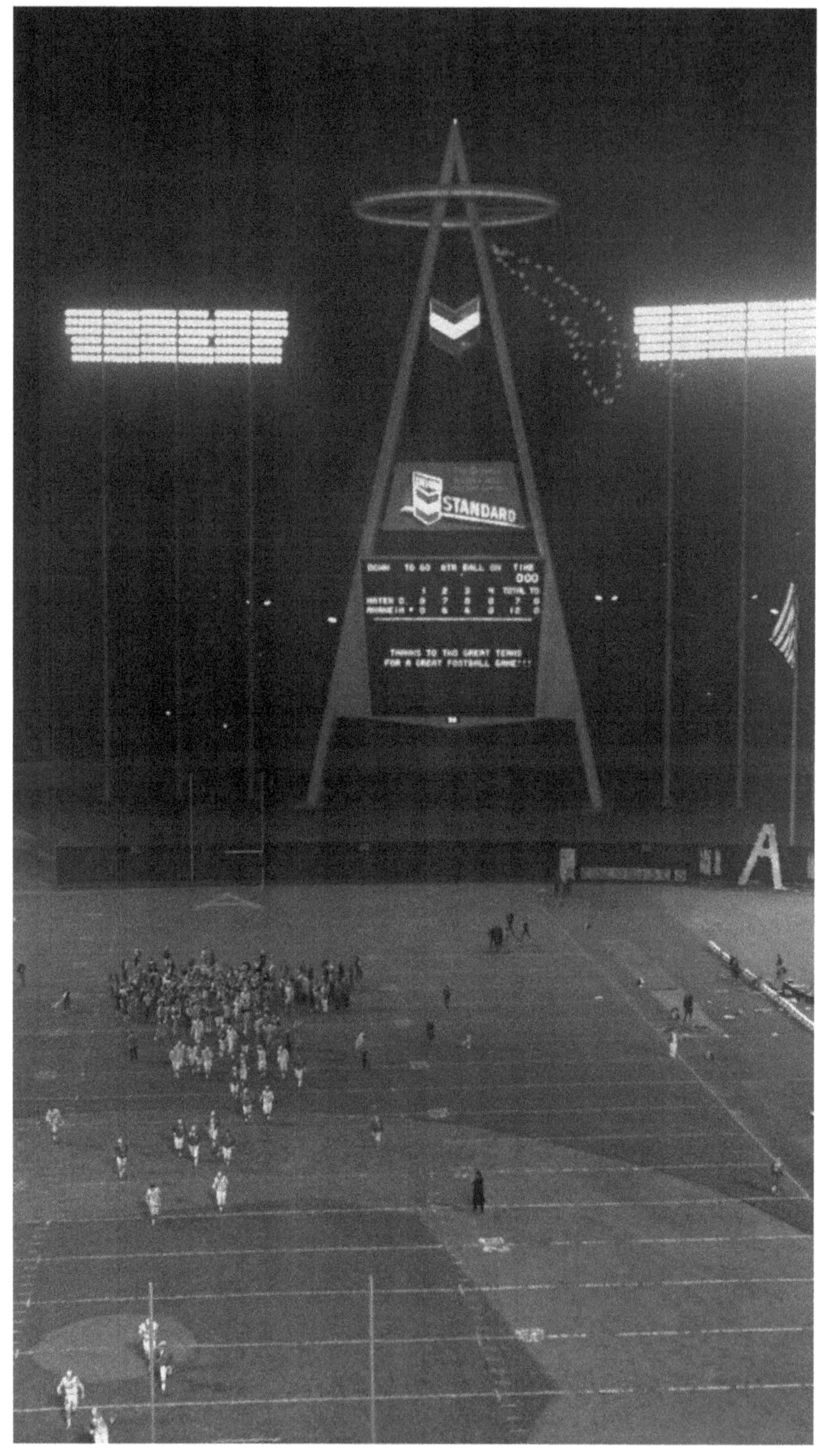

Long before the Rams' professional football team arrived at the "Big-A," the first football game of any kind was an Angelus League game held on November 3, 1966, between Anaheim's Servite Friars and Santa Ana's unbeaten Mater Dei Monarchs. Twenty thousand cheering fans saw the Monarchs run to a 36-6 victory. This was soon followed on December 9 by one of the most anticipated local high school games ever, when the unbeaten Anaheim High School Colonists played in a CIF semifinal match-up with the equally unbeaten Mater Dei Monarchs. A total of 32,808 excited fans watched this battle of the two Orange County High School titans, a non-championship game record. After a hard-fought first half and a second half that featured an 83-yard Anaheim drive, Coach Clare Van Hoorebeke's proud Colonists marched off the field with a 12-7 victory.

Anaheim's civic leaders had discussed a convention center as far back as the 1930s. It was not until the arrival of Disneyland in 1955 and the desire to attract more year-round business that the idea became reality. Announced in 1964, the $14.5 million Anaheim Convention Center was opened in July 1967. This early view shows the new space age facility tucked into the corner of orange groves south of Katella Avenue. Today, the largest facility of its kind on the West Coast, the Anaheim Convention Center anchors one of Southern California's most visited tourist resort areas.

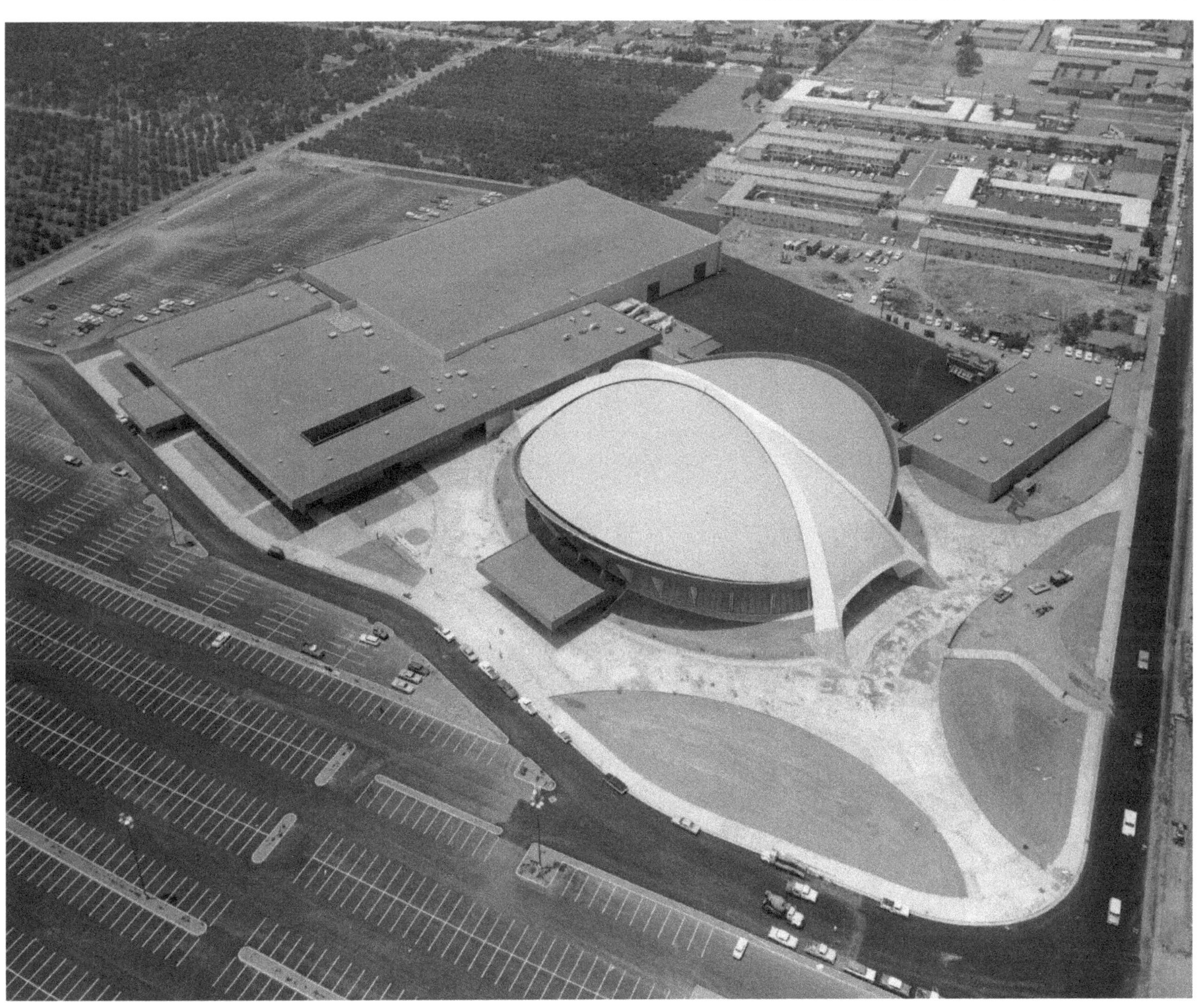

At the Anaheim Convention Center "flying saucer" arena, Mickey and friends are arm in arm in spring 1967. The partnership between Disneyland, the Anaheim Convention Center, and the many tourist-oriented hotels and businesses in the resort area has moved Anaheim's, and much of Orange County's economy far away from the agriculture of their founding. Now the center of a multi-billion-dollar tourist and entertainment complex, Anaheim has become an international destination.

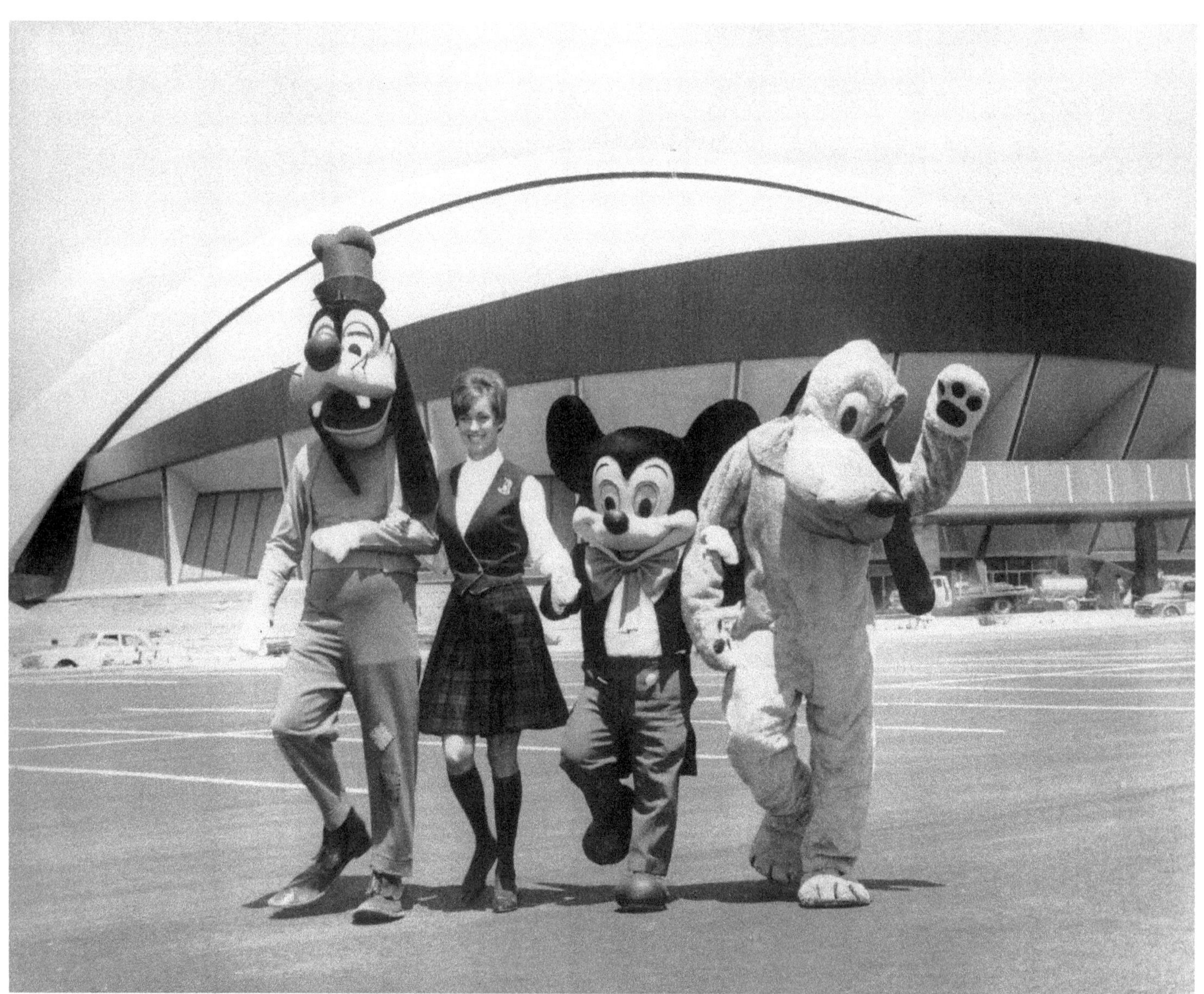

The Anaheim Amigos were one of the Anaheim Convention Center Arena's first tenants. The Amigos, a team of the newly created American Basketball Association (ABA), played but one season in Anaheim before leaving for the Los Angeles Sports Arena. Unable to secure a national television contract, the ABA dissolved in 1967.

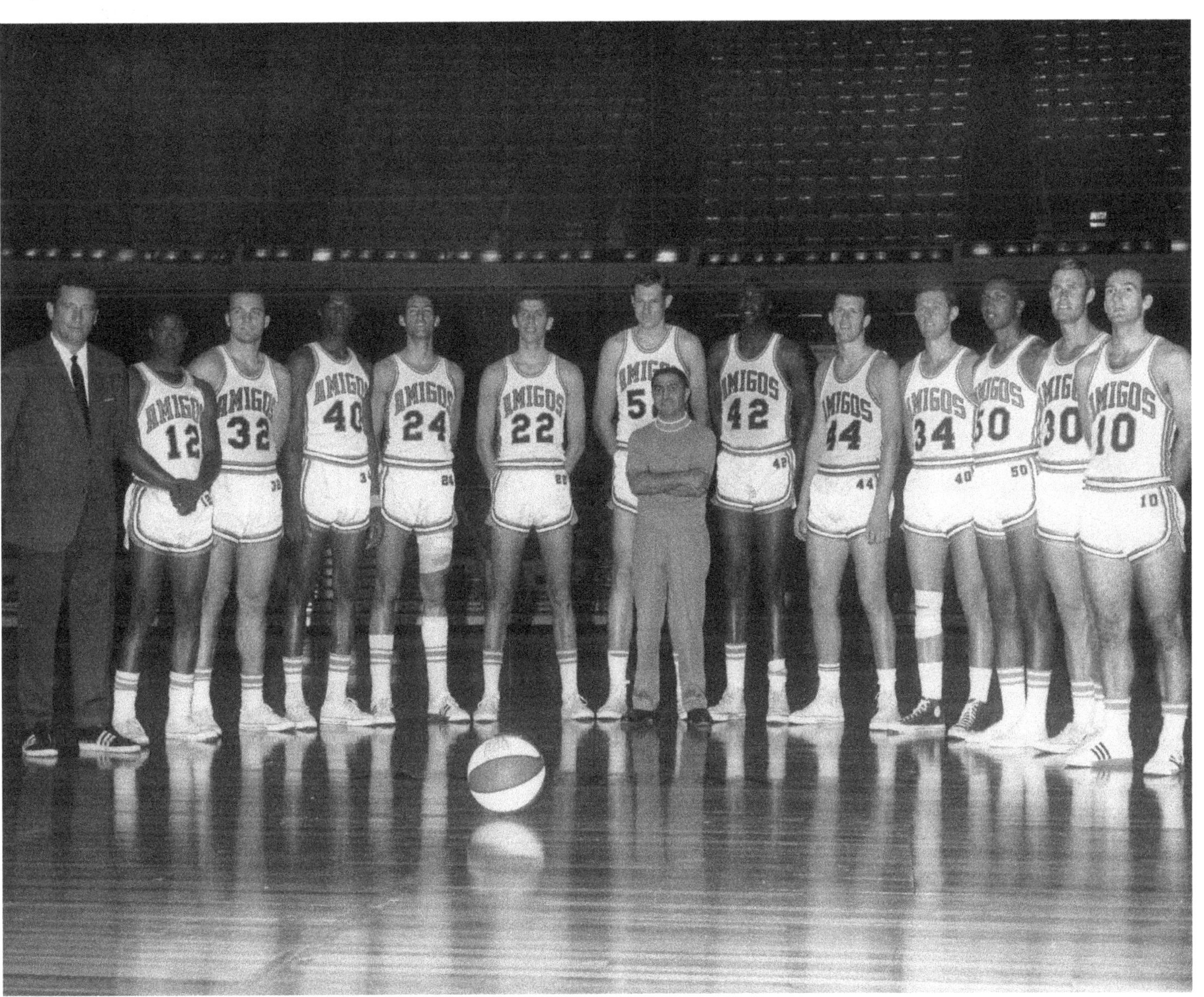

The 1968 Mobil Economy Run, a 41-car competition, left Anaheim for Times Square, New York, on Sunday, April 7. One of the drivers was sixty-six-year-old Gertrude Blair DeWitt, who had driven taxicabs in New York City for 38 years. Her passenger was Anaheim City Councilman Orda L. "Chuck" Chandler, who planned on boosting Orange County's tourist attractions on the 3,000-mile course. "Anna," Anaheim's 600-pound elephant mascot who had earlier "washed" Ms. DeWitt's taxi, poses for the camera.

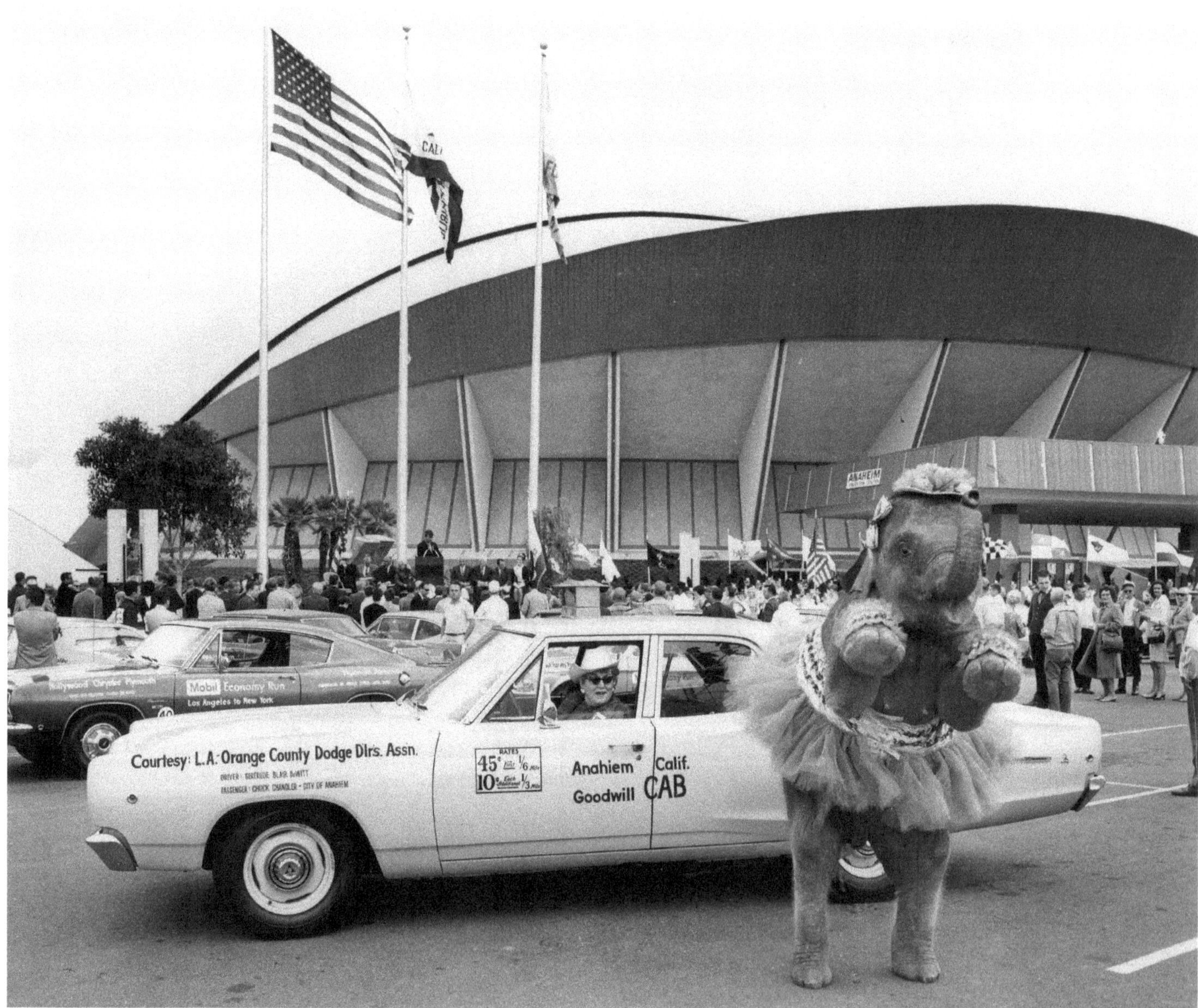

Impresario Tommy Walker produced the Anaheim Stadium 1968 Fourth of July Spectacular. High school bands, antique automobiles, a hot-air balloon, and a number of stage acts were included, culminating in an impressive fireworks display. The "Big-A" continues to this day to be a popular venue for outdoor shows of all kinds.

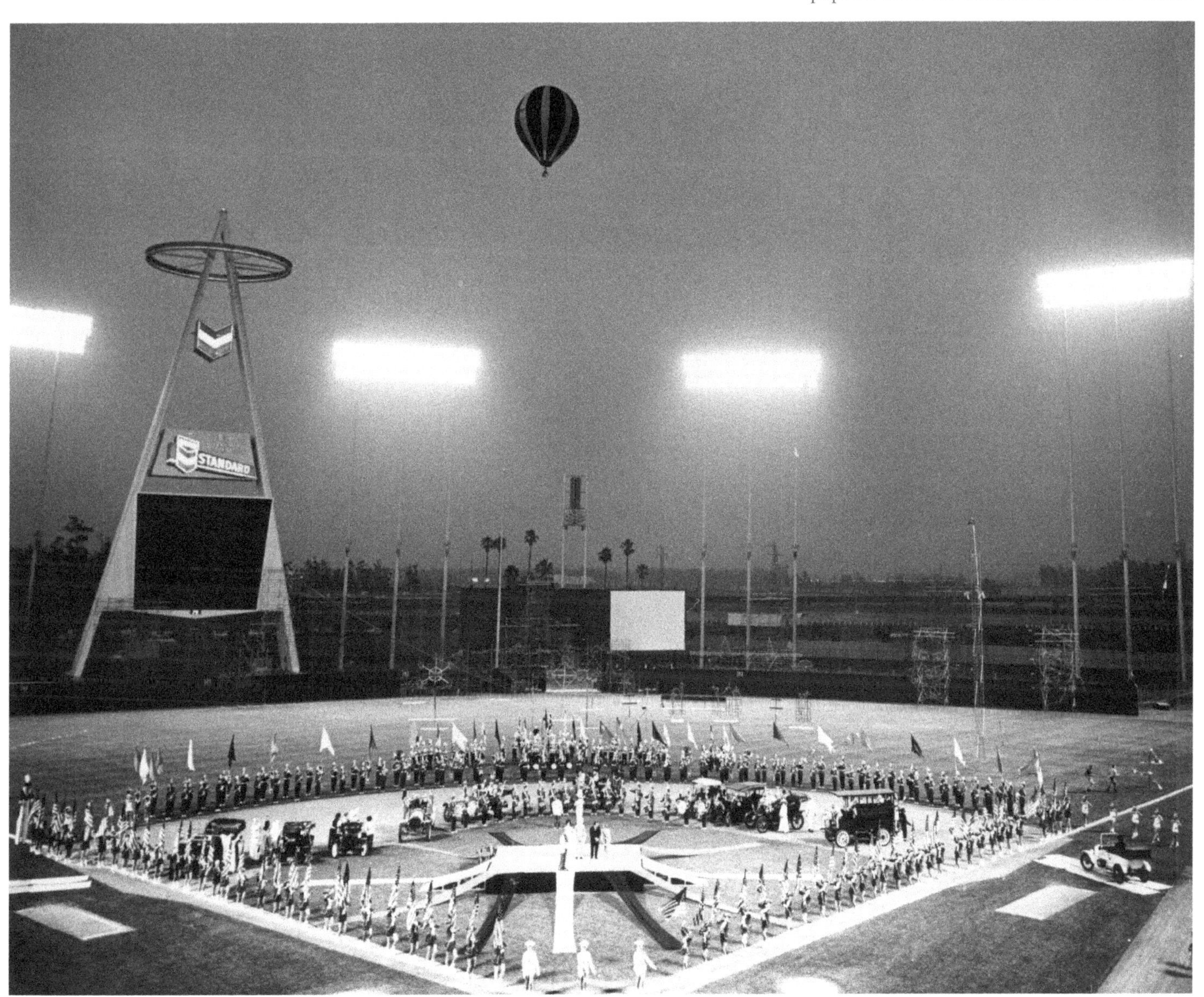

Before the Los Angeles Rams took up permanent residence at the Anaheim Stadium in August 1980, the field was occasionally used for exhibition games. In November 1970, the 49ers and the Rams played to a sold-out crowd. In 1980, the stadium was enlarged by 27,000 seats to accommodate the larger crowds of football fans that followed the Rams' move from Los Angeles.

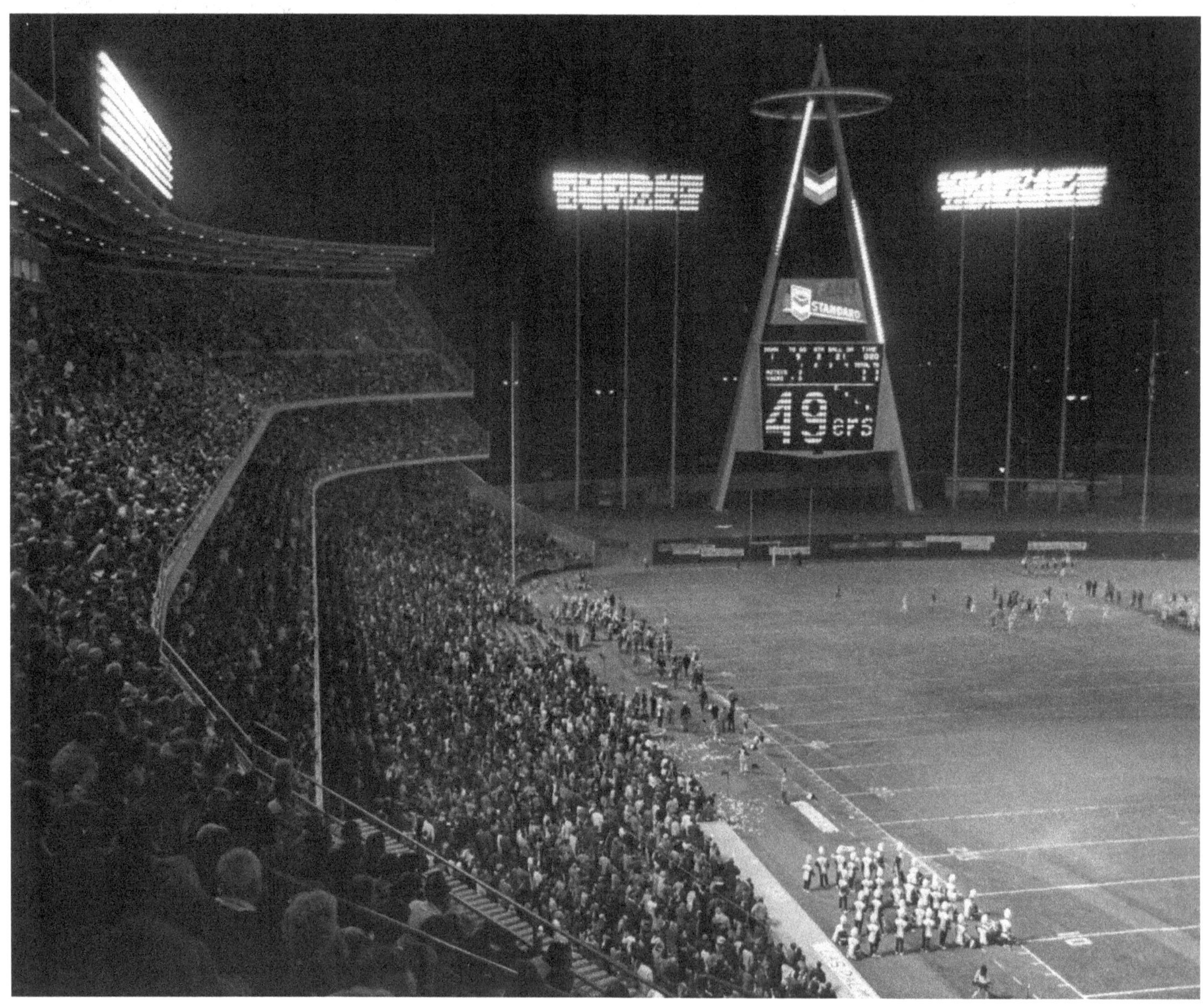

President Richard Nixon, an Orange County native, attended an Angel's game on April 6, 1972. Anaheim's mayor, Jack Dutton, also an Anaheim native, greets Nixon in this view. Dutton played key roles in persuading Gene Autry to move his Angel's ball club to Anaheim in 1966 and arranging the construction of the Anaheim Convention Center.

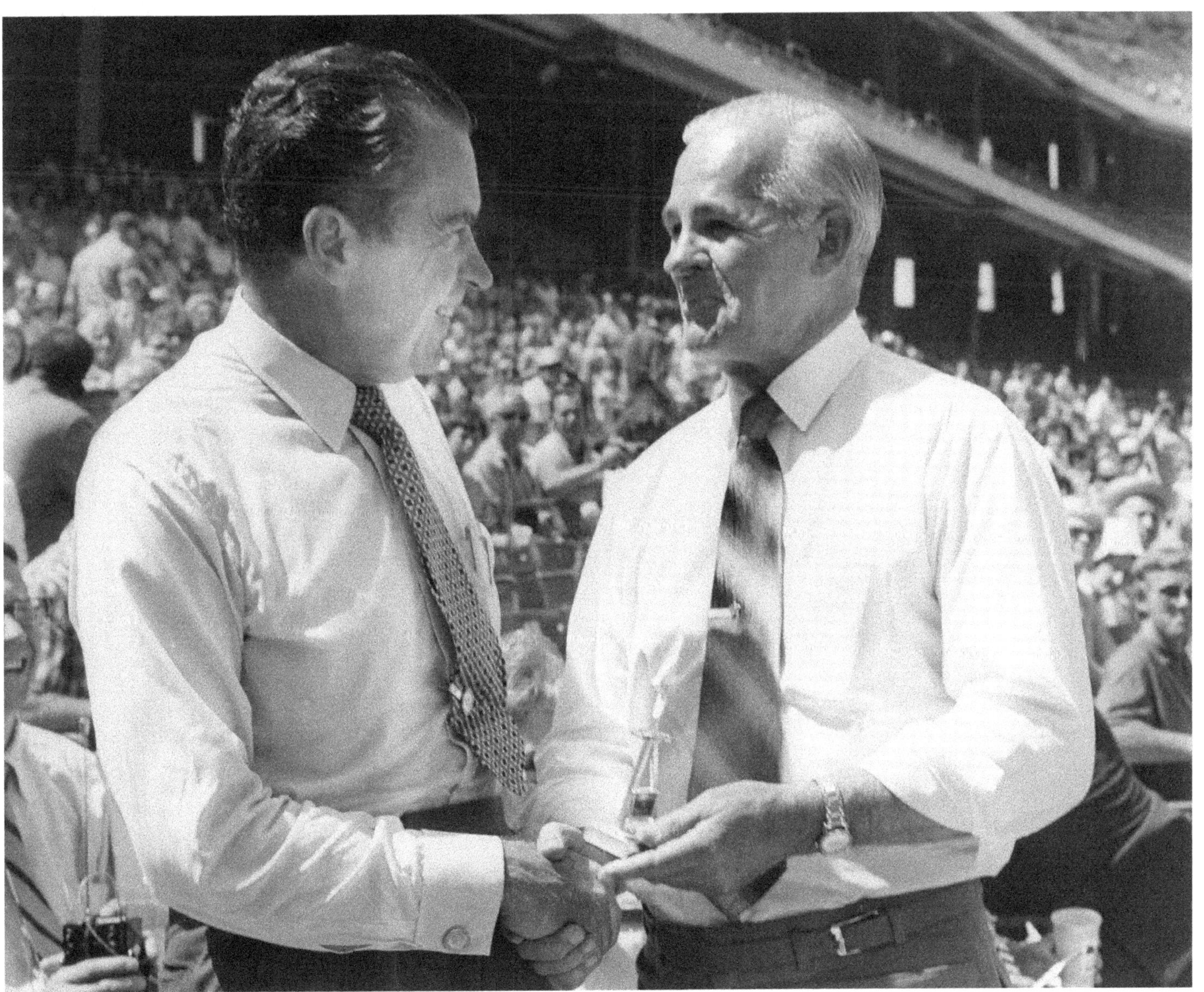

In order to bolster the finances of the "Big-A," the City of Anaheim offered this unique outdoor venue for many kinds of uses, from rock concerts to large religious meetings. In 1970, the Assembly of Men of Goodwill used the field for their exercises, and in June 1970, the British rock group "the Who" played to a crowd of more than 30,000 fans. Motor sport shows also grew in popularity and the loud but very well attended events are held yearly.

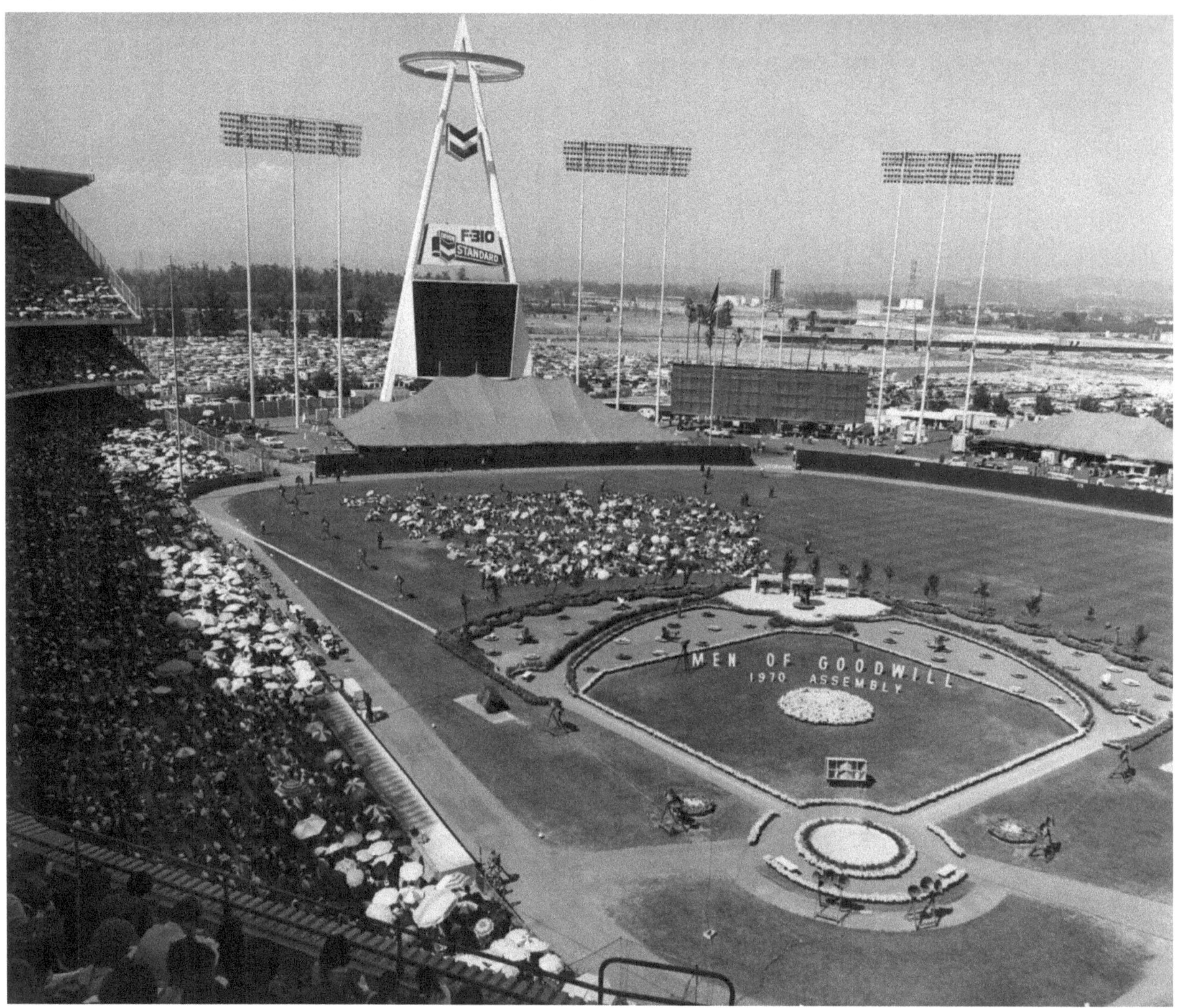

The Osmond Brothers ham it up for the camera before their September 8, 1972, show at the Big-A. It was reported that 95 percent of the 30,000 fans were mothers and daughters. The wholesome Osmonds were a big change from the early rock concerts with their widely reported security and drug use problems.

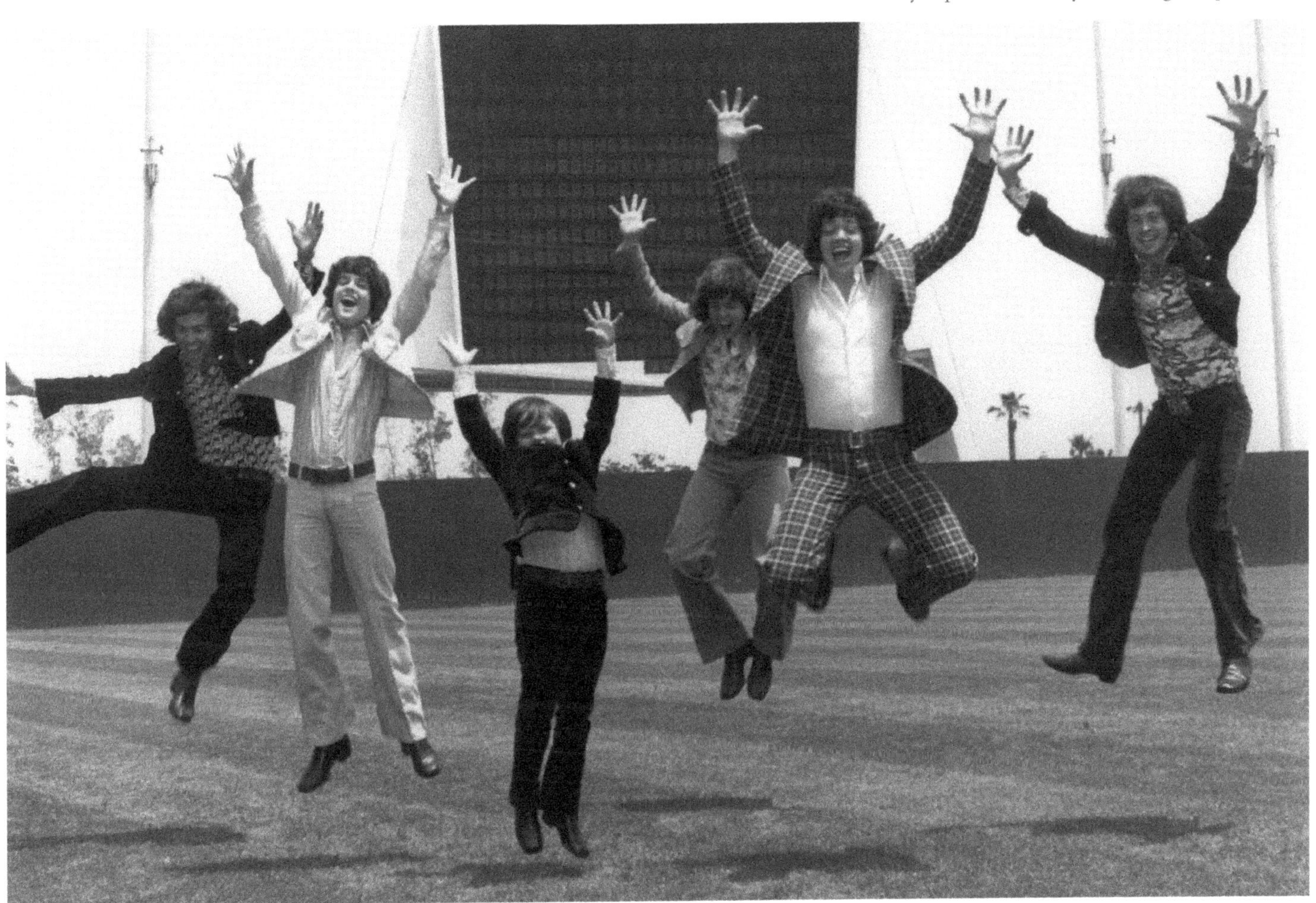

Notes on the Photographs

These notes, listed by page number, attempt to include all aspects known of the photographs. Each of the photographs is identified by the page number, photograph's title or description, photographer and collection, archive, and call or box number when applicable. Although every attempt was made to collect all available data, in some cases complete data was unavailable due to the age and condition of some of the photographs and records.

II **Anaheim Aerial View**
Anaheim Public Library
p1164

VI **Sister City Program**
Anaheim Public Library
pio-007

X **George Hansen**
Anaheim Public Library
p457

2 **Langenberger's Store**
Anaheim Public Library
p97

3 **Ontiveros And Wife**
Anaheim Public Library
p171

4 **Anaheim Hotel**
Anaheim Public Library
p61

6 **Center Street**
Anaheim Public Library
p10140

7 **Commercial Hotel**
Anaheim Public Library
p442

8 **Planters Hotel**
Anaheim Public Library
p270

9 **Fourth Of July Parade**
Anaheim Public Library
p87

10 **Planters Hotel**
Anaheim Public Library
p263

11 **Saint Boniface**
Anaheim Public Library
p7055

12 **Planters Hotel**
Anaheim Public Library
p63

13 **Dreyfus Winery**
Anaheim Public Library
p6838

14 **Koenig Vineyard**
Anaheim Public Library
p43

15 **Dr. Bullard**
Anaheim Public Library
p15405

16 **Bullard Bottling Wine**
Anaheim Public Library
p9743

18 **Center Street**
Anaheim Public Library
p283

19 **Dreyfus Winery**
Anaheim Public Library
p41

20 **Fritz Ruhmann Building**
Anaheim Public Library
p250

21 **Backs Store**
Anaheim Public Library
p24

22 **Wallop's Grocery Store**
Anaheim Public Library
p49

23 **West Center Street**
Anaheim Public Library
p272

24 **Langenberger's Vineyard**
Anaheim Public Library
p94

25 **Santa Ana Rail**
Anaheim Public Library
p5969

26 **Hudson Real Estate**
Anaheim Public Library
p440

27 **Fashion Stables**
Anaheim Public Library
p273

28 **Palace Market**
Anaheim Public Library
p16214

29 **Center Street**
Anaheim Public Library
p246

30 **Anaheim Landing**
Anaheim Public Library
p338

31 **Visitor Tents**
Anaheim Public Library
p671

32 **Vacation Cottage**
Anaheim Public Library
p5470

33 **Walnut Street**
Anaheim Public Library
p625

34 **Cajon Canal**
Anaheim Public Library
p13377

35 **Installing Water Tower**
Anaheim Public Library
p488

36 **Center Street**
Anaheim Public Library
p447

37 **Stagecoach**
Anaheim Public Library
p10493

38 **Triumphal Arch**
Anaheim Public Library
p936

39 **Rabbit Hunting Party**
Anaheim Public Library
p164

40 **Citizen's Bank**
Anaheim Public Library
p492

41 **Boston Bakery**
Anaheim Public Library
p627

42 **Mable Street**
Anaheim Public Library
p15894

43 **Metz Block Building**
Anaheim Public Library
p701

44 **Boyd Hardware**
Anaheim Public Library
p248

45 **Center Street**
Anaheim Public Library
p257

46 **Electric Anaheim**
Anaheim Public Library
p438

48 **Electric Streetlights**
Anaheim Public Library
p268

49 **Del Campo Hotel**
Anaheim Public Library
p1439

50 **Knights Of Pythias**
Anaheim Public Library
p398

51 **First Presbyterian Church**
Anaheim Public Library
p10588

52 **Second City Hall**
Anaheim Public Library
p699

53 **Fire Laddies**
Anaheim Public Library
p112

54 **Kroeger Building**
Anaheim Public Library
p837

55 **Southern Pacific Railroad**
Anaheim Public Library
p3920

56 **Trained Ostrich**
Anaheim Public Library
p91

57 **Rural Free Delivery**
Anaheim Public Library
p589

58 **Del Campo Hotel**
Anaheim Public Library
p297

60 **Seale's Grocery**
Anaheim Public Library
p5694

61 **Local Business Owners**
Anaheim Public Library
p200

62 **Federman Block Building**
Anaheim Public Library
p5653

63 **Central School**
Anaheim Public Library
p714

64 **Blacksmith Shop**
Anaheim Public Library
p633

65 **Wells Fargo**
Anaheim Public Library
p267

66 **St. Catherine's Orphanage**
Anaheim Public Library
p499

67 **Over Anaheim**
Anaheim Public Library
p266

68 **Blacksmith Shop**
Anaheim Public Library
p771

71 **Peerless Bar**
Anaheim Public Library
p23

72 **Young Baseball Players**
Anaheim Public Library
p558

74 **Sprinkling Streets**
Anaheim Public Library
p6599

75 **Evergreen Nursery**
Anaheim Public Library
jh011

76 **Commercial Hotel**
Anaheim Public Library
p656

77 **Company E**
Anaheim Public Library
p75

78 **Ice Depot**
Anaheim Public Library
p11461

79 **Rail On Center Street**
Anaheim Public Library
p16110

80 **Orange County Preserving Company**
Anaheim Public Library
p2576

81 **Philadelphia Street**
Anaheim Public Library
p2574

82 **Mule-Drawn Wagon**
Anaheim Public Library
p10577

83 **Chilie's Place**
Anaheim Public Library
p591

84 **Modern Powerhouse**
Anaheim Public Library
p575

85 **Dr. Johnston's Home**
Anaheim Public Library
p8349

86 **Napolean Hart's Place**
Anaheim Public Library
p752

87 **Knights Of Pythias**
Anaheim Public Library
p8821

88 **Exchange Bar**
Anaheim Public Library
p10697

90 **Favorite Saloon**
Anaheim Public Library
p11057

91 **Buster Brown Shoes**
Anaheim Public Library
p757

92 **Horseless Carriages**
Anaheim Public Library
p697

93 **Broadway School**
Anaheim Public Library
p6080

94 **Union Brewing Float**
Anaheim Public Library
p602

95 **May Day**
Anaheim Public Library
p6888

96 **El Camino Real**
Anaheim Public Library
p759

97 **Mission Ice Cream Parlor**
Anaheim Public Library
p6880

98 **Funeral Procession**
Anaheim Public Library
p450

99 **Anaheim Carnival**
Anaheim Public Library
p806

100 **Anaheim Carnival**
Anaheim Public Library
p10971

101 **Medium Car Road Race**
Anaheim Public Library
jh072

102 **Fine Silver Loving Cup**
Anaheim Public Library
p754

104 **First Christian Church**
Anaheim Public Library
jh067

105 **Motor Sweeper**
Anaheim Public Library
p711

106 **Carnival Parade**
Anaheim Public Library
p6352

107 **Street Sweeper**
Anaheim Public Library
p8366

108 **Hardware Store**
Anaheim Public Library
p30

109 **Salem Evangelical Church**
Anaheim Public Library
p2566

110 **Orange Advertisement**
Anaheim Public Library
p11245

111 **Faculty Picnic**
Anaheim Public Library
p7142

112 **Roadster**
Anaheim Public Library
p6968

113 **Upholstery Shop**
Anaheim Public Library
p995

114 **Ingram Brothers**
Anaheim Public Library
p818

115 **Fire Truck**
Anaheim Public Library
p587

116 **1916 Flood**
Anaheim Public Library
p15027

117 **Anaheim Cemetery**
Anaheim Public Library
p2

118 **Anaheim Steam Laundry**
Anaheim Public Library
p3563

119 **Liberty Bond Drive**
Anaheim Public Library
p1414

120 **Kusumoto's Barber Shop**
Anaheim Public Library
an-01-188

121 **Lee's Service Station**
Anaheim Public Library
p11961

122 **Memorial Day Parade**
Anaheim Public Library
p803

124 **California Theatre**
Anaheim Public Library
p8819

125 **Gerrard Brothers & Hanson Grocery Store**
Anaheim Public Library
p10610

126 **Angelina Hotel**
Anaheim Public Library
p3532

127 **American Savings Bank**
Anaheim Public Library
p6799

128 **Valencia Orange Show**
Anaheim Public Library
p2382

129 **Egyptian Settings**
Anaheim Public Library
p2159

130 **Orange Show Interior**
Anaheim Public Library
p2371

131 **Moorish Arch**
Anaheim Public Library
p2325

132 **Orange Show Parade**
Anaheim Public Library
p2184

133 **Boston Bakery**
Anaheim Public Library
p3351

134 **American Savings Bank**
Anaheim Public Library
p3506

135 West Center Street
Anaheim Public Library
p100

136 Warren Hodges
Anaheim Public Library
p394

138 Rimpau's Orange Grove
Anaheim Public Library
p228

139 Big Train And Babe Ruth
Anaheim Public Library
p16491

140 Friends Motoring
Anaheim Public Library
p8815

141 City Band
Anaheim Public Library
p6267

142 Street Technology
Anaheim Public Library
p3545

143 Bethel Baptist Church
Anaheim Public Library
p2344

144 German Methodist
Anaheim Public Library
p11

145 Halloween Parade
Anaheim Public Library
p140

146 Armistice Day Parade
Anaheim Public Library
p2415

147 Christmas Decorations
Anaheim Public Library
p11489

148 Pioneer Home
Anaheim Public Library
p154

149 Long Beach Earthquake
Anaheim Public Library
p13920

150 Public Parks
Anaheim Public Library
p285

151 Park Amphitheater
Anaheim Public Library
p2399

152 Hotel Valencia
Anaheim Public Library
p261

153 New Post Office
Anaheim Public Library
p12692

154 Packing House
Anaheim Public Library
p6706

155 Orange Tree To New York
Anaheim Public Library
p982

156 Orange County Flood
Anaheim Public Library
p315

157 Los Angeles Street
Anaheim Public Library
p8351

158 East Center Street
Anaheim Public Library
p7766

159 Second Public Park
Anaheim Public Library
p12213

160 Halloween Parade
Anaheim Public Library
p90

162 La Palma Park
Anaheim Public Library
p12227

163 Air Raid Lookout
Anaheim Public Library
photo by Betzsold Studio, courtesy of Brad Pettigrew
pio-0010

164 Orange Production
Anaheim Public Library
an-001-102

165 Orange Packing House
Anaheim Public Library
p12787

166 Granada Fruit Company
Anaheim Public Library
p3657

167 Railroad Station
Anaheim Public Library
p15327

168 Santa Ana Street
Anaheim Public Library
p7094

169 Henry Brothers Drug Store
Anaheim Public Library
p3175

170 Center Street
Anaheim Public Library
p3177

171 Jack Benny
Anaheim Public Library
p12722

172 Halloween Parade
Anaheim Public Library
p6147

173 East Center Street
Anaheim Public Library
p12234

174 Fire Truck
Anaheim Public Library
p11520

175 Downtown Shoppers
Anaheim Public Library
p10668

176 Disney's Dream
Anaheim Public Library
p13393

179 Aerial Of Disneyland
Anaheim Public Library
p843

180 Monorail
Anaheim Public Library
p13029

181 Submarine Voyage
Anaheim Public Library
p103258

182 Halloween Parade
Anaheim Public Library
p2949

183 Bookmobile
Anaheim Public Library
p431

184 Check Your Speed
Anaheim Public Library
p11509

185 South Los Angeles Street
Anaheim Public Library
p10671

186 Sargeants 3
Anaheim Public Library
p10667

187 Angels Billboard
Anaheim Public Library
p10312

188 Big A
Anaheim Public Library
p568

189 Anaheim Stadium
Anaheim Public Library
p15068

190 Angels League Game
Anaheim Public Library
pio-002

191 Convention Center
Anaheim Public Library
p8962

192 Flying Saucer
Anaheim Public Library
p7211

193 Anaheim Amigos
Anaheim Public Library
p10311

194 Mobil Economy Run
Anaheim Public Library
pio-003

195 Fourth Of July Spectacular
Anaheim Public Library
p16618

196 Exhibition Game
Anaheim Public Library
ppio-0040

197 Richard Nixon
Anaheim Public Library
p6737199 Osmond Brothers
Anaheim Public Library
pio-005

198 Men Of Goodwill
Anaheim Public Library
p6747

HISTORIC PHOTOS OF ANAHEIM

Anaheim is an American city quintessentially founded upon change. From its birth to the present, Anaheim has consistently built and reshaped its appearance, ideals, and industry. Through changing fortunes, Anaheim has continued to grow and prosper by overcoming adversity and maintaining the strong, independent culture of its citizens.

Historic Photos of Anaheim captures this journey through still photography selected from the finest archives. From Anaheim as the birthplace of the Los Angeles Vineyard Society to its becoming home of the world-famous Disneyland, *Historic Photos of Anaheim* follows life, government, education, and events throughout the city's history.

This volume captures unique and rare scenes through the lens of hundreds of historic photographs. Published in striking black and white, these images communicate historic events and everyday life of two centuries of people building a unique and prosperous city.

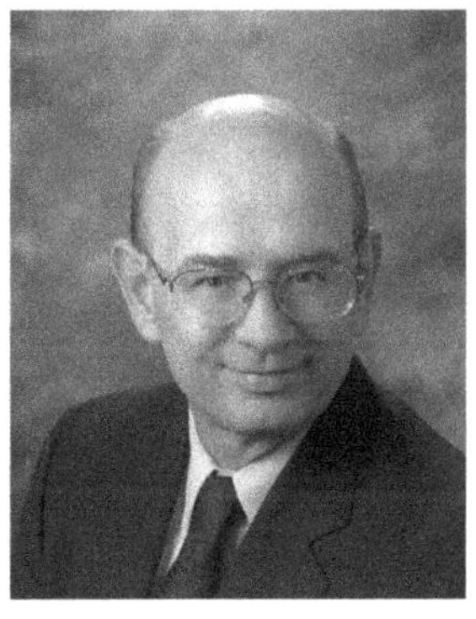

An Anaheim native, Stephen J. Faessel was born in 1950 of parents active in the local citrus industry. Faessel supported local history as past chairman of the Orange County Historical Commission and as a member of the Board of Directors of the Anaheim Museum, as past president of the Anaheim Historical Society, and as president of the Mother Colony Household. Faessel has also crossed the division between historical preservation and civic growth as a member of the Anaheim Planning Commission and as past chairman of the Anaheim Public Utility Board, where he also served as its unofficial historian. In addition to his interest in local history, Faessel serves as the vice president of the Anaheim Community Foundation and as a board member of the Charitable Foundation of the Native Sons of the Golden West, which provides financial assistance to children with craniofacial birth defects. Faessel lives in Anaheim with Susan, his wife of thirty-four years.

WWW.TURNERPUBLISHING.COM

www.ingramcontent.com/pod-product-compliance
Lightning Source LLC
LaVergne TN
LVHW070459120826
845154LV00019BA/31

* 9 7 8 1 6 8 3 3 6 9 4 7 9 *